Understanding Mastercam

Kelly Curran
Fox Valley Technical College

Jon Stenerson
Fox Valley Technical College

Upper Saddle River, New Jersey
Columbus, Ohio

Library of Congress Cataloging-in-Publication Data

Curran, Kelly
Understanding Mastercam/Jon Stenerson, Kelly Curran.
p. cm.
Includes index.
ISBN 0-13-020581-8
1. CAD/CAM systems. I. Stenerson, Jon. II. Title.
TS155.6 .S74 2002
670′.285--dc21

2001021679

Editor in Chief: Stephen Helba
Executive Editor: Ed Francis
Production Editor: Christine M. Buckendahl
Production Coordination: Lisa Garboski, bookworks
Design Coordinator: Robin G. Chukes
Cover Designer: Jeff Vanik
Cover photo: Stock Market
Production Manager: Brian Fox
Marketing Manager: Jimmy Stephens

This book was set in Minion by The Clarinda Company, and was printed and bound by Banta Book Group. The cover was printed by The Lehigh Press, Inc.

Pearson Education Ltd., *London*
Pearson Education Australia Pty. Limited, *Sydney*
Pearson Education Singapore Pte. Ltd.
Pearson Education North Asia Ltd., *Hong Kong*
Pearson Education Canada, Ltd., *Toronto*
Pearson Educación de Mexico, S.A. de C.V.
Pearson Education—Japan, *Tokyo*
Pearson Education Malaysia Pte. Ltd.
Pearson Education, *Upper Saddle River, New Jersey*

10 9 8 7 6 5 4 3 2 1
ISBN: 0-13-020581-8

To my wife, Sheryl, and my daughters, Megan and Melissa, for their patience, support, and inspiration.

Kelly Curran

To the few administrators who understand and support technical education.

Jon Stenerson

Preface

To compete in the global market, most manufacturers have seen the need to utilize computers to efficiently produce quality products. Computer numerical control (CNC) and computer-aided manufacturing (CAM) have gained a foothold in industry and have revolutionized the way manufacturers do business.

The ever-increasing popularity of CNC machines has created a need for people who are knowledgeable about programming CNC machines. There is a huge demand for people who are capable of programming, setting up, and operating CNC machine tools. They will continue to be in demand as long as they stay current with technology.

We decided to write this text when we were unable to find a practical, easy-to-understand book with enough examples and programming assignments. We thought it was essential to provide a clear, concise text that would enable students to learn the basics of Mastercam in a more independent and painless fashion.

The information in this textbook is based on our years of experience teaching CNC courses to students at Fox Valley Technical College in Appleton, Wisconsin, and industrial CNC courses for local business and industry, university and technical school students, and on-the-job trainees. We sincerely hope that our logical, easy-to-understand approach will enable readers to accomplish more than would otherwise be possible.

Thanks to the reviewers of this text for their helpful comments and suggestions: Paul Brennan, Monroe Community College; Joseph W. Johnson, College of Lake County; Richard Kibbe, Manufacturing Technology Publications; Brian LaBombard, St. Clair College; and Dan Ruesch, College of Lake County.

Kelly Curran
Jon Stenerson

Contents

CHAPTER 8

CHAPTER 9

CHAPTER

1

Mastercam's Working Environment

In this chapter you are introduced to Mastercam's working environment. While within the working environment you will construct a very basic part. Doing this allows you to get a feel for Mastercam's style of user interface. The commands you use in this exercise are used throughout the book. It is important that each exercise be done exactly as it is presented in this text. This will help you avoid errors, which may not become apparent until you are further along in the computer aided manufacturing process.

Objectives

Upon completion of this chapter the reader will be able to:

- Start Mastercam from the Windows environment
- Manipulate the hidden or pop-up menus to create geometry
- Identify the five main areas that make up Mastercam's working environment
- Save an exercise to a file name
- Get a previously saved program
- Exit Mastercam

WORKING IN THE WINDOWS ENVIRONMENT

In this chapter you will look at Mastercam's working environment and construct a simple part. The commands you use here will be used throughout the book, so please do each exercise exactly as it is presented. This chapter provides the basis for the rest of the book. A thorough understanding of it should guarantee your success in using Mastercam.

Once you have turned on your computer and allowed the computer system to boot up, you will notice a series of icons (pictures) appearing on the screen. Each of these icons represents a program that resides within your computer (see Figure 1–1). Your screen will vary somewhat, depending on the programs that are installed on your computer. Depending on the software installation process that was used, a Mastercam icon may be present on your screen. Look for an icon called **Mastercam Mill.** If it is present, move the mouse cursor over the top of this icon and double click the left mouse button. If the Mastercam Mill icon is not visible on the screen, use the directions that follow.

Notice the Start button in the lower left corner of the screen (see Figure 1–1). You can also use the Start button to start any program you want to use. The start button will give you several options. Choose the **programs** option by clicking on it with your left mouse button. You should see a list of program folders.

To start Mastercam Mill software, point to the folder called **Mastercam.** Click on **Mastercam Mill** option (see Figure 1–2).

Navigating in Windows is really quite simple, but if you need additional help you can use the Microsoft Windows handbook that is distributed along with the Windows software. The Windows interactive Help area found under the Start button can also be great help.

As you have probably noticed by now, clicking on Mill has launched Mastercam's programming software. Your screen should now look like the screen in Figure 1–3.

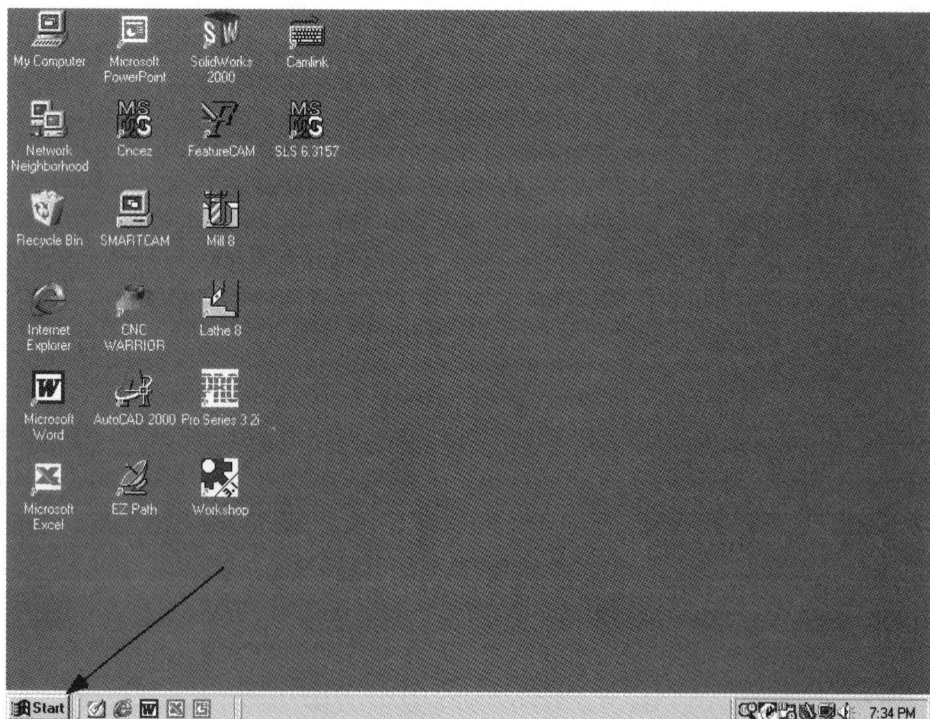

FIGURE 1–1
Various program icons and the start button.

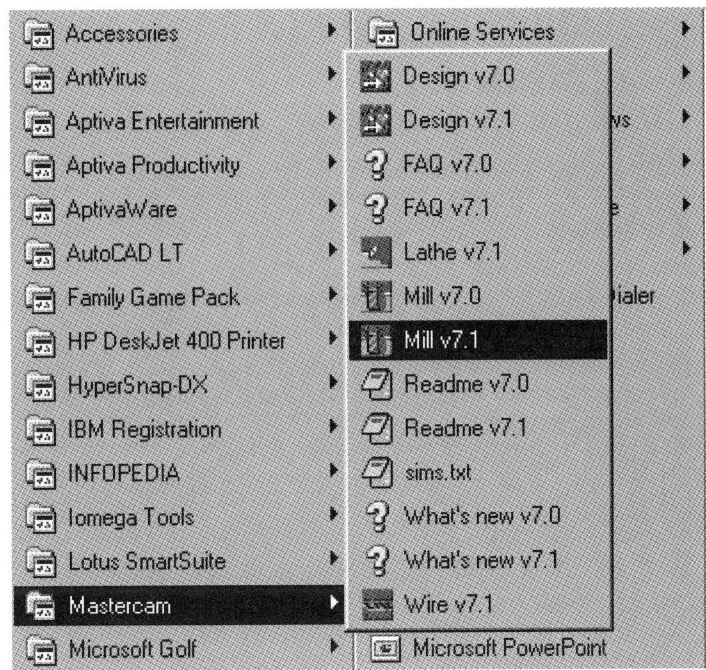

FIGURE 1–2
Mastercam folder and Mill program.

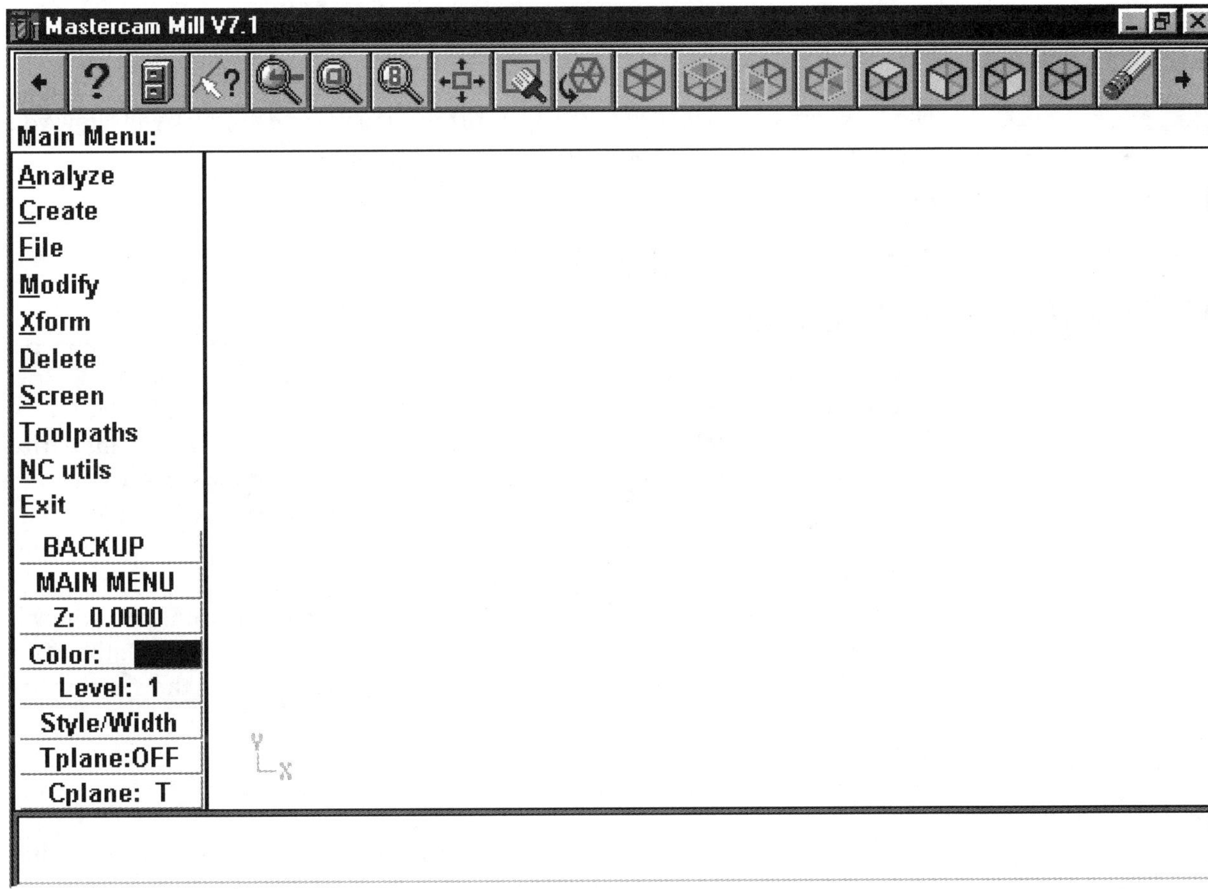

FIGURE 1–3
Mastercam Mill programming screen.

Establishing the Mastercam Viewing Window

If after launching Mastercam the screen does not cover the entire viewing area, it is possible to resize the screen by using the minimize, size, and maximize buttons. The minimize, size, and maximize buttons are located in the upper right corner of the screen (see Figure 1–4).

FIGURE 1–4
These buttons are used to adjust the size of the screen and to close the software.

The leftmost choice is the button that looks like an underscore. This is the minimize choice. By clicking on this button you can reduce Mastercam's working environment to a program icon along the bottom of the screen.

When you minimize the screen you don't leave the Mastercam working environment. To reestablish the full Mastercam working environment simply click on the Mastercam program icon on the bottom of your screen.

The middle choice looks like two rectangles. This is called the size option. This choice allows you to make the window any size you like. In the size option the program screen still appears on the screen but does not fill the entire screen.

When you are in the size condition, the middle choice will change to a single rectangle. This is the maximize button. By clicking the maximize button in the title bar you can utilize the entire viewing area for Mastercam's working environment. The X, which is located next to the minimize and maximize buttons, will allow you to quickly exit the Mastercam programming software.

UNDERSTANDING THE MASTERCAM WORKING ENVIRONMENT

If you have been following along with each step we have covered, you should now have Mastercam's Main Menu working environment on the screen. If not, follow through the steps below to get to this point before you continue. To summarize what you have done to this point, you used the Microsoft Windows environment to launch the Mastercam Mill software. You then used the maximize buttons to enlarge the Mastercam viewing screen to fill the entire screen. Practice opening and closing Mastercam and utilizing the minimize, size, and maximize options.

Now that you have entered into Mastercam's working environment you will notice that Mastercam is divided into five specific areas (see Figure 1–5): the Main Menu, the secondary menu, the display area, the tool bar, and the system dialogue box.

The Tool Bar

The tool bar is located across the top of the screen (see Figure 1–5). The tool bar consists of a series of icons. The Mastercam software has a user-friendly description built into each icon. When you place the mouse cursor over the top of any of the tool icons, a description of the icon appears.

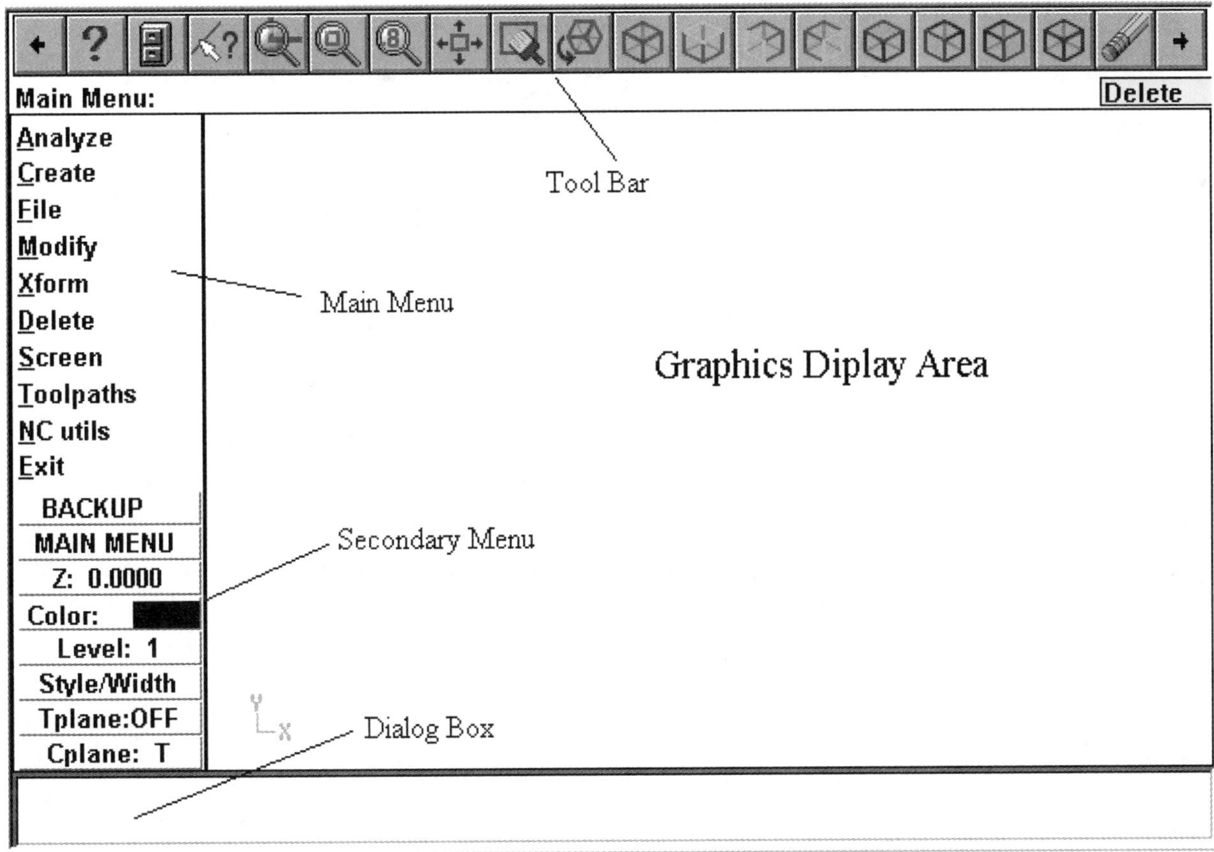

FIGURE 1–5
Main Menu, secondary menu, display area, tool bar, and system dialogue box.

Try placing the cursor over any of the tool icons in the tool bar. Do you see the prompt explaining what this tool is used for? To use a tool, you must place the mouse cursor over the icon you want to use and click the left mouse button. You will be using the tool icons in Chapter 2.

Graphics Display Area

The graphics display area is located in the middle of the screen. The graphic display area is where you can view and manipulate the geometry you construct. When you create geometry, modify geometry, or delete geometry, this is where it happens.

The System Dialogue Box

The system dialogue box is located across the bottom of the screen. If the system needs a response to a question, the dialogue box will prompt you for an answer. The dialogue box is a very helpful tool, especially for beginning users. The system dialogue box will help guide you in the use of the commands.

The Secondary Menu

The secondary menu is located on the lower left side of the screen command area. The secondary menu is used to change the working parameters. The working

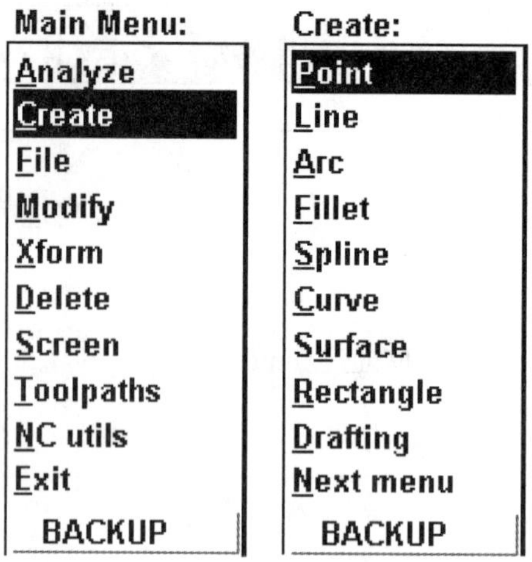

FIGURE 1–6 This figure shows what happens when the Create option is chosen. A submenu appears that presents the user with choices of what to create. In this case the user has selected Point.

Main Menu:	Create:
Analyze	Point
Create	Line
File	Arc
Modify	Fillet
Xform	Spline
Delete	Curve
Screen	Surface
Toolpaths	Rectangle
NC utils	Drafting
Exit	Next menu
BACKUP	BACKUP

parameters control the construction depth, geometry color, active level, mask level, tool plane, construction plane, and graphics view. When you get further into geometry construction, these options will be explained in more detail.

The Main Menu

The Main Menu area is located on the upper left side of the screen command menu area. The main menu area is where you can select the operation you wish to perform. Mastercam has structured the Main Menu screen using hidden or pop-up menus. To give you an example of this, click the **Create** button from the **Main Menu** screen area. Notice the new screen that pops up? This is called the Create: Menu (see Figure 1–6).

To go back to the Main Menu, select **Main Menu** from the Main menu area. In this instance, you could have also used the BACKUP selection from the Main Menu, which would step you back to the previous menu.

In Mastercam there are two ways to pick a menu option from the screen command menu area. The first is the pick method using the mouse cursor and left mouse key. The second is to type the first underlined letter of the command as it appears in the command box; for example, Type **C** for create.

Now you can use what you have just learned to create and save a rectangular geometry file.

CREATING A RECTANGLE IN MASTERCAM

As you do this exercise try to concentrate on the different methods of selecting commands and the overall Mastercam process instead of every keystroke. Mastercam has a very good menu system that will help guide you through geometry creation. From the **Main Menu** click the **Create** button. From the Create menu select **Rectangle** (see Figure 1–7).

You are using the Create/Rectangle function to create a 5 × 3 rectangle with the lower left corner of the rectangle located at X0, Y0. After selecting the rectangle function you will see that it allows you to create the rectangle using different methods. You will use the 1-Point method (see Figure 1–8).

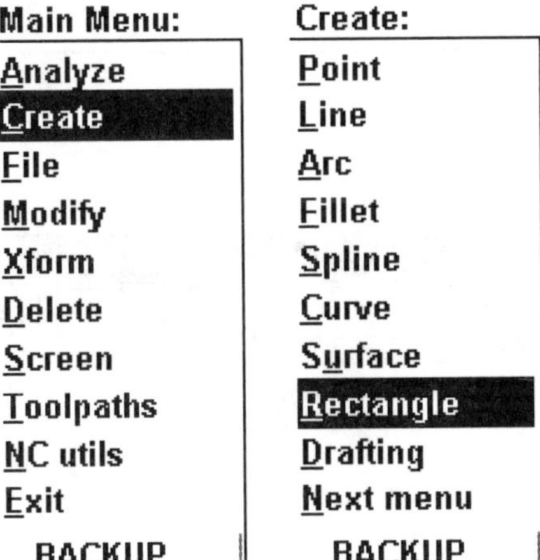

FIGURE 1–7
In this figure the Create option was again chosen, but then the user chose the Rectangle option.

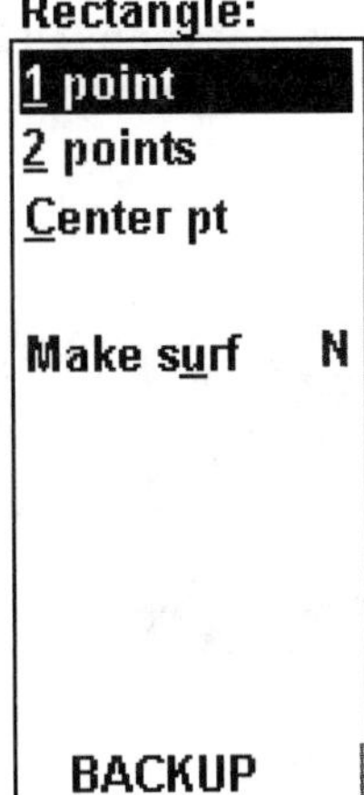

FIGURE 1–8
The user has chosen 1 point from the Create/Rectangle menu.

Select **1 Point** from the Rectangle menu.

Notice in the dialogue box along the bottom of the screen that Mastercam is prompting you for a solution to the 1 point menu selection (see Figure 1–9).

FIGURE 1–9
This figure shows the prompt for creating a rectangle with 1 point.

Create rectangle (1): Enter the lower left corner

You want the lower left corner of the rectangle to be X0, Y0. You need to specify this by typing in the X coordinate first and then the Y coordinate with a comma between the two coordinates. Start typing **0,0** and press **enter.** Notice how Mastercam switches the dialogue box to an input coordinate box (see Figure 1–10).

FIGURE 1–10
The user has entered 0,0 for the lower left coordinates of the rectangle.

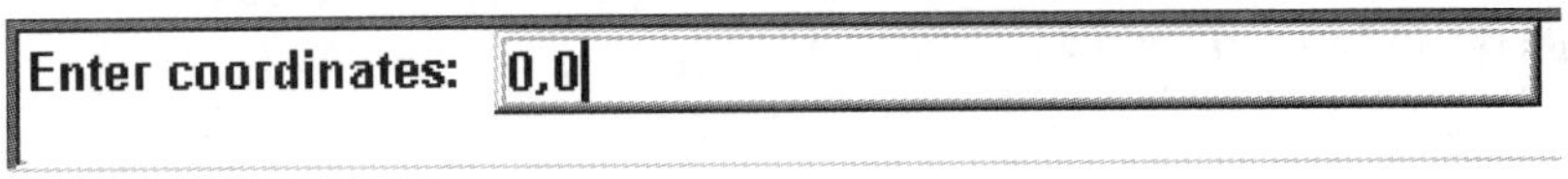

Enter coordinates: 0,0

Now that you have established the origin of the rectangle, you must enter the width of the rectangle. Notice in the dialogue box along the bottom of the screen that Mastercam is prompting you for a solution to the width of the rectangle. The width of the rectangle refers to the distance or size of the rectangle along the X axis (horizontally). You need a 5 × 3 rectangle. For the width enter a **5.,** in the dialogue box and press **Enter** (see Figure 1–11).

Now that you have established the width of the rectangle, you must enter the height of the rectangle. Notice in the dialogue box along the bottom of the screen that Mastercam is prompting you for a solution to the height of the rectangle. The height of the rectangle refers to the distance or size of the rectangle along the Y axis

FIGURE 1–11
The user has entered 5 inches for the width.

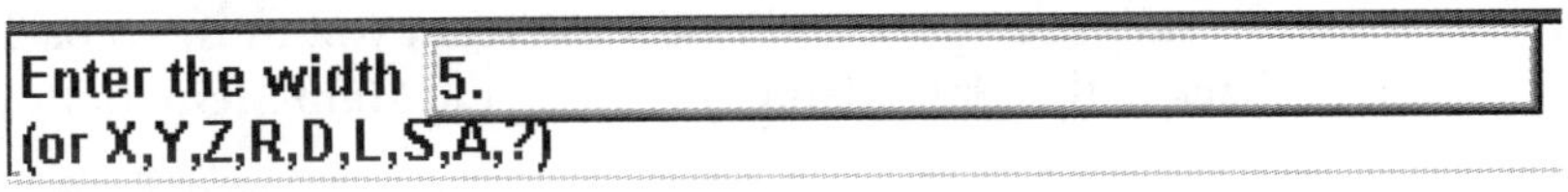

Enter the width 5.
(or X,Y,Z,R,D,L,S,A,?)

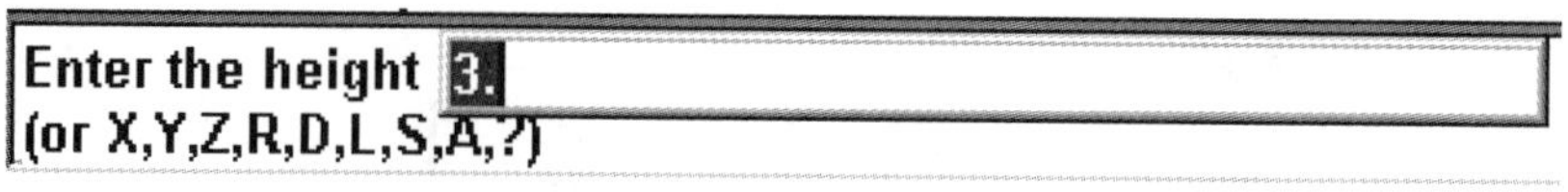

Enter the height 3.
(or X,Y,Z,R,D,L,S,A,?)

FIGURE 1–12
The user has entered 3 inches for the height.

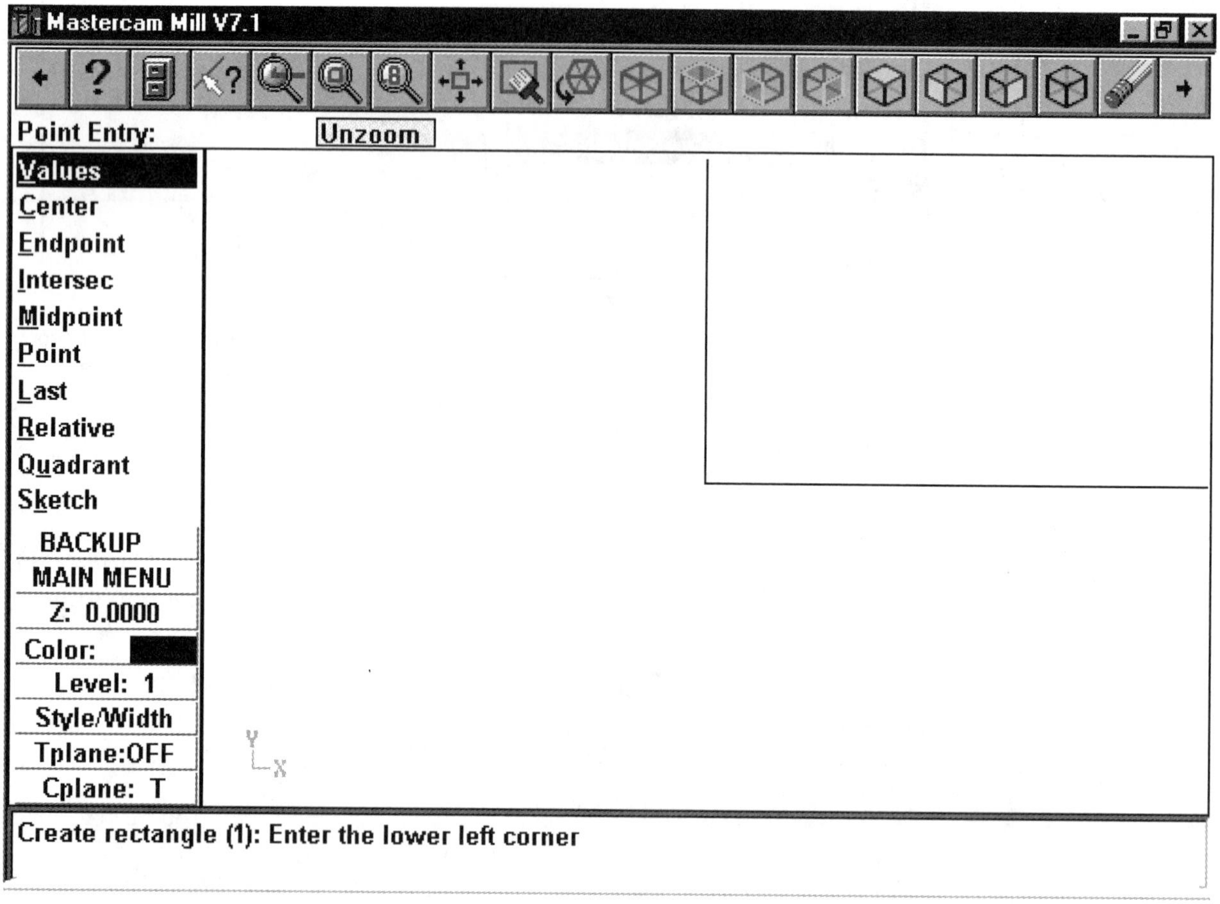

Mastercam Mill V7.1
Point Entry: Unzoom
Values
Center
Endpoint
Intersec
Midpoint
Point
Last
Relative
Quadrant
Sketch
BACKUP
MAIN MENU
Z: 0.0000
Color:
Level: 1
Style/Width
Tplane:OFF
Cplane: T
Create rectangle (1): Enter the lower left corner

FIGURE 1–13
This screen shows the completed rectangle. The lower left corner is located at 0,0. The rectangle is 5 inches wide and 3 inches high.

(vertically). You said that you needed a 5 × 3 rectangle. For the height, enter a **3.** in the dialogue box and press **Enter** (see Figure 1–12).

Your screen should now look like the screen in Figure 1–13. Notice that the rectangle doesn't fit the screen. There is a simple solution to this. Locate the **Fit** key in the toolbar along the top of the screen. Use the mouse to pick this key. The screen will resize itself to accept the full rectangle.

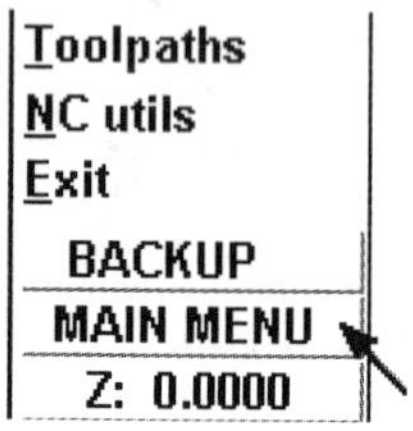

Toolpaths
NC utils
Exit
BACKUP
MAIN MENU
Z: 0.0000

FIGURE 1–14
The user chose Main Menu.

To Save Your Work

To save your work and exit Mastercam you must go back to the Main Menu. Go back to the Main Menu by clicking the **Main Menu** button in the Main Menu area (see Figure 1–14).

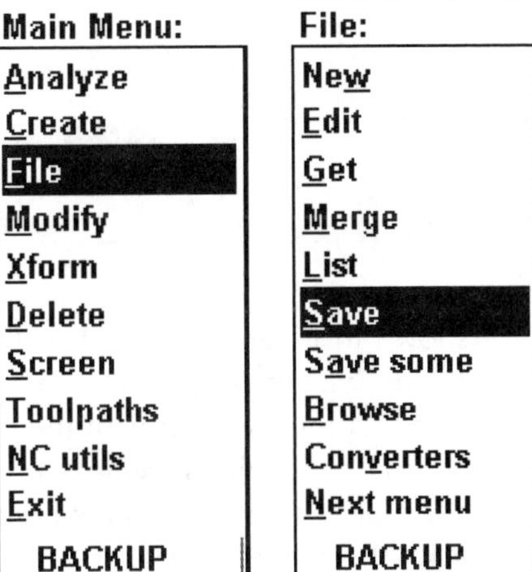

FIGURE 1–15
The user chose File and then Save to save the file.

From the Main Menu screen select **File.** From the File menu select the **Save** option. That is Main Menu/File/Save. Upon entering the Save option a file folder appears (see Figure 1–15).

This is the Mc7 file folder. Keeping files in a selected file folder or on a separate disk will help you to organize and keep track of your files. In the examples in this book all of the files will be saved to the A: drive. This will help keep the internal drive or C: drive free of unwanted files. It will also allow us to carry our files to a different computer or store the disk for safekeeping.

To change the target drive and directory you will need to work in the Save in: file area (see Figure 1–16).

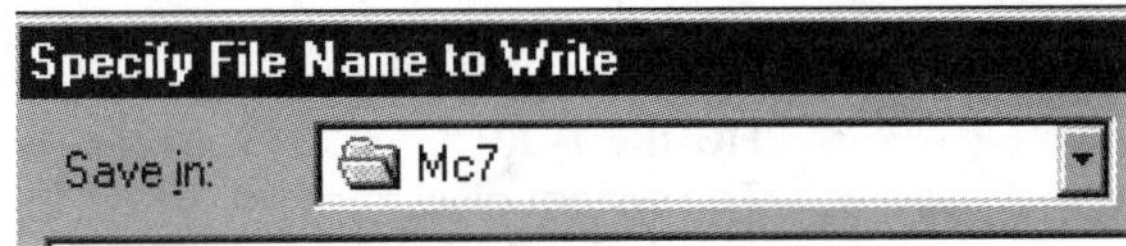

FIGURE 1–16
The user should click on the right down arrow of this area to be given additional choices of where to save the file.

Since you are going to save the file to the A: drive (this is the external drive of your computer) you need to place a formatted disk in the A: drive. Do this now. Click on the **down arrow** button on the right side of the "save in" file area as shown in Figure 1–16. Use the **up arrow** button to move up the list of target areas until the **3½ Floppy (A:)** appears (see Figure 1–17). Click on this option using the mouse cursor. The computer now checks to see if a disk is in the disk drive. Once the processor finds the disk you are ready to type your file name in. Use your first name as the name of this first file. Use the mouse cursor to click in the **File Name:** box

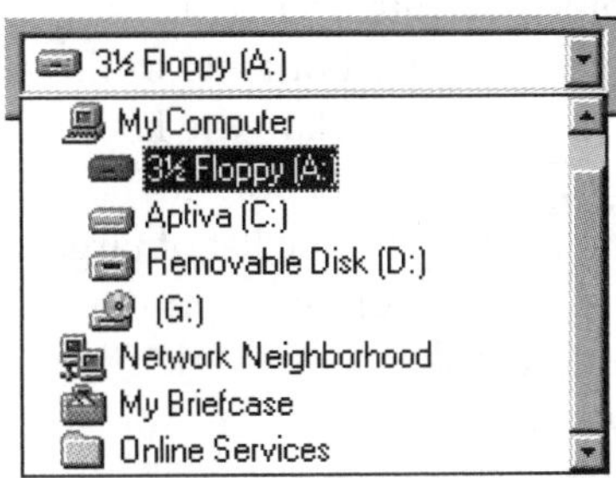

FIGURE 1–17
The user has chosen the A: drive.

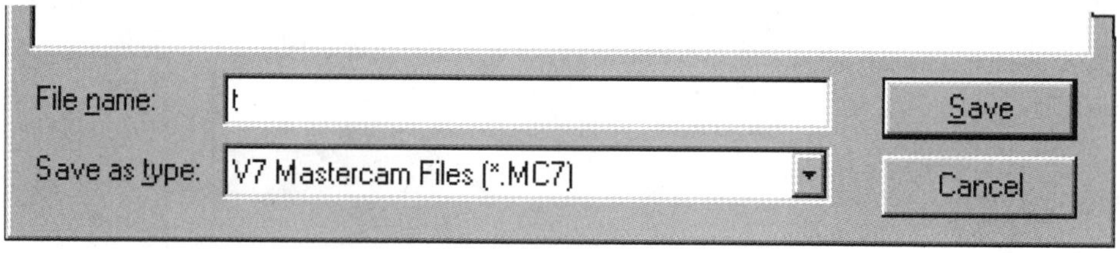

File name: t
Save as type: V7 Mastercam Files (*.MC7)
Save
Cancel

FIGURE 1–18
This figure shows where the user will enter the name of the file to which the work will be saved.

shown in Figure 1–18. This activates the box and allows you to type in your file name. Type your first name in the file name dialogue box now. Once you have finished typing your name in the box, you can either hit the **Enter** key on your keyboard or click the **Save** button also shown in Figure 1–18. Do either option now. Your file is now saved to the floppy disk in the A: drive.

If you need help at any time, Mastercam has an on-line help screen. Using the mouse to select the large question mark icon in the tool bar can access On-line Help. This includes frequently asked questions (FAQ) about the software.

Main Menu:
Analyze
Create
File
Modify
Xform
Delete
Screen
Toolpaths
NC utils
Exit

FIGURE 1–19
The user chose Main Menu and then Exit.

Exiting Mastercam

To exit Mastercam you must go back to the Main Menu area. Select the **Main Menu** button from the Main Menu area. Next, select the **Exit** option (see Figure 1–19). Remember you can also select options in Mastercam by typing the underlined letter in the option name. Try typing an E. To confirm that you wish to exit Mastercam you must select **Yes** from the confirmation box (see Figure 1–20). Use the mouse cursor to click in the **Yes** box. Remember, to exit Mastercam you need to click Main Menu/Exit/Yes.

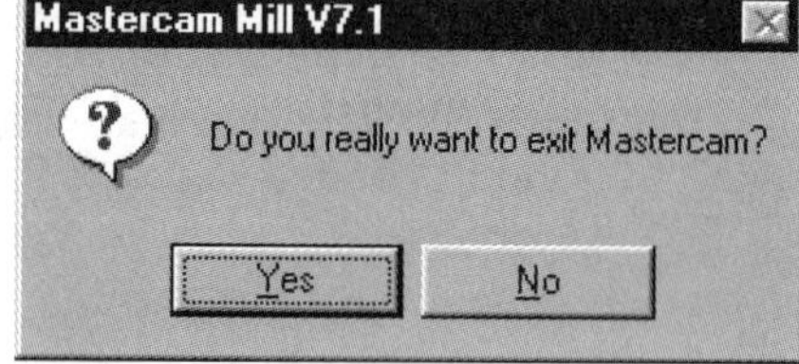

FIGURE 1–20
The system gives the user a chance to change his/her mind about exiting Mastercam.

To Get a Previously Saved File

Start Mastercam Mill software by clicking the **Start** button. Choose the **Programs** option. Point to the folder called **Mastercam.** Click on the **Mastercam Mill** option. From the Mastercam Main Menu screen select **File.** From the File menu select the **Get** option. That is Main Menu/File/Get (see Figure 1–21).

Upon entering, the Get option a file folder appears. This is the Look in file folder (see Figure 1–22).

You saved our file to the A: drive. To change our target drive and directory you need to work in the Look in: file area. Click on the **down arrow** button on the right side of the Look in: file area as shown in Figure 1–22. Use the **up arrow** button to move up the list of target areas until the **3-½ Floppy (A:)** appears (see Figure 1–17). Click on this option using the mouse cursor. The computer now checks to see if a disk is in the disk drive. Once the processor finds the disk, you are ready to type your file name in. You should have used your first name as the name of the first file. Use the mouse cursor to click on your file name. Once you have finished,

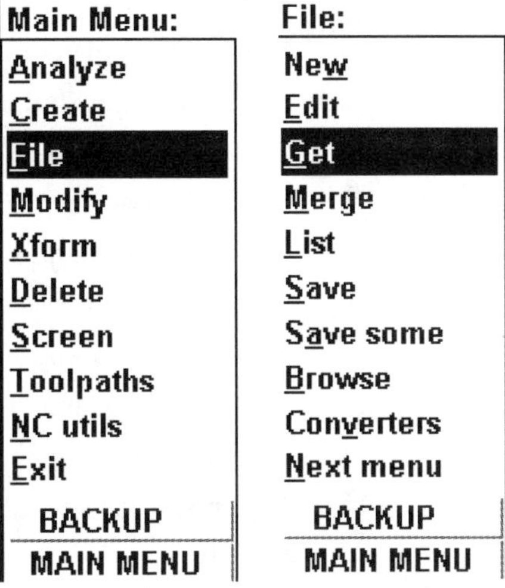

FIGURE 1–21
The user has chosen File and then Get from the submenu.

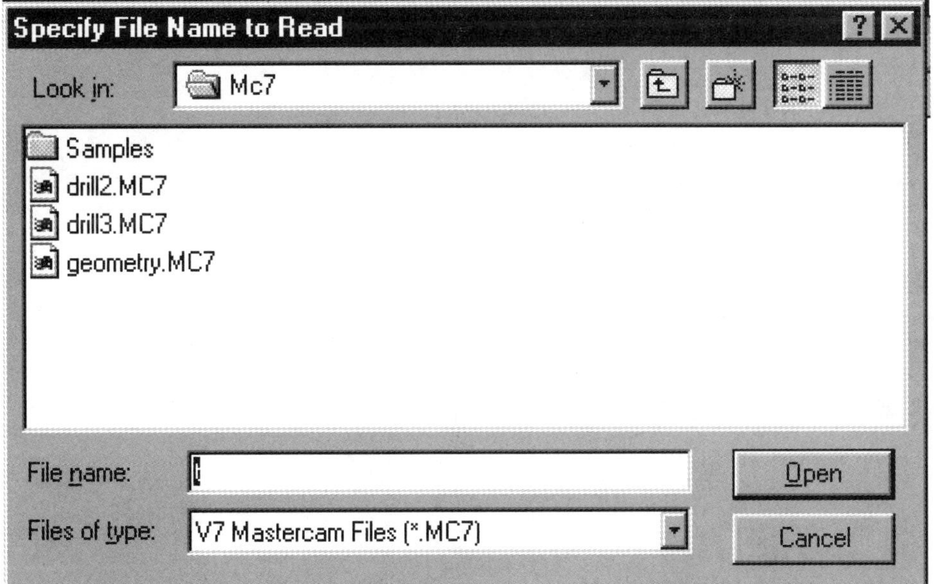

FIGURE 1–22
The screen that the user is presented with when retrieving a previously saved file.

and your name appears in the file name box, you can either hit the **Enter** key on your keyboard or click the **Open** button also shown in Figure 1–22. Do either option now. Your File should now appear on the screen.

Congratulations, you have now completed this chapter and you are ready to move on to the next chapter. If you are not thoroughly comfortable with what you did, go back and redo the exercises.

REVIEW QUESTIONS

1. What is an icon?
2. In the Microsoft Windows environment, where is the Start button located?
3. Where is the Mastercam tool bar located?

4. In Mastercam, where would you view the geometry?
5. What is the purpose of Mastercam's secondary menu?
6. In Mastercam, what is the purpose of the dialogue box?
7. Under which menu will you find the Create option?
8. Name the two methods of selecting a menu option.
9. Under which menu will you find the Rectangle option?
10. What is the purpose of the hot keys?
11. Under which menu will you find the Save option?
12. In which drive area does the 3½ floppy disk drive reside?
13. To exit Mastercam, which three command options do you need to select?
14. Which hot keys would you need to select to bring up the on-line help screen?
15. From Mastercam's Main Menu, which two options would you need to select to retrieve a previously saved file?

CHAPTER

2

Overview of the Mastercam CAD/CAM Process

This chapter takes you through an overview of how Mastercam is used to take a part from conception to generating numerical control (NC) code. It is not vital that you understand everything that is done in this chapter, but is important you understand the overall CAD/CAM process.

Objectives

Upon completion of this chapter you will be able to:

- Define the basic components of the Mastercam CAD/CAM process
- Use Mastercam Mill to create simple part geometry
- Apply machining commands to the part geometry
- Generate numerical control code to machine the part

PROCESS OVERVIEW

This section will lead you through a step-by-step procedure of how Mastercam can take you from a basic part conception to generating NC code able to machine the part. The part you are going to use in the procedure is shown in Figure 2–1. Once the part is designed you will contour mill the profile of the rectangle and drill the four holes.

FIGURE 2–1

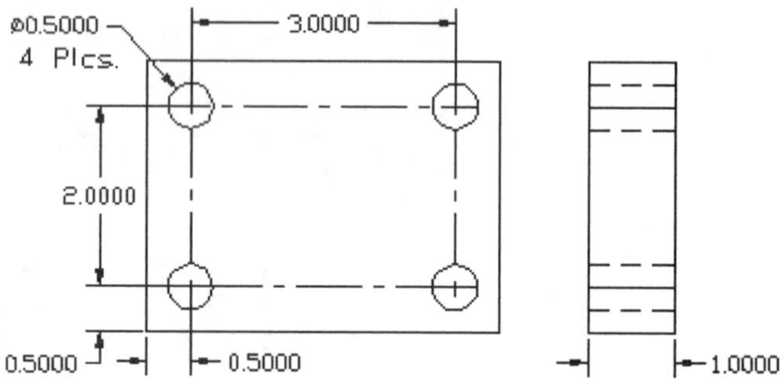

The CAD/CAM process involves four basic components: geometry definition, application of machining commands, setting the NC parameters, and post-processing.

FIGURE 2–2

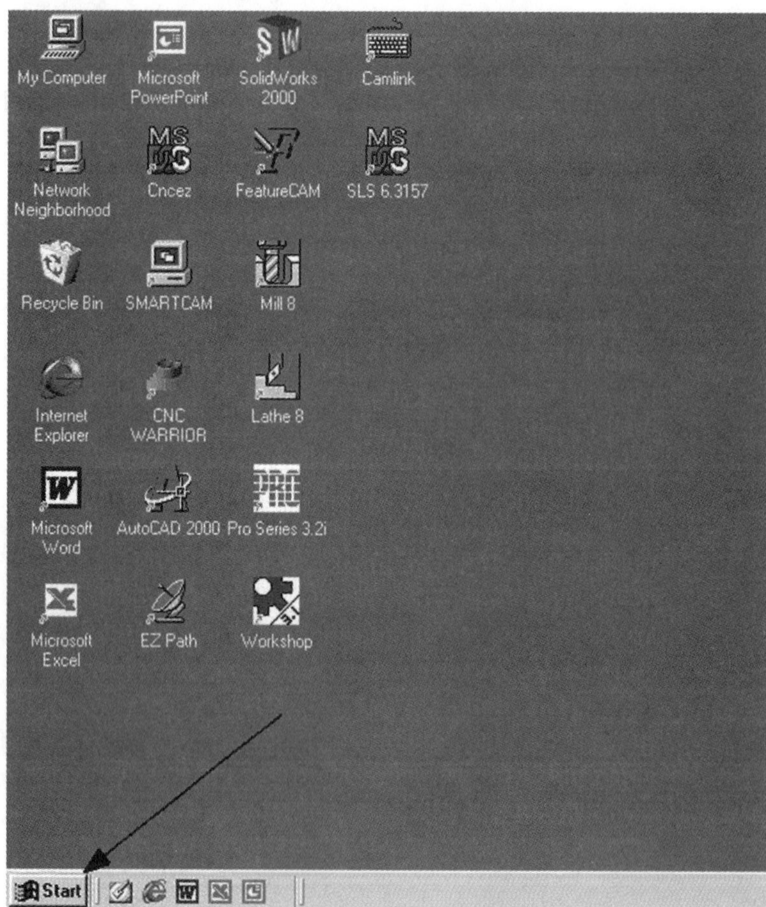

Design

CAD/CAM or computer-aided parts programming (CAPP) always begins with geometry definition or part design. In Mastercam you can create geometry in any one of the application areas. Mastercam Mill, Mastercam Lathe, and Mastercam Design all have part geometry creation capabilities built into them. If the part was originally drawn using another type of CAD or CAM system, Mastercam may be able import in this drawing, using a file converter. This would allow us to bypass the Mastercam design phase of the part.

Please follow the step-by-step procedures that follow carefully. Don't become concerned if you don't understand everything that you are doing. This is really just an overview of the Mastercam CAD/CAM process.

At this point you are assuming that Mastercam has been previously set up or installed into your computer.

Once you have turned on your computer and allowed the system to boot up you will notice a series of icons (pictures) appearing on the screen. Each one of these icons is a program that resides within your computer (see Figure 2–2). Depending on the software installation process that was used, a Mastercam icon may be present on your screen. Look for an icon called **Mastercam Mill.** If it is present, move the mouse cursor over the top of this icon and double click the left mouse button. If the Mastercam Mill icon is not visible on the screen, use the directions that follow.

Notice the Start button in the lower left corner of the screen (see Figure 2–2). You can use the Start button to open any program you want to use. To start the Mastercam Mill software click the **Start** button using the left mouse button, and then point to the area called **programs.** Now click on the **Mastercam Mill** option (see Figure 2–3).

As you have probably noticed by clicking on Mill you have launched Mastercam's programming software. Your screen should now look like Figure 2–4.

If after launching Mastercam Mill the screen does not cover the entire viewing area, it is possible to resize the screen by using the minimize and maximize buttons. The minimize and maximize buttons are located in the upper right corner of the screen (see Figure 2–5). By clicking the maximize button on the title bar you

FIGURE 2–3

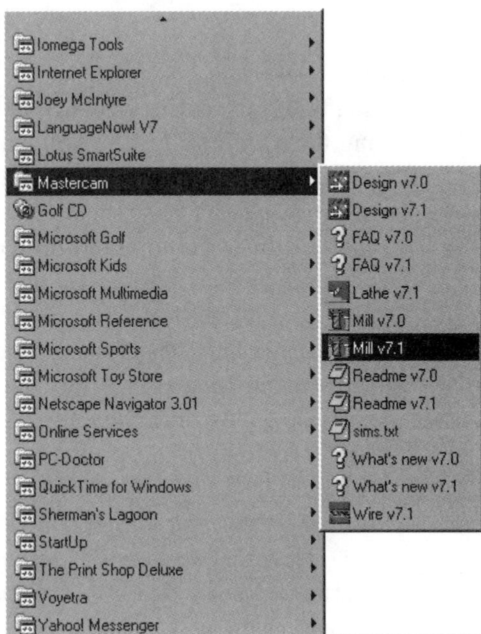

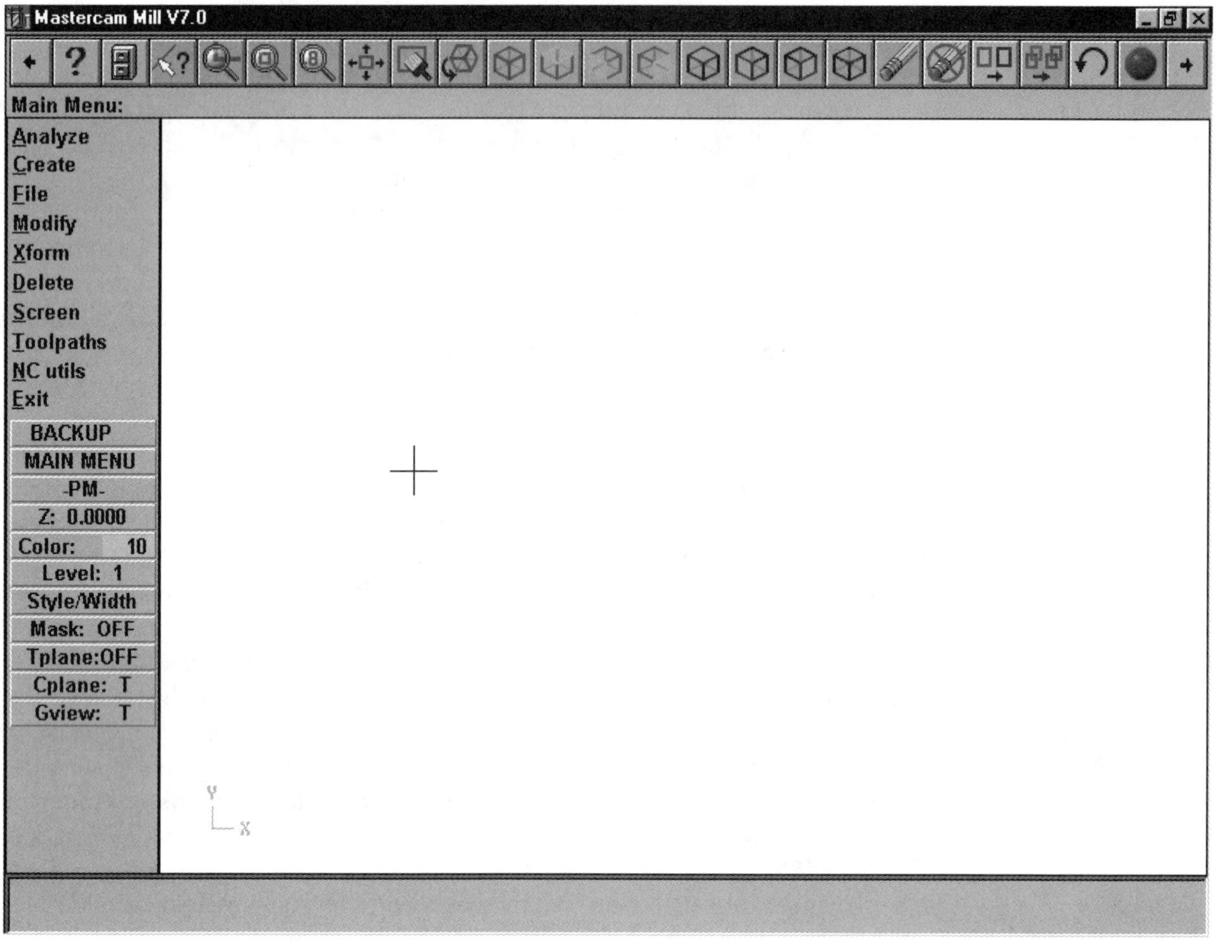

FIGURE 2–4

FIGURE 2–5

can utilize the entire viewing area for Mastercam's working environment. By clicking the minimize button you can reduce Mastercam's working environment to a title icon along the bottom of the screen. Remember, when you minimize the screen you don't leave the Mastercam working environment. To reestablish the full Mastercam working environment, simply click on the maximize button. The X, which is located next to the minimize and maximize buttons, will allow you to quickly exit the Mastercam programming software.

If you have been following along with each step you should now have Mastercam's Main Menu working environment on the screen. If not, follow the steps below to get us all to the same point before you proceed. Now let's reestablish what you have done to this point. You used the Microsoft Windows 95, 98, or NT environment to launch the Mastercam Mill software. You then used the maximize buttons to enlarge the Mastercam viewing screen.

Now that you are in Mastercam's working environment you will notice that Mastercam is divided into five specific areas (see Figure 2–6): the Main Menu, the secondary menu, the display area, the tool bar, and the system dialogue box.

FIGURE 2–6

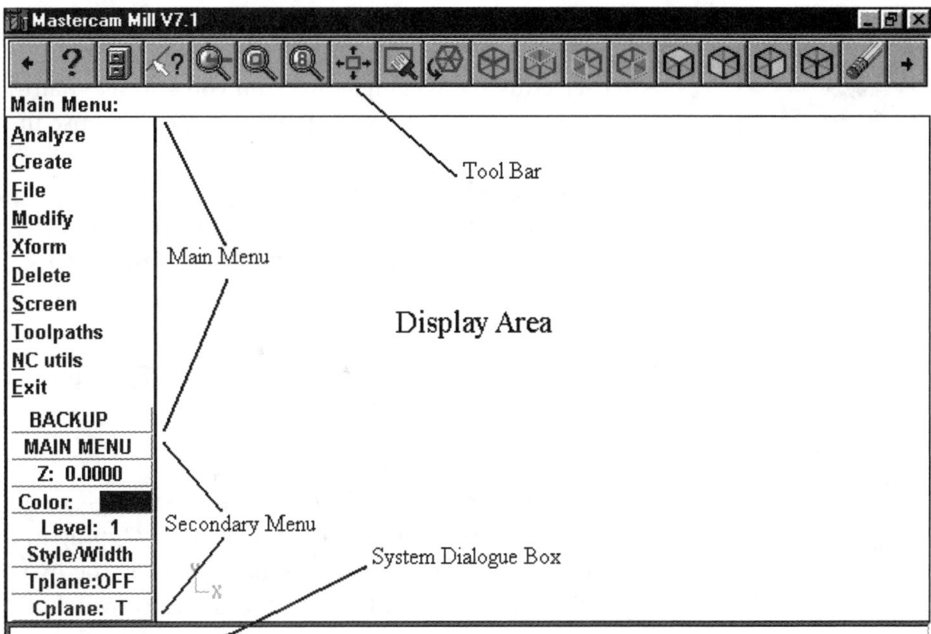

The Main Menu

The Main Menu area is located along the left side of the screen menu area. The Main Menu area contains the commands that you will use to do the majority of our geometry construction. Mastercam has structured the Main Menu screen using hidden or pop-up screens. To give you an example of this, click the **Create** button from the **Main Menu** screen area. Notice the new screen that pops up. This is called the Create: screen (see Figure 2–7).

To go back to the Main Menu, press the **Main Menu** button from the Main Menu. In this instance you could have also used the **BACKUP** button from the Main Menu, which would have stepped you back to the previous menu.

From the **Main Menu** click the **Create** button. From the Create menu select **Rectangle** (see Figure 2–8).

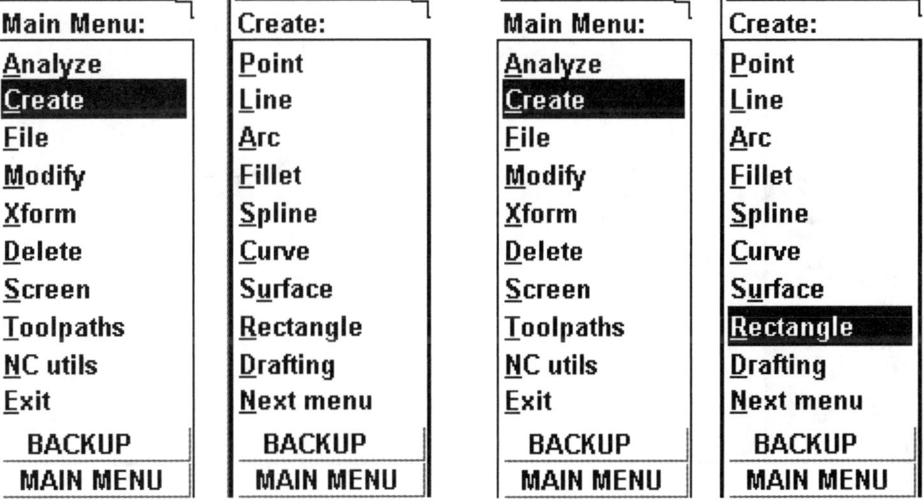

FIGURE 2–7

FIGURE 2–8

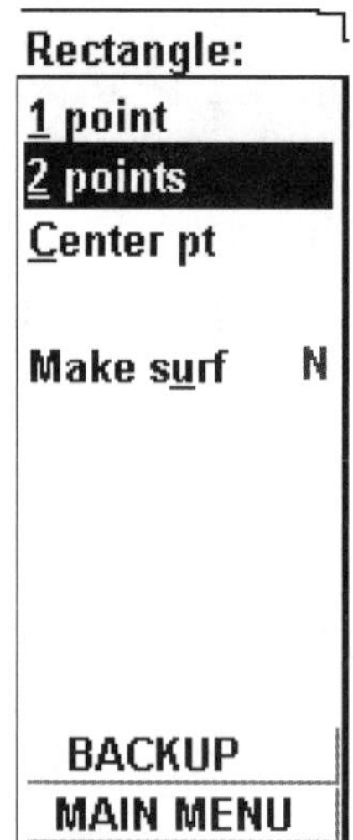

You are using the Create/Rectangle function to create a 4 × 3 rectangle with the lower left corner of the rectangle having the X and Y axes coordinate of 0, 0. After selecting the rectangle function you will see that this function allows you to create a rectangle using several methods. You will use the two-points method (see Figure 2–9).

Select **2 Points** from the Rectangle menu.

Notice in the dialogue box along the bottom of the screen that Mastercam is prompting you for a solution to the 2 points menu selection (see Figure 2–10).

Rectangle:
1 point
2 points
Center pt
Make surf N
BACKUP
MAIN MENU

FIGURE 2–9

FIGURE 2–10

Create rectangle (2): Enter the lower left corner

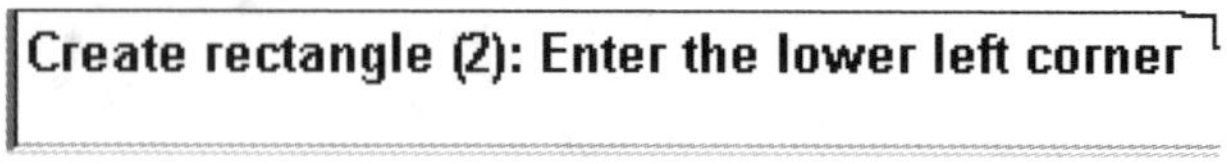

You want the lower left corner of the rectangle to be located at the coordinate position of X0, Y0. You need to specify this by typing in the X coordinate first and then the Y coordinate with a comma separating the two coordinates. Start by typing **0,0.** Notice that Mastercam automatically switches to the Point Entry mode (see Figure 2–11). Once you have typed **0,0,** press **Enter.**

FIGURE 2–11

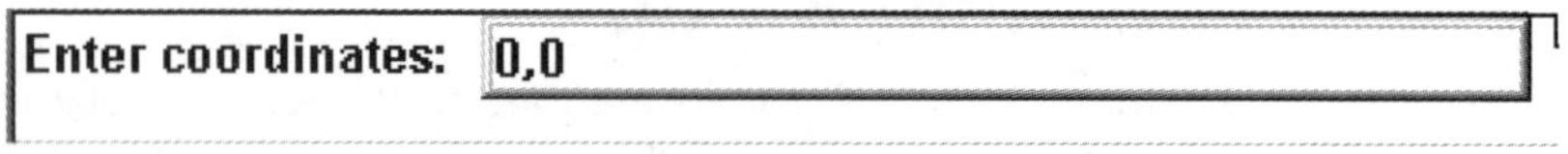

Enter coordinates: 0,0

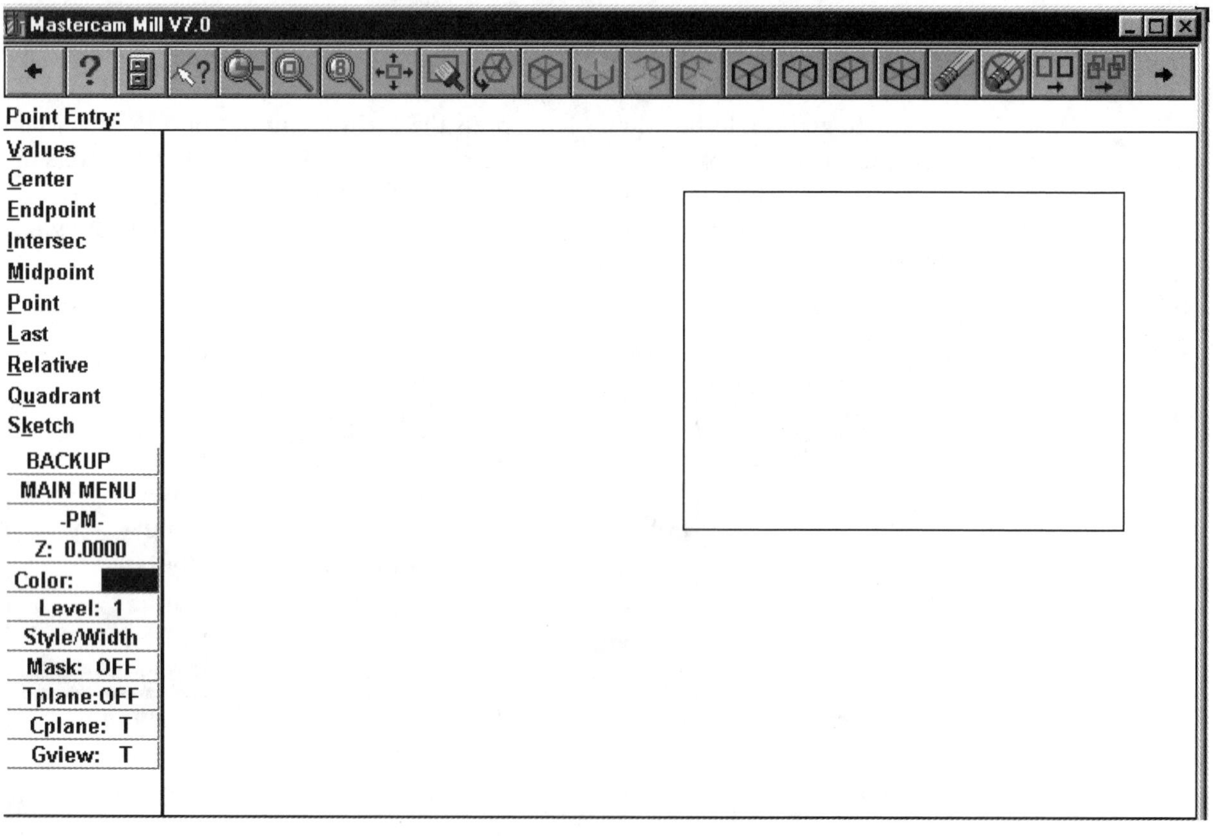

Mastercam Mill V7.0
Point Entry:
Values
Center
Endpoint
Intersec
Midpoint
Point
Last
Relative
Quadrant
Sketch
BACKUP
MAIN MENU
-PM-
Z: 0.0000
Color:
Level: 1
Style/Width
Mask: OFF
Tplane:OFF
Cplane: T
Gview: T

FIGURE 2–12

Now that you have established the origin of the rectangle you must enter the opposite corner of the rectangle. You will note that in the dialogue box along the bottom of the screen that Mastercam is tracking the width and height of the rectangle using the cursor snap. The width of the rectangle refers to the distance or size of the rectangle along the X axis (horizontally). The height of the rectangle refers to the distance or size of the rectangle along the Y axis (vertically). You said that you needed a 4 × 3 rectangle. It is very difficult to precisely locate coordinates using the cursor snap, so you will enter the coordinates using the keyboard. Type **4,3** in the dialogue box and press **Enter.**

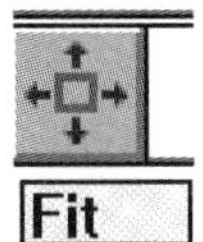

FIGURE 2–13
The Fit button resizes the screen to fit the part.

Your screen should now look like the screen in Figure 2–12.

Notice that the rectangle isn't centered nicely in the display area. There is a simple solution to this. Press the **Fit** button on the tool bar (Figure 2–13). The screen should resize itself to fit our rectangle.

After completing the rectangle you now must create the four 0.500-diameter drilled holes. You will create these circles using the Create/Arc modes. To go back to the Main Menu area, select **Main Menu** from the Main Menu area.

From the **Main Menu** click the **Create** button. From the Create menu select **Arc** (see Figure 2–14).

After selecting Arc, Mastercam gives you many options for creating arcs. From the Arc menu select **Circ pt+dia** (see Figure 2–15). This will allow us to create an arc or circle by specifying both the coordinate of the center point and the diameter of the circle or arc.

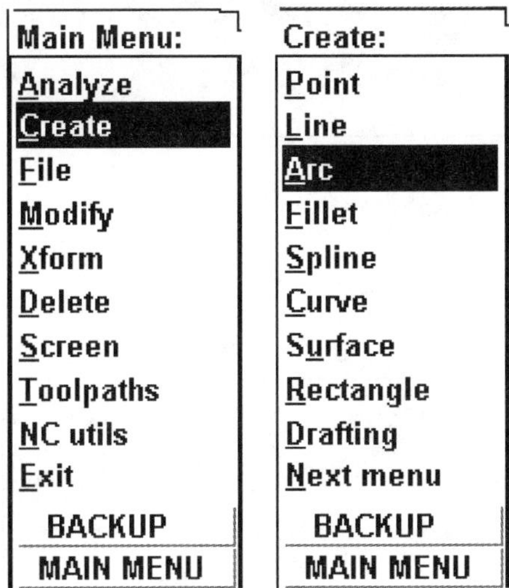

FIGURE 2–14

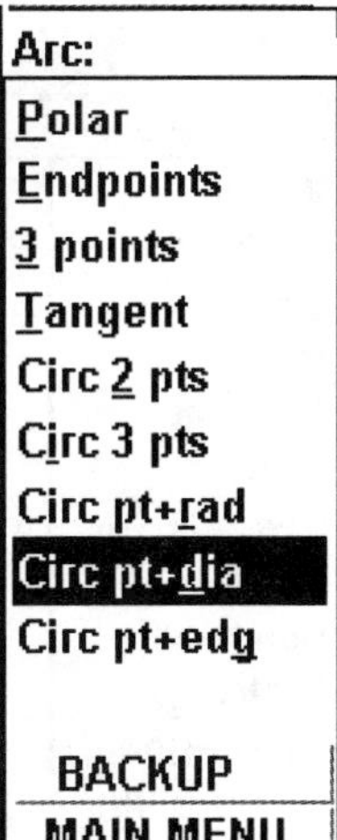

FIGURE 2–15

Notice in the dialogue box along the bottom of the screen that Mastercam is prompting you for a center point (see Figure 2–16). The center point coordinate of the first hole is X.500 and Y.500. Type **.5,.5** and press **Enter.**

Mastercam should now be prompting you for the diameter of the circle or arc (see Figure 2–17). Notice that the Mastercam software is defaulting to the last

FIGURE 2–16

Circle, with center/diameter: Enter the center point

FIGURE 2–17

Enter the diameter 1.
(or X,Y,Z,R,D,L,S,A,?)

diameter value that was input. This becomes useful to us when inputting multiple circles. If the software is not defaulting to .500, type **.5** for a .500-diameter hole and press **Enter.**

FIGURE 2–18

The first drilled hole should now be located in the lower left corner of the rectangle. Does the part now appear too big for the screen? If it does, click on the **Unzoom** button located in the tool bar (see Figure 2–18).

To reestablish what you did to create the first hole, you selected Main Menu/Create/Arc/Circ pt+dia.

Now let's finish the other three holes. Mastercam is still in the Circ pt+dia Creation mode. Notice how Mastercam is prompting you for the center position of the next hole. Type **.5,2.5** and press **Enter.** Notice how Mastercam is now defaulting to .5 for the diameter of the circle or arc. This was the last value that was input. Press **Enter** to accept the default. The second hole should now appear.

Finish putting in the last two holes using Figure 2–1 to calculate the hole positions. Follow the same procedure as the first two holes. The Mastercam screen should now look like Figure 2–19.

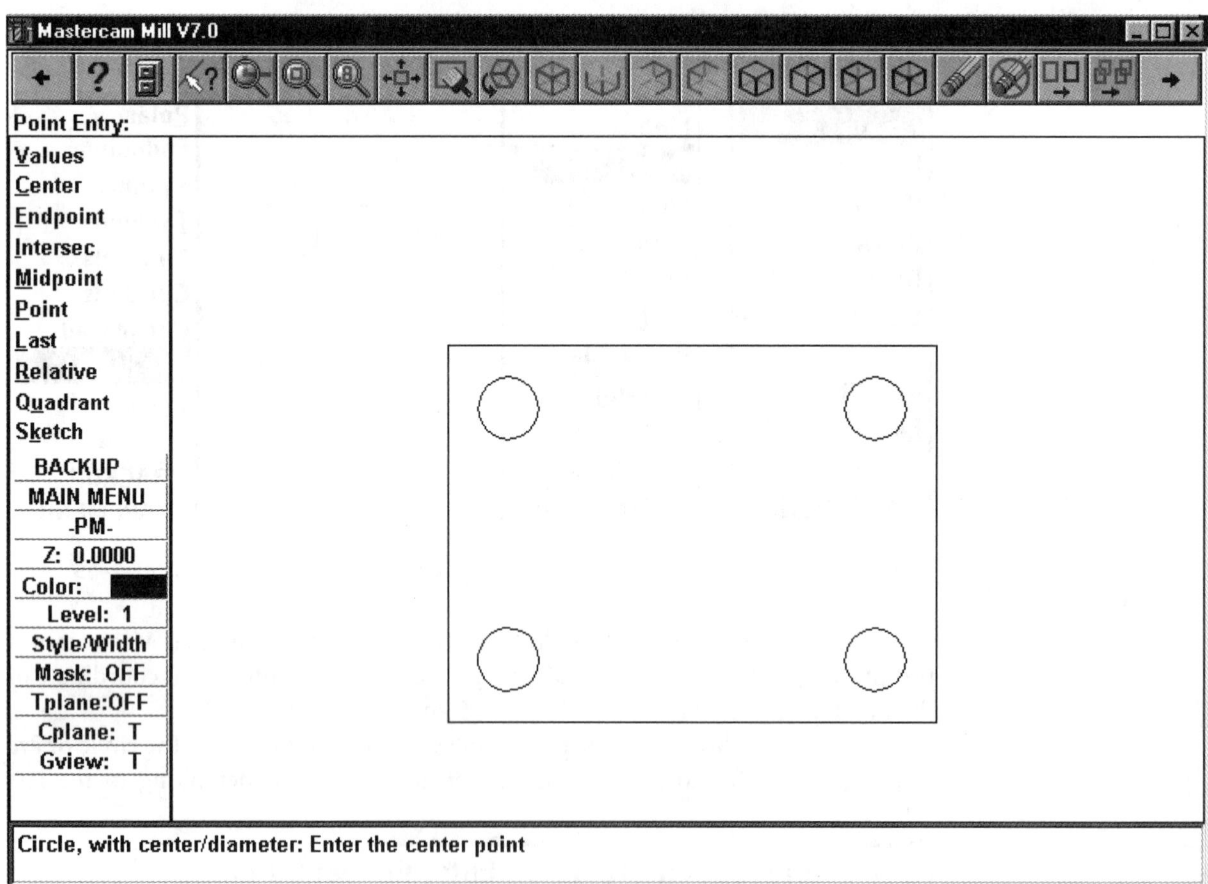

FIGURE 2–19

APPLYING MACHINING COMMANDS

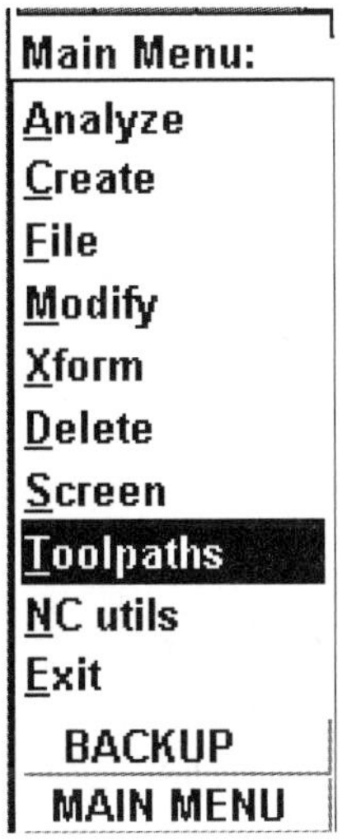

Now that you have established the part geometry, it is time to apply the machining commands. Some of the basic machining commands in Mastercam Mill include: contour machining, pocketing, drilling, point machining, and manual entry. In some instances the machining commands are referred to as modules. Do not get confused; this is just a matter of terminology. You will be using the Contour module to machine around the outside of the rectangle and the Drilling module to machine the 0.500-diameter holes.

To initiate the Contour module, return to the Main Menu by selecting the **Main Menu** button from the Main Menu area of Mastercam. From the Main Menu select **Toolpaths** (see Figure 2–20).

From the Toolpaths menu select **Contour** (see Figure 2–21). To reestablish how you got to the Contour machining module, you selected Main Menu/Toopaths/Contour.

Mastercam is now asking for a new file name under which to save the machining module (see Figure 2–22). Type **cadcam** with no slash between cad and cam and select the **Save** button.

Notice in the dialogue box at the bottom of the screen that Mastercam is prompting us to select Chain (see Figure 2–23). The Chain mode defines the individual members of the contour profile that you want to machine. Select **Chain** now from the Contour menu.

To begin defining the contour of the rectangle you want to machine, use the mouse cursor to select the **lower left corner of the rectangle** as shown in Figure 2–24.

Once you have selected this entity, Mastercam uses a chaining arrow (see Figure 2–25) to depict the starting entity of the chained contour. Mastercam is chaining in a clockwise direction. After picking the start point, Mastercam now

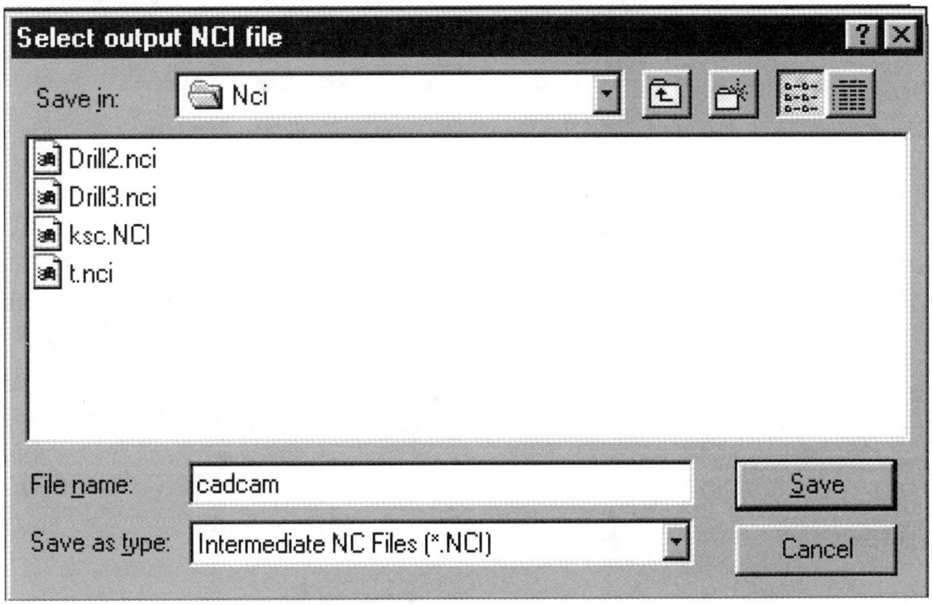

FIGURE 2–20

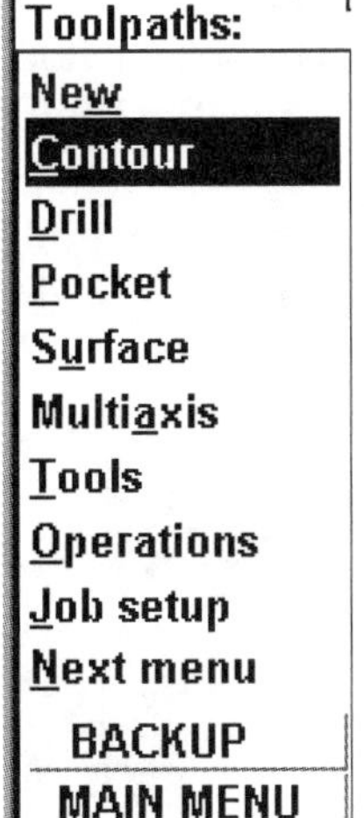

FIGURE 2–21

FIGURE 2–22

FIGURE 2–23

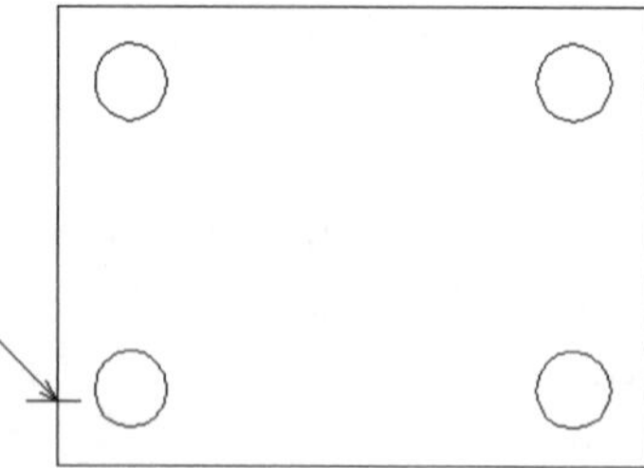

FIGURE 2–24

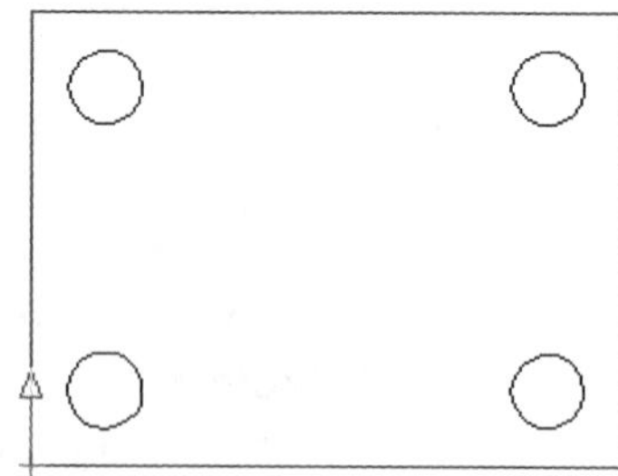

FIGURE 2–25

recognizes that this rectangle is one closed entity. This will allow us to start at a point, go around the contour, and end at the same point.

At this point you can select **Done** (see Figure 2–26) from the chaining menu. After selecting done, the Mastercam software automatically pulls up the Tool and Contour parameters menu (see Figure 2–27). These parameters will be covered in greater detail in the upcoming chapters.

The Tool Parameters box is the initial box that appears. The default tool parameter settings will work for this example. Compare the settings in Figure 2–27 with the actual settings on your screen. To machine around the rectangle you will use tool number 1, which is a .500 end mill. Open the contour module by clicking on the folder heading called **Contour Parameters** at the top of the framed area.

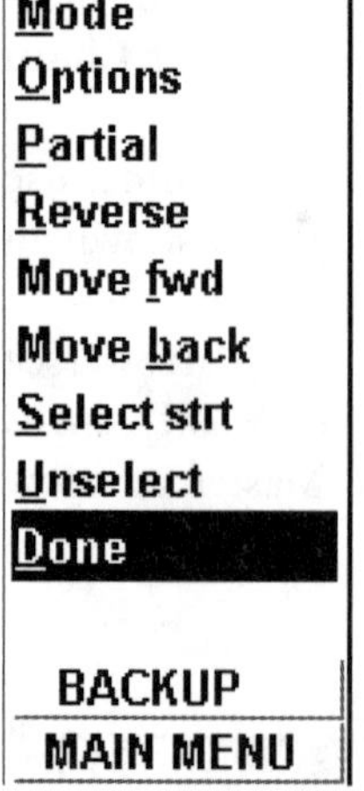

FIGURE 2–26

Contour - C:\MILL7\NCI\CADCAM.NCI Properties

Tool parameters | Contour parameters

Left 'click' on tool to select; right 'click' to edit or define new tool

Tool name				Tool dia	0.5	Corner radius	0.0
Tool #	1	Feed rate	2.0	Program #	0	Spindle speed	1200
Dia. offset	41	Plunge rate	2.0	Seq. start	100	Coolant	Off
Len. offset	1	Retract rate	2.0	Seq. inc.	2		Change NCI...

Comment

Home pos... Ref. point... Misc. values...

Rotary axis... T/C planes... Tool display...

OK Cancel

FIGURE 2–27

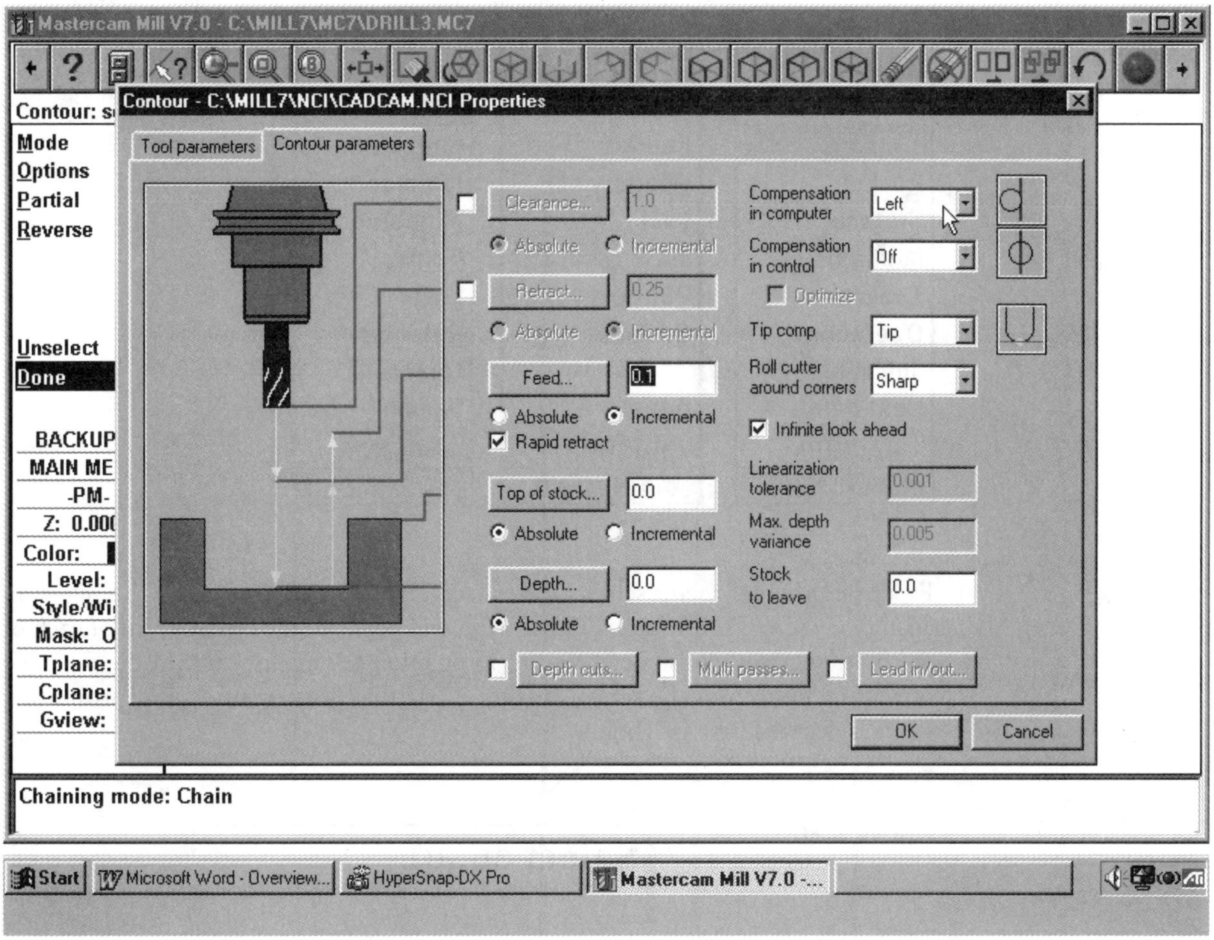

FIGURE 2–28

Looking at the Contour Parameters (Figure 2–28) you can see that these parameters have a great deal of control on the tool and the tool path. You will accept the Mastercam default parameters file by selecting the **OK** button now. Mastercam asks if it is OK to create a new tool. Select **OK** to confirm this. The screen should now be reverting back to the part geometry with the tool path appearing (Figure 2–29).

Now that you have completed the rectangular contour it is time to drill the holes. From the Toolpaths menu select **Drill.** From the Drill menu select **Manual.**

FIGURE 2–29

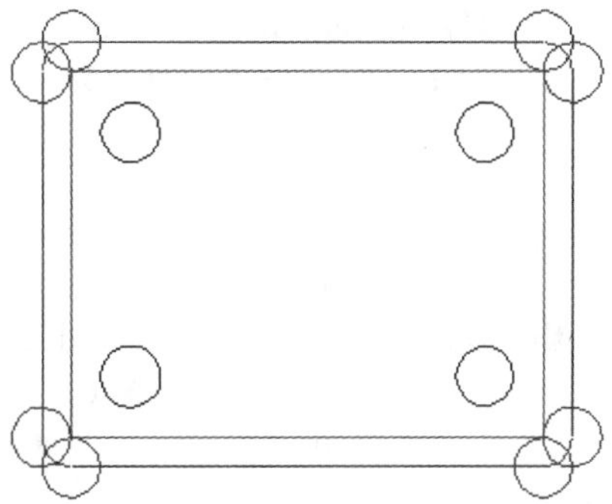

FIGURE 2–30

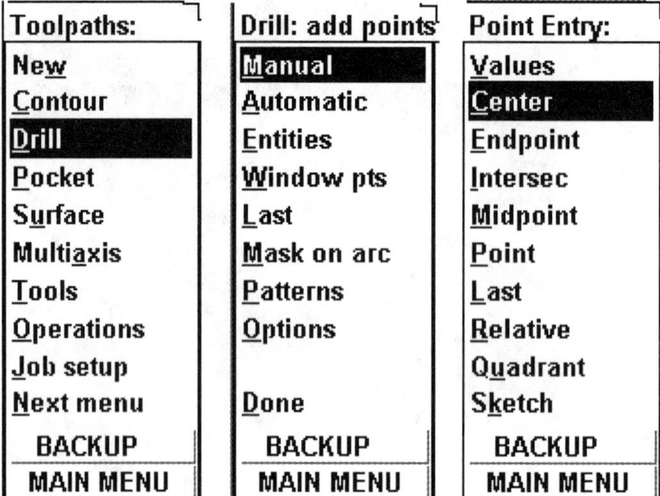

From the Manual menu select **Center** (see Figure 2–30). To review the selection again, they were Drill/Manual/Center. You will be using the center point of each of the holes that you constructed earlier to position the drill. Notice in the dialogue box at the bottom of the screen (Figure 2–31) that Mastercam is now prompting you to select the first arc (hole).

FIGURE 2–31

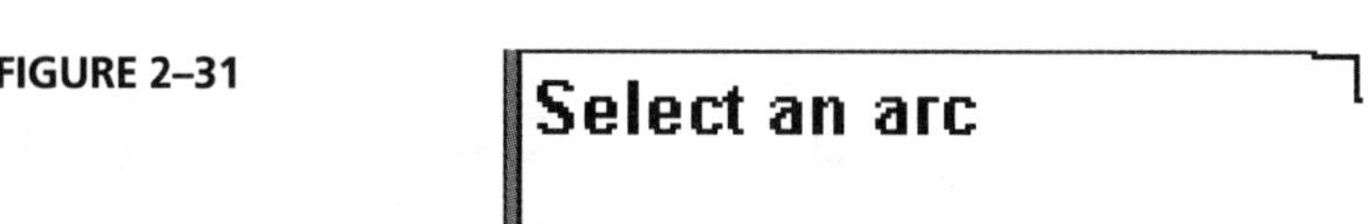

The Mastercam manual drill module will machine the holes in the same order you pick them. Using the mouse, select the **hole** that is located in the **lower left** corner first. By previously selecting Center from the Point Entry menu the software automatically snaps to the center of the first hole. To drill the next hole, select **Center** again from the Point Entry menu. Now select the **next hole** you would like to drill. Make sure that you select Center for each of the last two holes to assure that the drill uses the center of the hole to accurately position the tool. After you have finished picking the final hole, Mastercam prompts you to hit the **Esc** key, or the "escape" key. Now select **Done** from the Drill menu (Figure 2–32).

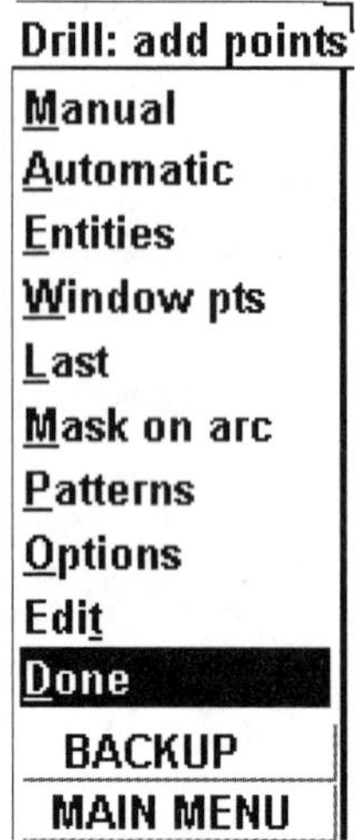

FIGURE 2–32

When the Tool Parameters menu appears, add tool number 2 by moving the mouse cursor to the **large tool parameters box** (see Figure 2–33) and press the **RIGHT** mouse button. When the pop up menu appears (Figure 2–34), use the mouse to select **Get tool** from library. Select tool number **141,** the 1/2 drill. Mastercam now shows us the newly created drill called tool number 2. Press **OK.** At the tool parameters, select **OK** again to accept the added tool. The completed tool path should now appear on the screen.

To complete the CAD/CAM process you must now convert or postprocess the tool path that you created into machine language or NC code. Go back to the Main Menu by selecting **Main Menu.** From the Main Menu select **NC Utils.** From the NC utils menu select **Post Proc.** From the Post proc menu select **Run** (see

FIGURE 2–33

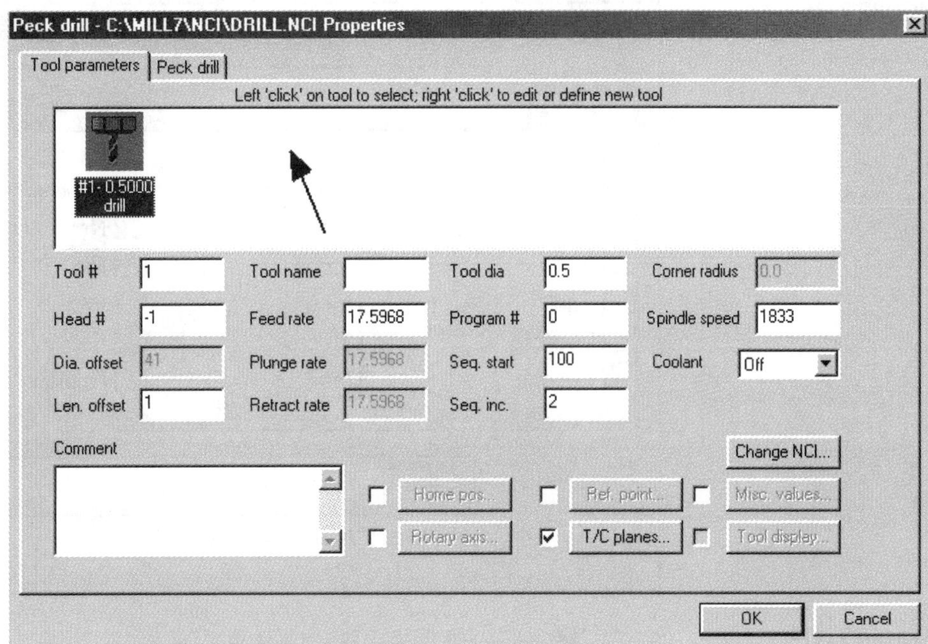

Get tool from library...
Create new tool...
Job setup...

FIGURE 2–34

Figure 2–35). To review the selections again, they were Main Menu/NC utils/Post proc/Run.

Mastercam now asks if you want to create the NCI tool file. Select **Yes.** Mastercam now wants to know which tool path file you want to postprocess (Figure 2–36). You called the file cadcam. Mastercam should be defaulting to the last active file, which was cadcam. If it is, select **Open.** If not, type **cadcam** and select **Open.** Mastercam now wants to know what file name it should assign to the machine language file (Figure 2–37). To keep all of the files consistent, name the file **cadcam** and press Save. The files you are creating all have different extensions, so there is no chance of overwriting any existing files named cadcam.

FIGURE 2–35

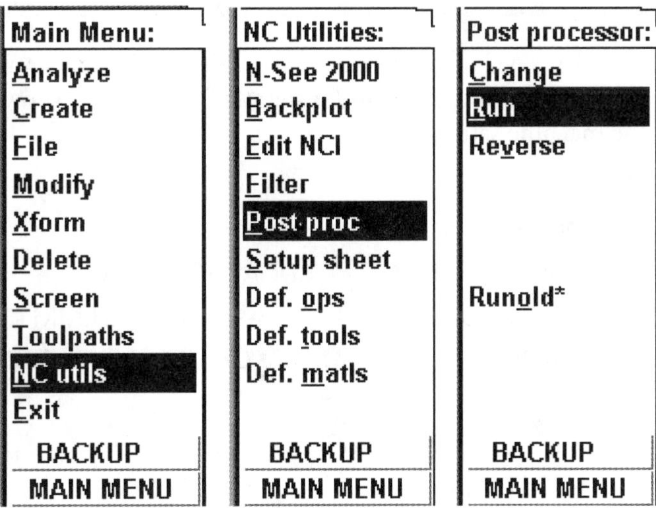

FIGURE 2–36

FIGURE 2–37

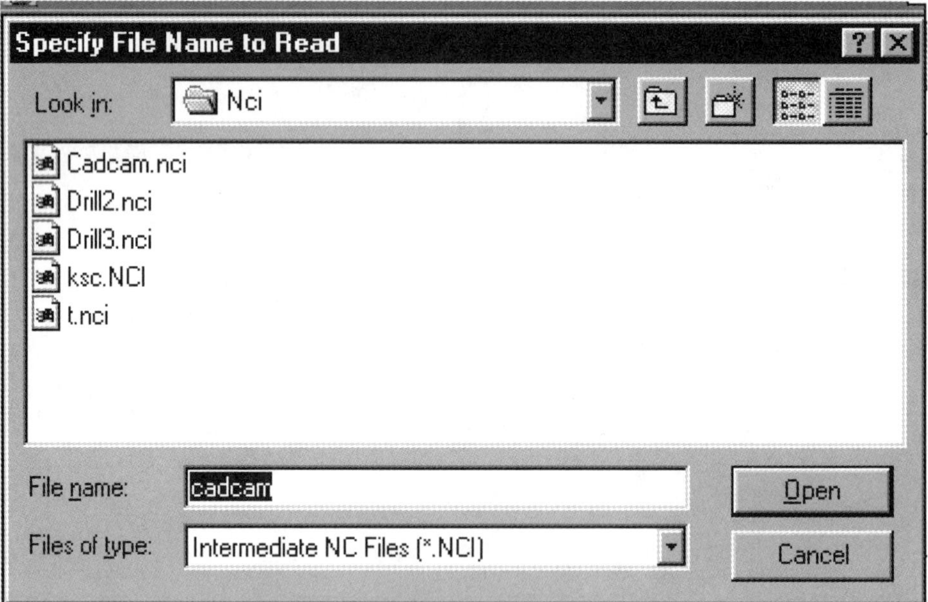

Your NC or numerical control file should appear and look similar to the NC file below. Your file may differ slightly from the one shown due to slight changes in the machine settings.

```
%
O0000
(PROGRAM NAME - CADCAM)
(DATE=DD-MM-YY - 17-08-98 TIME=HH:MM - 14:40)
(UNDEFINED TOOL - 1 DIA. OFF. - 41 LEN. - 1 DIA. - .5)
N100G20
N102G0G40G49G80G90
N104T1M6
N106G0G90G55X-.25Y0.S1200M3
```

```
N108G43H1Z.1
N110G1Z0.F2.
N112Y3.
N114G2X0.Y3.25I.25
N116G1X4.
N118G2X4.25Y3.J-.25
N120G1Y0.
N122G2X4.Y-.25I-.25
N124G1X0.
N126G2X-.25Y0.J.25
N128G0Z.1
N130M5
N132G91G28Z0.
N134M01
(UNDEFINED TOOL - 2 DIA. OFF. - 42 LEN. - 2 DIA. - .5)
N136T2M6
N138G0G90X.5Y.5S1833M3
N140G43H2Z.1
N142G99G81Z0.R.1F29.33
N144Y2.5
N146X3.5
N148Y.5
N150G80
N152M5
N154G91G0G28Z0.
N156M30
%
```

Exit the file editor by selecting the **X** or **Exit** icon in the upper right corner of the screen.

Now that you have finished this chapter, you should have a better understanding of the Mastercam CAD/CAM process. Keep the CAD/CAM process in mind as you go through the following chapters.

REVIEW QUESTIONS

1. Define the basic components of the Mastercam CAD/CAM process.
2. If the part were originally drawn using a separate CAD system, could you use it in Mastercam? If so how?
3. Mastercam's working environment is divided into five specific areas. Name them.
4. Once you have established the part geometry, what needs to be done next?

5. Which mode defines the individual members of the contour profile that you want to machine?
6. Which parameters have a great deal of control on the tool and the tool path.
7. To complete the CAD/CAM process you convert the tool path that you created into machine language or NC code. What is this process called?

CHAPTER

3

Creating Basic Geometry

In this chapter you are introduced to Mastercam's geometry construction area. Some, but not all, geometry construction is done in the design programming area of Mastercam. In later chapters we discuss the other methods by which we can create geometry. No matter which Mastercam method we use to create geometry, it is essential that the geometry we construct is correct in all phases, especially scale. Since the geometry we will be creating will be the basis for our tool path, the drafting model that we create is an essential part of the CAD/CAM process. The exercises in this chapter will be repeated in later chapters to help solidify the geometry construction process.

Objectives

Upon completion of this chapter you will be able to:

- Create lines, points, arcs
- Create circles, rectangles, fillets, chamfers
- Create polygons

USING THE CREATE MENU

Start Mastercam using the **Start** button and then under **Programs** point to the folder called **Mastercam.** Click on the **Mastercam Design v7.1** option (see Figure 3–1).

As noted earlier, part geometry can be created in the Design area of Mastercam and also in Lathe, Mill, and other machine areas of Mastercam. Once the part geometry has been completed the file is called up and the tool path is generated according to the geometry file. Since we will not be creating a tool path or code in this unit we will be using the Geometry construction area of Mastercam in this chapter.

CREATING LINES

All of the geometry construction starts with the **Create** menu. The Create menu is located in the Main Menu of Mastercam (see Figure 3–2). Once you have entered the Create menu select **Line.**

In review, the commands were Main Menu/Create/Line. Mastercam is a very powerful computer-aided drafting software and allows the user a number of different methods in which to create different geometry elements. Figure 3–3 is the Mastercam Line menu. Note the number of options Mastercam offers for line geometry creation. In this chapter we explore each of these options. Follow along with each line creation exercise that follows.

Creating a Horizontal Line

To create a horizontal line select the **Horizontal** option from the Line menu (see Figure 3–3). Next select **Values** from the Point Entry menu to input the coordinates for the start of the horizontal line.

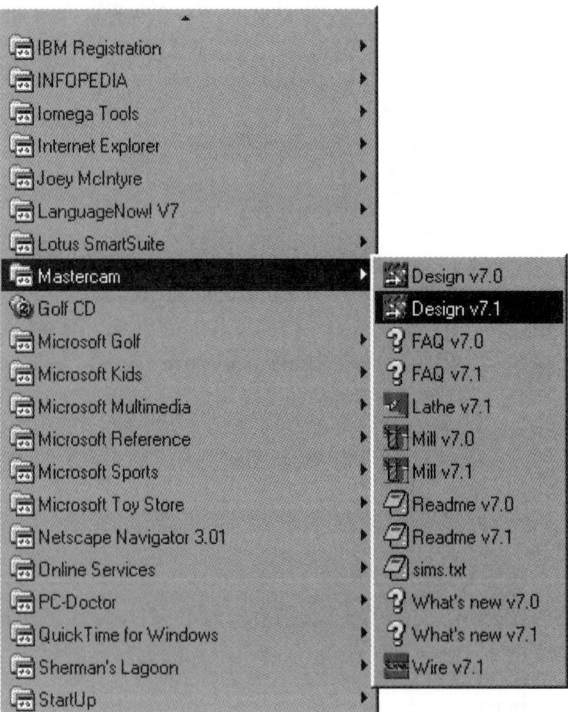

FIGURE 3–1
The user chose the Mastercam folder and then the Mastercam Design v7.1 option.

Main Menu:
Analyze
Create
File
Modify
Xform
Delete
Screen
Exit
BACKUP
MAIN MENU
Create:
Point
Line
Arc
Fillet
Spline
Curve
Surface
Rectangle
Drafting
Next menu
BACKUP
MAIN MENU

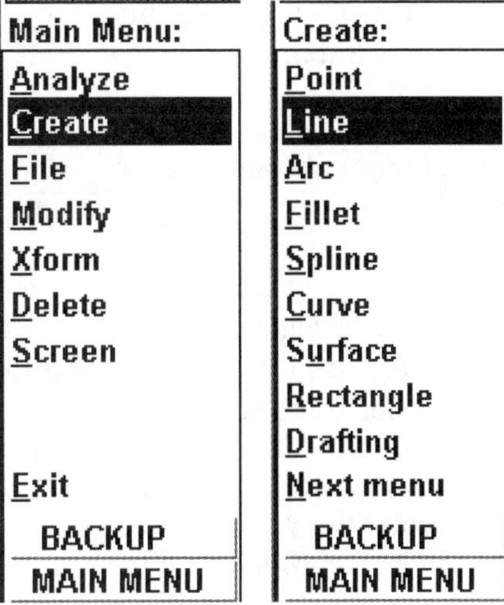

FIGURE 3–2
The user has chosen Create and then Line.

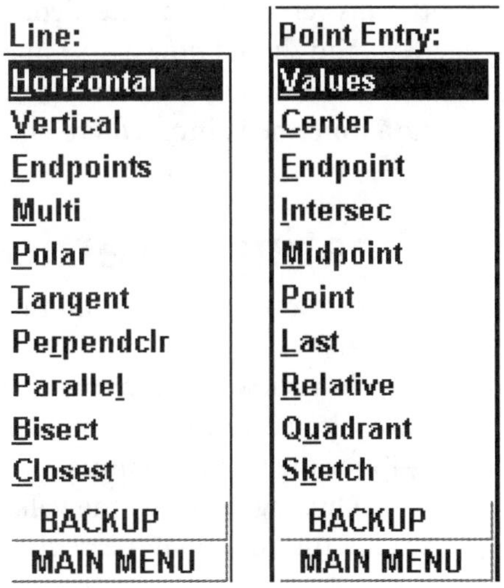

Line:
Horizontal
Vertical
Endpoints
Multi
Polar
Tangent
Perpendclr
Parallel
Bisect
Closest
BACKUP
MAIN MENU
Point Entry:
Values
Center
Endpoint
Intersec
Midpoint
Point
Last
Relative
Quadrant
Sketch
BACKUP
MAIN MENU

FIGURE 3–3
The user has chosen Horizontal and then Values.

In review, the commands were Create/Line/Horizontal/Values. Once you have selected Horizontal, Mastercam will prompt you for the first endpoint in the dialogue box (see Figure 3–4).

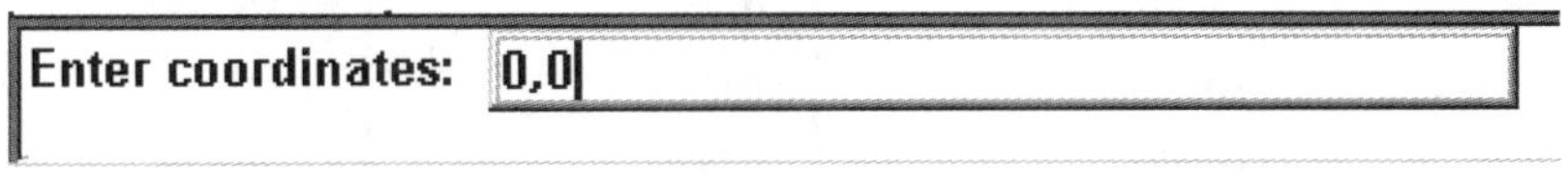

Enter coordinates: 0,0

FIGURE 3–4
The user has entered 0,0 for the first endpoint of the line.

Using the Value option from the Point Entry menu allows us to specify coordinates associated with the horizontal line we are creating. After selecting the Values option, specify the X-axis coordinate position of the endpoint of the line first, followed by a comma, and then the Y-axis coordinate position of the endpoint of the line. Type in **0,0** and press **Enter.** This will be the start point or origin of the first line.

You should now have a cross or what is called a cursor snap on your screen. That cursor snap is attached to the line you are creating. Select the **Values** option from the Point Entry menu to specify the coordinates associated with the endpoint of the horizontal line you are creating. Mastercam's dialogue box is now asking for the endpoint of the line (see Figure 3–5). Type **3** for the X-axis coordinate and press **Enter.**

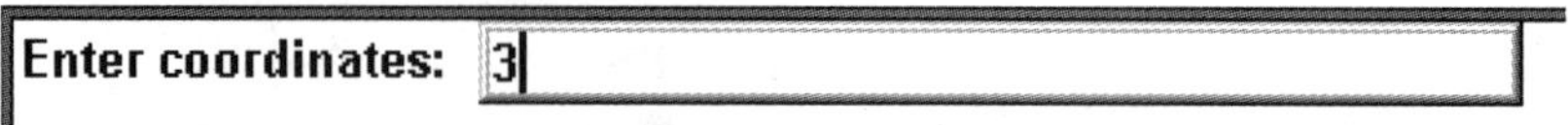

FIGURE 3–5
The user has entered 3 for the X-axis coordinate of the line.

Mastercam's dialogue box is now asking for the endpoint of the line on the Y axis (see Figure 3–6). Since the line is horizontal, Mastercam should be defaulting to 0. Accept this by pressing **Enter** on the keyboard or type in a **0** for the Y-axis coordinate and accept the 0 by pressing **Enter.**

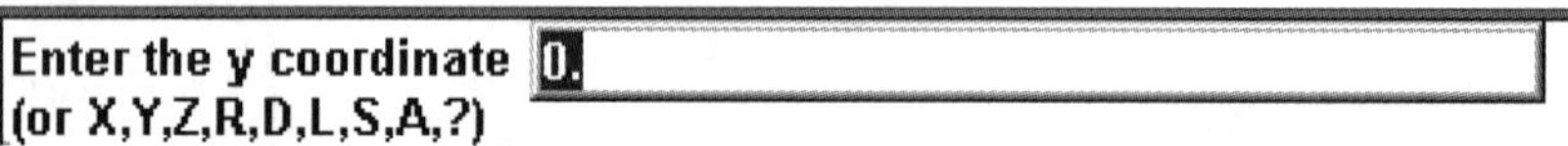

FIGURE 3–6
The user has accepted the default value of 0 for the Y-axis coordinate of the line.

Notice the importance of Mastercam's dialogue box. It will prompt you for the answers as they are needed.

You should now have a line in the Display area of your Mastercam screen.

In review, the commands were Create/Line/Horizontal using the Values option from the Point menu to enter the coordinates of the line.

Creating a Vertical Line

To create a vertical line from the Main Menu select **Create/Line/Vertical** (see Figure 3–7).

In review, the commands were Main Menu/Create/Line/Vertical. Once you have selected Vertical, Mastercam is prompting you in the dialogue box (see Figure 3–8) for the first endpoint.

Once again, using the Value option from the Point entry menu allows you to specify the coordinates associated with the vertical line you are creating. Specify

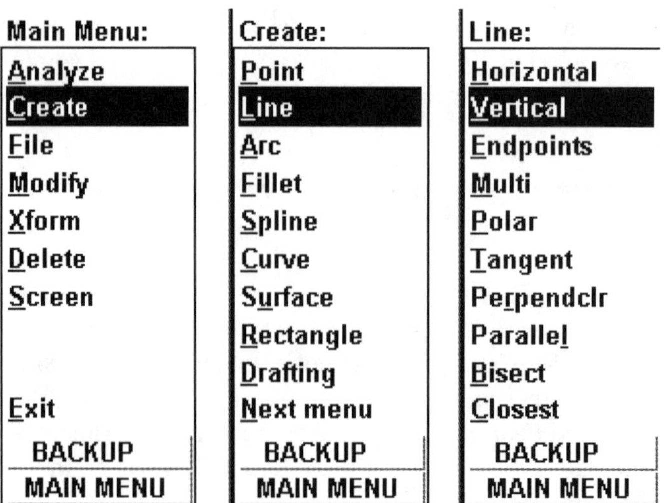

FIGURE 3–7
The user has chosen Create, Line, and Vertical for the line type.

Create line, vertical: Specify the first endpoint

FIGURE 3–8
The user has entered 1 for the X coordinate.

the X-axis coordinate position of the endpoint of the line first followed by a comma and then the Y-axis coordinate position of the endpoint of the line. Type in **1,1** and press **Enter** (see Figure 3–9). This will be the start point or origin of the vertical line.

FIGURE 3–9
The user has entered 1,1 for the first endpoint of the vertical line.

You should now have a cursor snap on your screen. That cursor snap is attached to the line you are creating. Select the **Values** option from the Point Entry menu to specify the coordinates associated with the end point of the vertical line. Mastercam's dialogue box is now asking for the endpoint of the line (see Figure 3–10). Type **1,3** for the endpoint coordinates of the vertical line.

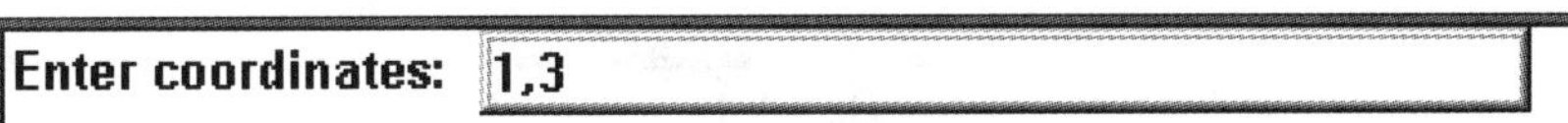

FIGURE 3–10
The user has entered 1,3 for the second endpoint.

Mastercam's dialogue box is now asking for the coordinate endpoint of the line on the X axis (see Figure 3–11). Since the line is vertical, the system knows it has to be 1 and is defaulting to 1. Accept the default by pressing **Enter** on the keyboard.

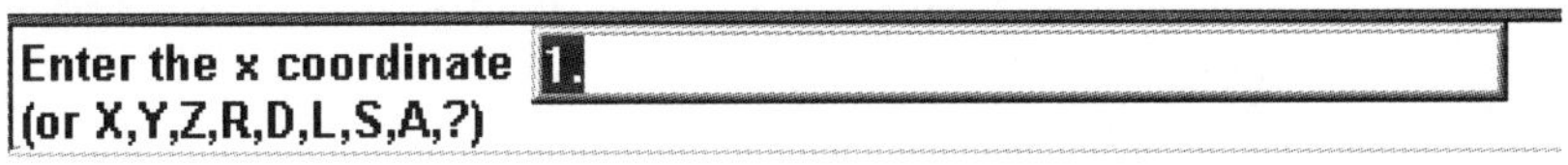

Enter the x coordinate 1.
(or X,Y,Z,R,D,L,S,A,?)

FIGURE 3–11
The user accepted the default of 1 for the X value.

You should now have a vertical line in the Display area of your Mastercam screen.

In review, the commands were Create/Line/Vertical using the Value option from the Point menu to enter the coordinates of the line.

Creating a Line Using Endpoints

To create a Line using endpoints, from the Main Menu select **Create/Line/Endpoints** (Figure 3–12).

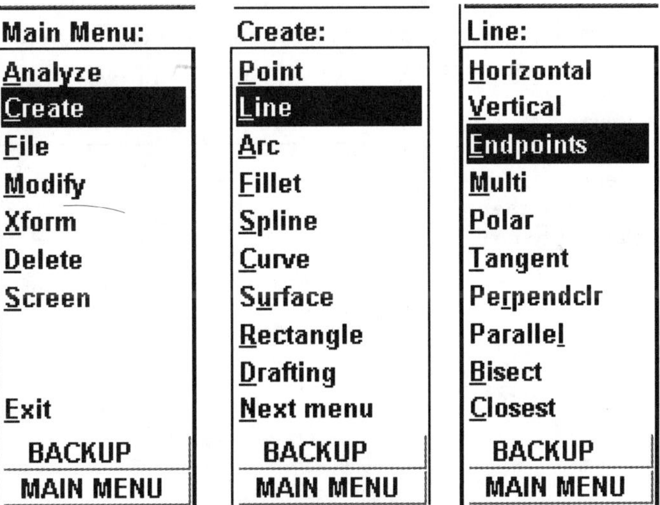

FIGURE 3–12
The user chose Create from the Main Menu, then Line and Endpoints.

In review, the commands were Main Menu/Create/Line/Endpoints. Once you have selected Endpoints, Mastercam is prompting you for the first endpoint in the dialogue box (see Figure 3–13).

FIGURE 3–13
The system prompts the user to enter the coordinates of the first endpoint.

Create line, endpoints: Specify the first endpoint

To begin specifying the first endpoint, type **2,2** and press **Enter** (see Figure 3–14). Notice that Mastercam automatically goes into a coordinate input mode without selecting it from the menu. 2, 2 will be the start point or origin of the new line.

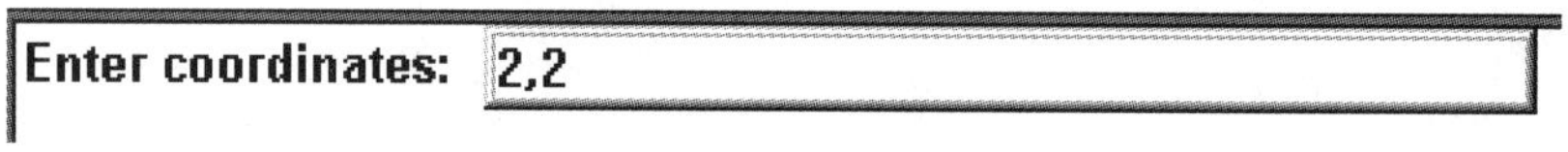

FIGURE 3–14
The user has entered 2,2 for the first endpoint.

Enter coordinates: 2,2

You should now have a cursor snap on your screen. That cursor snap is attached to the line you are creating. Mastercam's dialogue box is now showing the polar coordinates of the cursor position. To specify the coordinates of the endpoint, type **4,4.** Again, notice that the dialogue box automatically switches over to the coordinate input mode (see Figure 3–15). Press **Enter** to accept 4, 4 as our line endpoint.

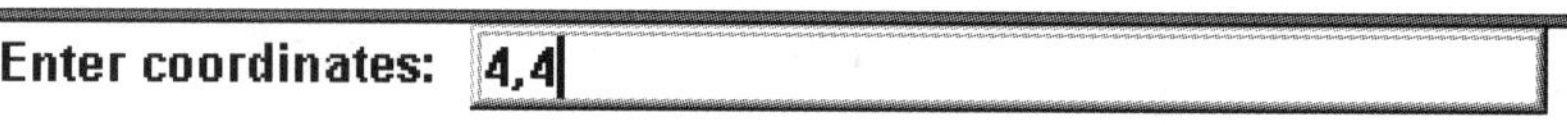

FIGURE 3–15
The user entered 4,4 for the second endpoint.

If you have made a mistake, you may need to erase an entity. In Chapter 1 we talked about the tool bar. The tool bar is located along the top of the screen. In the tool bar we have a Delete option. Move the mouse to the **pencil eraser** as shown in Figure 3–16. When you place the mouse cursor over the top of any of the tool icons, a description of the icon appears.

FIGURE 3–16
The delete option in the tool bar.

The icon description should be Delete. Select the **Delete** icon using the left mouse button. Once the Eraser icon has been selected, Mastercam will prompt you for the entity you want to erase. Use the mouse to move the cursor snap over the angled line (see Figure 3–17) you just created. You want to erase this entity. Click the left mouse button and the line will disappear.

FIGURE 3–17
The user has chosen the line as the element to be deleted.

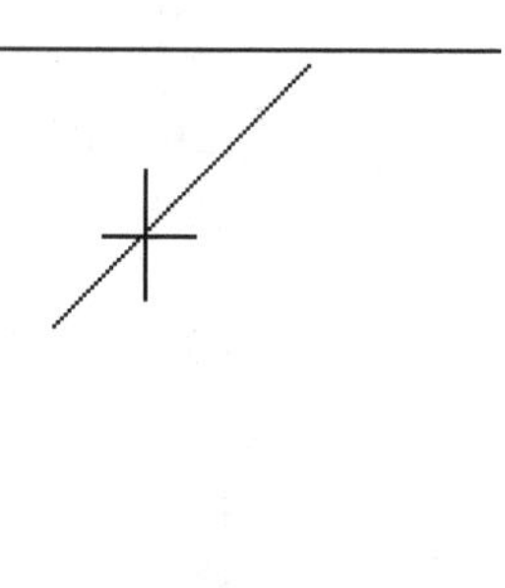

FIGURE 3–18
The unerase option button.

If you make a mistake and erase the wrong entity, you can restore the entity by selecting the Un-Erase option from the tool bar (see Figure 3–18). If you don't see this icon click on the next page arrow. The page arrows are the arrows located at the far ends of the toolbar. Find the **Un-delete** icon and click on it using the left mouse button to restore the line that you erased.

Before we continue on with line creation, let's get to know more about some of the other tool bar applications.

FIGURE 3–19
The zoom button.

Zoom

In many cases when you are creating geometry you need to enlarge a part of the drawing. The Zoom function allows you to specify a windowed area to zoom in on (see Figure 3–19). By entering the two corner points of the rectangular window you can enlarge this area.

The window is a rectangular box and the zoom window area becomes the center of the Graphics area. Find the Zoom icon (you may have to use the Next Page arrows). Click on the **Zoom** icon. The cursor snap should now appear. Using the mouse, move the cursor to the lower left corner of the vertical line (see Figure 3–20). Use the left mouse button to click on this point. Now move the mouse to the upper right corner of the vertical line. Notice the window you are creating. Use the left mouse button to click when the window surrounds the vertical line.

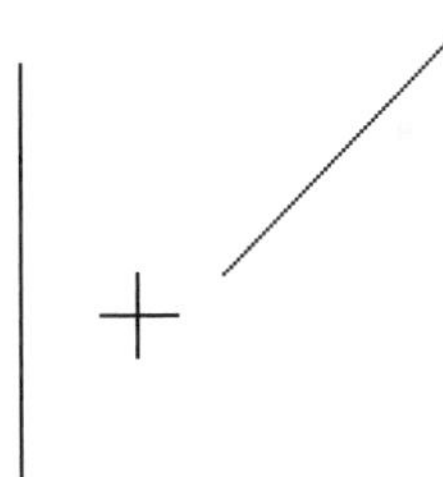

FIGURE 3–20
The user has specified the lower left corner of the area to be zoomed.

UnZoom

The unzoom function (see Figure 3–21) enlarges the display screen. This will give us the impression that we are backing up, enabling us to see more of the graphics screen. Select the **UnZoom** icon in the toolbar. Selecting the Unzoom icon gives us a display scale factor of 0.5. Notice that the screen appears to be backing up. Press the **Unzoom** button again. All of the lines should now appear on the screen.

FIGURE 3–21
The Unzoom button.

Unzoom 0.8

Selecting the **Unzoom 0.8** icon, which is to the right of the **Unzoom** icon, gives you a display scale of 0.8. This allows you to use either scale factor when you want to resize your screen. Try the **Unzoom 0.8** option also.

Use the **Fit** icon (see Figure 3–22) to reestablish all of the lines on the graphics screen.

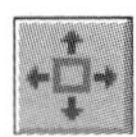

FIGURE 3–22
The fit icon.

Creating Multiple Lines

Find the Main Menu by clicking on **Main Menu** or by hitting the **Escape** key. You may have to select one of these options more than once to back up to the Main Menu. From the Main Menu select **Create/Line/Multi** to create multiple lines (Figure 3–23).

In review, the commands were Main Menu/Create/Line/Multi. Once you have selected Multi, Mastercam will prompt you for the first endpoint coordinate in the dialogue box. Once again we will use **Values** from the Point Entry menu, but this time we will use the cursor snap to create multiple lines. We want to start the line from the upper endpoint of the angled line. To make sure that we have started the multiple line from the endpoint of the angled line we need to use the endpoint snap. This will insure that we are creating perfect mathematical geometry. This is very important because we will be using this geometry to create tool path. From the Point Entry menu select **Endpoint** (see Figure 3–24).

Main Menu:	Create:	Line:
Analyze	Point	Horizontal
Create	Line	Vertical
File	Arc	Endpoints
Modify	Fillet	Multi
Xform	Spline	Polar
Delete	Curve	Tangent
Screen	Surface	Perpendclr
	Rectangle	Parallel
	Drafting	Bisect
Exit	Next menu	Closest
BACKUP	BACKUP	BACKUP
MAIN MENU	MAIN MENU	MAIN MENU

FIGURE 3–23
The user has chosen Create from the Main Menu, then Line, and then Multi.

Point Entry:
Values
Center
Endpoint
Intersec
Midpoint
Point
Last
Relative
Quadrant
Sketch
BACKUP
MAIN MENU

FIGURE 3–24
The user has chosen Endpoint from the Point Entry menu.

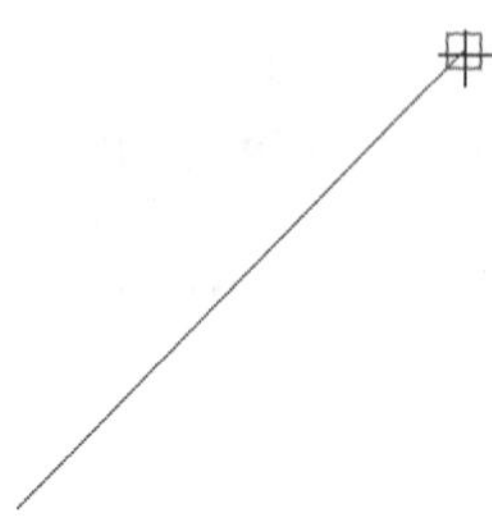

FIGURE 3–25
The user has used the mouse to position a crosshair over the end of the line.

The Mastercam dialogue box is now asking you to select the endpoint of the entity from which you want the line to start. You will use the mouse cursor to select the entity. Place the cursor over the angled line. You want to have the cursor closer to the upper end of the line than to the lower end (see Figure 3–25). This will insure that Mastercam knows which end you want to choose. Use the left mouse button to select the end when you have the mouse cursor in position.

You are now connected to the upper endpoint of the angled line. When you have the mouse positioned where you want the endpoint of the line, press the left mouse button. Use the mouse cursor and practice creating lines using the mouse and the Endpoint selection. Create a figure that resembles Figure 3–26.

You are now going to close the figure that you have created. With the line still connected to the cursor select the **Endpoint** function from the Point Entry menu (see Figure 3–27).

The Mastercam dialogue box is now asking you to select the endpoint of the entity where you want the line to end. You will use the mouse cursor to select the en-

FIGURE 3–26
The user has created two additional lines using the mouse.

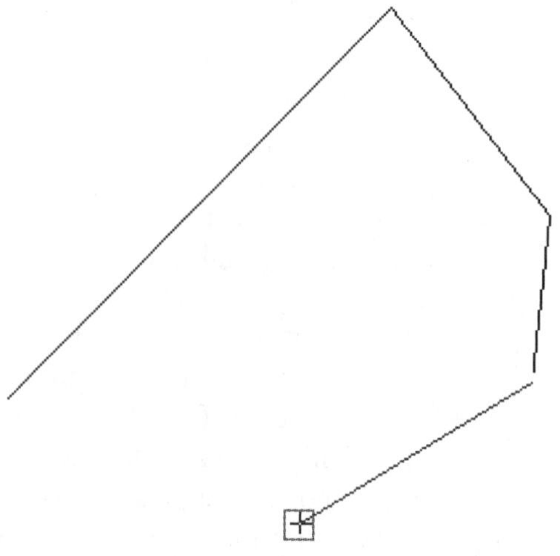

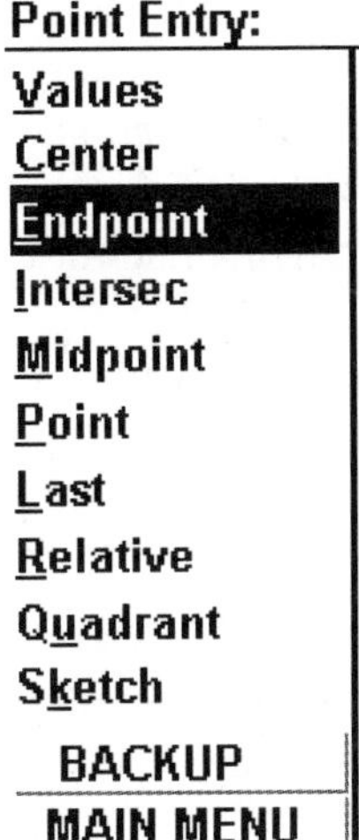

FIGURE 3–27
The user selected the Endpoint option from the Point Entry menu.

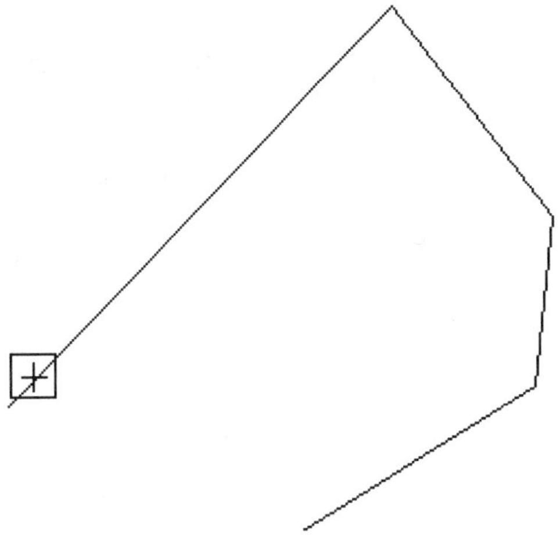

FIGURE 3–28
The user has selected the lower left side of the line.

tity. Place the cursor over the lower end of the angled line. You must have the cursor closer to the lower end of the line than to the upper end of the line (see Figure 3–28) to assure that Mastercam knows which end of the line you want to choose. Use the left mouse button to select the end when you have the mouse cursor in position. The figure you created should now be closed. To stop creating lines hit the **Esc** or the escape key on the keyboard.

Creating Lines with Polar Entries

From the Main Menu select **Create/Line/Polar** to create lines specified by an angle and a line length (Figure 3–29).

In review, the commands were Main Menu/Create/Line/Polar. Once you have selected Polar, Mastercam will prompt you in the dialogue for the start point of the line or the endpoint coordinate.

FIGURE 3–29
The user selected the Create, Line, and Polar options.

Main Menu:
Analyze
Create
File
Modify
Xform
Delete
Screen
Exit
BACKUP
MAIN MENU

Create:
Point
Line
Arc
Fillet
Spline
Curve
Surface
Rectangle
Drafting
Next menu
BACKUP
MAIN MENU

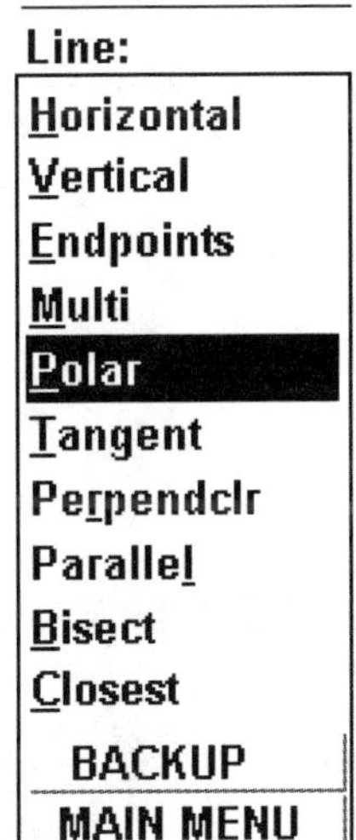

In this exercise we will use Mastercam's smart cursor system. Place the cursor snap over the upper end of the vertical line. Notice how the snap or crosshair converts to a box and the option in the Point Entry menu automatically shifts to Endpoint (see Figure 3–30). Accept the entry by clicking the left mouse button.

If you have done this correctly, the crosshair should be precisely on the end of the line. If the cursor snap is not precisely located on the end of the line hit **Esc** and try doing it again by selecting **Polar.** Once you have correctly located the start point of the line, Mastercam will prompt you for the line angle (Figure 3–31).

We would like a 45-degree-angle line. Type **45** and press **Enter.**

FIGURE 3–30 The user used the mouse to snap the end of the line.

Enter the angle in degrees 45.
(or X,Y,Z,R,D,L,S,A,?)

FIGURE 3–31 The user entered 45 degrees for the angle.

Now enter the length of the angled line. You want the line length to be 1 inch. Type **1** and press **Enter.** Your graphic screen should now look like the one in Figure 3–32. If it doesn't look like it is connected, click on the **Repaint** icon in the tool bar. This updates the screen.

The next line geometry construction exercise will be to create a line tangent to a circular feature. To use the tangent line function correctly we must first create a circular object, then we can create a line that is tangent to it.

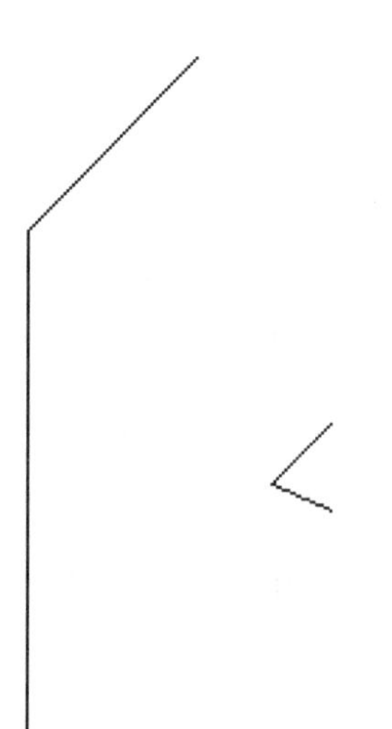

FIGURE 3–32 The user entered 1 inch for the length of the line. This figure shows the result.

Creating a Circle

From the Main Menu select **Create/Arc/Circ pt+rad** (see Figure 3–33) to create a circle specified by its center point coordinate and its radius value.

In review, the commands were Create/Arc/Circ pt+rad. Once you have selected Circ pt+rad, Mastercam will prompt you in the dialogue box for the center point coordinate.

Type in a center point coordinate of **-1,1** and press **Enter.** Notice how Mastercam automatically shifts into the Value point entry mode. Mastercam, in the dialogue box, will prompt you for the radius value of the circle. Type **.5** for a .5 radius circle and press **Enter.** Use the **Fit** icon to resize the screen. Your screen should now look like Figure 3–34.

Main Menu:	Create:	Arc:
Analyze	Point	Polar
Create	Line	Endpoints
File	Arc	3 points
Modify	Fillet	Tangent
Xform	Spline	Circ 2 pts
Delete	Curve	Circ 3 pts
Screen	Surface	Circ pt+rad
	Rectangle	Circ pt+dia
	Drafting	Circ pt+edg
Exit	Next menu	
BACKUP	BACKUP	BACKUP
MAIN MENU	MAIN MENU	MAIN MENU

FIGURE 3–33 The user chose Create, Arc, and Circ pt+rad.

FIGURE 3–34

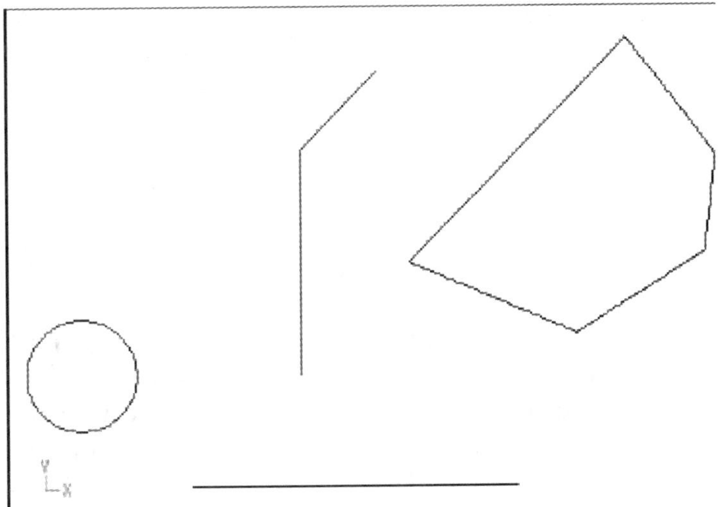

Creating Tangent Lines

From the Main Menu select **Create/Line/Tangent** to create a line tangent to an arc or circle (Figure 3–35).

In review, the commands were Main Menu/Create/Line/Tangent. Once you have selected Tangent, Mastercam, under the Tangent menu, will prompt you for the type of tangent line you want to create. Select **Angle** (see Figure 3–36) to create an angular line that will be tangent to the circle.

Mastercam, in the dialogue box, is now asking you to select the arc that you want the line to be tangent to. Use the mouse to select any part of the right side of the circle. Once you have picked the arc, Mastercam will prompt you for the line angle. You want the line to be tangent to the circle and at a 30-degree angle. Type **30** and press **Enter.** Once you have entered in 30, Mastercam wants to know the length of the line. Type **2,** for a 2-inch line and press **Enter.** Mastercam, in the dialogue

Main Menu:	Create:	Line:
Analyze	Point	Horizontal
Create	Line	Vertical
File	Arc	Endpoints
Modify	Fillet	Multi
Xform	Spline	Polar
Delete	Curve	Tangent
Screen	Surface	Perpendclr
	Rectangle	Parallel
	Drafting	Bisect
Exit	Next menu	Closest
BACKUP	BACKUP	BACKUP
MAIN MENU	MAIN MENU	MAIN MENU

FIGURE 3–35
The user chose Create, Line, and Tangent.

FIGURE 3–36
The user chose Angle from the Tangent menu.

FIGURE 3–37

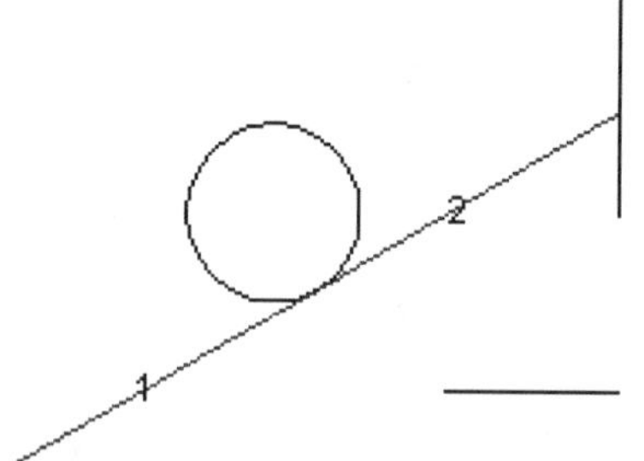

box, wants to know which line you want to keep. Internally, Mastercam has created two lines, each tangent to the circle, and each 2 inches long (see Figure 3–37).

You need to use the mouse cursor to select the line that you want to *keep*. Select the upper line (2 in Figure 3–37) using the mouse cursor. Your graphic screen should now look like Figure 3–38.

FIGURE 3–38

Creating Perpendicular Lines

From the Main Menu select **Create/Line /Perpendclr** to create a line perpendicular to an arc or line (Figure 3–39).

In review, the commands were Main Menu/Create/Line/Perpendclr. Once you have selected Perpendclr, Mastercam needs to know the circumstances of the perpendicular line that you want to create. The Point option allows you to create a line perpendicular to another line, spline, arc, or curve, through a specified point. The Arc option allows you to create a line perpendicular to another line and tangent to an arc or circle. Select **Point** from the Perpendicular menu (see Figure 3–40).

Mastercam, in the dialogue box, is now asking you to select the line, arc, or spline to which you want the line to be perpendicular. Use the mouse to select the horizontal line. Once you have picked the line, Mastercam will prompt you to specify an endpoint.

Main Menu:
Analyze
Create
File
Modify
Xform
Delete
Screen
Exit
BACKUP
MAIN MENU

Create:
Point
Line
Arc
Fillet
Spline
Curve
Surface
Rectangle
Drafting
Next menu
BACKUP
MAIN MENU

FIGURE 3–39
The user chose Create, Line, and Perpendclr.

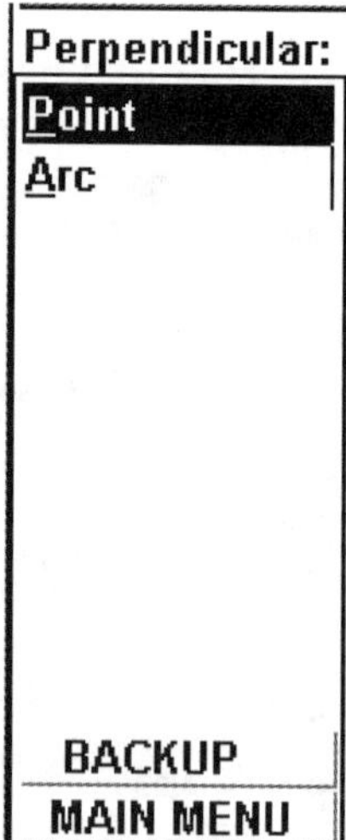

FIGURE 3–40
The user chose Point from the Perpendicular menu.

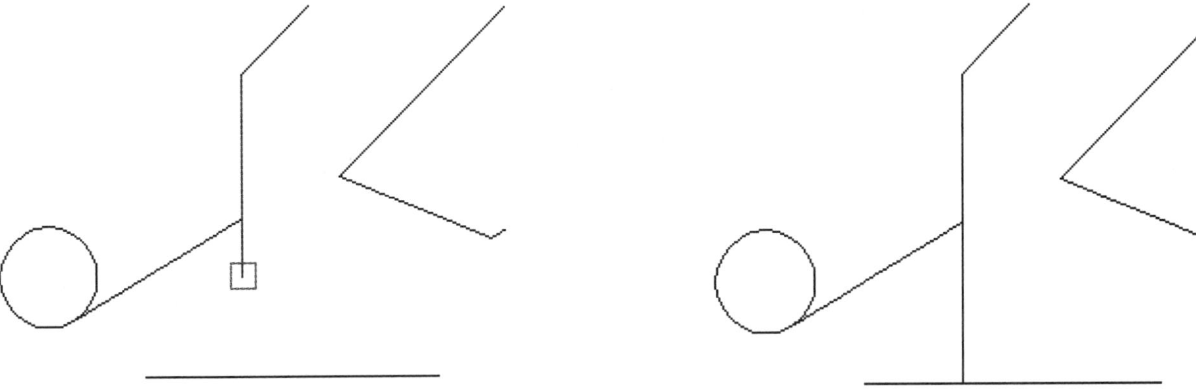

FIGURE 3–41

FIGURE 3–42

There are a number of ways to specify the endpoint, including inputting the coordinate values . We are going to use the endpoint cursor snap. Select **Endpoint** from the Point Entry menu. Once you have selected Endpoint, Mastercam wants you to select the endpoint of the entity. Use the mouse to select the bottom of the vertical line on your graphics screen (see Figure 3–41). Now Mastercam will want to know the length of the perpendicular line. Type **1** for a 1-inch line and press **Enter.**

You should now have a line that is perpendicular to the horizontal line and connected to the vertical line (see Figure 3–42).

Creating Parallel Lines

From the Main Menu select **Create/Line/Parallel** to create a line parallel to another line (see Figure 3–43).

In review, the commands were Main Menu/Create/Line/Parallel. Once you have selected Parallel, Mastercam needs to know the type of parallel line you want to create (see Figure 3–44). The Point option allows you to create a line parallel to

Main Menu:	Create:	Line:
Analyze	Point	Horizontal
Create	Line	Vertical
File	Arc	Endpoints
Modify	Fillet	Multi
Xform	Spline	Polar
Delete	Curve	Tangent
Screen	Surface	Perpendclr
	Rectangle	Parallel
	Drafting	Bisect
Exit	Next menu	Closest
BACKUP	BACKUP	BACKUP
MAIN MENU	MAIN MENU	MAIN MENU

FIGURE 3–43
The user chose Create, Line, and Parallel.

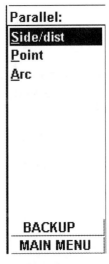

FIGURE 3–44
The user chose Side/dist from the Parallel menu.

FIGURE 3–45

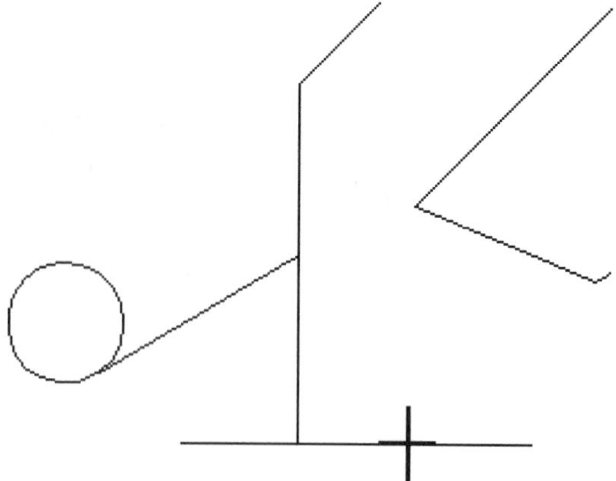

another line through a specified point. The Arc option allows you to create a line parallel to another line and tangent to an arc or circle. Side/Dist allows you to create parallel lines that are offset a specified distance and direction from an existing line. Select **Side/Dist** now.

Mastercam, in the dialogue box, is now asking you to select the line to which you want the new line to be parallel. Use the mouse to select the horizontal line you created earlier (see Figure 3–45). Once you have picked the line, Mastercam will prompt you to specify the offset direction. We would like the new line to be below the original. Use the mouse to select a point anywhere below the original horizontal line. Now Mastercam wants to know the offset distance. Type **1** or accept the default of one by pressing **Enter.** Click on the **Fit** icon to display all of the entities.

You should now have a parallel line 1 inch below the original horizontal line. Notice, in the dialogue box, Mastercam is prompting you to select another line. This comes in handy when you are creating multiple lines. To exit this line creation mode you can either press the **Esc** key on the keyboard or select **Main** from the Main Menu.

Creating Bisected Lines

From the Main Menu select **Create/Line/Bisect** to create a line that bisects the angle formed by two intersecting lines (see Figure 3–46).

FIGURE 3–46
The user chose Create, Line, and Bisect.

Main Menu:	Create:	Line:
Analyze	Point	Horizontal
Create	**Line**	Vertical
File	Arc	Endpoints
Modify	Fillet	Multi
Xform	Spline	Polar
Delete	Curve	Tangent
Screen	Surface	Perpendclr
	Rectangle	Parallel
	Drafting	**Bisect**
Exit	Next menu	Closest
BACKUP	BACKUP	BACKUP
MAIN MENU	MAIN MENU	MAIN MENU

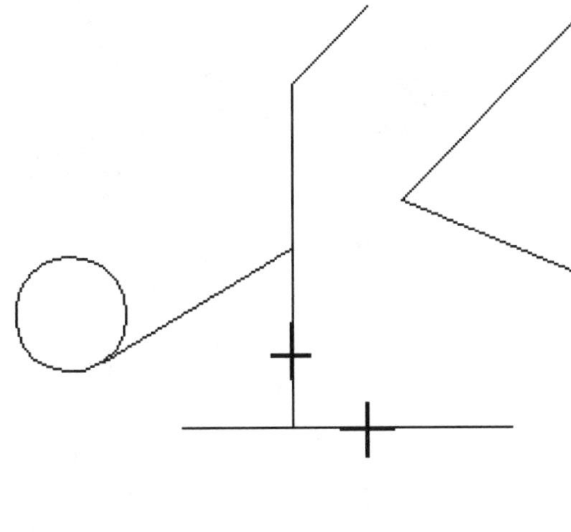

FIGURE 3–47

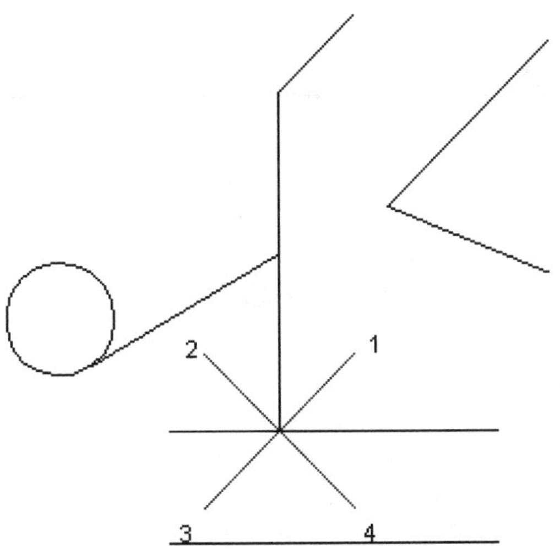

FIGURE 3–48

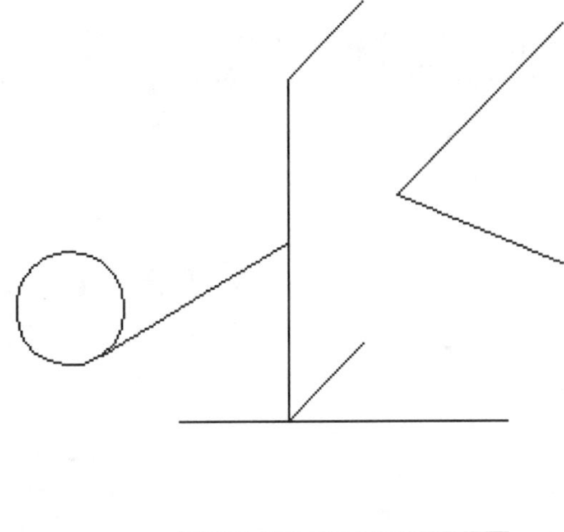

FIGURE 3–49

In review, the commands were Main Menu/Create/Line/ Bisect. Once you have selected Bisect, Mastercam will prompt you in the dialogue box to select the two lines you want to bisect. Using the mouse, select the first horizontal line and the perpendicular line you just created (see Figure 3–47).

Once you have picked the two lines, Mastercam needs to know the length of the line. Type **1** or accept the default of 1 by pressing **Enter.** Mastercam now wants to know which line you want to keep. Internally, Mastercam has created four lines, each bisecting the two lines, and each line is 1 inch long (see Fig ure 3–48).

You need to use the mouse to select the line that you want to keep. Select the upper-right line (1) using the mouse cursor. Your graphic screen should now look like Figure 3–49.

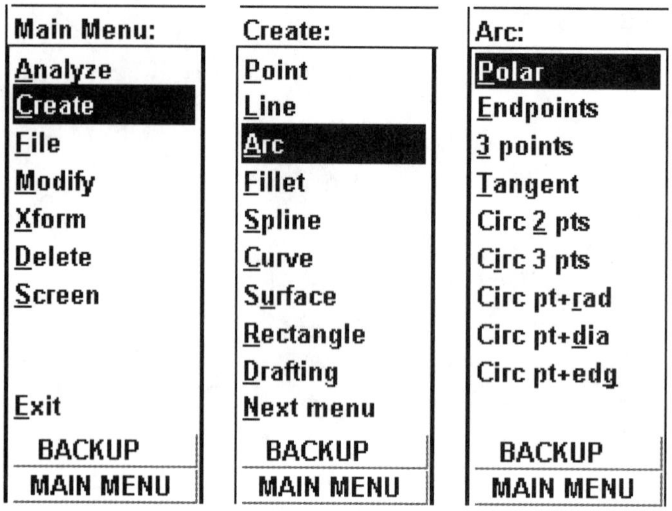

FIGURE 3–50
The user chose Create, Arc, and Polar.

Main Menu:	Create:	Arc:
Analyze	Point	Polar
Create	Line	Endpoints
File	Arc	3 points
Modify	Fillet	Tangent
Xform	Spline	Circ 2 pts
Delete	Curve	Circ 3 pts
Screen	Surface	Circ pt+rad
	Rectangle	Circ pt+dia
	Drafting	Circ pt+edg
Exit	Next menu	
BACKUP	BACKUP	BACKUP
MAIN MENU	MAIN MENU	MAIN MENU

CREATING ARCS AND CIRCLES

The Arc command is used to create arcs and circles. Like the line commands, Mastercam provides many different ways in which to create arc and circles.

Creating a Circle Using Polar Coordinates

From the Main Menu select **Create/Arc/Polar** to create a circle using polar coordinate for the center point (see Figure 3–50).

Using polar coordinates, Mastercam allows you to select four options for creating arcs. The option you select will depend on how you want to locate the arc or circle (see Figure 3–51). We want to locate the circle using the center point. This is typically how we would locate an arc or circle. Select the **Center pt** option from the Polar menu. You will be inputting the particular coordinate value of the center point of the arc so either select **Values** from the Point Entry menu or just begin typing in the coordinates.

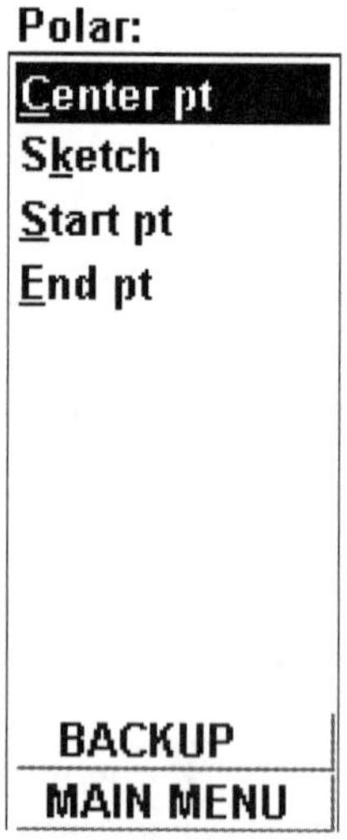

Polar:
Center pt
Sketch
Start pt
End pt
BACKUP
MAIN MENU

FIGURE 3–51
The user chose Center pt from the Polar menu.

In review, the commands were Main Menu/Create/Arc/ Polar/Center pt/Values. If you selected Values, Mastercam will prompt you in the dialogue box to input the coordinate value of the center of the arc. Locate the center of the circle at the coordinates of 3,3. Type **3,3** in the dialogue box and press **Enter.** The circle you are creating has a 1-inch radius. The Mastercam dialogue box is now prompting you for the radius value of the circle. Type **1** and press **Enter.**

Arcs can be described as partial circles, portions of circles that have a start point and an endpoint. Mastercam, in the dialogue box, wants you to enter the initial angle. The initial angle is the start angle for the arc. You are creating a circle. Circles have neither a start point nor an endpoint, so accept the default of **0** by pressing **Enter.**

Mastercam, in the dialogue box, wants you to now enter the final angle. The final angle is the end angle for an arc. Accept the default of **0,** because a circle has neither a start point nor an endpoint. Press **Enter.**

Your graphic screen should now look like Figure 3–52.

FIGURE 3–52

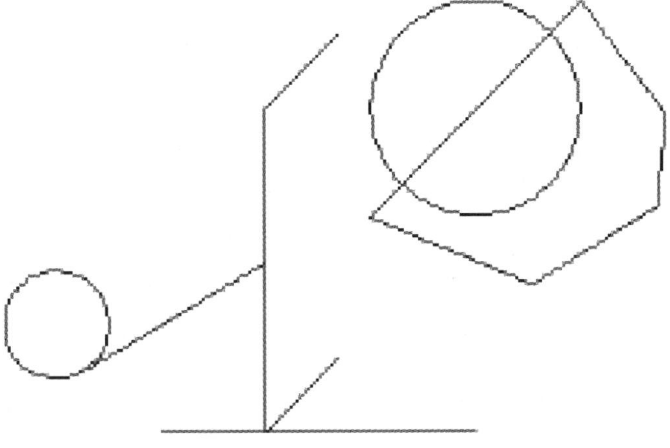

Creating an Arc Using Endpoints

From the Main menu select **Create/Arc/Endpoints** to create an arc using two known endpoints (see Figure 3–53).

After you select Endpoints, Mastercam gives you many different selection options under the Point Entry menu. We will be using the Values entry method. You can select Values from the Point Entry menu, or just begin typing in the coordinates of the first endpoint of the arc and Mastercam will automatically select the Values method for you. In review, the commands were Main Menu/Create/Arc/Polar/Endpoints/Values.

If you selected Values from the Point Entry menu, Mastercam will prompt you (in the dialogue box) to input the coordinate value of the arc endpoint. Type in the coordinates **-1,4** for the starting point for the arc and press **Enter.**

Mastercam, in the dialogue box will now prompt you to input the coordinate value of the second point of the arc. Type **0,2** for the second point and press **Enter.** Mastercam, in the dialogue box, will now prompt you to input the radius value of the arc. Type **2** for an arc with a 2-inch radius. There should be two complete circles in your screen now (see Figure 3–54).

FIGURE 3–53
The user chose Create, Arc, and Endpoints.

Main Menu:	Create:	Arc:
Analyze	Point	Polar
Create	Line	Endpoints
File	Arc	3 points
Modify	Fillet	Tangent
Xform	Spline	Circ 2 pts
Delete	Curve	Circ 3 pts
Screen	Surface	Circ pt+rad
	Rectangle	Circ pt+dia
	Drafting	Circ pt+edg
Exit	Next menu	
BACKUP	BACKUP	BACKUP
MAIN MENU	MAIN MENU	MAIN MENU

FIGURE 3–54

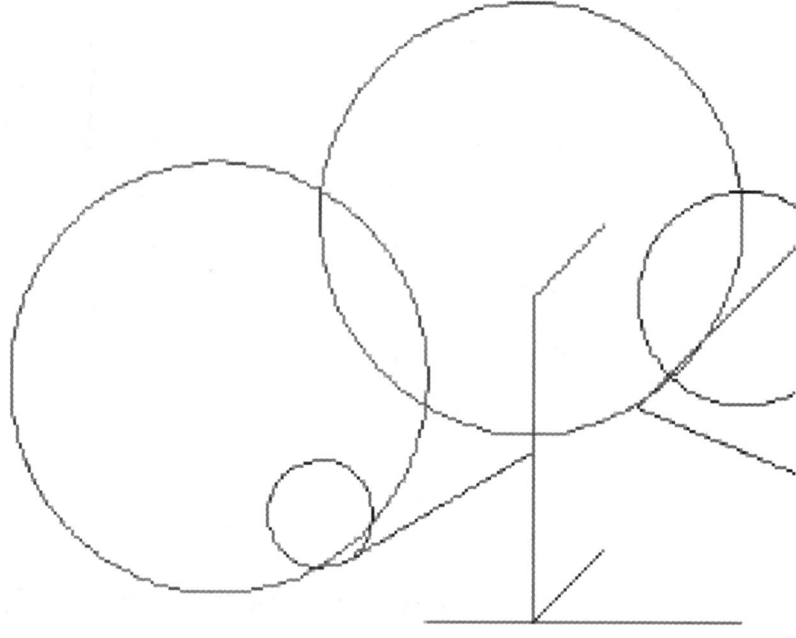

FIGURE 3–55

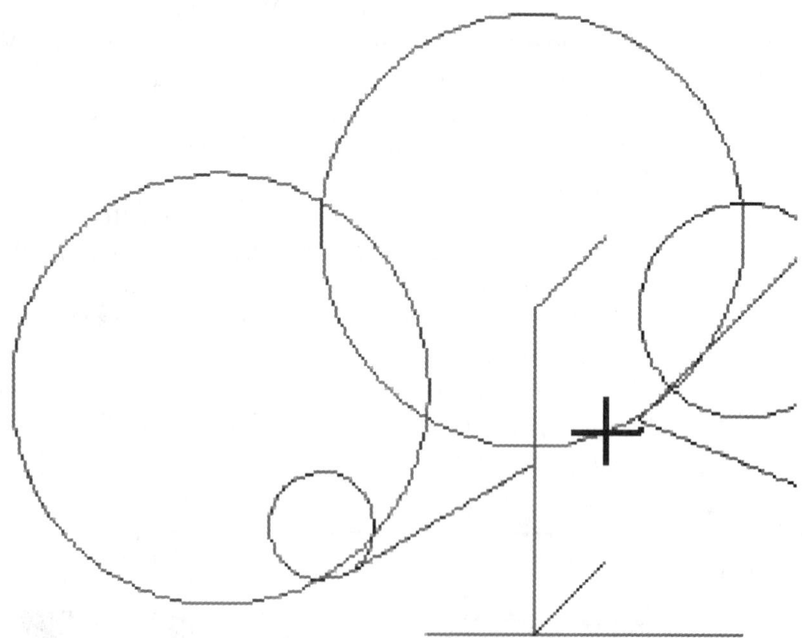

These circles should be of a different color than the other entities on the screen. The reason they are a different color is because they are only possible solutions to the values you suggested; they are not real entities yet. The two circles are actually four arcs. It is your job now to pick the arc that you want. To pick the desired arc, you need to place the mouse cursor as close to the desired arc as possible. Use Figure 3–55 to place the cursor snap in position to save the arc you want.

Your graphic screen should now look like Figure 3–56. If your screen has some blips or parts of the residual arcs left on the screen, select the **Repaint** icon (see Figure 3–57) located up in the Tool Bar.

FIGURE 3–57

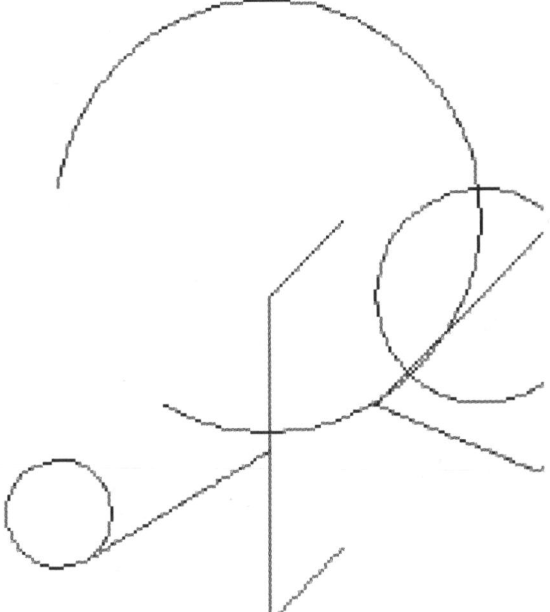

FIGURE 3–56

FIGURE 3–58
The user chose Create, Arc, and 3 points.

Main Menu:	Create:	Arc:
Analyze	Point	Polar
Create	Line	Endpoints
File	Arc	3 points
Modify	Fillet	Tangent
Xform	Spline	Circ 2 pts
Delete	Curve	Circ 3 pts
Screen	Surface	Circ pt+rad
	Rectangle	Circ pt+dia
	Drafting	Circ pt+edg
Exit	Next menu	
BACKUP	BACKUP	BACKUP
MAIN MENU	MAIN MENU	MAIN MENU

These blips are not part of the drawing, they are just drawing marks and would disappear when a new entity was created or the file was closed out. Select the **Fit** icon from the tool bar to show all of the entities.

Creating a Three-Point Arc

From the Main Menu select **Create/Arc/3 Point** to create an arc that passes through 3 points (see Figure 3–58).

After you select Endpoints, Mastercam gives you many different selection options under the Point Entry menu. The three-point method of creating an arc is best illustrated using the Sketch option. Select **Sketch** from the Point Entry menu. In review, the commands were Main Menu/Create/Arc/3 point/Sketch. Use the mouse and the left mouse (pick) button to select three pick points that are similar to the positions that are shown in Figure 3–59.

FIGURE 3–59

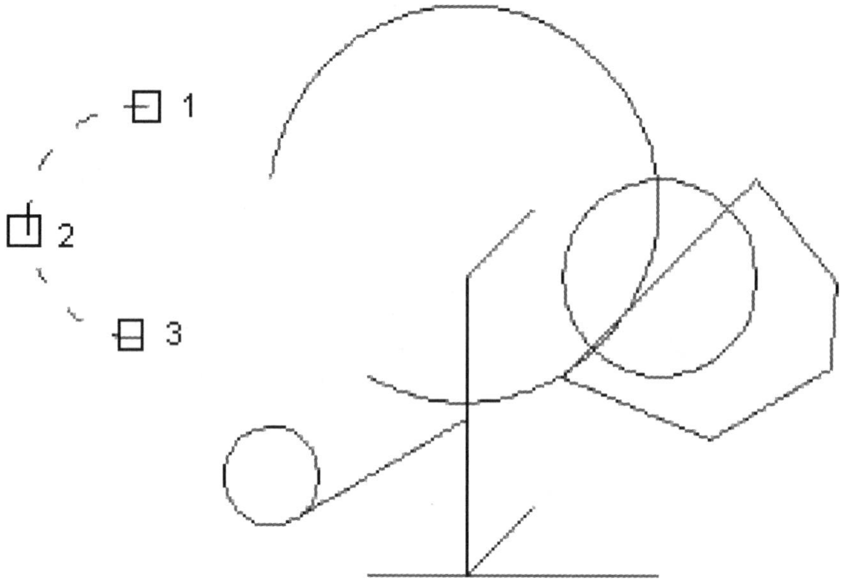

Note that after you input the first two points, an arc appears. The arc is not solved until the third point is input. Using the Sketch method to input coordinates is a quick and easy way of creating free-form geometry, but it is usually impractical for most types of geometry creation.

Creating a Tangent Three-Point Arc

From the Main Menu select **Create/Arc/Tangent** to create an arc that is Tangent to up to three lines or arcs (Figure 3–60).

After you select Tangent, Mastercam gives you six options under the Tangent menu (see Figure 3–61).

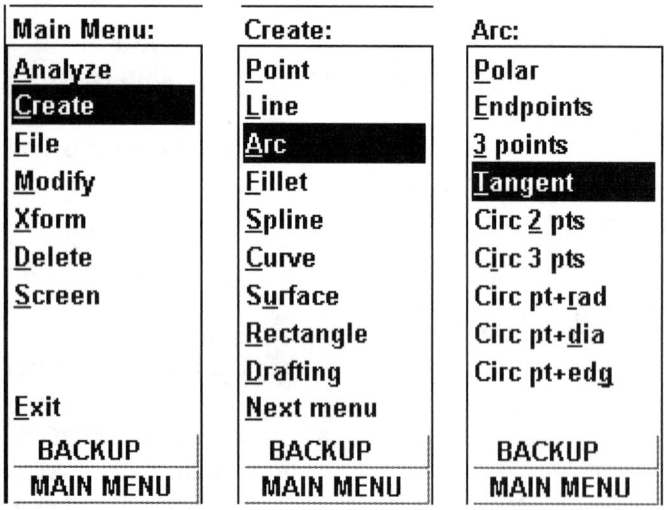

Main Menu:
- Analyze
- Create
- File
- Modify
- Xform
- Delete
- Screen
- Exit
- BACKUP
- MAIN MENU

Create:
- Point
- Line
- Arc
- Fillet
- Spline
- Curve
- Surface
- Rectangle
- Drafting
- Next menu
- BACKUP
- MAIN MENU

Arc:
- Polar
- Endpoints
- 3 points
- Tangent
- Circ 2 pts
- Circ 3 pts
- Circ pt+rad
- Circ pt+dia
- Circ pt+edg
- BACKUP
- MAIN MENU

FIGURE 3–60
The user chose Create, Arc, and Tangent.

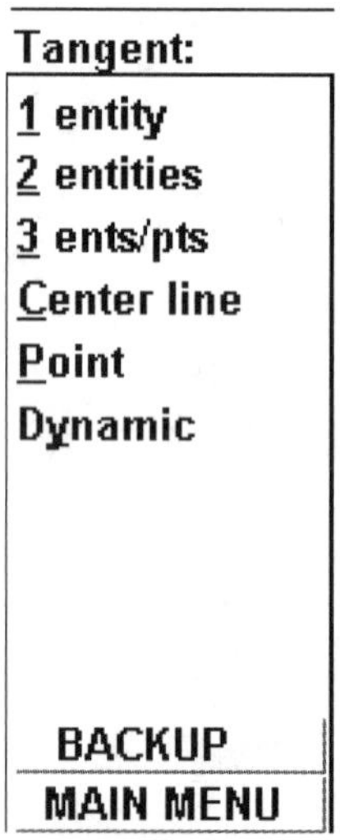

Tangent:
- 1 entity
- 2 entities
- 3 ents/pts
- Center line
- Point
- Dynamic
- BACKUP
- MAIN MENU

FIGURE 3–61
Options in the Tangent menu.

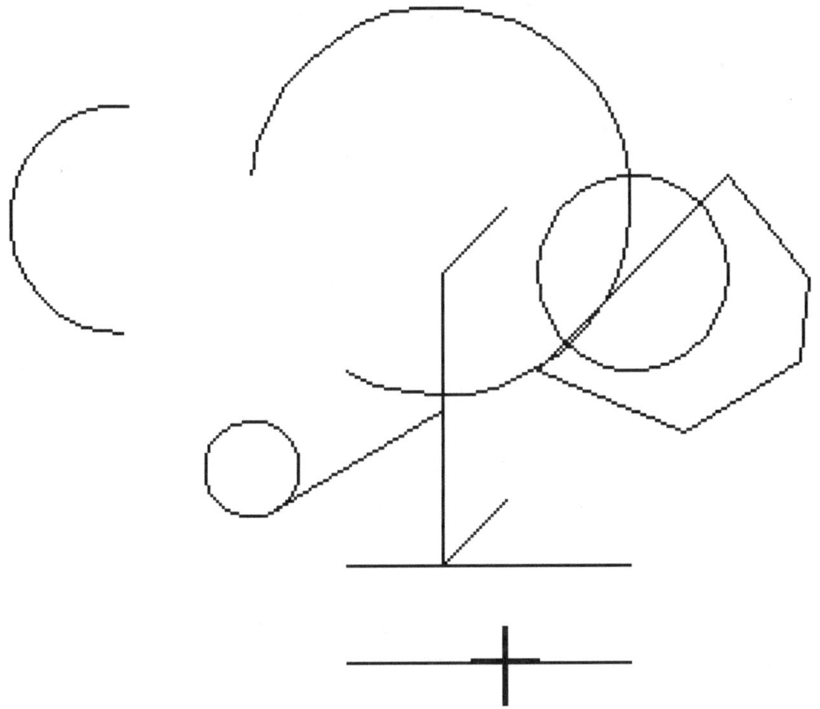

FIGURE 3–62

Point Entry:
Values
Center
Endpoint
Intersec
Midpoint
Point
Last
Relative
Quadrant
Sketch
BACKUP
MAIN MENU

FIGURE 3–63
The user chose the Midpoint option from the Point Entry menu.

The first option, 1 entity, allows you to create a 180-degree arc tangent to a selected entity. Select **1 entity** now. Mastercam, in the dialogue box, is prompting you select the entity to which you want the arc to be tangent.

Using the mouse, select the parallel horizontal line (see Figure 3–62) that you created earlier in the exercise.

Once you have selected the entity, Mastercam (in the dialogue box) will prompt you to select the exact point along the entity to which you want the arc to be tangent. The Point Entry option allows you to precisely locate the tangency point on the entity.

You are going to locate the tangency point at the exact midpoint of the line entity that you selected. From the Point Option menu select **Midpoint** (see Figure 3–63). In review, the commands were Main Menu/Create/Arc/Tangent/Midpoint.

Using the mouse you select **Midpoint** from the Point Option menu. At this point you must reselect the same horizontal line entity that you had selected earlier. Mastercam, in the dialogue box, will now prompt you to input the radius value of the arc. Type in **1** for an arc with a 1-inch radius and press **Enter.**

Two complete circles should be on your screen now (see Figure 3–64). These circles should be of a different color than the other entities on the screen because they are only possible solutions; they are not yet real entities. The two circles are actually four arcs. It is your job now to pick the arc that you want. To pick the desired arc, place the mouse cursor as close to the desired arc as possible. Use Figure 3–64 to place the cursor snap in the correct position to save the arc numbered 1.

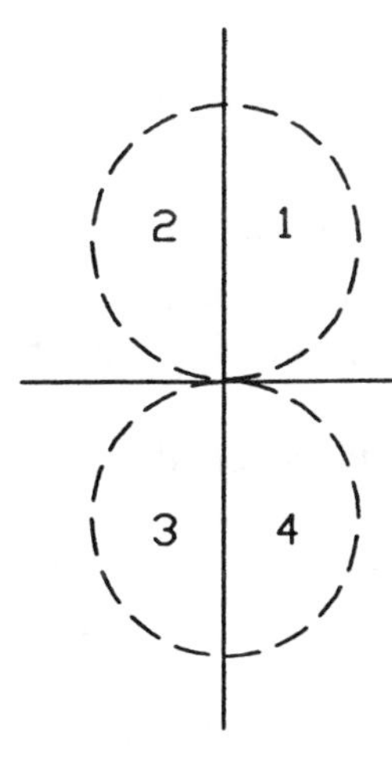

FIGURE 3–64

FIGURE 3–65

FIGURE 3–66

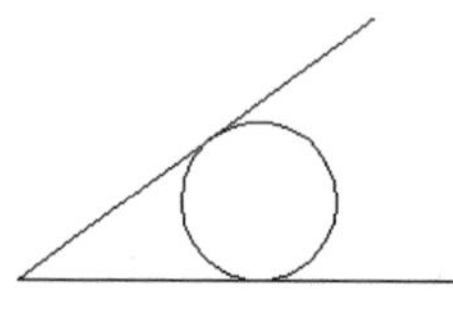

FIGURE 3–67

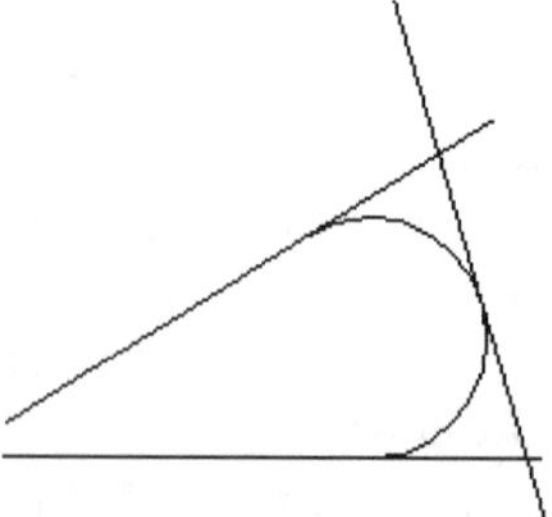

The entities on the screen should now look like Figure 3–65. To end this arc creation segment, press the **Esc** key on the keyboard or select **Main Menu.**

The second tangent arc creation option is the tangent to two entities option (see Figure 3–66).

The third option of creating a tangent arc is an arc that is tangent to three entities (see Figure 3–67).

The fourth option to create a tangent arc is to create an arc that is tangent to a line with the center point of the arc existing on another line (see Figure 3–68).

The fifth option of creating a tangent arc is the creation of an arc that is tangent to an entity and passes through a given point (see Figure 3–69).

The sixth option of creating a tangent arc is the dynamic creation of an arc that can be tangent at any point on an entity and allows you to manipulate the endpoint using the mouse cursor or point menu options (see Figure 3–70).

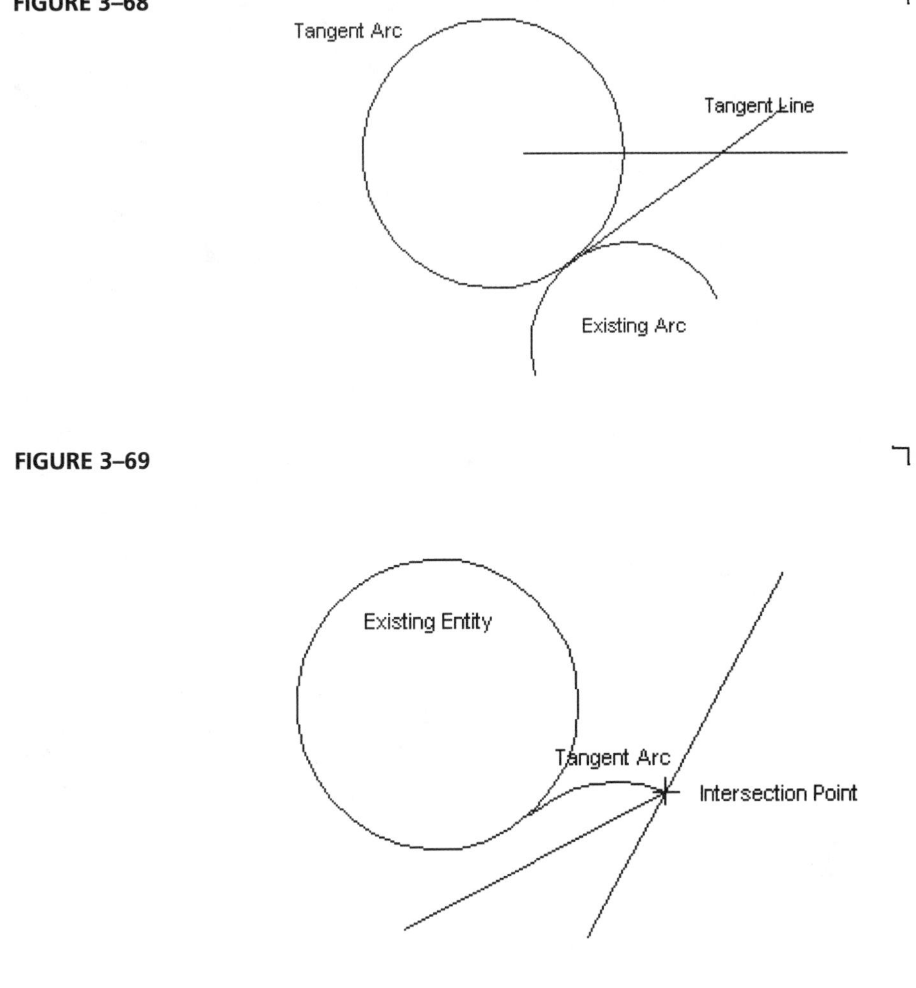

FIGURE 3–68

FIGURE 3–69

FIGURE 3–70

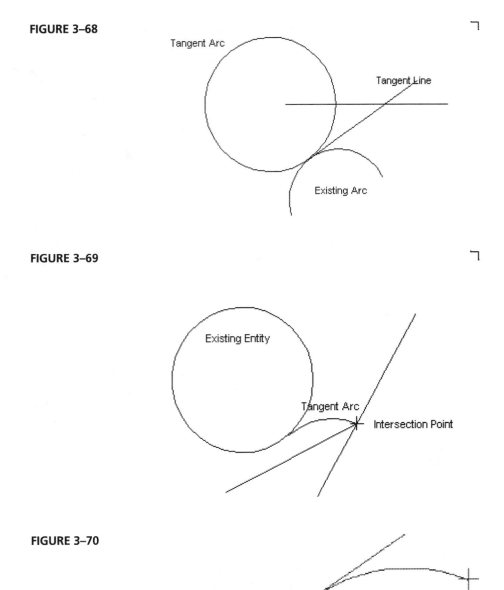

Now that we have finished the tangent arc section of arc creation, it is time to clear the screen of all of the entities that you have created up to this point. Go back to the Main Menu by clicking on the **Main Menu** button. From the Main menu select **Delete/Window** (see Figure 3–71). This will allow you to delete entities that reside within a window you create with the mouse cursor.

After you select Window, Mastercam allows you to create a window around the entities you wish to delete. Use the mouse to select a point (1) in the lower left portion of the screen (see Figure 3–72). Pull the window up around all of the entities to point 2. Once the entities are surrounded, click the left mouse button to erase the entities that are in the windows. If you look back at Figure

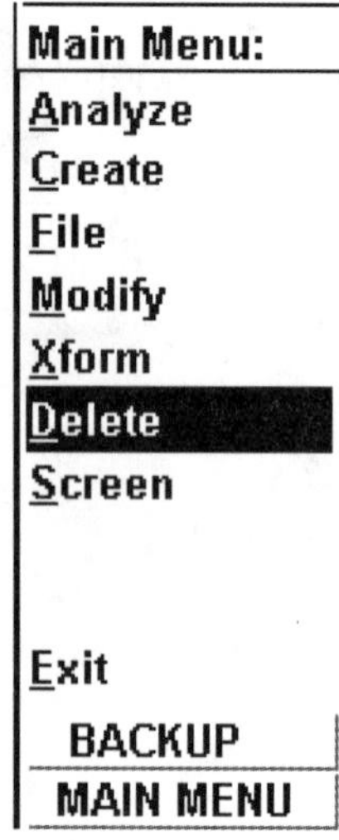

FIGURE 3–71
The user chose Delete and Window.

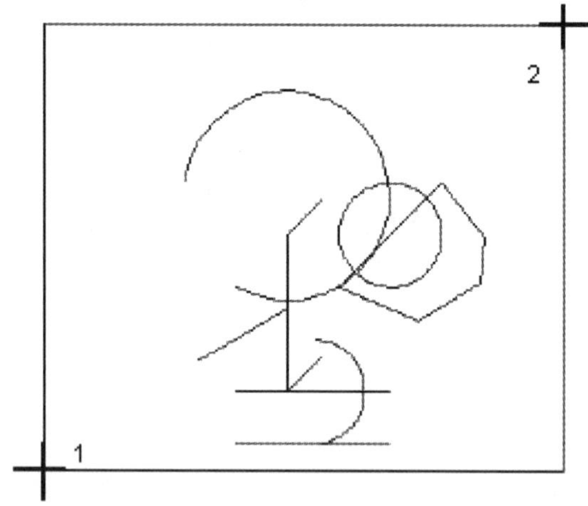

FIGURE 3–72

3–71 under the **Delete** menu, you will see that you could have also used the All option to delete all of the entities, but now you know how to use the Window option.

Creating a Two-Point Circle

From the Main Menu select **Create/Arc/Circ 2 pts** to create an arc using two points that make up the circle's diameter (see Figure 3–73).

After you select Circ 2 pts, Mastercam prompts you to select the first point in the creation of the two-point circle. Mastercam allows you to use the full Point Entry menu to select or create points (see Figure 3–74).

We will use the Values point entry method. Remember, you don't need to select Values from the Point Entry menu. If you start typing in the values, Mastercam goes into the Values mode automatically.

In review, the commands were **Main Menu/Create/Arc/Circ 2 pts/.** Type in the coordinates of **1,1** for the first point in the two-point circle and press **Enter.** Mastercam, in the dialogue box, will now prompt you to input the second point of the two-point circle. The two points of the two-point circle must lie 180 degrees apart. After entering the first point you now have a dynamic representation of the

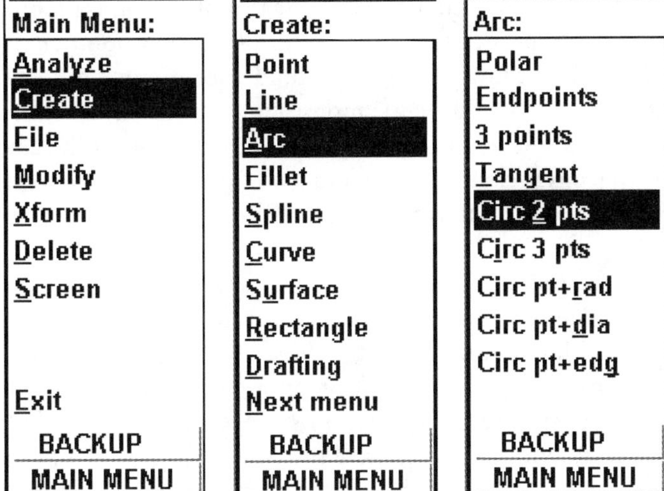

FIGURE 3–73
The user chose Create, Arc, and Circ 2 pts.

Point Entry:
Values
Center
Endpoint
Intersec
Midpoint
Point
Last
Relative
Quadrant
Sketch
BACKUP
MAIN MENU

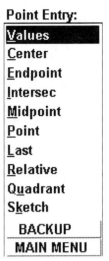

FIGURE 3–74
The user chose Values from the Point Entry menu.

possible circle solutions. By moving the mouse you can come up with an endless number of solutions. Type in **-1,1** and press **Enter** for a circle that passes through the coordinates at -1, 1 and 1, 1.

Creating a Three Point-Circle

From the Main Menu select **Create/Arc/Circ 3 pts** to create an arc using three points that make up the circle's diameter (see Figure 3–75).

After you select Circ 3 pts, Mastercam prompts you to select the first point in the creation of the three-point circle.

Mastercam also allows you to use the full Point Entry menu to select or create points for the three-point circle. In review, the commands were Main Menu/Create/Arc/Circ 3 pts/Center. Mastercam, in the dialogue box, is now prompting you to

FIGURE 3–75
The user chose Create, Arc and Circ 3 pts.

Main Menu:
Analyze
Create
File
Modify
Xform
Delete
Screen
Exit
BACKUP
MAIN MENU

Create:
Point
Line
Arc
Fillet
Spline
Curve
Surface
Rectangle
Drafting
Next menu
BACKUP
MAIN MENU

Arc:
Polar
Endpoints
3 points
Tangent
Circ 2 pts
Circ 3 pts
Circ pt+rad
Circ pt+dia
Circ pt+edg
BACKUP
MAIN MENU

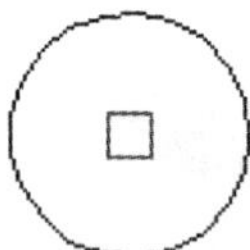

FIGURE 3–76

select the arc that you want Mastercam to snap to the center point of. You want one of the three points of the circle to pass through the center of the two-point circle that you just created. From the Point Entry menu you could select Center, but let's utilize Mastercam's smart mouse ability. Move the mouse cursor to the circle in the graphics screen (see Figure 3–76). As you move the mouse cursor around the circle's perimeter, notice how the circle changes color and a box appears in the center of the circle. When the box is around the center point of the circle press the left mouse button.

You have just captured the center of the circle.

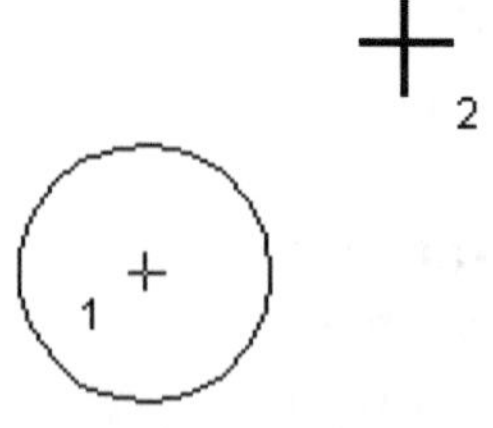

FIGURE 3–77

Mastercam, in the dialogue box, will now prompt you to input the second point of the three-point circle. The three points of the three-point circle, unlike the two-point circle, can be in any configuration other than a straight line. Use the mouse cursor to pick a point approximately at position 2 in Figure 3–77.

After you input the second point, Mastercam allows you to create a dynamic representation of the arc. By moving the mouse you can come up with an endless number of solutions. To create point three, use the mouse cursor to pick a point around the position of point 3 in Figure 3–78.

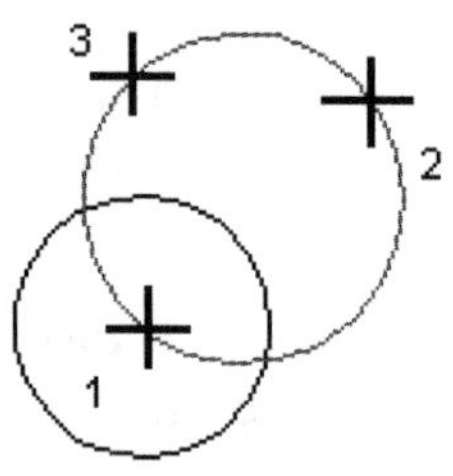

FIGURE 3–78

Creating a Circle Using Radius and Center Point Values

From the Main Menu select **Create/Arc/Circ pt+rad** to create a circle with a given center point and a known radius (see Figure 3–79).

After you select Circ pt+rad, Mastercam prompts you to select the center point in the creation of the circle.

Mastercam also allows you to use the full Point Entry menu to select or create a center point for the circle. You want the center of this circle to have the same center point as the larger circle you created earlier. Use the smart cursor to select the center of the second circle (see Figure 3–80).

In review, the commands were Main Menu/Create/Arc/Circ pt+rad. Mastercam, in the dialogue box, will now prompt you to input the radius of the circle. Type in **2,** and press **Enter.**

FIGURE 3–79
The user chose Create, Arc, and Circ pt+rad.

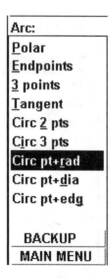

Main Menu:	Create:	Arc:
Analyze	Point	Polar
Create	Line	Endpoints
File	Arc	3 points
Modify	Fillet	Tangent
Xform	Spline	Circ 2 pts
Delete	Curve	Circ 3 pts
Screen	Surface	Circ pt+rad
	Rectangle	Circ pt+dia
	Drafting	Circ pt+edg
Exit	Next menu	
BACKUP	BACKUP	BACKUP
MAIN MENU	MAIN MENU	MAIN MENU

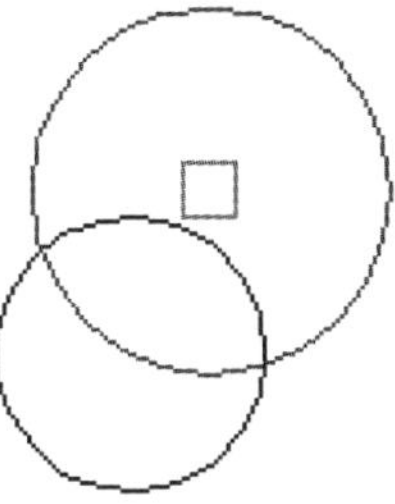

FIGURE 3–80

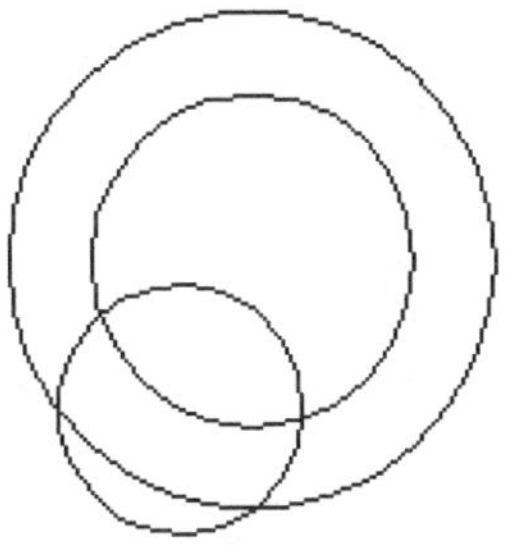

FIGURE 3–81

Your graphic screen should now look like Figure 3–81. Creating circles with the same center point is something that is very common in the machining and designing industry.

Creating a Circle Using Diameter and Center-Point Values

From the Main Menu select **Create/Arc/Circ pt+dia** to create a circle with a given center point and a known diameter (see Figure 3–82).

After you select Circ pt+dia, Mastercam prompts you to select the center point in the creation of the circle.

Mastercam also allows you to use the full Point Entry menu to select or create a center point for the circle. You want the center of this circle to be at the intersection point of the two largest circles. Use the smart mouse again to select the intersection of the two circles (see Figure 3–83). As you move the mouse cursor to the intersection point notice how the circle changes color and a box appears at the intersection point of the circles. When the box is around this point, press the left mouse button.

You have just captured the intersection point of the two circles.

In review, the commands were Main Menu/Create/Arc/Circ pt+dia using the smart mouse to select the intersection point. Mastercam, in the dialogue box, is

FIGURE 3–82
The user chose Create, Arc, and Circ pt+dia.

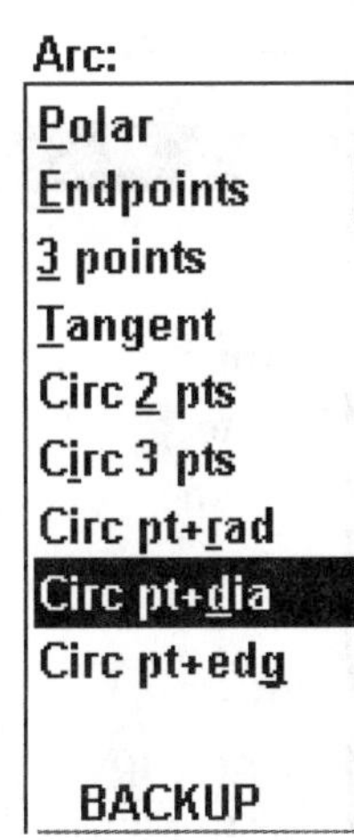

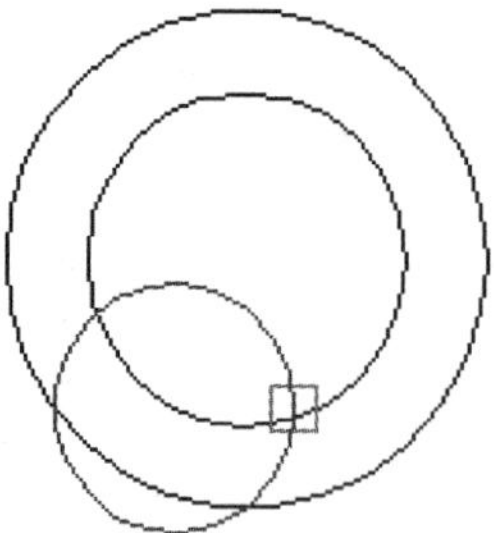

FIGURE 3–83

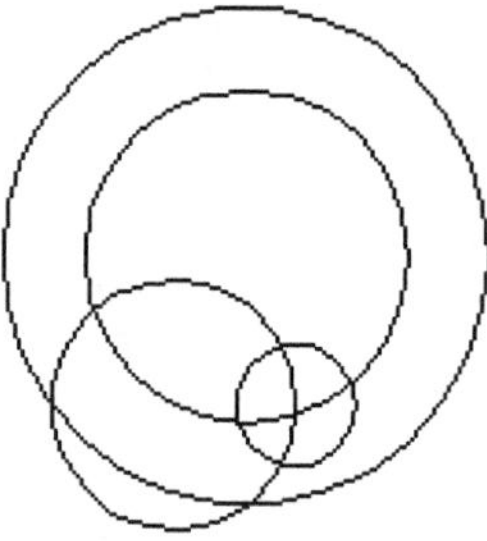

FIGURE 3–84

now prompting you to enter the diameter of the circle. Type in **1,** and press **Enter.** The graphics screen should now look like Figure 3–84.

Creating a Circle Using a Center Point and a Point on a Circumference

From the Main Menu select **Create/Arc/Circ pt+edg** to create a circle with a given center point and a point on the circumference (see Figure 3–85).

After you select Circ pt+edg, Mastercam prompts you to select the center point in the creation of the circle.

You want the center of this circle to be at the axes coordinates of 3.5 and 2. Type in **3.5,2,** and press **Enter.**

After entering the center point you now have a dynamic representation of the possible circle solutions. By moving the mouse you can come up with an endless number of solutions to the edge point. Select a point similar to the edge point position in Figure 3–86.

Before you go onto creating rectangles, you will want to erase all of the entities on the graphics screen.

From the tool bar select the **Delete** icon (Figure 3–87). Next, from the menu screen, select **All.** From the All menu select **Entities.**

When asked for a confirmation to delete all entities, select **Yes.**

FIGURE 3–85
The user chose Create, Arc, and Circ pt+edg.

Main Menu:	Create:	Arc:
Analyze	Point	Polar
Create	Line	Endpoints
File	Arc	3 points
Modify	Fillet	Tangent
Xform	Spline	Circ 2 pts
Delete	Curve	Circ 3 pts
Screen	Surface	Circ pt+rad
	Rectangle	Circ pt+dia
	Drafting	Circ pt+edg
Exit	Next menu	
BACKUP	BACKUP	BACKUP
MAIN MENU	MAIN MENU	MAIN MENU

FIGURE 3–86

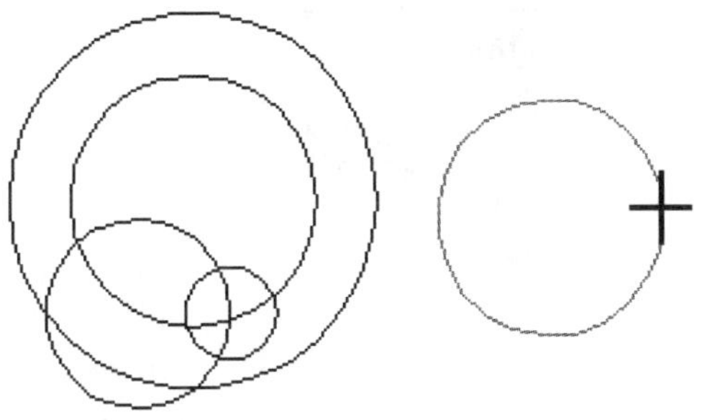

FIGURE 3–87
The user used the delete tool, and chose All and Entities from the menus.

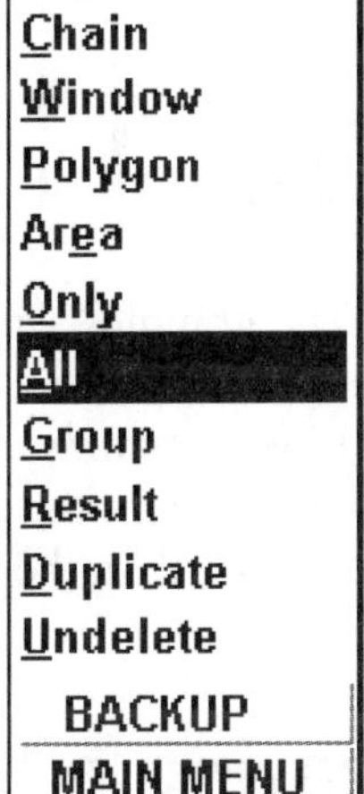

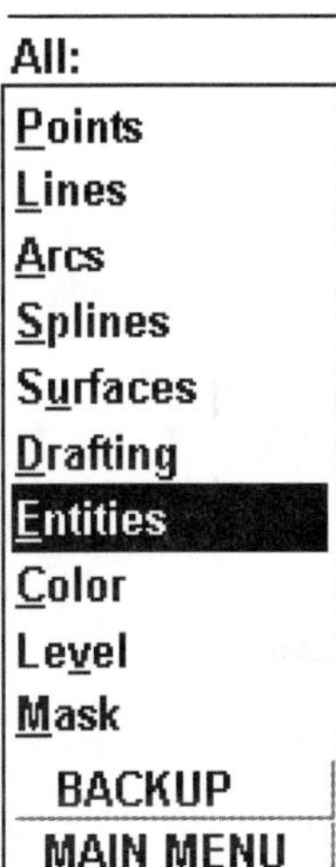

CREATING RECTANGLES, CHAMFERS, FILLETS, AND POLYGONS

The Create/Rectangle command is used to create a rectangle. As with the Line and Arc commands, Mastercam provides a number of different ways in which to create rectangles. The first method we explore is the one-point method.

Creating a Rectangle Using One Point

From the Main Menu select **Create/Rectangle/1 point** (see Figure 3–88) to create a rectangle by establishing a corner point and giving the width and height of the rectangle.

After you select 1 point, Mastercam prompts you to enter the lower left corner of the rectangle. Mastercam allows you to use the full Point Entry menu to select or create a point for the rectangle. We want the lower left corner of the rectangle to be at the X and Y axes coordinate position of 0, 0. Type in **0,0** and press **Enter.** Mastercam, in the dialogue box will now prompt you to enter the width of the rectangle. The width of the rectangle is the length of the rectangle along the X axis. Type in **2** and press **Enter.**

Mastercam, in the dialogue box, will now prompt you to enter the height of the rectangle. The height of the rectangle is the length of the rectangle along the Y axis. Type in **1** and press **Enter.**

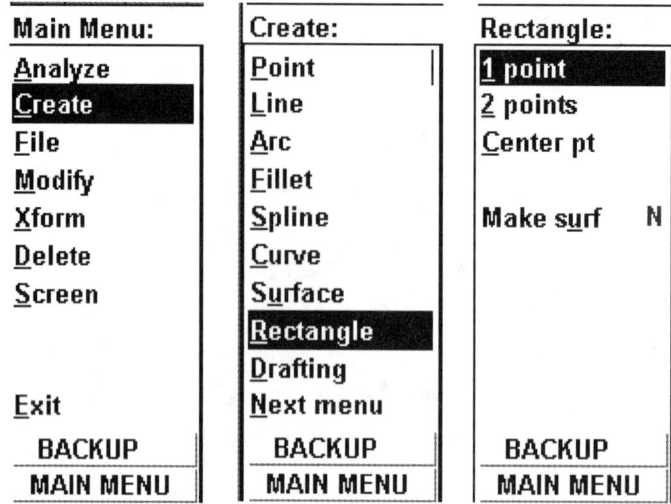

FIGURE 3–88 The user chose Create, Rectangle, and 1 point.

FIGURE 3–89

The graphics screen should now show a rectangle with a width of 2 and a height of 1 (see Figure 3–89).

When creating a rectangle, if you were to input negative numbers for the width and height, the corner point of the rectangle would now be the upper right corner rather than the lower left corner.

Creating a Rectangle Using Two Points

From the Main Menu select **Create/Rectangle/2 points** (see Figure 3–90) to create a rectangle by establishing the lower left and upper right corners of the rectangle.

After you select 2 points, Mastercam prompts you to enter the lower left corner of the rectangle. Mastercam allows you to use the full Point Entry menu to select or create a point for the rectangle. For this exercise you will use the mouse to select the lower left corner of the rectangle. Use the mouse to select a point somewhere above the existing rectangle. Mastercam now allows you to finish creating the rectangle by entering the opposite corner of the rectangle. Notice on the screen that you have a dynamic representation of the possible solutions to the rectangle. Use the mouse to select a position for the upper right corner of the rectangle.

FIGURE 3–90 The user chose Create, Rectangle, and 2 points.

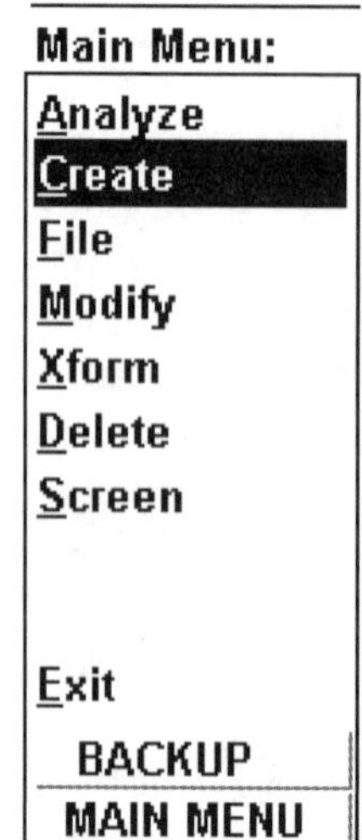

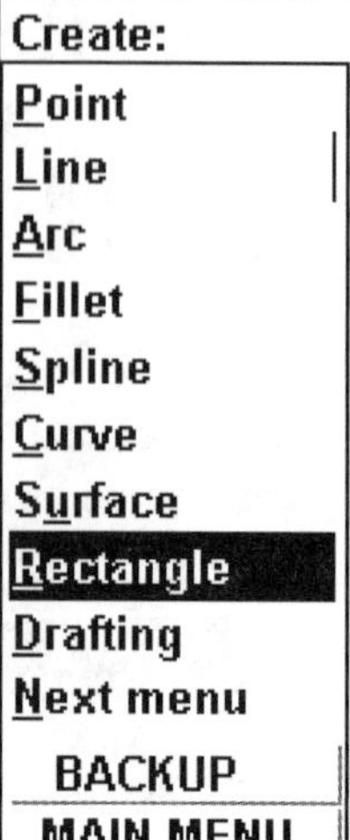

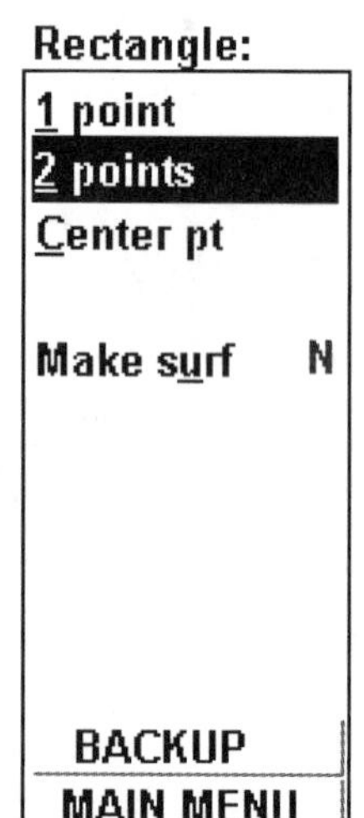

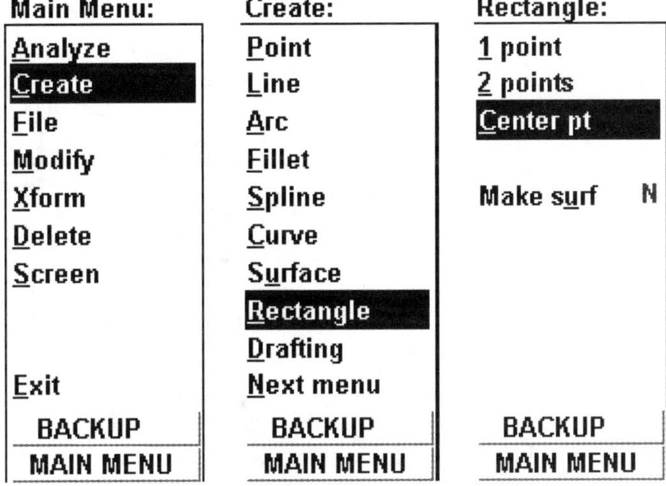

FIGURE 3–91 The user chose Create, Rectangle, and Center pt.

Point Entry:
Values
Center
Endpoint
Intersec
Midpoint
Point
Last
Relative
Quadrant
Sketch
BACKUP
MAIN MENU

FIGURE 3–92 The user chose Relative from the Point Entry menu.

Creating a Rectangle by Specifying the Center Point

From the Main Menu select **Create/Rectangle/Center pt** (see Figure 3–91) to create a rectangle by establishing the center point of the rectangle.

After you select Center pt, Mastercam prompts you to enter the center point of the rectangle. Mastercam allows you to use the full Point Entry menu to select or create a point for the rectangle. For this exercise we will use the Relative option (see Figure 3–92). Select **Relative** from the Point Entry menu.

We are going to locate the center of this rectangle relative to the upper right corner of the first rectangle we created. After you select relative, Mastercam wants to know how you want to select the entity you want to be relatively located from. We want to use the intersection point of the two lines that make up the upper right corner of the existing triangle (see Figure 3–93). Use the smart mouse to select this intersection point.

Now that you have selected the intersection point that you are going to use as the relative position of the center of the rectangle, Mastercam wants to know what type of coordinates you want to use to finish the rectangle (see Figure 3–94).

The first option, Rectang, allows you to enter the *incremental* distance along the X and Y axes from the intersection point to the center point of the new rectangle.

FIGURE 3–93

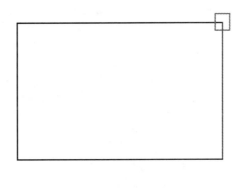

Rectang
Polar

BACKUP
MAIN MENU

FIGURE 3–94
The user chose Polar from the menu.

FIGURE 3–95

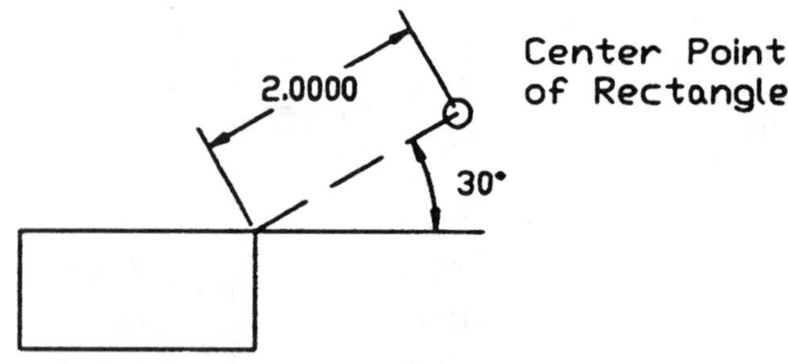

The second option, Polar, allows you to enter a coordinate specified by a distance along a specified angle (see Figure 3–95).

Select **Polar** from the entry menu. Mastercam now prompts you, in the dialogue box, for the relative distance. Type **2,** and press **Enter.**

Mastercam is now prompting you, in the dialogue box, for the relative angle. Type **30,** and press **Enter.**

Mastercam, in the dialogue box, will now prompt you to enter the width of the rectangle. Type in **2** and press **Enter.** Mastercam, in the dialogue box, will now prompt you to enter the height of the rectangle. Type in **1** and press **Enter.** The rectangle should now appear on the screen. If it doesn't, you may have to select the **Fit** icon from the toolbar.

The Make Surf N rectangle option deals with surfacing and will not be covered in this text.

Creating Chamfers

The chamfer command places an angled line with two given lengths between two nonparallel lines (see Figure 3–96).

From the Main Menu select **Create/Next Menu/Chamfer** to create a chamfer with set distances (Figure 3–97).

After you select Chamfer, Mastercam prompts you in the dialogue box to enter the distances of the chamfer legs. The default lengths of the chamfer is appearing in the dialogue box now. Next we would like to change the chamfer length. To change the distances, select **Distances** from the Chamfer menu (see Figure 3–98).

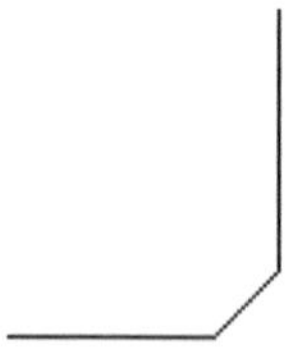

FIGURE 3–96

After you select Distances, Mastercam prompts you in the dialogue box to enter the distances of the first leg of the chamfer. The first distance should be set to .375. Type **.375** and press **Enter.**

Mastercam, in the dialogue box, will now prompt you to enter the distance of the second leg of the chamfer. To create a 45-degree chamfer we need to make both legs of the chamfer equal. The second distance should also be set to .375. Type **.375** and press **Enter.**

Now that you have set the lengths of the chamfer, you need to select the entities you want to apply the chamfer to. Mastercam, in the dialogue box, is asking you to select the first entity.

Main Menu:
Analyze
Create
File
Modify
Xform
Delete
Screen
Exit
BACKUP
MAIN MENU

Create:
Chamfer
Letters
Pattern
Ellipse
Polygon
Primsol
Eplot*
Gear*
Htable*
Shapes*
BACKUP
MAIN MENU

FIGURE 3–97
The user chose Create, Next menu, and Chamfer.

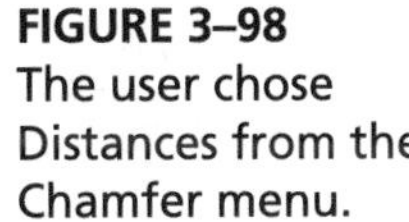
FIGURE 3–98
The user chose Distances from the Chamfer menu.

FIGURE 3–99

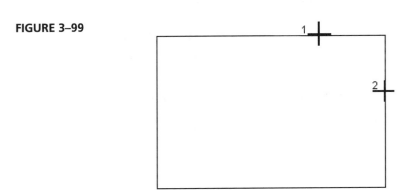

Select the upper horizontal line on the large rectangle (see Figure 3–99) we created earlier. The line should change colors, indicating that you have selected it. Now that you have selected the first entity, Mastercam is asking you in the dialogue box to select the second entity (see Figure 3–99).

When inputting the length of the chamfer legs it is important to remember that the length of the legs don't have to be equal, but the order that you pick the entities directly corresponds to the order in which you input the values; i.e., the distance of the first leg corresponds to the first entity picked.

The chamfer should now appear in the upper right corner of the rectangle (see Figure 3–100).

Creating a Fillet

The fillet command places a radius of a given size between two nonparallel lines. The fillet command operates in much the same way as the chamfer command.

From the Main Menu select **Create/Fillet** to create a fillet with a set radius (see Figure 3–101).

FIGURE 3–100

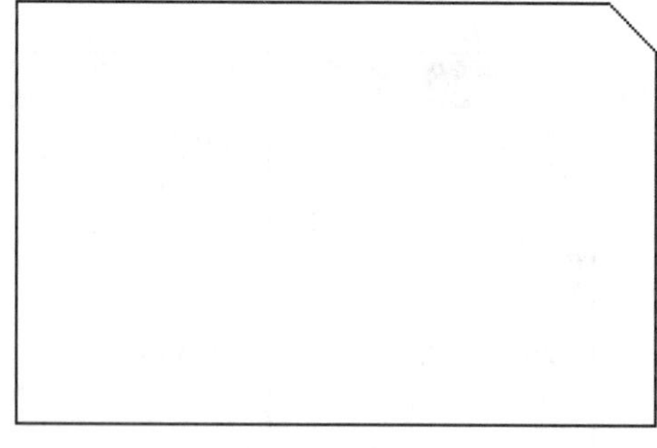

Main Menu:
Analyze
Create
File
Modify
Xform
Delete
Screen
Exit
BACKUP
MAIN MENU

Create:
Point
Line
Arc
Fillet
Spline
Curve
Surface
Rectangle
Drafting
Next menu
BACKUP
MAIN MENU

FIGURE 3–101
The user chose Create and Fillet.

FIGURE 3–102
The user chose Radius from the menu.

After you select Fillet, Mastercam prompts you in the dialogue box to select the entity to apply the fillet to. But, we first want to change the radius size of the fillet. To change the radius, select **Radius** from the menu (see Figure 3–102).

After you select Radius, Mastercam prompts you in the dialogue box to enter the radius of the fillet. The fillet radius should be set to .50. Type **.50** and press **Enter.**

Now that you have set the radius, you need to select the entity you want to apply the fillet to. Mastercam, in the dialogue box, is asking you to select the first entity.

Select the upper horizontal line on the large rectangle (see Figure 3–103). The line should change colors, indicating that you have selected it. Now that you have selected the first entity, Mastercam in the dialogue box is asking you to select the second entity (see Figure 3–103).

The fillet should now appear in the upper left corner of the rectangle.

Before you go on to creating a polygon, you will want to erase all of the entities on the graphics screen.

From the tool bar select the **Delete** icon. Next, from the menu screen, select **All.** From the All menu select **Entities.** When asked for a confirmation to delete all entities, select **Yes.**

FIGURE 3–103

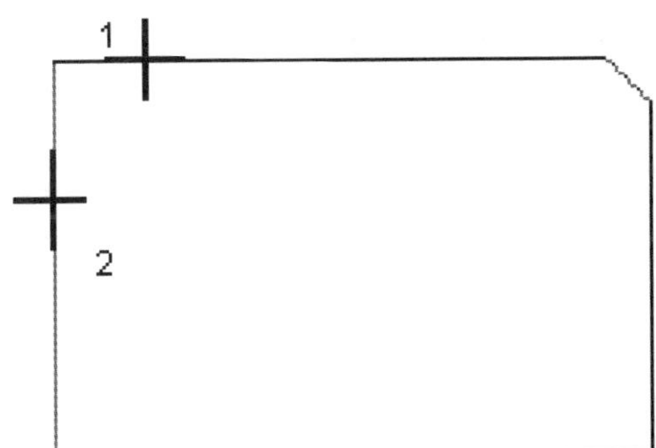

Creating a Polygon

From the Main Menu select **Create/Next Menu/Polygon** (see Figure 3–104) to create a polygon by inputting data related to the type and size polygon you wish to create.

After you select Polygon, Mastercam prompts you in the dialogue box to enter the data necessary to create the polygon (see Figure 3–105).

No. Sides
The total number of sides of the polygon.

Radius
The distance from the center of the polygon to the edge (see Figure 3–106).

Start angle
The start angle of the base of the polygon measured on the X axis (see Figure 3–106).

Measure Cnr Y
This switch allows you to input the radius distance either from the center of the polygon to the flat or the radius distance from the center of the polygon to the corner point (see Figure 3–106). Toggle Y for the center to the corner measurement. Toggle N for the center to the flat measurement.

Main Menu:
Analyze
Create
File
Modify
Xform
Delete
Screen
Exit
BACKUP
MAIN MENU

Create:
Point
Line
Arc
Fillet
Spline
Curve
Surface
Rectangle
Drafting
Next menu
BACKUP
MAIN MENU

Create:
Chamfer
Letters
Pattern
Ellipse
Polygon
Primsol
Eplot*
Gear*
Htable*
Shapes*
BACKUP
MAIN MENU

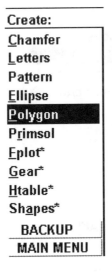

FIGURE 3–104
The user chose Create, Next menu, and Polygon.

No. sides
Radius
Start angle
Meas crnr Y
Make NURBS N
Center pt
BACKUP
MAIN MENU

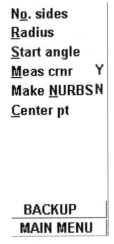

FIGURE 3–105
Submenu when the Polygon option is chosen.

FIGURE 3–106

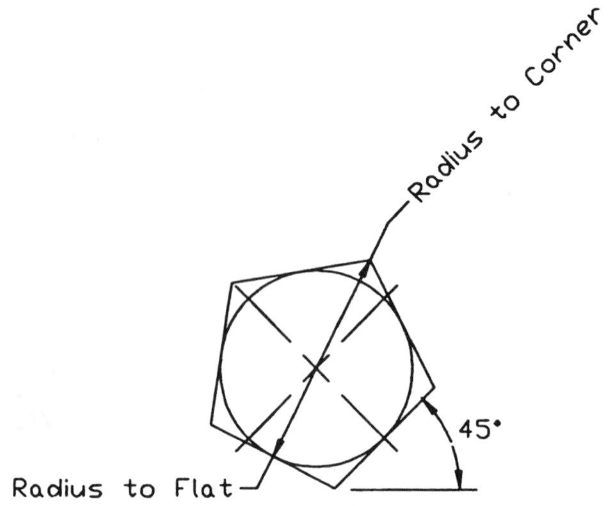

Make NURBS N
This switch allows you to make the polygon a single entity or leave the polygon as a multiple-line entity; toggle Y for yes, to make it one entity. Toggle N for no, keep it multiple entities.

Ctr Point
Select the center of the polygon using the Point Entry menu.

From the Polygon menu select **No. sides** (see Figure 3–107). Mastercam, in the dialogue box, should now be prompting you to input the number of sides. Type in **5** and press **Enter.**

From the Polygon menu now select **Radius** (see Figure 3–108). Mastercam, in the dialogue box, should now be prompting you to input the radius. Type in **1** and press **Enter.**

From the Polygon menu select **Start angle** (see Figure 3–109). Mastercam, in the dialogue box, should now be prompting you to input the starting angle. Type in **30** and press **Enter.**

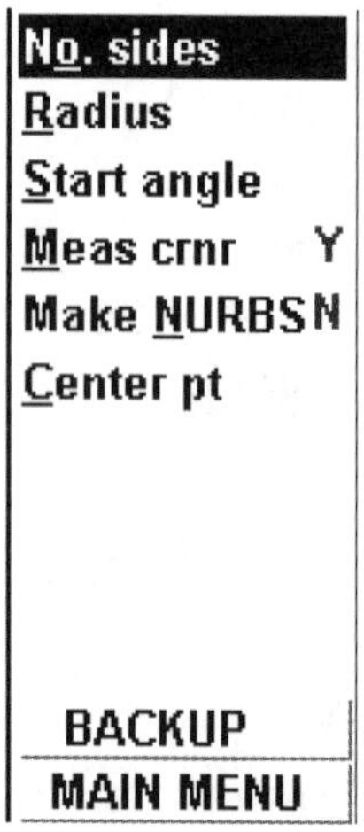

No. sides
Radius
Start angle
Meas crnr Y
Make NURBS N
Center pt
BACKUP
MAIN MENU

FIGURE 3–107
The user chose the No. sides option.

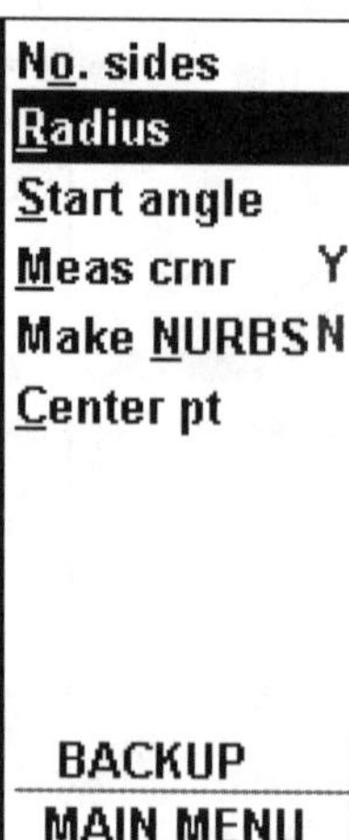

FIGURE 3–108
The user chose the Radius option.

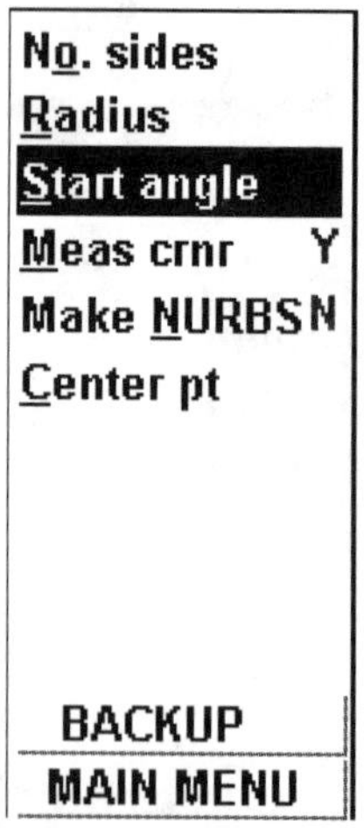

No. sides
Radius
Start angle
Meas crnr Y
Make NURBS N
Center pt
BACKUP
MAIN MENU

FIGURE 3–109
The user chose the Start angle option.

FIGURE 3–110
The user chose the Meas crnr option.

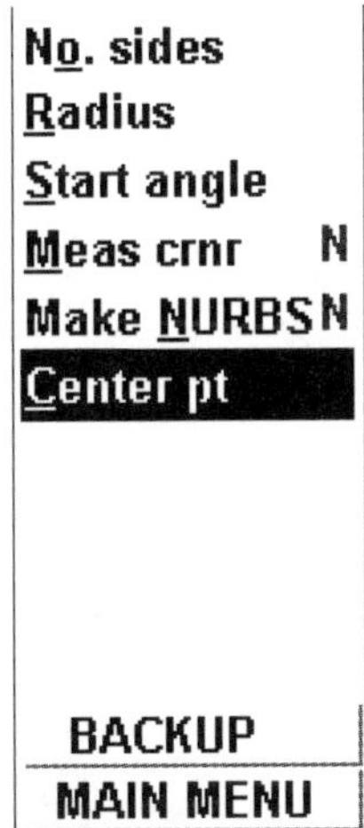

FIGURE 3–111
The user chose the Center pt option.

From the Polygon menu select **Meas crnr** (see Figure 3–110). Notice how Mastercam toggles the Y to an N.

Leave the selection at N for the center to the flat measurement.

Notice also that Mastercam, in the dialogue box, tells you whether you are measuring to the polygon corner or the flat.

Leave the make Nurbs set to N. Leave the polygon as a multiple line entity.

From the Polygon menu select **ctr Point** (see Figure 3–111). Mastercam, in the dialogue box, should now be prompting you to select the center point of the polygon. Mastercam allows you to use the full Point Entry menu to select the center point for the polygon. Use the mouse to select a point anywhere in the center of the screen.

Your polygon should now appear on the screen. This concludes our chapter on basic geometry construction. We have not covered every aspect of geometry construction, but we have covered the basics. Eventually we will touch on most of the aspects of two-dimensional geometry construction. Please use the next chapter to sharpen your geometry construction skills.

REVIEW QUESTIONS

1. All of the new geometry construction starts with which Main Menu option?
2. Explain the Point Entry menu.
3. How does the Value option differ from the Endpoint option?
4. In which areas can you find the Delete option?
5. What occurs when you place the mouse cursor over the top of the icons in the tool bar?
6. What function in Mastercam allows you to enlarge a portion of the graphics display area?

7. What two methods can be used to resize the screen to accommodate all of the geometry that has been created?
8. What does the cursor snap look like?
9. Which option allows you to create parallel lines that are offset from an existing line?
10. What two items are needed to create a line using polar coordinates?
11. Which tool bar icon is used to redraw or update the screen?
12. To end a specific geometry creation segment you need to press the ____________ key or select ____________ from the menu area.
13. What abilities does Mastercam's smart mouse give you?
14. What do you have to keep in mind when creating chamfers with unequal leg lengths?
15. When creating a polygon there are two ways to specify the radial size of the polygon. What are they?

CHAPTER

4

Creating and Modifying Existing Geometry

This chapter describes how to create geometry and modify existing geometry. In the preceding chapters you used the Create function to draw simple objects, lines, and circles. In this chapter you will refine your drawing techniques to increase your efficient use of the the Mastercam creation function.

Objectives

Upon completion of this chapter you will be able to:

- Use different techniques to select entities
- Use the tool bar options to create entities and to delete and undelete objects
- Use the Modify function to edit entities
- Use the Xform function to edit and create entities
- Use the Create function to develop letters

FIGURE 4–1

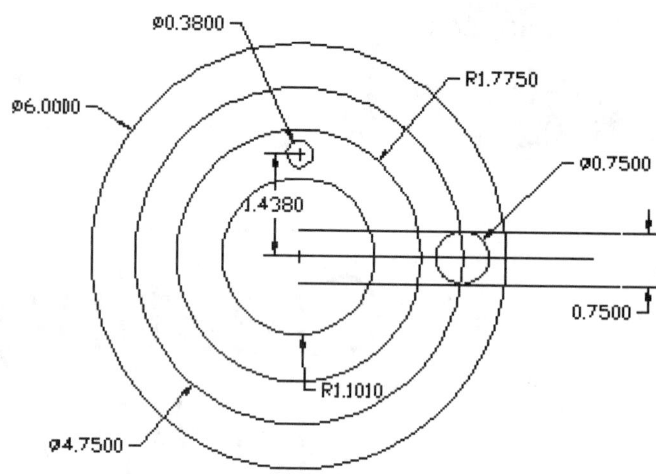

AN OVERVIEW

In the first exercise you will concentrate on editing geometry that has already been created. But, before you edit geometry you will use some of the Create commands that you learned in Chapter 2 and also some new create commands to generate the geometry in Figure 4–1. You are going to need to continue to review Figures 4–1 and 4–2. Concentrate and understand what you are doing; don't just go through the motions of typing in commands on the keyboard. By the time you are finished with this section, Figure 4–1 should evolve into Figure 4–2. By the end of this chapter you should feel very comfortable creating and editing geometry in Mastercam.

CREATING THE PART SHOWN IN FIGURE 4–2

Once you have turned on your computer and allowed the system to boot up, click **Start** using the left mouse button, and then point to the folder called **Mastercam.** Click on the **Mastercam Design** option. From the Mastercam Main Menu area select **File/New** to start a new file. Choose **Yes** to initialize geometry and operations.

Creating Circles

All of the geometry construction starts with the Create menu. To create the 6-inch and the 4.75-diameter circles, select **Main Menu/Create/Arc/Circ pt+dia.** The dialogue box will prompt: Circle with Center/Diameter: Enter the center point. Type **0,0** as the center point. Press **Enter.** Enter **6.0** for the diameter. Press **Enter.**

Mastercam automatically assumes that you want to create another circle. The dialogue box is prompting: Circle with Center/Diameter: Enter the center point. The center point of the next circle is the same as that of the last circle. Select **Last** from the Point Entry menu. Enter **4.75** for the diameter. Press **Enter.**

Now you need to create circles with radius values. To create the 1.101 and 1.775 radius circles select **Main Menu/Create/Arc/Circ pt+rad.** The dialogue box

FIGURE 4–2

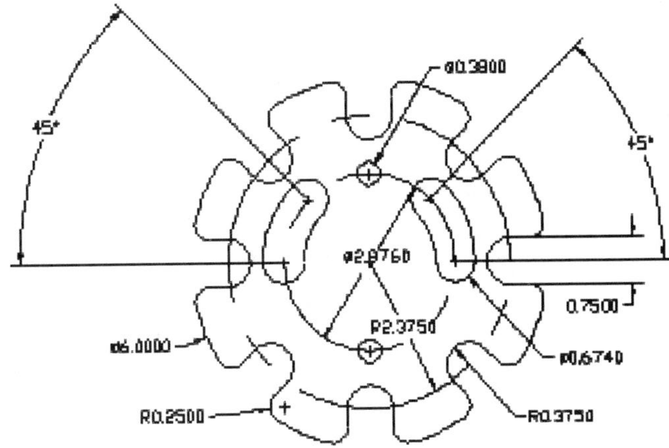

will prompt Circle with Center/Radius: Enter the center point. Select **Center** from the Point Entry menu.

Next the dialogue box will prompt: Select an arc. Select the edge of any of the circles that you have already created.

The dialogue box will prompt: Enter the Radius. Type in **1.101.** Press **Enter.**

Mastercam automatically assumes that you want to create another circle right away. The dialogue box is prompting: Circle with Center/Radius. Enter the center point. The center point of this circle is the same as that of the last circle. Select **Last** from the menu.

The dialogue box will prompt: Enter the Radius. Type **1.775.** Press **Enter.**

You should now have four concentric circles on the screen. Next you will create the .380-diameter circle. To create the .380-diameter circle select **Main Menu/Create/Arc/Circ pt+dia.** The dialogue box will prompt: Circle with Center/Diameter. Enter the center point. Type **0,1.438** for the center point. Press **Enter.** Enter the diameter. Type **.380.** Press **Enter.**

Creating Horizontal Lines Using the Offset Command

FIGURE 4–3

Let's try another method of creating geometry. Start with the horizontal line that runs through the center of the circles. Use the icons in the tool bar to bypass the Main Menu and Create commands. To create this horizontal line, use the mouse to select the **Create-Line-Horizontal** icon from the tool bar (see Figure 4–3). If you don't see the Horizontal line icon, page to the next tool bar screen using either the Next Page (arrow) or Previous Page icons at the ends of the tool bar. Once you have found the **Horizontal line** icon, use the mouse to select it.

The dialogue box should now be prompting: Select the first endpoint. The line starts at the center point of the circles. Use the smart mouse to snap to the center of the circles. Move the mouse cursor to the edge of one of the large circles. When the box surrounds the center of the circles, click the left mouse button. Your line should start from the center of the circle. Drag the line out beyond the right side of the largest circle (see Figure 4–4) and click the left mouse button.

The dialogue box is now prompting: Enter the Y coordinate. Accept the default value of **0** by pressing **Enter.** If you ever want to undo the last entity you

FIGURE 4–4

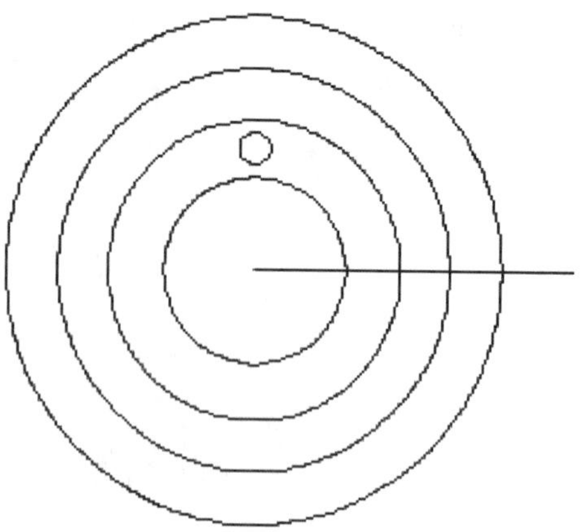

FIGURE 4–5

FIGURE 4–6

FIGURE 4–7

FIGURE 4–8

created, select the Undo icon from the tool bar (see Figure 4–5). This will eliminate the last entity you created as long as you have not exited the create area that you are currently in.

You will now use the Create-Line-Parallel icon from the tool bar (see Figure 4–6). If you don't see it in the present tool bar menu, use the Page icons located in either corner of the tool bar. Select the **Create-Line-Parallel** icon now.

Upon selecting the Parallel Line icon, the Parallel options menu appears (see Figure 4–7).

You want to create offset copies of the existing centerline, so activate the **Side/dist** option. Mastercam, in the dialogue box, is now prompting you to select the line you wish to use. Use the mouse to select the horizontal centerline you just created. Mastercam is now prompting you to select the direction in which you would like to offset. Use the mouse to place the cursor anywhere above the existing horizontal line. Click the left mouse button. Mastercam is now prompting you to input the parallel line distance. You need a total slot width of .75, so the offset distance from the centerline will be .375. Type **.375** and press **Enter.** When you have completed this, the new line should appear.

The Mastercam dialogue box should now be prompting you to select the line. Use the mouse to select the original horizontal centerline. Mastercam is prompting you to select the direction in which you want to offset. Use the mouse to place the cursor anywhere below the existing horizontal line. Click the left mouse button. Mastercam is now prompting you to input the parallel line distance. You need a total slot width of .75, so the offset distance from the centerline will be .375. Accept the .375 default by pressing **Enter** or type **.375** and press **Enter.** When you have completed this, the new line should appear.

You should now have the three horizontal lines on the screen.

Creating the Circle for the Slot

Next you will create the .75-diameter circle, which along with the horizontal lines creates the slot. (Be careful not to select the Create-Arc-Endpoints icon). To create the .75-diameter circle, select the **Create-Arc** icon from the tool bar (see Figure 4–8). If you don't see it, use the Page keys located in either corner of the tool bar.

From the Arc menu select **Circ pt+dia.** The dialogue box will prompt: Circle with Center/Diameter. Enter the center point. Using the smart mouse, surround the intersection point of the horizontal centerline and the 4.75-diameter circle (see Figure 4–9).

FIGURE 4–9

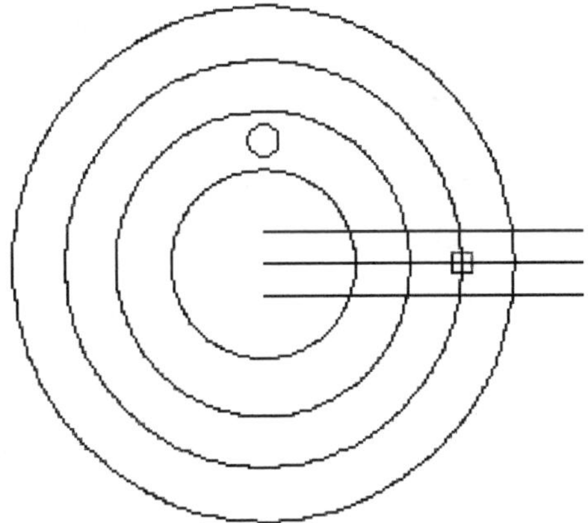

FIGURE 4–10

The dialogue box will be prompting: Enter the diameter. Type **.75** and press **Enter.** Your screen should now have all of the entities that Figure 4–1 has. You no longer need the original horizontal centerline. Use the Delete function from the tool bar to erase it now. Next select the **Repaint** icon to update the screen (see Figure 4–10).

Trimming 1 Entity

You have created the geometry of Figure 4–1. Now it is time to begin modifying this geometry. You will use the Trim 1 entity function to trim the horizontal lines from the circle to create the slot.

The Trim 1 entity function trims away a single entity at the intersection point of another entity. Select **Main Menu/Main Menu/Modify/Trim/1 entity.** The dialogue box will prompt: Trim (1) select entity to trim. Use the mouse to select the part of the horizontal line (P1) you want to keep (see Figure 4–11).

The dialogue box will prompt: Trim (1) select entity to trim to. Use the mouse to select the entity (circle P2) you want to use as the cutting line (see Figure 4–11). The line should now be trimmed from the .75-diameter circle to the left.

The dialogue box will be prompting: Trim (1) select entity to trim. Use the mouse to select the part of the horizontal line (P3) you want to keep (see Figure 4–11).

The dialogue box will prompt Trim (1) select entity to trim to. Use the mouse to select the entity (Circle P4) you want to use as the cutting line (see Figure 4–11).

FIGURE 4–11

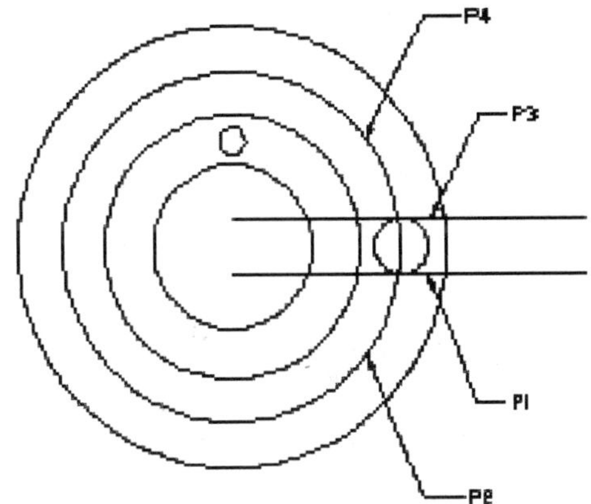

FIGURE 4–12

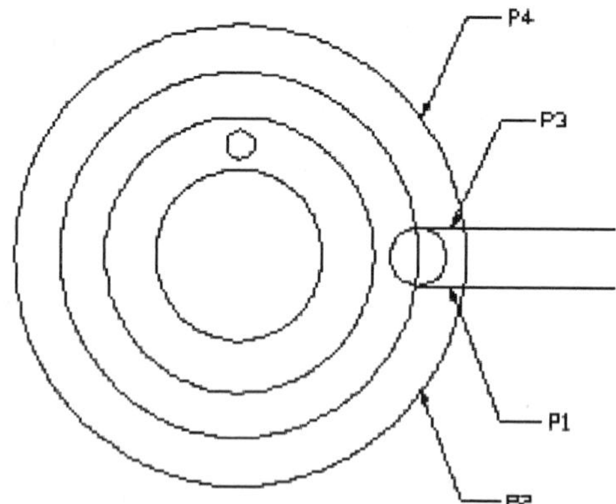

The line should now be trimmed. The first pick you make when trimming an entity is the part of the entity you want to keep. The second pick is the cutting line.

Now you will trim the parts of lines that are outside the circle. The dialogue box will be prompting: Trim (1) select entity to trim. Use the mouse to select the part of the horizontal line (P1) you want to keep (see Figure 4–12).

The dialogue box will prompt: Trim (1) select entity to trim to. Use the mouse to select the entity (circle P2) you want to use as the cutting line (see Figure 4–12). The line should now be trimmed from the 6.0-diameter circle to the right.

Trim (1) select entity to trim. Use the mouse to select the part of the horizontal line (P3) you want to keep (see Figure 4–12).

The dialogue box will prompt: Trim (1) select entity to trim to. Use the mouse to select the entity (circle P4) you want to use as the cutting line (see Figure 4–12).

The lines that extended beyond the circle should now be trimmed. You will again use the Trim 1 entities function to trim the 6-inch diameter circle from the two horizontal lines. This will open up the slot. The dialogue box will be prompting: Trim (1) select entity to trim.

Use the mouse to select the part of the circle (P1) you want to keep (see Figure 4–13).

The dialogue box will be prompting: Trim (1) select entity to trim to. Use the mouse to select the entity (line P2) you want to use as the cutting line (see Figure 4–13). The circle should now be trimmed to where the center horizontal line was. This leaves the slot one-half open. Now let us trim the other half of the slot.

The dialogue box will be prompting: Trim (1) select entity to trim. Use the mouse to select the part of the circle (P3) you want to keep (see Figure 4–13).

FIGURE 4–13

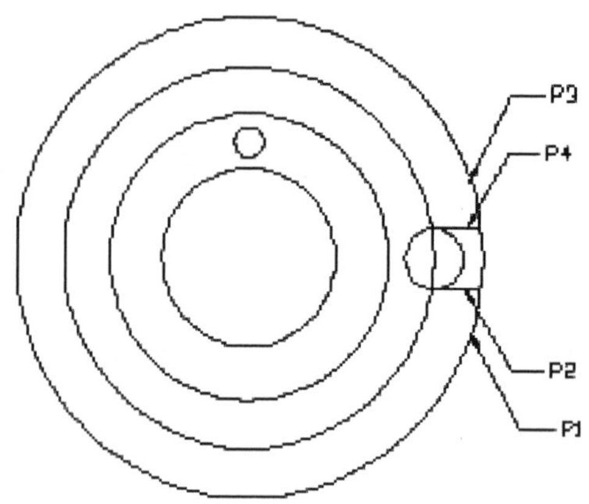

FIGURE 4–14

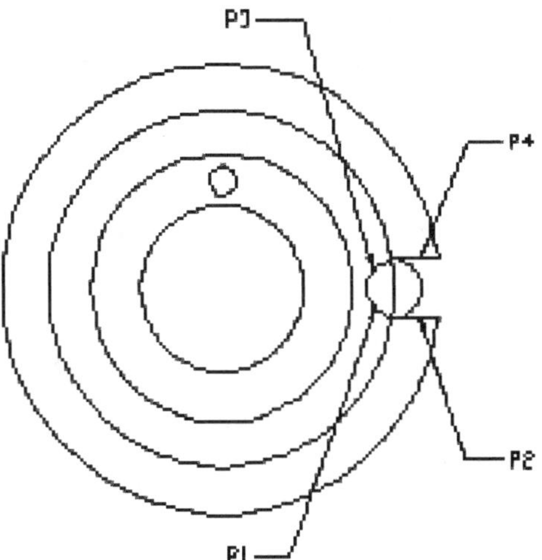

The dialogue box will prompt: Trim (1) select entity to trim to. Use the mouse to select the entity (line P4) you want to use as the cutting line (see Figure 4–13). The slot should now be fully open.

Now finish the slot by trimming away half of the .75-diameter circle. The dialogue box will be prompting: Trim (1) select entity to trim. Use the mouse to select the part of the circle (P1) you want to keep (see Figure 4–14).

The dialogue box will be prompting: Trim (1) select entity to trim to. Use the mouse to select the entity (line P2) you want to use as the cutting line (see Figure 4–14). One-half of the circle should now be trimmed away.

Now finish the slot by trimming away the other half of the .75-diameter circle. The dialogue box will prompt: Trim (1) select entity to trim. Use the mouse to select the part of the circle (P3) you want to keep (see Figure 4–14).

The dialogue box will be prompting: Trim (1) select entity to trim to. Use the mouse to select the entity (line P4) you want to use as the cutting line (see Figure 4–14). You should now be left with just one open slot.

Using the Rotate Function

The rotate function takes existing entities and copies and rotates the entities around a selected point. Now you will use the one slot to create 8 slots using the Rotate function. To rotate entities using the Rotate command, select **Main Menu/Xform/Rotate.** Mastercam is now asking you to pick the entities you wish to rotate. Select the three entities that make up the slot (see Figure 4–15).

Once you have picked the three entities that make up the slot, select **Done** from the menu area. Mastercam will now prompt you for the Origin or Point you wish to rotate the slot around. You would like to rotate around the center point of the part. From the Rotate menu select **Point.** Next use the smart mouse to select the center of any of the large circles. The Rotate attribute box should now appear on the screen (see Figure 4–16).

You need to make seven copies of the original slot. Make sure that the Copy option is active. The Copy attribute should have a dot in the selection circle. If it doesn't, use the mouse to activate the **copy selection** circle. Next activate the number of steps option by using the mouse to activate the **Number of Steps** dialogue option. Type **7** in the Number of Steps dialogue box. According to Figure 4–2, the slots are located 45 degrees apart. Activate the **Rotation Angle** option and type **45**

FIGURE 4–15

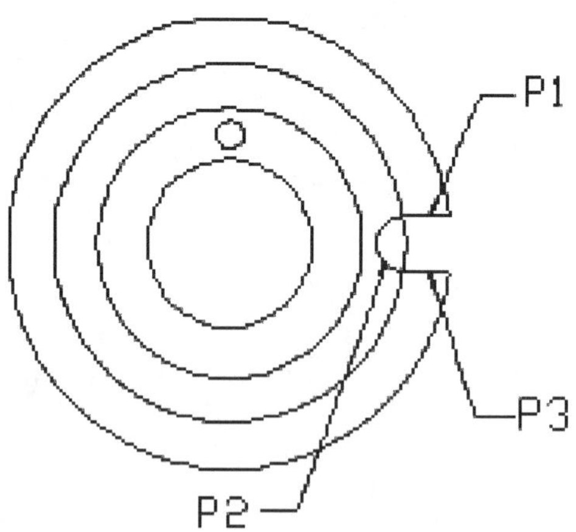

FIGURE 4–16

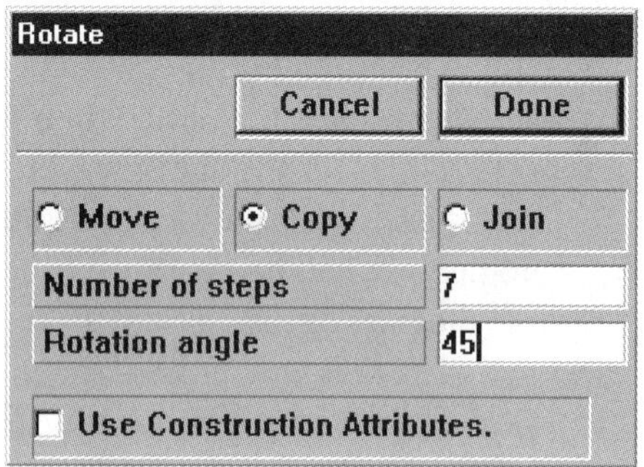

FIGURE 4–17

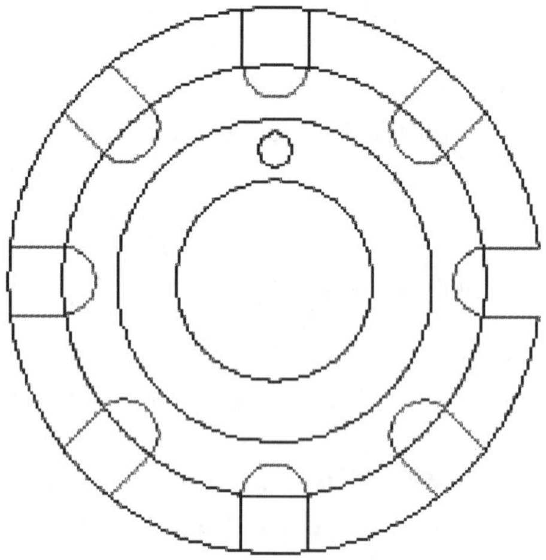

in this dialogue box and press **Enter.** Now select **Done.** The new slots should now appear on the screen (see Figure 4–17).

Using the Mirror Function

The mirror function takes existing entities and makes a copy of the selected entities and places them on the opposite side of a mirror line. The object that you are going to mirror is the .380-diameter circle. You could simply draw this circle in, but let's do it to illustrate the Mirror command.

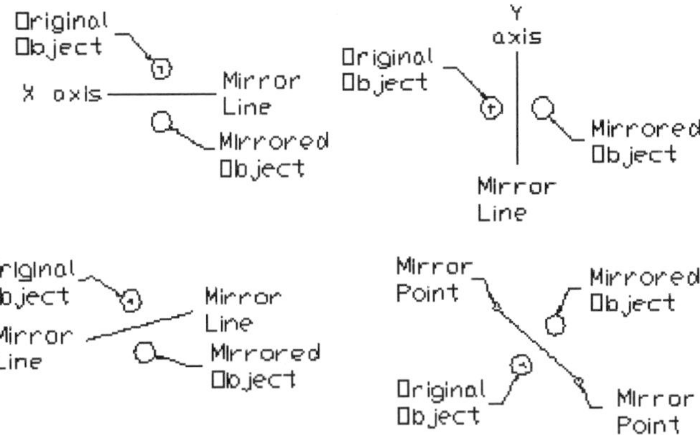

FIGURE 4–18

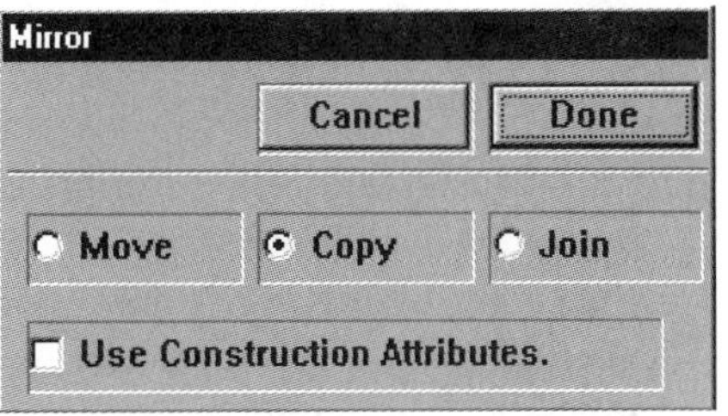

FIGURE 4–19

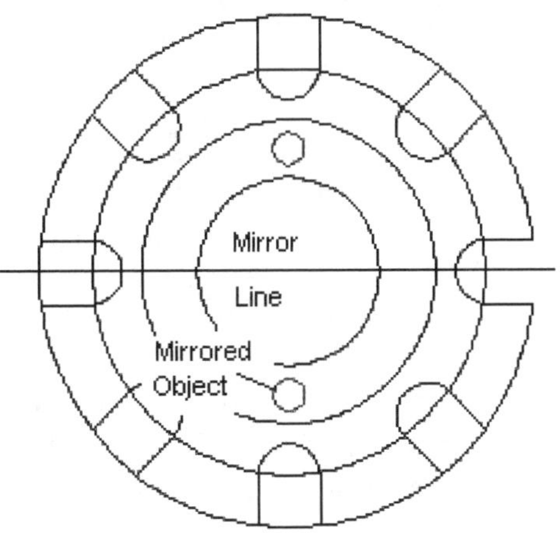

FIGURE 4–20

To mirror entities using the Mirror command select **Main Menu/Xform/ Mirror.** Mastercam is now asking you to pick the entities you wish to mirror. Select the .38-diameter circle. Once you have picked the circle, select **Done** from the menu area. Mastercam will now be prompting you to select X axis, Y axis, Line, or 2 points. These selections make up the mirror line you wish to use (see Figure 4–18).

You want to mirror about the X axis. Select **X axis** from the Mirror menu. The Mirror attribute box should now appear on the screen (see Figure 4–19). Make sure that the **Copy** attribute has a dot in the selection circle. This means that the copy option is active. If it is not active, use the mouse cursor to select the circle. Now select **Done.** The mirrored circle should now appear (see Figure 4–20).

FIGURE 4–21

Now you will create the radial slots. To create the slots, you must have two construction lines and a construction circle. The construction lines will be lines that run from the center of the part to the center of the two circles that make up the slot. To create the first line at a 45-degree angle, select the **Create-Line-Polar** icon from the tool bar (see Figure 4–21).

FIGURE 4–22

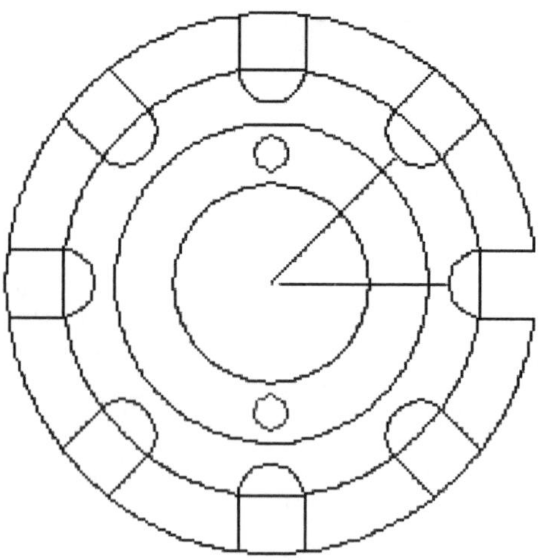

Mastercam will prompt: Create, line Polar: Specify an endpoint. The first endpoint of the line starts at the center of the part. Use the smart mouse to select the center of any of the main circles of the part. Mastercam will prompt: Enter the angle in degrees. Type **45** and press **Enter.** Enter the line length. Type **2** and press **Enter.** Now you will create the other polar line. Mastercam will be prompting you: Create line Polar, specify endpoint. When the smart mouse creates a box around the center point of the part accept this center point by clicking on the left mouse button. Enter the angle in degrees. Type **0** and press **Enter.** Enter the line length. Accept the default of **2** by pressing **Enter.** You should now have two construction lines (see Figure 4–22).

Now you need to create the construction circle. The construction circle is the radial centerline of the slots. To create the circle, select the **Create-Arc** icon from the tool bar. From the Arc menu select **Circ pt+rad.** The dialogue box will be prompting: Circle with Center/Radius. Use the smart mouse to select the center of the main circles.

The dialogue box will prompt: Enter the Radius. Type **1.438.** Press **Enter.** The two construction lines and the radial centerline should now appear on the screen (see Figure 4–23).

FIGURE 4–23

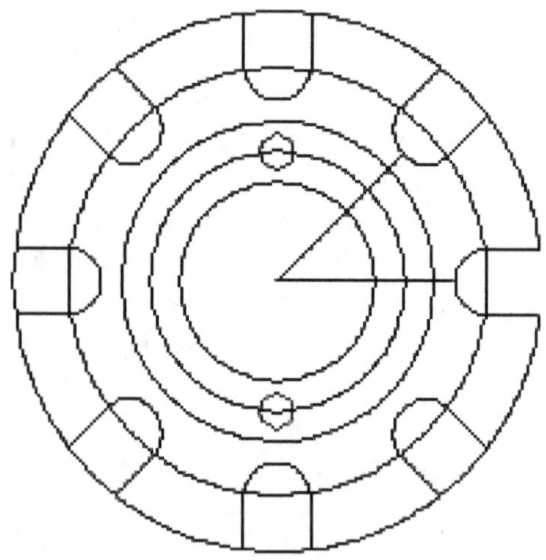

FIGURE 4–24

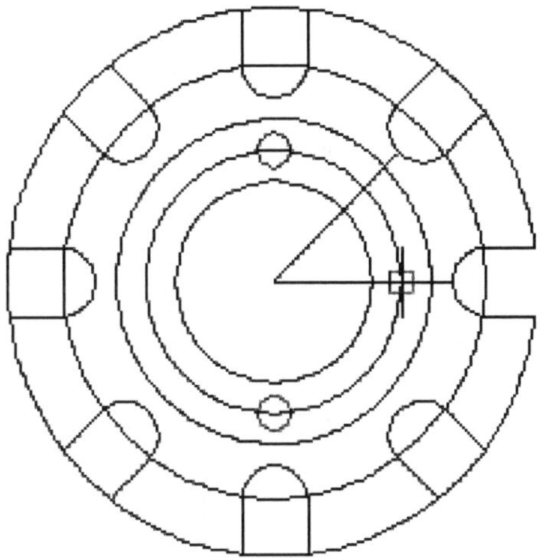

Now create the two circles that make up the radial slot. Select the **Create-Arc** icon from the tool bar. Notice that since you are already in the Create-Arc function, you cannot get the Arc menu to pop up. Press the **Esc** key on the keyboard until the Arc menu appears. From the Arc menu select **Circ pt+dia.** The dialogue box will be prompting: Enter the center point. Using the smart mouse select the intersection point of the line at angle 0 and the 1.438-radius circle (see Figure 4–24).

The dialogue box will prompt: Enter the diameter. Type **.674** and press **Enter.** Remember that if you make a mistake, you can undo the last command by selecting the Undo icon from the tool bar.

The dialogue box will prompt Circle with Center/Diameter. Enter the center point. Using the smart mouse select the intersection point of the line at angle 45 and the 1.438-radius circle (see Figure 4–25).

The dialogue box will be prompting: Enter the diameter. Accept the default of **.674** by pressing **Enter.** The screen should now look like Figure 4–26.

Trim 3 Entity

You will now use the Trim 3 entity function to trim the unwanted entities and leave the radial slot. The Trim 3 entity function trims away three entities at the

FIGURE 4–25

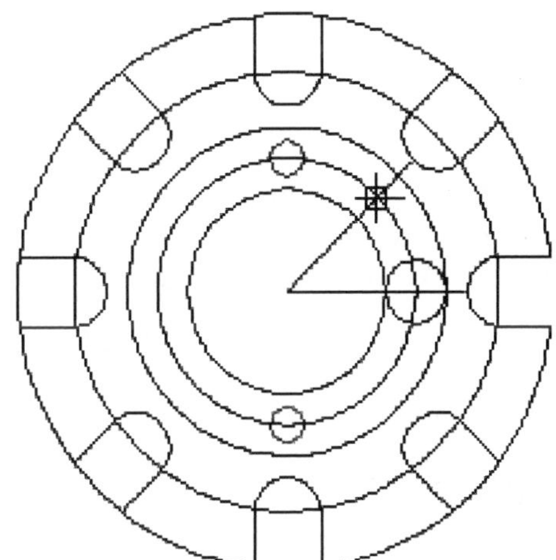

FIGURE 4–26

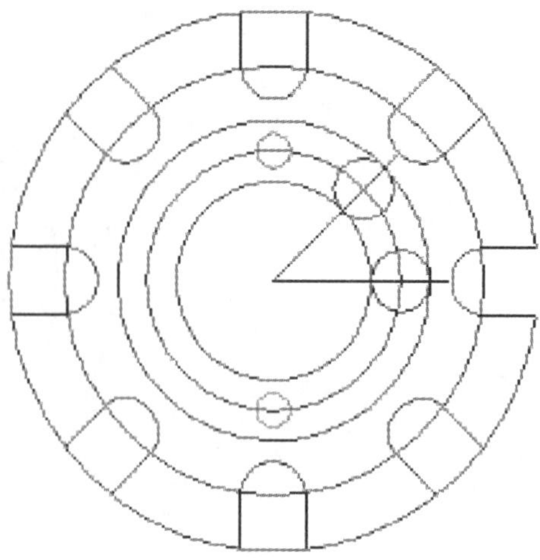

FIGURE 4–27

intersection points of the other entities. Select the **Modify-Trim-3 entities** icon (see Figure 4–27).

The dialogue box will prompt: Trim (3) select the first entity to trim. Use the mouse to select the part of the circle (P1) you want to keep (see Figure 4–28).

The dialogue box will prompt: Trim (3) select the second entity to trim. Use the mouse to select the second part of the circle (P2) that you want to keep (see Figure 4–28).

The dialogue box will be prompting: Select entity to trim to. Use the mouse to select the part of the circle (P3) you want to trim to (see Figure 4–28).

The top part of the slot should now be trimmed from the large circles (see Figure 4–29).

The slot should now appear on the screen by itself. Erase the two polar construction lines using the **Delete** function from the tool bar.

Now you will trim the bottom portion of the circle. You will use the Trim 1 entity function to trim the unwanted entities from the radial slot. Select the **Modify-Trim-1-entities** icon. The dialogue box will be prompting: Select entity to trim to. Use the mouse to select the part of the circle (P1) you want to keep (see Figure 4–30). Now select the entity you want to trim to (P2).

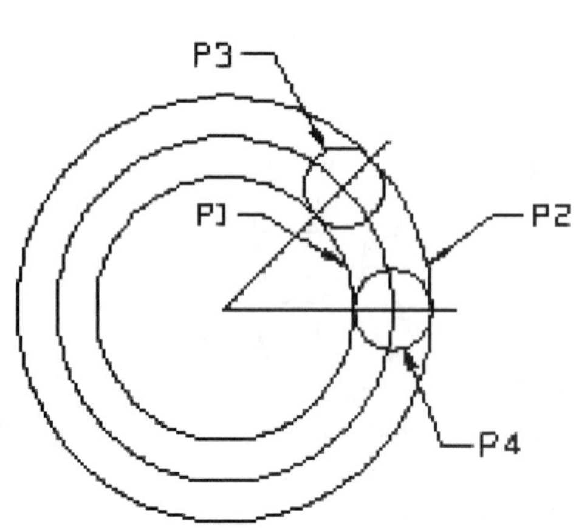

FIGURE 4–28

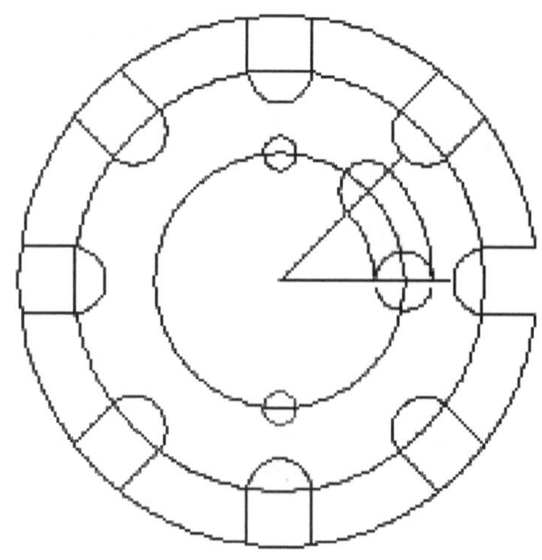

FIGURE 4–29

FIGURE 4–30

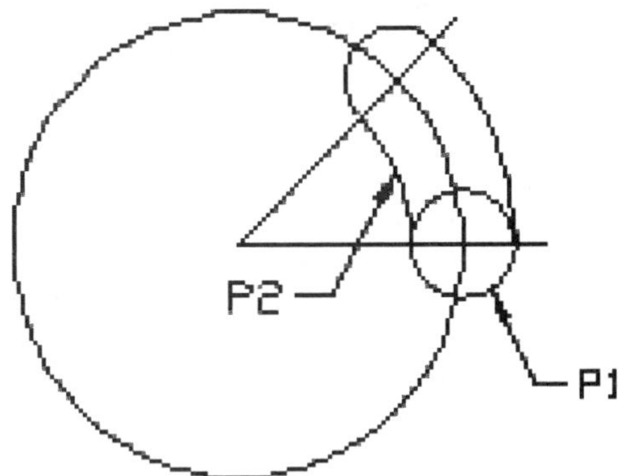

Rotating the Slot

FIGURE 4–31

You are going to use the Rotate function again to copy and rotate the existing slot to create the other slot. To rotate entities using the Rotate command, select the **Xform-Rotate** icon (see Figure 4–31).

Notice that there are many icons in the tool bar that speed up the design function of Mastercam. If you don't recognize an icon, hold the mouse cursor over the icon and read the description.

Mastercam should be prompting you: Select entities to rotate. Select the four entities that make up the slot. Select **Done** from the menu area. Mastercam will now be prompting you for Origin or Point. You want to rotate around the center point of the radial arc. Select **Point** from the Rotate menu. Next you want to use the smart mouse to select the center of any of the main circles that make up the part. The Rotate attribute box should now appear on the screen (see Figure 4–32).

You want to make one copy of the original slot. Make sure that the **Copy** option is active. The Copy attribute should have a dot in the selection circle. Activate the **Steps** option by using the mouse to activate the Steps dialogue option. Type in a **1** in the Steps dialogue box. The slots are located 135 degrees apart (90 + 45). Activate the **Rotation Angle** dialogue box and type **135.** Now select **Done.** The new slot should now appear on the screen (see Figure 4–33).

Trimming or Dividing a Curve from Two Entities

The Divide command trims a line or curve from two other lines or curves. You will now trim the 6-inch circle from each of the webs that join the slots. You need to do this before you can fillet the slots.

FIGURE 4–32

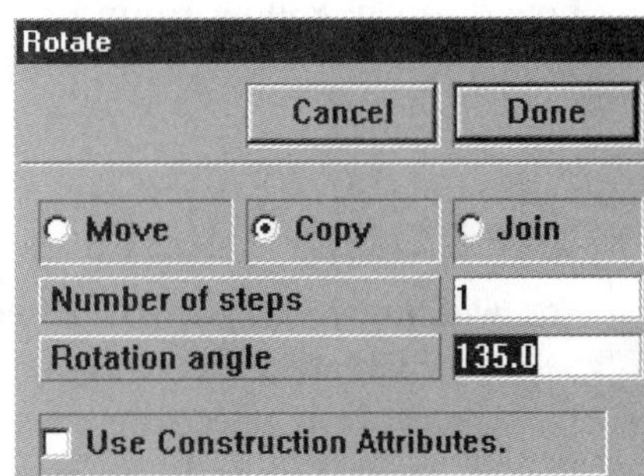

FIGURE 4–33

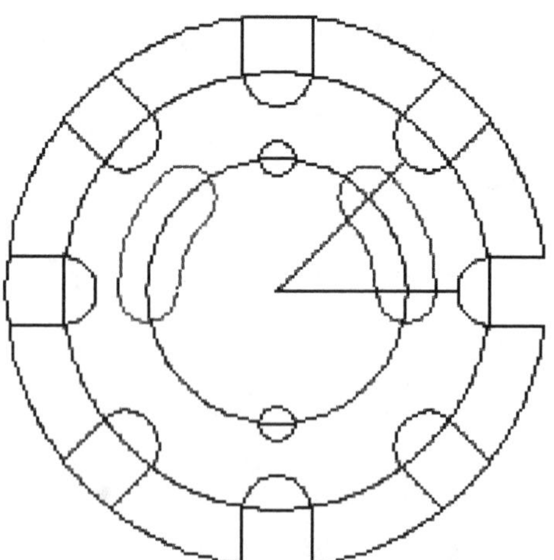

FIGURE 4–34

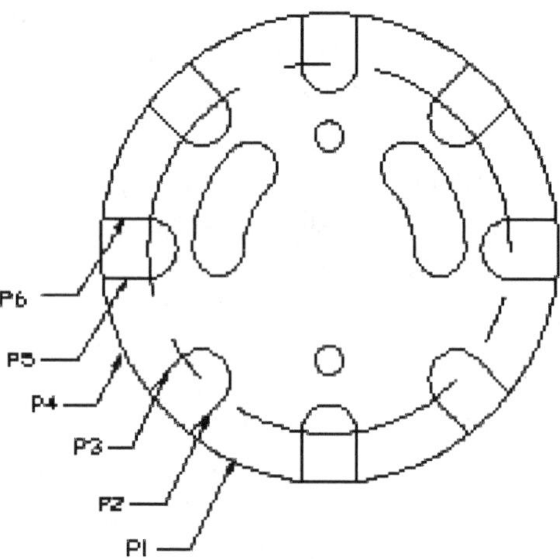

To divide the circle you need to select **Main Menu/Main Menu/ Modify/Trim/Divide.** Mastercam will now be prompting you to Select curve to divide. Select the 6-inch-diameter circle at P1 (see Figure 4–34). The dialogue box will prompt: Select the first dividing curve. Mastercam now wants the cutting plane line. Select the line at P2 (see Figure 4–34). Select the second dividing curve. Mastercam now wants the other cutting plane line. Select the line at P3 (see Figure 4–34). The slot should now be open. Mastercam will prompt you to Select curve to divide. Select the 6-inch diameter circle at P4 (see Figure 4–34). Select the first dividing curve. Mastercam now wants the cutting plane line. Select the line at P5 (see Figure 4–34). Select the second dividing curve. Mastercam now wants the other cutting plane line. Select the line at P6 (see Figure 4–34). The second slot should now be open. Follow around the rest of the part and finish opening up all of the slots.

Creating Fillets

FIGURE 4–35

You will now finish the part by creating the fillets on the outer edges of the slots. Select the **Create-Fillet** icon on the tool bar (see Figure 4–35).

Before you select the entity to fillet, check the dialogue box to make sure that the fillet radius is equal to .250. If it is not equal to .250, select **Radius**

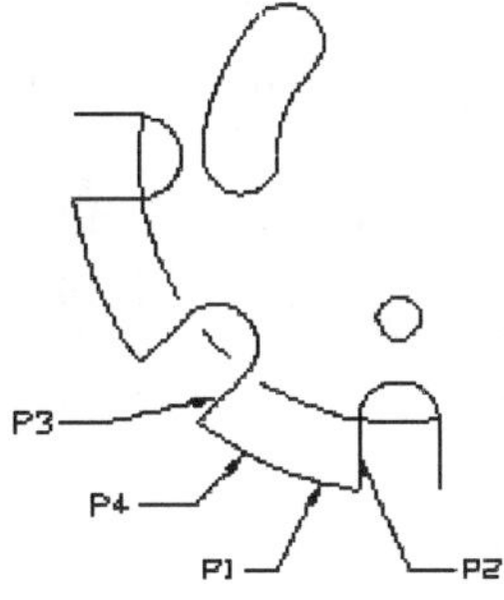

FIGURE 4–36

from the menu and enter **.250.** The dialogue box will prompt: Fillet, Select an entity. Select entity P1 (see Figure 4–36). Fillet, Select another entity. Select entity P2.

The corner should now have a fillet showing. Mastercam is now prompting: Fillet, Select an entity. Select entity P3 (see Figure 4–36). Fillet, Select another entity. Select entity P4. Again, the corner should have a fillet showing. Complete all of the remaining fillets. Congratulations, the part should now be complete and you are ready to do the final tutorial in this chapter.

CREATING FIGURE 4–37

This is the last design tutorial in this chapter. In this exercise you are not going to be provided with every keystroke as in the previous tutorial. If you have been keeping track of the commands, this should not be a problem. If you find yourself getting lost, go back in this chapter or previous chapters to review the information associated with the command(s) in question.

Select **File/New** to start a new file. Choose **Yes** to initialize geometry and operations. Because all of the dimensions originate from the vertical centerline of the part and the center of the large radii, you will use this position as the part origin (see Figure 4–37).

Creating Circles

Create the two 3-inch- and the 1.5-inch-radius circles by selecting the **Create-Arc** icon.

From the Arc menu select **Circ pt+rad.** The dialogue box will prompt: Circle with Center/Radius: Enter the center point. Type **-3,0** as the center point. Press **Enter.**

Enter the Radius. Type in **3.0.** Press **Enter.** Use the **Alt+F1** hot keys or the Fit icon to resize the display area. Mastercam automatically assumes that you want to create another circle. The dialogue box is prompting: Circle with Center/Radius: Enter the center point. Type **3,0.** Press **Enter.**

Enter the Radius. Type **3.0.** Press **Enter.**

FIGURE 4–37

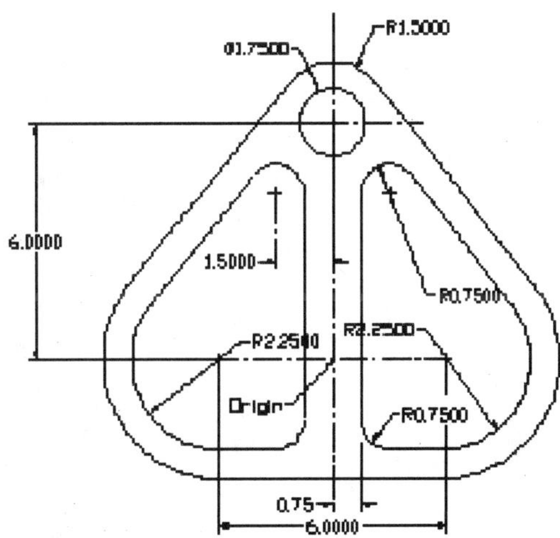

Use the **Alt+F1** hot keys or the Fit icon to resize the display area. Mastercam automatically assumes that you want to create another circle. The dialogue box is prompting: Circle with Center/Radius: Enter the center point.

Type **0,6** Press **Enter.** The dialogue box will be prompting: Enter the Radius. Type **1.5.** Press **Enter.** Use the **Alt+F1** hot keys or the Fit icon to resize the display area.

Creating Tangent Lines

Create the three tangent lines by selecting the **Create-Line** icon. From the line menu select **Tangent.** From the Tangent menu select **2 Arcs.** The dialogue box will be prompting: Select an Arc. Use the mouse to select the 3.0-inch-radius circle on the left. The dialogue box will be prompting: Select an Arc. Use the mouse to select the 1.50-inch-radius circle. The dialogue box will be prompting: Select an Arc. Use the mouse to select the 3.0-inch-radius circle on the right. The dialogue box will prompt: Select an Arc. Use the mouse to select the 1.50-inch-radius circle. The dialogue box will be prompting: Select an Arc. Use the mouse to select the 3.0-inch-radius circle on the right. The dialogue box will be prompting: Select an Arc. Use the mouse to select the 3.0-inch-radius circle on the left. The outside of the figure should now be closed.

Trimming the Circles

Select the **Modify-Trim-1 Entity** icon to begin trimming the circles from the tangent lines. The dialogue box will prompt: Select an Entity to trim. Use the mouse to select the trim entities shown in Figure 4–38. Trim the entities in the order shown. Remember the first pick you make when trimming an entity is the part of the entity you want to keep. The second pick is the cutting line. The profile of the part should now be complete.

Creating Line Vertical

Create the centerline of the part by selecting the **Create-Line-Vertical** icon. Use the smart mouse to select the center of the 1.5-inch-radius arc. Use the mouse to drag

FIGURE 4–38

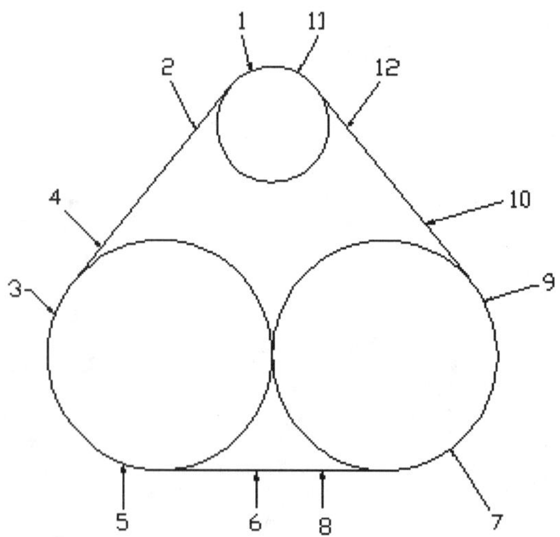

FIGURE 4–39

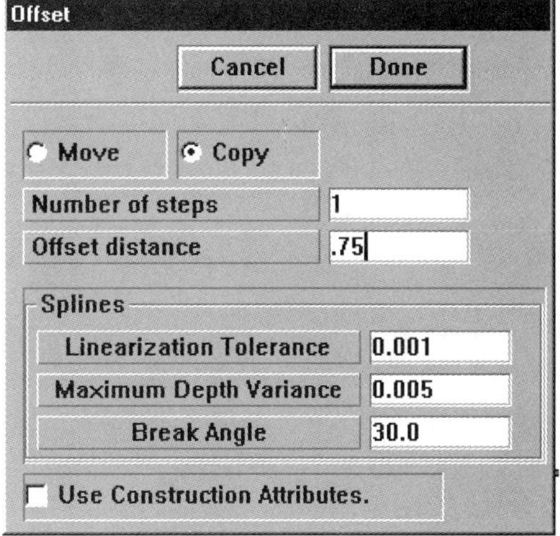

the line down beyond the bottom of the part. Click the left mouse button to end the line. At the X-axis coordinate prompt, press **Enter** to accept the default of 0.

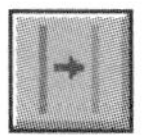

Creating Offset Geometry

You are going to begin creating the inside portion of the object by selecting the **Xform-Offset** icon. The Offset attributes box should appear on the screen (see Figure 4–39). You will create a single offset copy of some of the entities that make up the outside profile of the part. Make sure that the **Copy** button is selected. You will make only one copy of each of the entities. Enter a **1** in the "Number of steps" dialogue area. Note that the wall thickness between the outer profile and the inner pockets is .75 inches. Enter **.75** in the "Offset distance" dialogue area. When you have completed the entries, select **Done.**

The dialogue box will prompt: Select a line, arc, or spline to offset. Use the mouse to select the first entity shown in Figure 4–40. The dialogue box will prompt: Indicate the offset direction. Place the mouse cursor to the inside the figure and press the left mouse key. The first entity should now be copied and offset. Finish offsetting the other entities shown in Figure 4–40.

FIGURE 4–40

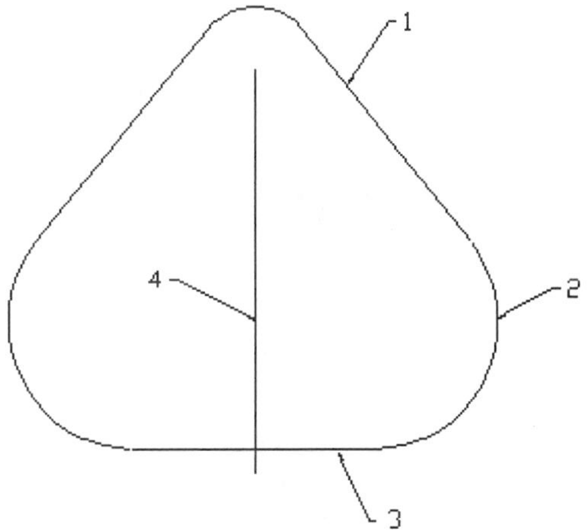

FIGURE 4–41

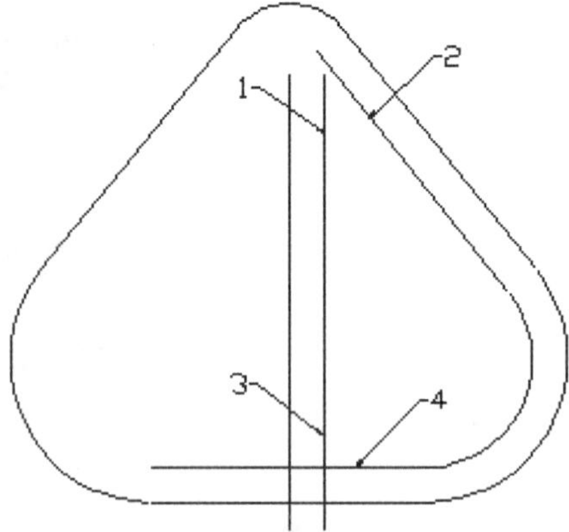

Filleting the Unfinished Corners

Now you will begin finishing the right side of the inner figure by selecting the **Create-Fillet** icon. Before you begin, you need to change the size of the fillet radius. Select **Radius** from the Fillet menu. The dialogue box will prompt: Enter the fillet radius. Type **.75** and press **Enter.** The dialogue box will prompt Fillet, select an entity. Use the mouse to select the entities shown in Figure 4–41.

Mirror and Copy

Now that you have finished one pocket you can begin the other pocket by selecting the **Xform-Mirror** icon. Use the mouse to select all of the entities that make up the right-hand pocket. When you have finished selecting the entities, select **Done** from the Mirror menu. The dialogue box will be prompting: Mirror: mirror about. You want to select **Y axis.** The Mirror attribute box should now appear on the screen. Make sure that the **Copy** button is selected. When you have finished, select **Done.**

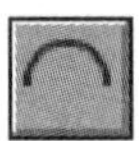

Creating a Circle

Create the final 1.75-inch-diameter circle by selecting the **Create-Arc** icon. From the Arc menu select **Circ pt+dia.** The dialogue box will be prompting: Circle with Center/diameter: Enter the center point. Type **0,6** as the center point. Press **Enter.**

Enter the diameter. Type **1.75.** Press **Enter.**

Deleting the Centerline

To delete the construction centerline (line number 4 in Figure 4–40) select the **Delete** icon. Deleting this line will give you room to create the lettering and complete this part. Delete the line now. The part should now resemble Figure 4–42 without the lettering.

You will now use the Main Menu/Create/Next Menu/Letters command to create lettering. Creating letters is really quite simple. Letters can be created in linear and radial configurations. After you have completed this exercise try creating

FIGURE 4–42

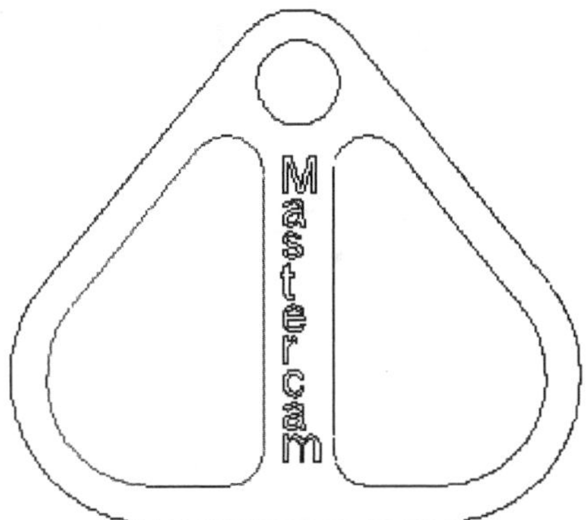

some different style and size lettering strings on your own. To begin creating the lettering, select **Main Menu/Create/Next Menu/Letters.** From the Letters menu select **TrueType.**

The Font attributes box should now appear on the screen (see Figure 4–43). You are going to create Regular Arial letters of a 10-point size. Use the mouse to highlight these choices. Once these choices have been highlighted, select **OK.**

The dialogue box will now prompt: Enter letters. Use the keyboard to type **Mastercam.** Press **Enter.** The dialogue box will now prompt Enter Letter height. Type **.75.** Press **Enter.** Mastercam will now be prompting us for the direction. Select **Vertical.** The dialogue box will now be prompting Enter Letter spacing. Type **.1.** Press **Enter.** The dialogue box will now prompt Enter Starting Location of letters: Type **-375, 4.5.** Press **Enter.** The letter string should now appear on the screen.

Congratulations, you have finished the final design tutorial. Now it's time for you to practice. Do the exercises at the end of this chapter. Save these exercises to a diskette for use later on in the textbook. If you get stuck, check back in this chapter or previous chapters for help.

FIGURE 4–43

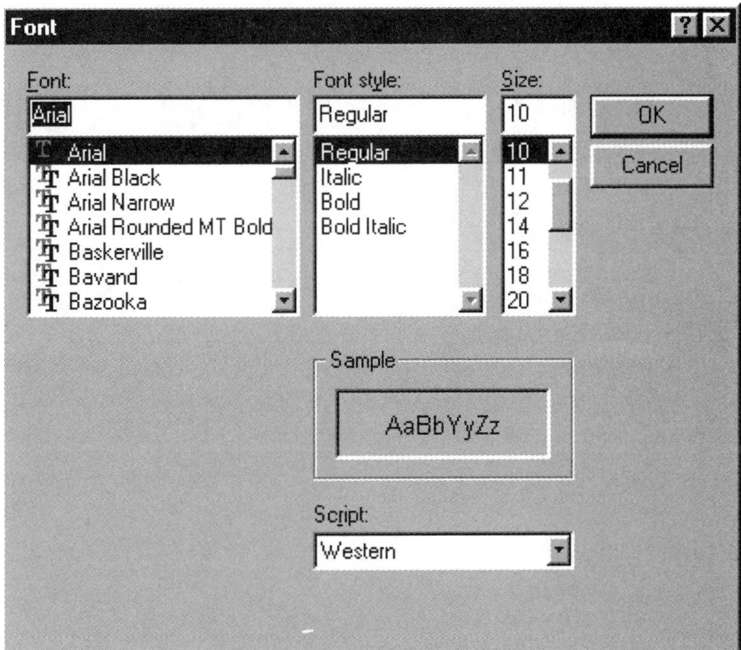

REVIEW QUESTIONS

Complete questions 1–5 by correctly identifying the tool bar icons shown below.

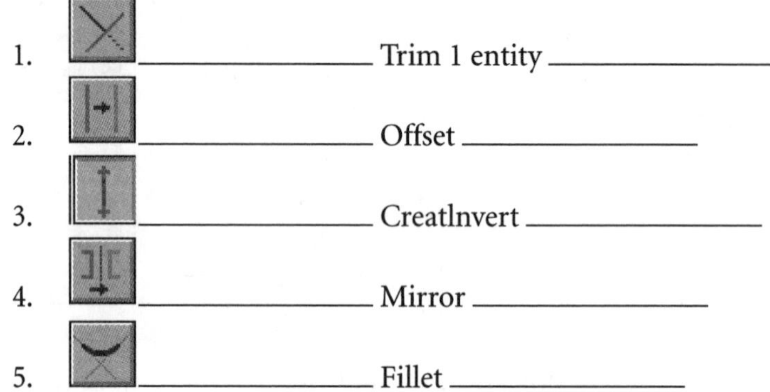

1. ________________ Trim 1 entity ________________
2. ________________ Offset ________________
3. ________________ CreatInvert ________________
4. ________________ Mirror ________________
5. ________________ Fillet ________________
6. To create copies of an existing entity you could use the ____________ command(s).
7. To move to the next or previous set of tool bar options, you could use the ____________ icon.
8. When trimming an entity, the first pick you make is the part of the entity you want to ____________.
9. What function(s) could you use to create a series of entities in a circular pattern?
10. Name the four directions or methods for creating mirrored images.
11. Under which menu heading will you find the Rotate function?
12. Starting with the Main Menu, name the other menu you would need to select to get to the letters command.

PRACTICE EXERCISES

EXERCISE 4–1

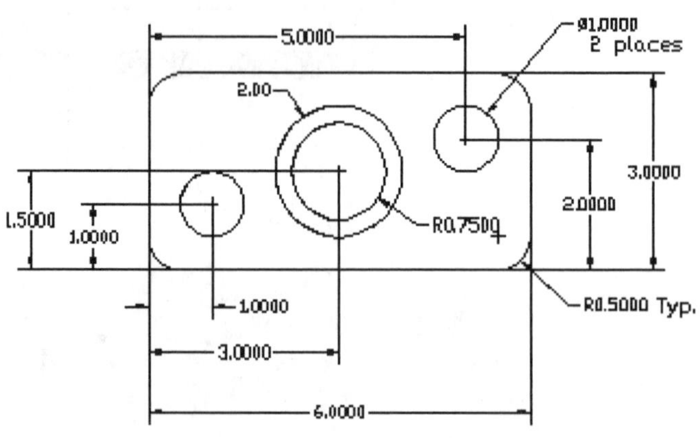

EXERCISE 4–2

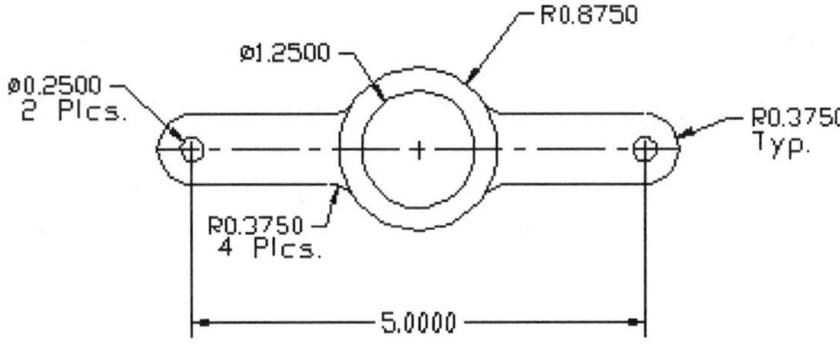

EXERCISE 4–3

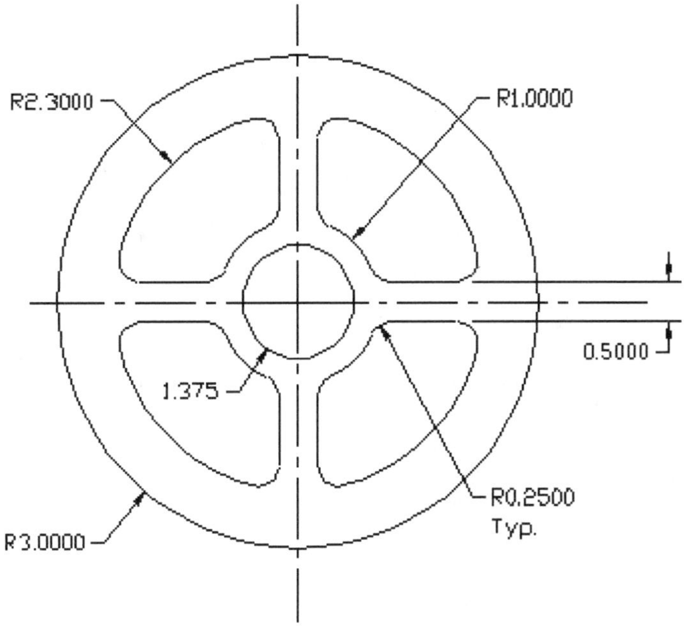

CHAPTER

5

Tooling Fundamentals

The choice of which cutting tools to use on numerical control machines is an important one. Numerical control machines are highly productive and efficient machines, but if the cutting tools cannot hold up under extreme conditions, the machine's efficiency and accuracy will be greatly diminished.

Objectives

Upon completion of this chapter, the reader will be able to:

- Describe the term "grade" as it applies to insert choice
- Explain which factors to consider when selecting tool nose radius
- Name three insert shapes in order of increasing strength
- State two factors to consider when selecting insert shapes
- Describe what the size of an insert is based on
- State how insert size and depth of cut are interrelated
- Describe the purpose and function of the different rake angles
- Choose inserts for various applications
- Describe how tool holders are identified

FUNDAMENTALS OF TOOLING

With today's CNC technology, machines can be operated by people with very little training. However, to be promoted to a CNC programmer, one must know the fundamentals of carbide cutting tools. Tooling is crucial to the success of a machine shop. A great machine with poor tooling will perform very poorly. Because good tooling techniques are vital to productivity, this chapter concentrates on the fundamentals of carbide cutting tools.

Cemented Carbide

Cemented carbide, or tungsten carbide, is a form of powdered metallurgy. Fine powders consisting of tungsten carbide and other hard metals bonded with cobalt are pressed into required shapes and then sintered.

Sintering is the heating of the carbide materials to approximately 2500°F. At this temperature the cobalt melts and flows around the carbide materials. Cobalt acts as the binder that holds the carbide particles together. After the carbide insert cools, the insert is almost as hard as a diamond.

The hardness and physical properties of cemented carbides allow them to operate at high cutting speeds and feeds with very little tool deformation. However, the great hardness of carbide is also its Achilles' heel. Extremely hard materials are also very brittle, which can cause problems under certain machining conditions. Through the use of different mixtures of hard materials, carbide manufacturers have come up with different grades of carbide materials. Selecting the proper grade for the machining application is important for economy and productivity.

Selection of Carbide Tool Grade

Carbide tools come in a variety of grades, based on the carbide's wear resistance and toughness. As an insert becomes harder or more wear resistant, it becomes brittle (less tough).

If you used a very hard, wear-resistant insert on a material that has an uneven or interrupted surface (interrupted cut), the insert would most likely break. The ANSI/ISO standards organizations have devised systems of grading carbide based on the carbide insert's application and physical makeup. These systems differ and can be quite confusing. Carbide manufacturers help clarify matters by putting cross-reference charts in their catalogues (see Figure 5–1).

Coatings for Carbide Inserts

Carbide is a very hard, durable cutting tool, but it still wears. The wear resistance of cemented carbide can be increased greatly by using coatings.

Wear-resistant coatings can be applied to the carbide substrate (base material) through the use of plasma coating or vapor deposition. The coating that is deposited is very thin but very hard.

The most common types of coatings include titanium carbide (TiC), titanium nitride (TiN), and aluminum oxide (AlO). Aluminum oxide is a very wear-

Grade selections

grades	composition and application	ISO
PVD TiN (titanium nitride) coated carbide grades		
KC710	**composition:** A PVD coated grade that has good toughness and thermal shock resistance with good crater wear resistance and resistance to buildup on the cutting edge. **application:** Greatly improved productivity when cutting a variety of steels and tool steels over a broad range of feeds at moderate to high speeds.	M15-M25 P15-P25
KC720	**composition:** A tough, durable PVD coated carbide grade. **application:** Developed for cutting high-temperature alloys, stainless steels, and low-carbon steels at low to moderate speeds. Its unique mechanical and thermal shock resistant properties, and resistance to edge buildup, enable KC720 to deliver superior performance and reliability on difficult operations, like interrupted cuts, and when milling high-temperature alloys with coolant.	K25-K35 M30-M40 P25-P45
KC730	**composition:** A PVD coated carbide grade. **application:** For milling cast and ductile irons, high-temperature alloys, aerospace materials, refractory metals, and 200 and 300 series stainless steels. The substrate offers superior thermal deformation resistance, depth of cut notch resistance, and edge strength. The uniformly dense PVD coating increases wear resistance, reduces problems with edge buildup, and provides an unusually good combination of properties for machining difficult-to-machine materials and aluminum.	K05-K15 M05-M15
New "M" multi-coating milling grades		
KC725M	**composition:** A patented, multi-layer, PVD coated, TiN/TiCN/TiN. **application:** A new milling grade engineered for high productivity wet milling of carbon, alloy and austenitic stainless steels. The high thermal shock resistance of the tough carbide substrate combined with the patented multi-layer coating provides long and reliable tool life in aggressive milling operations using coolant. It is the higher speed companion to KC720 in wet steel milling.	M15-M35 P20-P35
KC792M	**composition:** A PVD/CVD coated grade. **application:** Developed for 400-900 sfm milling of steels. Cobalt enriched, it is deformation resistant in interrupted cutting. The patent pending PVD over CVD coatings allow for thicker coatings than possible with other CVD coatings, as well as desirable compression stresses in the coatings to counteract thermal crack propagation. KC792M is the higher speed companion to KC710 for dry steel milling.	M25-M30 P30
KC992M	**composition:** A multi-layered ceramic CVD coated with $TiCN/Al_2O_3$ carbide. **application:** Designed to mill grey cast iron, with or without coolant, at medium speeds and feed rates with honed geometry inserts. Nodular irons with machinability index of 68-78 and BHN below 300 can also be machined up to 600 sfm and equivalent chiploads with T-land versions of insert geometries.	K10-K25
Uncoated carbide grades		
K313	**composition:** An unalloyed WC/Co fine-grained grade. **application:** Exceptional edge wear resistance, combined with very high edge strength and abrasion resistance, delivers high-speed metal removal rates with lighter chip loads when machining nonmetals and nonferrous metals including aluminum, stainless steels, and titanium materials.	K05-K15 M10-M20

FIGURE 5–1
Kennametal's grade system chart gives grade selection choices for machining applications. If a depth of cut of 3⁄16 of an inch is required, an insert with a 3⁄8-inch inscribed circle should be used. Insert thickness also affects the feed rate. If an insert is going to be used for continuous, heavy-feed roughing cuts, an insert of greater thickness should be selected. *(Courtesy of Kennametal Inc.)*

resistant coating used in high-speed finishing and light roughing operations performed on most steels and all cast irons. Titanium nitride coatings are very hard and have the strength characteristics to perform well under heavy rough-cutting conditions. All three coatings will perform well on most steels as well as on cast iron.

Diamond-Coated Inserts

Coated cutting tools have been around for years. Titanium and boron nitride materials have driven the coated cutting tool industry. The newest material to make its presence known is the polycrystalline diamond, or PCD. PCD tools are becoming widely accepted as tooling solutions for difficult-to-machine materials. The PCD material has the hardness of a diamond and the friction coefficient of Teflon. This combination has resulted in a remarkable increase in tool life. Diamond-coated tools are still being tested quite extensively, and manufacturers have not even published recommended speeds and feeds for their cutting tools. Diamond-coated tools are still in the infancy stage, but from all indications they could be the predominant cutting tool of the future.

Tool Nose Radius

Along with selecting the proper grade of insert, other factors, such as nose radius, are also important when choosing the proper tool.

The nose radius of the tool directly affects tool strength and surface finish, as well as cutting speeds and feeds. The larger the nose radius, the stronger the tool. If the tool radius is too small, the sharp point will make the surface finish unacceptable and the life of the tool will be shortened.

Larger nose radii will give a better finish and longer tool life and will allow for higher feed rates to be used. However, if the tool nose is too large, it can cause chatter. It is always good machining practice to select an insert with a tool nose radius as large as the machining operation will allow.

Insert Shape

Indexable inserts, also known as throwaway inserts, come in many shapes. Inserts are clamped in tool holders and provide cutting tools with multiple cutting edges. After the cutting edges are worn to a point where they can no longer be used, they are discarded.

When selecting an insert shape many factors must be taken into consideration:

What geometric features are required on the workpiece
What lead angle can be used
What operation needs to be performed
How to get the maximum number of cutting edges
What required strength is needed to do the job

Figure 5–2 shows the characteristics of different shaped inserts in order of their strength. Round inserts have the greatest strength as well as the greatest num-

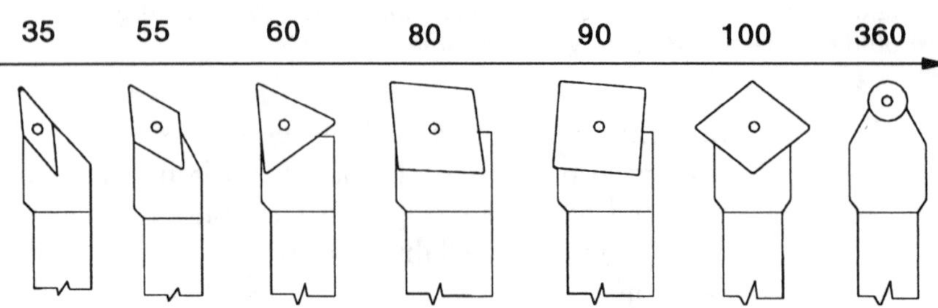

FIGURE 5–2 The shape of the insert will have a great effect on the strength of the tool. Select the largest included angle that will cut the part.

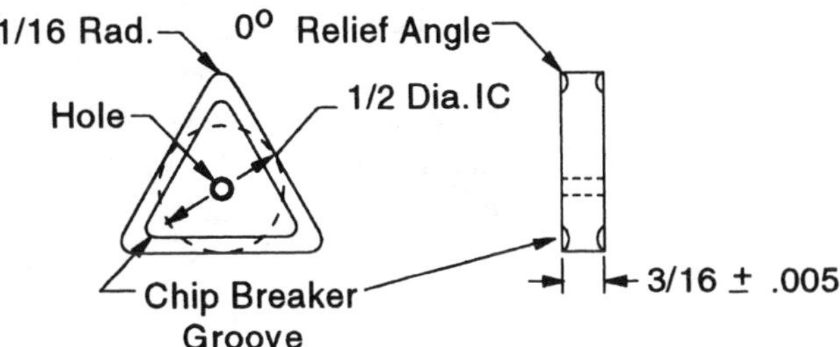

FIGURE 5–3
This figure is a diagram of a typical triangular insert.

ber of cutting edges, but the round configuration limits the operations that can be performed.

Square or 90-degree inserts have less strength and fewer cutting edges than round inserts, but are a little more versatile.

Triangular inserts (see Figure 5–3) are more versatile than square inserts, but as the included angle is reduced from 90 degrees to 60 degrees it becomes weaker and more likely to break under heavy machining conditions.

Diamond-shaped inserts are probably the most commonly used shape. Diamond-shaped inserts range from a 35-degree to an 80-degree included angle. Diamond-shaped inserts are much more versatile than square and round inserts. It is good machining practice to select the largest included angle insert that will properly cut the shape of the part because the insert will be stronger.

Insert Size

The size of the insert is based on the inscribed circle (IC, which is the largest circle that will fit inside the insert), the insert thickness, and the tool nose radius (see Figure 5–3).

The depth of cut possible with an insert depends greatly on the insert size. The depth of cut should always be as great as the conditions will allow. A good rule of thumb is to select an insert with an inscribed circle twice that of the depth of cut.

Rake Angles

The rake angle, or back rake angle, is the angle at which the chips flow away from the cutting area (see Figure 5–4). There are three principal rake angles: negative, positive, and neutral.

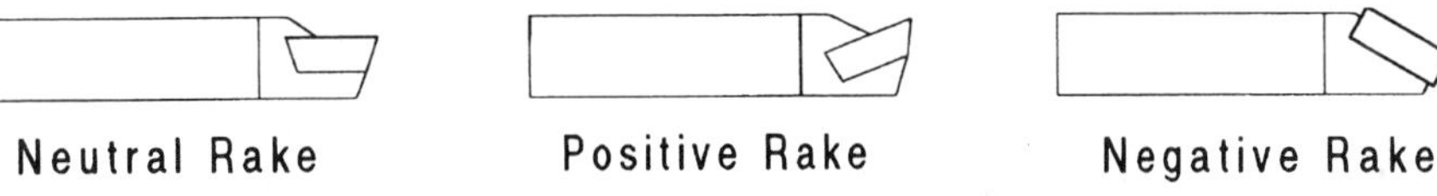

FIGURE 5–4
Side view of back rake angles.

When selecting the proper rake tool holder, it is essential to look at the machining conditions. Negative rake holders are economically a good choice because they hold neutral rake inserts. Neutral rake inserts have twice as many cutting edges as positive rake inserts because they can be turned over and used. Another advantage is that negative rake tool holders provide more support for the cutting edges of the insert. Under normal operating conditions negative rake inserts are also a little stronger because of the compressive strength of carbide. Negative rake holders should be used when the tool and the work are held very rigidly and when high machining speeds and feeds can be maintained. More horsepower is required to cut with negative rake tool holders, which is why there is an increasing trend toward the use of positive rake cutting.

Positive rake cutting is more of a shearing effect than the pushing effect generated by negative rake. Positive rake holders generate less cutting force and have less of a tendency to chatter.

Horsepower requirements are greatly reduced with positive cutting tools. Lower horsepower consumption is an important factor with today's smaller machines. Smaller machines are built with lower horsepower and less rigidity than the older manual machines.

The only drawback to positive rake cutting tools is their inability to stand up to harder materials. Eight to 10 years ago positive rake tool holders were considered unsuitable for machining steels because of cutting-edge weakness. However, recent advances in carbide technology have produced tougher substrate materials that provide greater edge strength. Some carbide companies have even gone as far as to recommend positive rake holders whenever possible.

Positive rakes should be used when machining softer materials because the chips are able to flow away from the cutting edge freely and the cutting action is more of a peeling effect. Positive rake cutting can be very successful on long, slender parts or other operations that lack rigidity.

Lead Angle

The lead angle, or side-cutting edge angle, is the angle at which the cutting tool enters the work (see Figure 5–5). The lead angle can be positive, negative, or neutral. The tool holder always dictates the amount of lead angle a tool will have.

Tool holders should always be selected to provide the greatest amount of lead angle that the job will allow. There are two advantages to using a large lead angle.

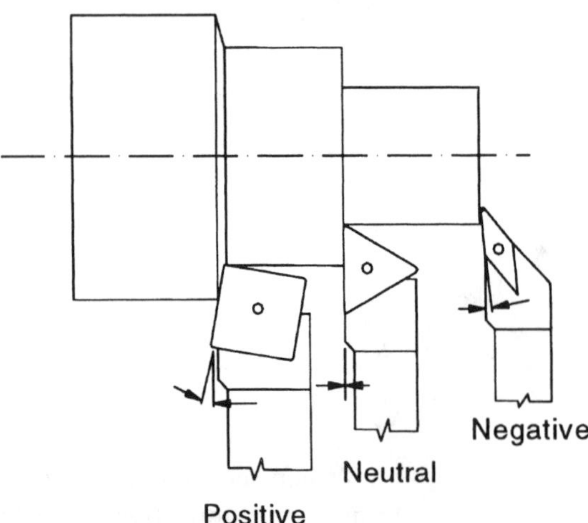

FIGURE 5–5
The lead or side-cutting edge angle is determined by the tool holder type. The lead angle can be positive, neutral, or negative.

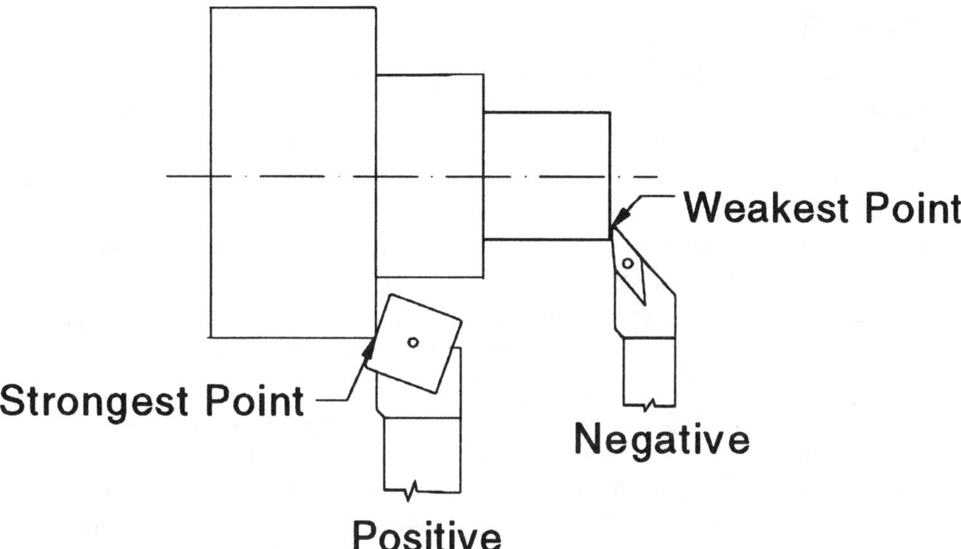

FIGURE 5–6
The effect of the lead angle on the strength of the insert. Increasing the lead angle will greatly reduce tool breakage when roughing or cutting interrupted surfaces.

First, when the tool initially enters the work, it is at the middle of the insert where it is strongest, instead of at the tool tip, which is the weakest point of the tool. Second, the cutting forces are spread over a wider area, reducing the chip thickness (see Figure 5–6).

INSERT SELECTION

Now that we have covered some aspects of carbide tool selection, let's look at the questions that we need to answer when selecting the proper insert grade and style. One of the first considerations is the material to be machined.

Machinability of Metals

Machinability describes the ease or difficulty with which a metal can be cut. Machining involves removing metal at the highest possible rate and at the lowest cost per piece. The structures of different materials can pose problems for the machinist. Materials that are easy to machine have high machinability ratings and therefore cost less to machine. Materials that are difficult to machine have lower machinability ratings and cost more to machine.

The machinability of a material has a direct correlation to the material's hardness, or its ability to resist penetration or deformation. A number of tests measure the hardness of a material, but the most common test for machinability is Brinell. Brinell hardness, or BHN, is stated as a number: the higher the BHN number, the harder the material. Hardness, although a major factor affecting machinability, is not the only factor that determines machinability.

Steels

Steels are generally classified based on their carbon content and their alloying elements. Plain carbon steels have only one alloy, carbon, mixed with iron. Carbon has a direct effect on a steel's hardness. Plain carbon steel's machinability is directly reflected in its carbon content. Alloy steels, on the other hand, have carbon and other alloying elements mixed with iron. These alloying elements can give steel the characteristic of being not only hard, but tough. The major concern with machining alloy steels is their tendency to work harden, a phenomenon that occurs when too much heat from the cutting process is developed in the steel. The heat changes the properties of the steel, making it hard and difficult to machine. Great care must be taken when machining some alloy steels.

Plain carbon steel is divided into three categories: low carbon, medium carbon, and high carbon. Low-carbon steels have a carbon content of 0.10 to 0.30% and are relatively easy to machine. Medium-carbon steels have a carbon content of 0.30 to 0.50%. They are relatively easy to machine, but because of the higher carbon content, they have a lower cutting speed than that of low-carbon steel. High-carbon steels have a carbon content of 0.50 to 1.8%. When the carbon content exceeds 1.0%, high carbon steel becomes quite difficult to machine.

Stainless Steel

Stainless steels have carbon, chromium, and nickel as alloys. Stainless steels are a very tough, shock-resistant material and are difficult to machine. Work hardening can be a problem when machining stainless steels. To avoid work hardening, use lower speeds and increased feed rates. Chip control is sometimes a problem when machining stainless because of its toughness and its unwillingness to break.

Cast Iron

Cast iron is a broad classification for gray, malleable, nodular, and chilled-white cast iron. This grouping is in order of its machinability. Gray cast iron is relatively easy to machine, while chilled-white cast iron is sometimes unmachinable. Cast iron does not produce a continuous chip because of its brittleness.

The machinability of any material can be affected by factors such as heat treatment. Heat treating can either harden or soften a material. The condition of the material at the time of machining should be taken into consideration when deciding a material's machinability.

INSERT SELECTION PRACTICE

Figure 5–7 shows a typical lathe part. We can choose an appropriate insert for the part using the Kennametal grade system chart (Figure 5–1), the insert identification system shown in Figure 5–8, and the other information found previously in the chapter.

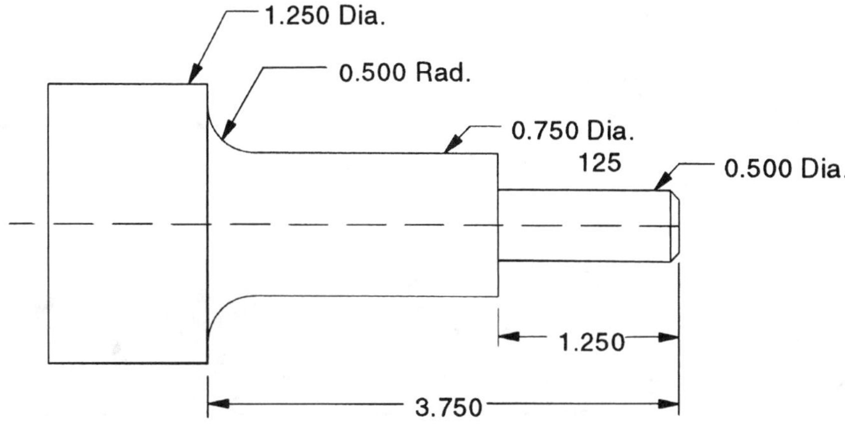

FIGURE 5–7
Typical lathe part.

1. What type of material is being cut? Would you use a cast iron or a steel grade? *Answer:* The material used for the part is 1018 cold rolled steel, so a steel cutting grade would be appropriate.
2. How hard is the material? How does this affect the grade? *Answer:* The material is a low-carbon alloy steel of only 200 Brinell hardness. A moderate hardness grade would be a good choice.
3. What is the condition of the material? Does the surface show evidence of scale or hard spots? How does this affect the selection of the grade, insert shape, rake angle, and nose radius? *Answer:* The material is cold rolled steel, which has little or no scale. Again, a general-purpose insert of moderate hardness and strength would be applicable.
4. What shape insert do we need to perform this job? *Answer:* For roughing this part, we would like to use a larger angled insert such as an 80-degree diamond. The finishing tool needs to have a little smaller angle to cut the radius. A 55–degree diamond or triangular insert would be a good choice for finishing the part.
5. How rigid is the machining setup? How does this affect the rake angles and nose radius? *Answer:* As you can see from the part print, the part has a small, turned diameter on the end. This small diameter may tend to deflect and chatter. A positive rake insert with a 1⁄32- or 1⁄16-inch tool nose radius would probably be the best choice.
6. What are the surface finish requirements of the part? How does this affect the nose radius? *Answer:* The surface finish requirement of the part is 125. A 125 finish is a standard machine finish that can be held using a 1⁄32- or 1⁄16-inch tool nose radius. Slowing down the feed rate will also help to acquire the 125 finish requirement.

Turning Insert Identification

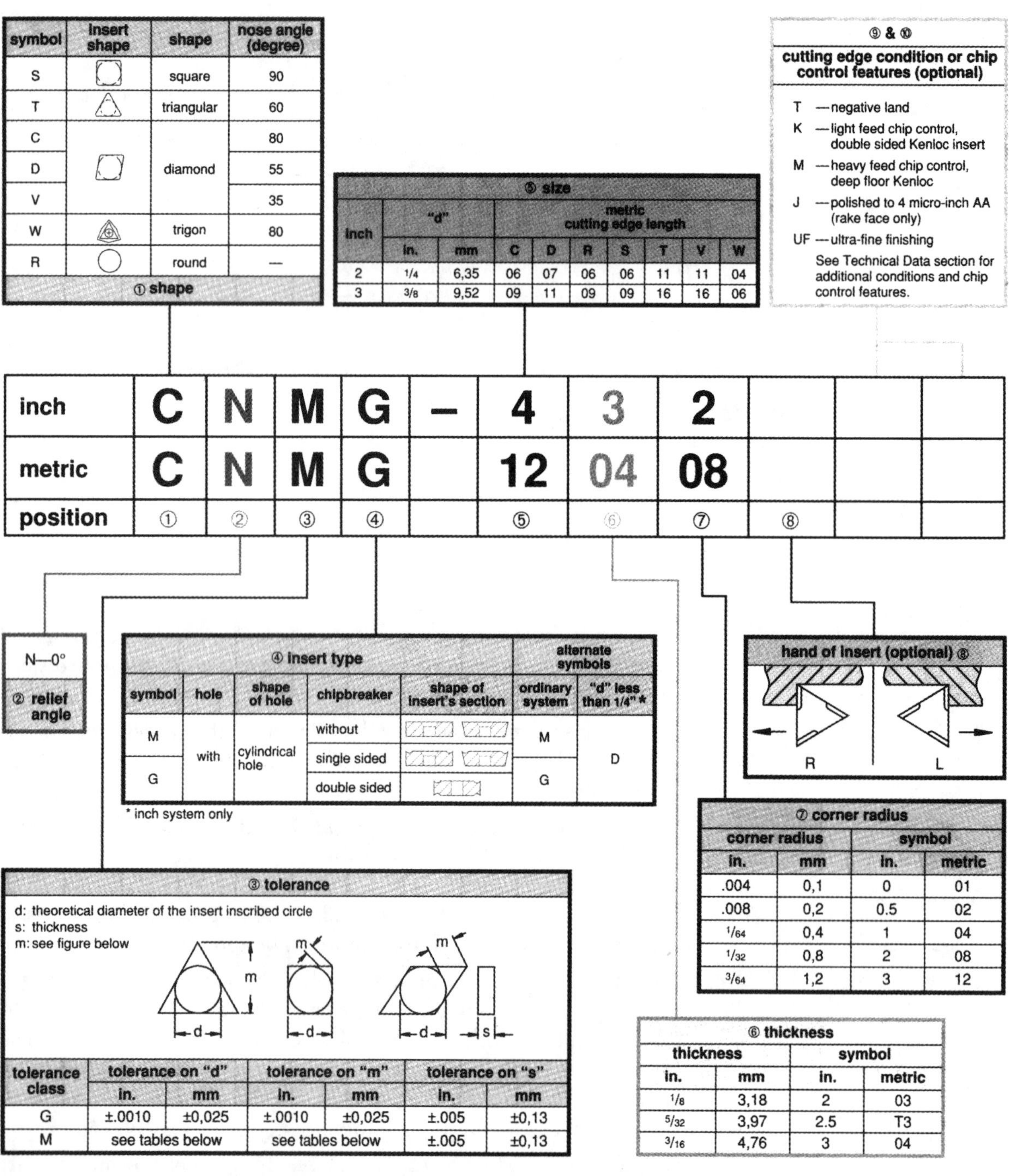

symbol	insert shape	shape	nose angle (degree)
S		square	90
T		triangular	60
C		diamond	80
D		diamond	55
V		diamond	35
W		trigon	80
R		round	—
① shape			

⑤ size									
inch	"d"		metric cutting edge length						
	in.	mm	C	D	R	S	T	V	W
2	1/4	6,35	06	07	06	06	11	11	04
3	3/8	9,52	09	11	09	09	16	16	06

⑨ & ⑩

cutting edge condition or chip control features (optional)

- T —negative land
- K —light feed chip control, double sided Kenloc insert
- M —heavy feed chip control, deep floor Kenloc
- J —polished to 4 micro-inch AA (rake face only)
- UF —ultra-fine finishing

See Technical Data section for additional conditions and chip control features.

inch	C	N	M	G	–	4	3	2			
metric	C	N	M	G		12	04	08			
position	①	②	③	④		⑤	⑥	⑦	⑧		

N—0°
② relief angle

④ insert type					alternate symbols	
symbol	hole	shape of hole	chipbreaker	shape of insert's section	ordinary system	"d" less than 1/4" *
M	with	cylindrical hole	without		M	D
			single sided			
G			double sided		G	

* inch system only

hand of insert (optional) ⑧	
R	L

⑦ corner radius			
corner radius		symbol	
in.	mm	in.	metric
.004	0,1	0	01
.008	0,2	0.5	02
1/64	0,4	1	04
1/32	0,8	2	08
3/64	1,2	3	12

③ tolerance

d: theoretical diameter of the insert inscribed circle
s: thickness
m: see figure below

tolerance class	tolerance on "d"		tolerance on "m"		tolerance on "s"	
	in.	mm	in.	mm	in.	mm
G	±.0010	±0,025	±.0010	±0,025	±.005	±0,13
M	see tables below		see tables below		±.005	±0,13

⑥ thickness			
thickness		symbol	
in.	mm	in.	metric
1/8	3,18	2	03
5/32	3,97	2.5	T3
3/16	4,76	3	04

"d"		± tolerance on "d" class "M" tolerance					
		shapes S,T,C,R&W		shape "D"		shape "V"	
inch	metric	inch	mm	inch	mm	inch	mm
1/4	6,35	.002	0,05	.002	0,05	.002	0,05
3/8	9,52						

"d"		± tolerance on "m" class "M" tolerance					
		shapes S,T,C,R&W		shape "D"		shape "V"	
inch	metric	inch	mm	inch	mm	inch	mm
1/4	6,35	.003	0,06	.004	0,11	.007	0,18
3/8	9,52						

FIGURE 5–8
Insert identification system. *(Courtesy of Kennametal Inc.)*

Near-Net-Shape Tooling Products

Toolholder Identification System

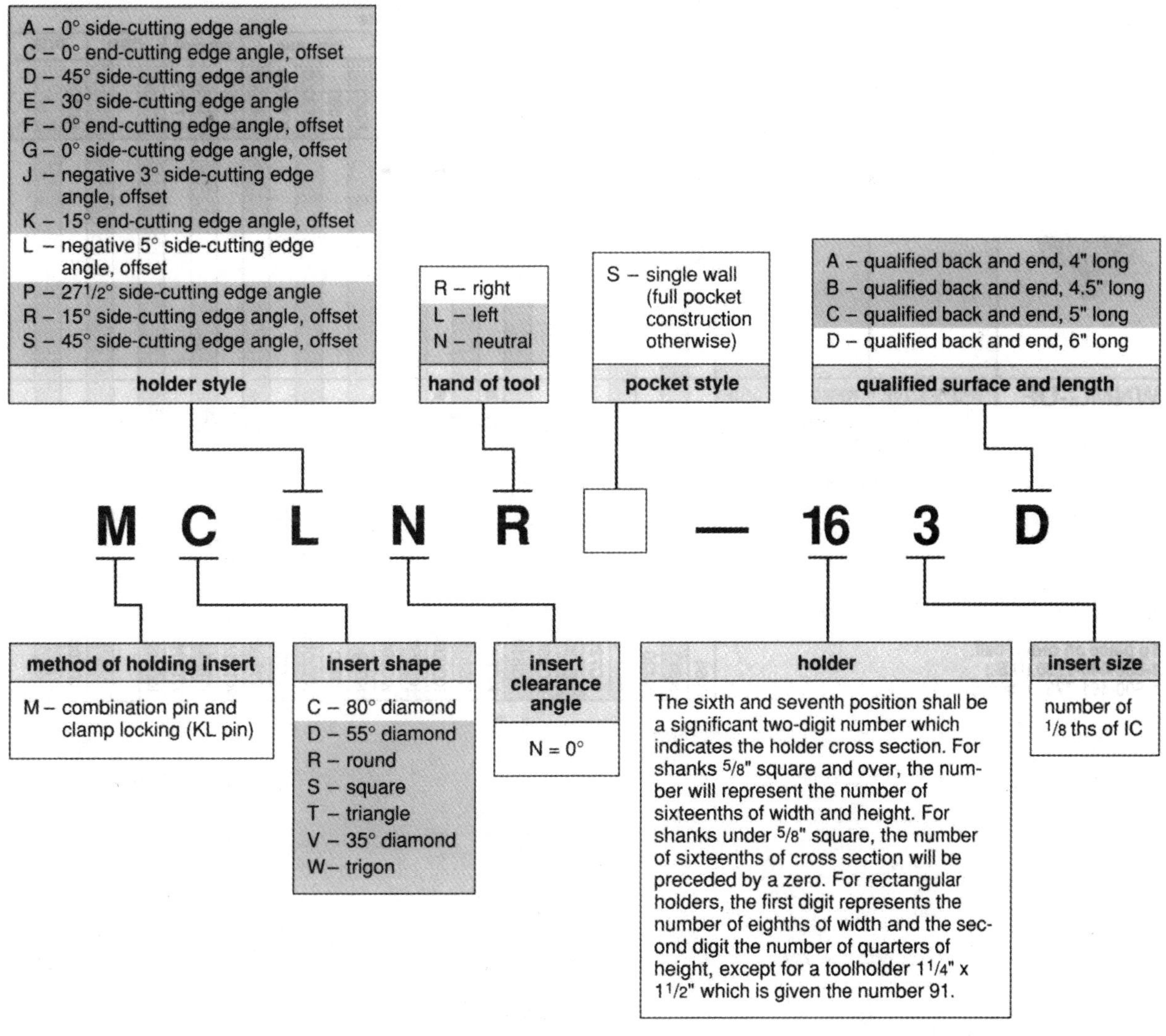

FIGURE 5–9
Tool holder identification system. *(Courtesy of Kennametal Inc.)*

TOOL HOLDER STYLE AND IDENTIFICATION

Carbide manufacturers and the American Standards Association have created a tool holder identification system for indexable carbide tool holders (see Figure 5–9). Because a huge variety of holders are available, we cannot include all of the holder types in this text.

TOOLS AND TOOL HOLDERS

Milling and drilling tools will make up the majority of the types of tools used on the machining center. This section discusses standard types of tools and tool holders used on milling machines.

High-Speed Steel Drills

The two basic types of high-speed drills are the twist drill and the spade drill. The high-speed steel twist drill is the most commonly used tool for producing holes.

Twist drills are great for rapidly producing holes that do not have to be very accurate in size or position. If the holes must be very accurate in size they are drilled to a smaller size and either reamed, milled, or bored to size. If the position of the hole must be very accurate, the drilled hole must be milled or bored on location.

Twist drills are made with two or more flutes and come in a variety of styles (see Figure 5–10). Twist drills have either a straight or tapered shank. Straight-shank drills are common up to ½ inch in diameter and are held in drill chucks.

FIGURE 5–10 Twist drills are the most common hole-producing tools in the machine shop. *(Courtesy of Kennametal, Inc.)*

Larger drills typically have a tapered shank with a tang on the end (see Figure 5–11). The tang keeps the tapered shank drill from slipping under the higher torque conditions associated with drilling large holes.

FIGURE 5–11 The tang on the end of the tapered shank drives the drill. *(Courtesy of Kennametal, Inc.)*

Center or Spotting Drills

When drilled holes need to be accurately located, it is advisable to center or spot drill the holes prior to drilling. This is achieved with center or spotting drills (see Figure 5–12). These drills are short, stubby, and rigid and do not flex or deflect like longer drills. The spot drill produces a small startpoint that is accurately located. When the hole is drilled, the drill point will follow the starting hole that the spot

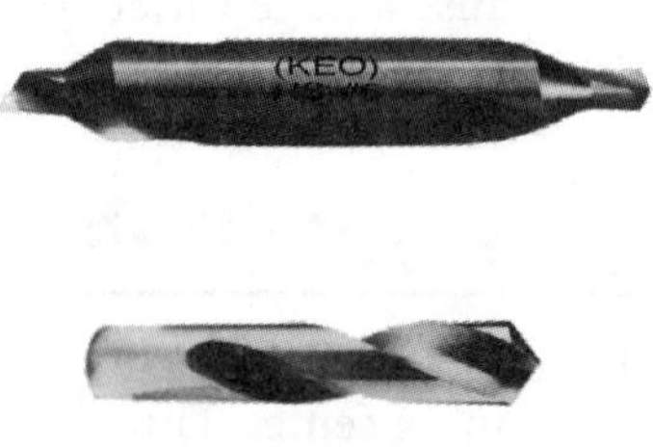

FIGURE 5–12 Center and spotting drills come in a variety of sizes. The short, stubby design of the drills allows them to accurately locate holes. *(Courtesy of Kennametal, Inc.)*

FIGURE 5–13
Spade drills are a two-piece tool consisting of the blade and the holder. Spade blades and holders increase productivity because one holder can be used to drill holes of many different diameters simply by changing blades. *(Courtesy of Kennametal, Inc.)*

drill made. This method can produce holes that are reasonably accurate in location.

Spade Drills

The spade drill has a flat blade with sharpened cutting edges (see Figure 5–13). The spade cutting tool is clamped in a holder and can be resharpened many times. Spade drills typically are used for drilling very large diameter holes. They can lower tooling costs because standard blade holders can hold a variety of sizes of blades. Designed to drill holes in one pass, spade drills require approximately 50% more horsepower than twist drills. Spade drilling also requires a rigid machine and setup.

Carbide Drills

Carbide-tipped twist drills have been around for many years. They are basically carbon steel drills with a piece of tungsten carbide brazed into them. They look similar to a spade drill but are usually made in smaller diameters. Solid carbide drills are just that: a solid carbide cutting tool in a twist configuration. Solid carbide drills are typically found in small diameters because of the cost of the carbide materials.

One of the newer innovations in carbide drilling technology is carbide insert drills (see Figure 5–14). These drills incorporate indexable or replaceable inserts and can remove metal 4 to 10 times faster than a high-speed steel drill. Carbide insert drills need a very rigid setup and a machine with substantial horsepower.

Auxiliary Hole-Producing Operations

Drilling may be the most common method of producing holes, but it is not the most accurate. In some cases, holes may need a very accurate size, location, or finish. If an accurate-size hole is needed, reaming may be the quickest method.

FIGURE 5–14 Carbide insert drills allow you to drill hard materials at feeds and speeds much higher than those of conventional drills. When the carbide insert drill becomes dull, the carbide inserts can be indexed or replaced. *(Courtesy of Kennametal, Inc.)*

A reamer is a cylindrical tool similar in appearance to the drill (see Figure 5–15). Reamers produce holes of exact dimension with a smooth finish. Reaming can be done only after a slightly smaller hole has been drilled in the part. The reamer follows the drilled hole, so inaccuracies in location cannot be corrected by reaming. If accurate location is needed as well as size, boring may be necessary. Reamers are a quick way of producing accurately sized small holes. However, boring can produce holes of any size and in the exact location.

FIGURE 5–15 Reamers consistently produce accurately sized holes. Reamers should be run at half the speed and twice the feed of the same size drill. *(Courtesy of Kennametal, Inc.)*

Boring

Boring is done with an offset boring head and cutting tool. Figure 5–16 illustrates a variety of boring heads that can use high-speed steel tools as well as carbide tools. The offset boring head holds the tool and can be adjusted to cut any size hole within its range. The boring head is rotated and fed down into the piece, removing material (see Figure 5–17). Boring accurately produces holes of any size and in the exact location.

Boring, like reaming, can be done only on previously prepared holes. As a general rule, for best results, the boring tool should be as short and as large in diameter as possible. When using a high-speed steel tool, the diameter-to-length ratio should be no greater than 5 to 1. For example, if a 1-inch-diameter boring bar is used, no

FIGURE 5–16 The offset boring head can be adjusted to cut any size hole within its size range. *(Courtesy of Kennametal, Inc.)*

FIGURE 5–17
Boring bars are tools used to do the cutting in a boring operation. Carbide boring tools need a rigid setup to operate properly. *(Courtesy of Kennametal, Inc.)*

more than 5 inches should be sticking out. Carbide has a 3 to 1 recommended ratio. Reducing the ratio insures against chatter, because as the tool overhang becomes greater, the amount of force it takes to flex the boring bar decreases greatly.

Tapping

Tapping is the process of producing internal threads by using a preformed threading tool known as a tap. Tapping can be done only on previously drilled holes. There are many different types of taps (see Figure 5–18). The most common type of tap used on the machining center is the spiral pointed gun tap, which is especially useful for tapping holes that go through the workpiece or holes with sufficient space for chips. Chip clearance is especially important when tapping. If chips clog the hole, a broken tap often results.

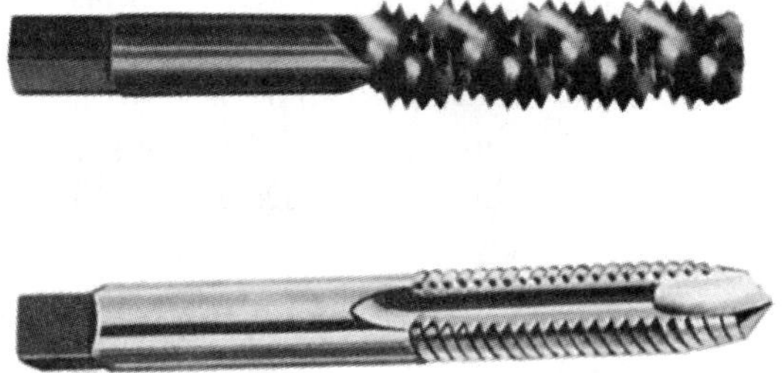

FIGURE 5–18
The two most common types of machine taps used on CNC machines are the spiral fluted tap and the gun tap. The spiral flutes on each allow lubricant or coolant to reach the end of the tap. Gun taps push the chips ahead of the tap, so you must consider the amount of chip clearance available. *(Courtesy of Kennametal, Inc.)*

FIGURE 5–19
The spring-loaded tapping head allows the tap to feed down at its own rate. *(Courtesy of Kennametal, Inc.)*

There are two ways to tap on Computer Numerical Control (CNC) machines. One way uses a special tapping head. The tapping head is spring loaded, and the lead of the tap provides the primary feed (see Figure 5–19). The secondary or programmed feed need only be approximate, because the spring-loaded head allows the tap to float up and down at the lead rate of the thread. The lead of the tap is the distance that the thread travels in one revolution (see Figure 5–20).

The second type of tapping is called rigid tapping. This doesn't need special holders, but precise feed and rpm synchronization is needed to insure undamaged threads. Some machines are not capable of such synchronization. In either case, the feed of the tap needs to be calculated. The feed for tapping is calculated by dividing 1 inch by the number of threads per inch. The quotient is then multiplied by the revolutions per minute of the spindle. For example, for a ¼-20 UNC tap running at 250 rpm, ½ × 250 = 0.05 × 250 rpm = 12.5 inches per minute feed rate. Most modern machining centers are equipped with tapping cycles, which feed the tap down to the programmed depth and then automatically reverse the spindle and feed up, unscrewing the tap from the hole.

Tools for Milling

Milling cutters are classified by the type of relief they have ground on the cutting edges and by the method in which they are mounted. When selecting the best milling cutter for a particular operation, four things must be taken into consideration; the kind of cut to be made, the material to be cut, the number of parts to be machined, and the type of machine available.

End Mills

One of the most frequently used tools on a machining center is the end mill (see Figure 5–21). End mills are made from two types of materials: solid carbide and high-speed steel. End mills are ground with a relief on the sides and ends just behind the cutting edges. They come in two or more flutes. Two-fluted or end-cutting end mills can be used for plunging. The teeth on the end come together much like those of a drill. Two considerations determine the number of flutes a milling cutter should have: Does the end mill need to be end cutting for a plunging operation,

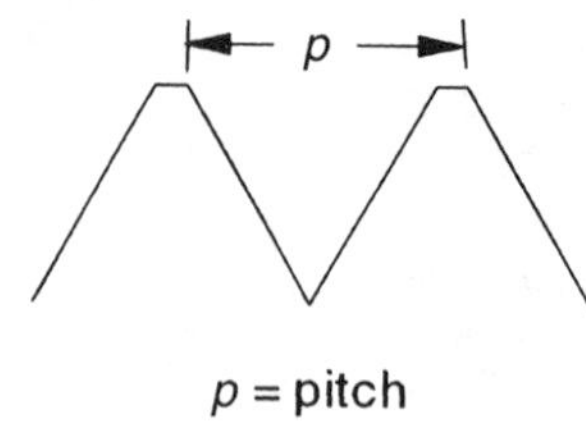

FIGURE 5–20
The lead for a single lead thread is the same as the pitch of the thread. The pitch is the distance from a point on one thread to the same point on the next thread.

FIGURE 5–21 End mills are manufactured with two or more flutes. The two-flute, double end mill is used for plunging and profiling. Ball end mills have a radius ground on the end of the tool and are used for milling radii in slots or contouring the bottom surfaces of mold cavities. The multifluted roughing end mill, or hog mill, has scallops or grooves around the body of the tool and can remove three times as much material as standard end mills. *(Courtesy of Kennametal, Inc.)*

and what is the depth of cut going to be? Increasing the number of teeth on the end mill greatly reduces the chip clearance area to prevent clogging. End mills can be used for profile cutting, slotting, cavity cutting, or face milling, although face milling is usually done with a shell milling cutter. End mills are typically held in solid-type holders with set screws for positive holding (see Figure 5–22).

Shell End Mills

Shell end milling cutters are designed to remove large amounts of material. They are sometimes referred to as face mills because of their ability to make large facing cuts. Shell end mills range in size from 1¼ to 6 inches and up. They have a hole for mounting on an arbor and a key way to receive a driving key (see Figure 5–23). Shell-end mills are available in high-speed steel as well as carbide. The carbide shell mill has indexable carbide inserts that can be indexed or thrown away when they become dull.

Shell end mills represent a potential savings to machine shops because several different cutter sizes and materials can be used with one mounting arbor. This reduces the number of arbors required.

Climb and Conventional Milling

In milling there are two basic directions you can feed: into the rotation of the cutter or with the rotation of the cutter (see Figure 5–24). Feeding with the rotation of the cutter is known as *climb milling.* In climb milling, the cutter is attempting to climb onto the workpiece.

On most manual machines, not equipped with backlash eliminators, climb milling is unheard of. If there is any slack or backlash between the screw and nut

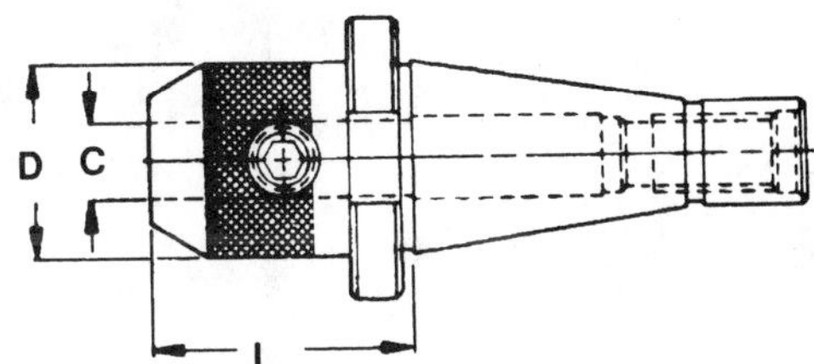

FIGURE 5–22 End mill tool holders use set screws to positively locate on the flats that are located on end mills. This positive locking-style holder keeps the end mill from slipping during machining operations. *(Courtesy of Kennametal, Inc.)*

FIGURE 5–23
Shell end mills are designed to remove large amounts of material. Facing operations are usually performed with these types of tools, which are available in high-speed steel or indexable carbide. *(Courtesy of Kennametal, Inc.)*

driving the table, the workpiece would be pulled into the cutter, possibly causing tool breakage, a spoiled workpiece, and serious injury to the operator. However, CNC machines are equipped with ball screws, and backlash is all but eliminated, thus allowing climb milling.

Climb milling is desirable in most cases because it takes less horsepower to cut in this fashion. Other benefits of climb milling are better surface finishes, less tool deflection, and extended tool life, and the chips are discarded away from the

FIGURE 5–24
Climb milling and conventional milling represent the two directions of feed associated with milling. When climb milling, the outer scale of the material is cut first. In conventional milling, the inside of the material is cut first.

cutter. Feeding against the rotation of the cutter is known as conventional milling. The conventional milling chip has no thickness at the beginning, but builds in size toward the exit of the cutter. Conventional milling is recommended on materials with a hard outer scale, such as cast steels or forgings. If the tool needs to extend out of the holder a greater than normal length, it may be best to conventional cut. This will cause the tool to flex and stay in the flexed position, avoiding chatter.

Cutting Tools for Turning

Modern turning machines use tool holders with indexable inserts. The tool holders on CNC machines come in a variety of styles, each suited for a particular type of cutting operation. The machining operations discussed in this chapter include facing, turning, grooving, parting, boring, and threading.

Facing

Facing operations involve squaring the face or end of the stock. The tool needs to be fed into the stock in a direction that will push the insert toward the pocket of the holder (see Figure 5–25).

Turning

Turning operations remove material from the outside diameter of the rotating stock. Rough turning removes the maximum amount of material from the workpiece and should be done with an insert with a large included angle.

The large included angle will insure that the tool has the proper strength to withstand the cutting forces being exerted. Profile turning uses an insert with a smaller included angle. If the finish profile warrants the use of a small, sharp-angled insert, a series of semi-finish passes are necessary to insure against tool breakage (see Figure 5–26).

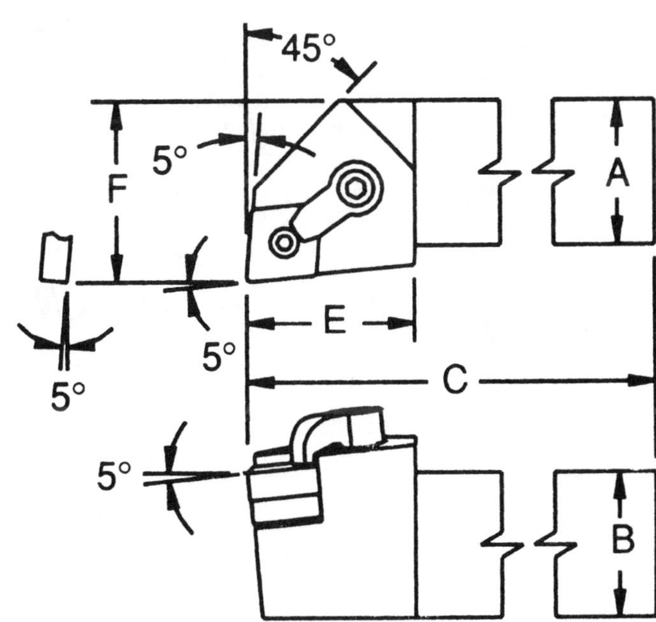

FIGURE 5–25 Tool style L can be used for turning and facing using an 80-degree diamond insert. *(Courtesy of Kennametal Inc.)*

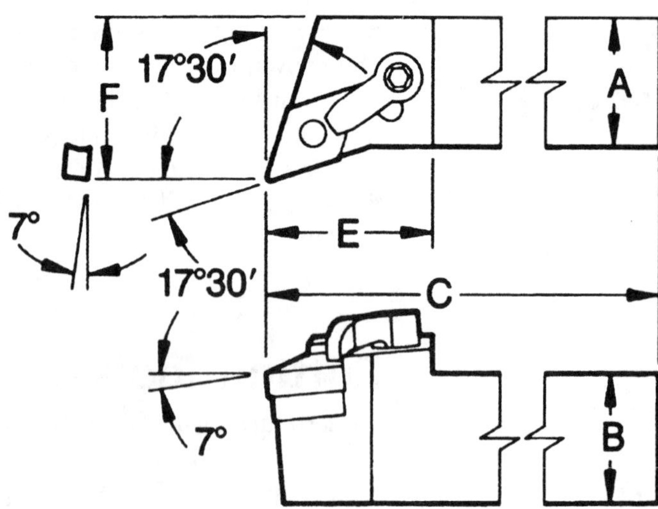

FIGURE 5–26
Tool style Q is used for profile turning using a 55-degree diamond insert. *(Courtesy of Kennametal Inc.)*

Grooving

For internal and external grooving the tool is fed straight into the workpiece at a right angle to its centerline. The cutting insert is located at the end of the tool. Grooving operations include thread relieving, shoulder relieving, snap-ring grooving, O-ring grooving, and oil reservoir grooving (see Figure 5–27).

Parting

Parting is a machine operation that cuts the finished part off of the rough stock. This operation is similar to grooving. The tool is fed into the part at a right angle to the centerline of the workpiece and is fed down past the centerline of the work, thus separating it from the rough stock. The parting tool has a carbide insert located at the end of the tool and has a slight back taper along the insert for clearance (see Figure 5–28).

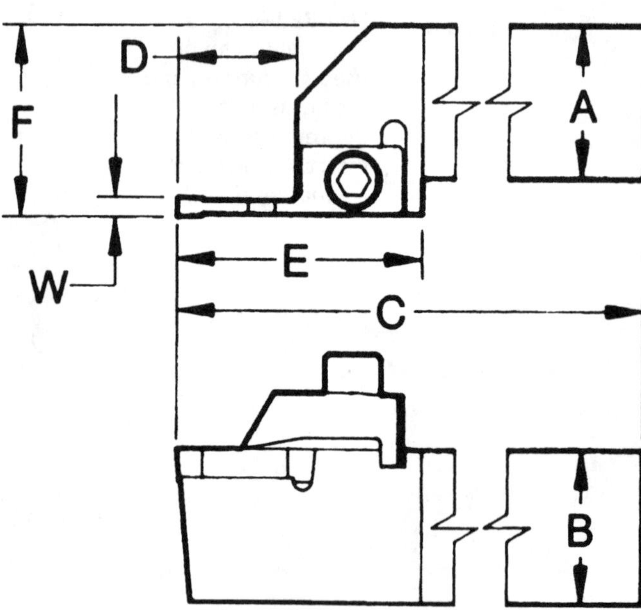

FIGURE 5–27
Tool style NG for grooving. *(Courtesy of Kennametal Inc.)*

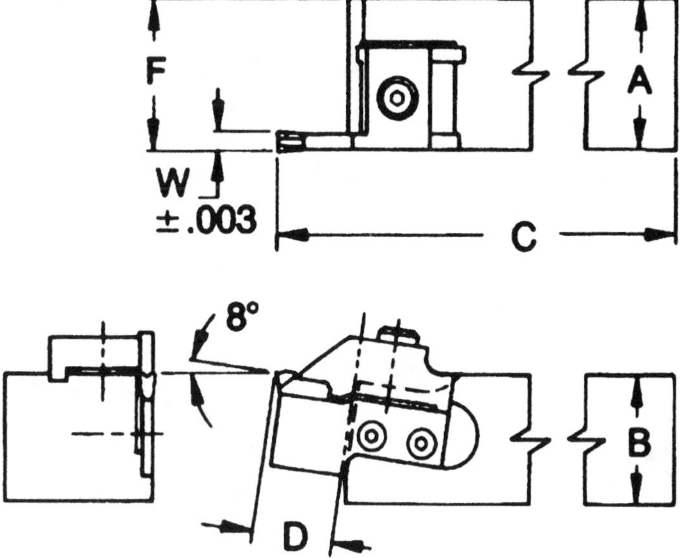

FIGURE 5–28
Tool style KGSP for parting. *(Courtesy of Kennametal Inc.)*

Boring

Boring is an internal turning operation that enlarges, trues, and contours previously drilled or existing holes. Boring is done with a boring bar (see Figure 5–29).

Threading

Threading is the process of forming a helical groove on the outside or inside surface of a cylinder or cone. Threads can be cut in several different manners, but for this tooling section we will concentrate on single-point threading tools (see Figure 5–30). Single-point threading tools are typically 60-degree carbide inserts clamped in a tool holder. The threading tool is fed into the work and along the part at a feed rate equal to the pitch. (The pitch of a thread is the distance from the one thread to the next.) On single start threads, the pitch can be calculated by dividing 1 inch by the number of threads. For example, if you had eight threads per inch, the calculation would appear as ⅛ or .125.

Presetting Tools

Presetting tooling involves setting the cutting point of the tool in relation to a predetermined dimension. Modern tool presetting is done with a toolset arm (see Figure 5–31), which is equipped with sensors.

FIGURE 5–29
LP style boring bar using a standard 55-degree diamond insert. *(Courtesy of Kennametal Inc.)*

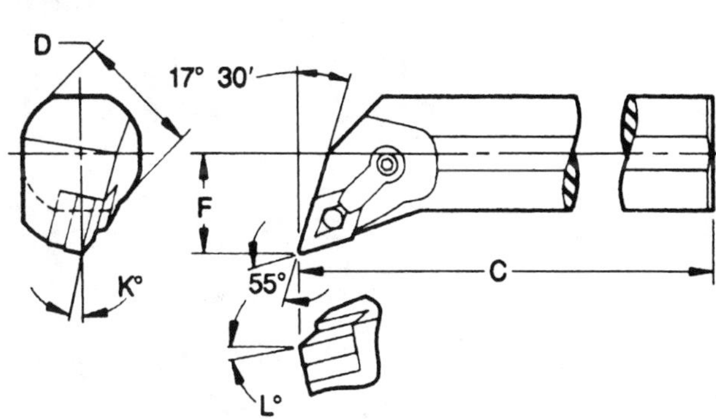

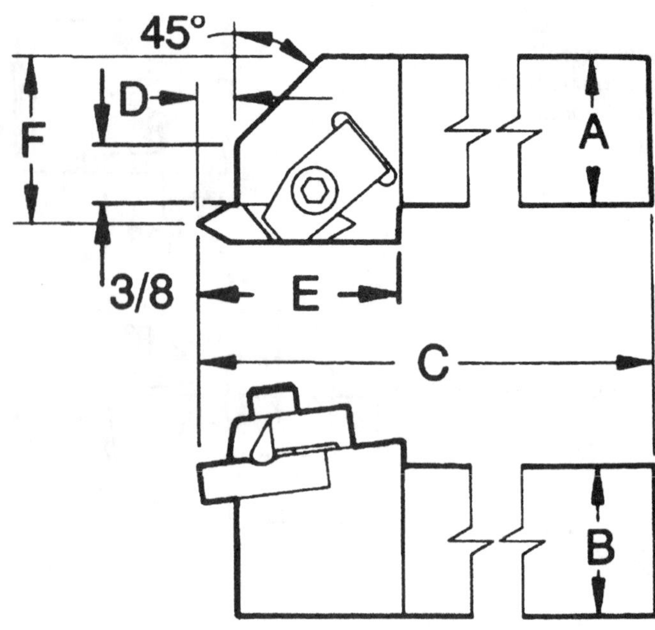

FIGURE 5–30
NS style threading tool. This style holder can be equipped with different angled threading inserts for different types of threads. *(Courtesy of Kennametal Inc.)*

The operator simply moves each tool close to the sensor and touches off the tool on the X and Z sensor to set the dimension. When the tool tip comes in contact with the sensors, the offset dimension is recorded in an offset page. When all the tools are measured, the operator uses one premeasured tool and touches off on the end of the workpiece. The control then uses this information to determine where the workpiece is located and also calculates and adjusts for the different tool tip locations.

Some controls can use the tool measurement arm to check tools automatically between cutting operations to be sure tools have not been worn, damaged, or broken during cutting.

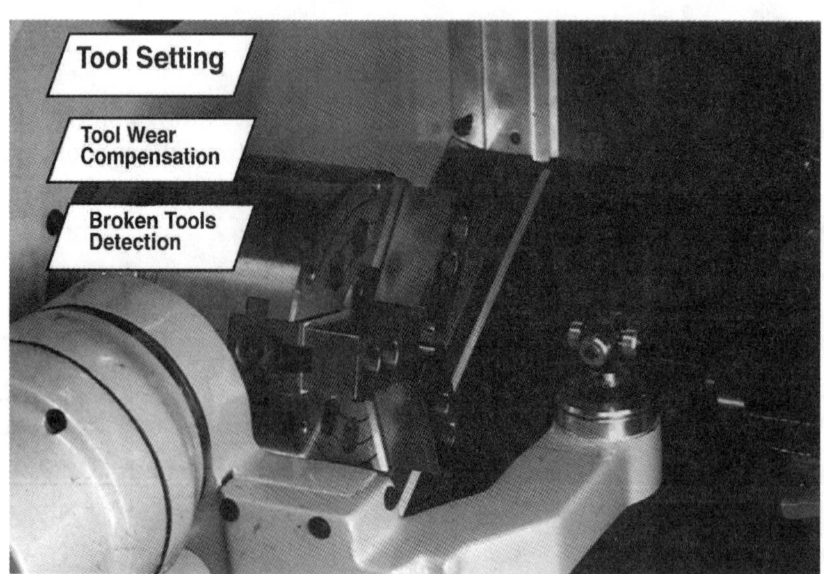

FIGURE 5–31
The tool presetting arm greatly reduces the time required to measure tools. *(Courtesy of Yamazaki Mazak Corporation.)*

CHAPTER

6

Creating 2D Tool Paths in Mastercam Mill

In this chapter you are going to go through step-by-step procedures of how to use Mastercam to generate NC code from a basic part print. Mastercam offers four levels of mill tool-path programming. Entry is a basic system of programming that concentrates on two-dimensional machining. Mill level 1 supports two-dimensional machining, as well as basic three-dimensional tool-path creation. Mill level 2 includes all of the functions of mill level 1 as well as advanced three-dimensional surfacing capabilities. Mill level 3 contains all of the surfacing capabilities of mill level 2 plus multiaxis (4-axis and 5-axis simultaneous) tool-path generation.

This textbook concentrates on the machining capabilities of Mastercam Entry.

Objectives

Upon completion of this chapter you will be able to:

- Define the basic components of the Mastercam Mill module
- Use Mastercam Mill to create part geometry
- Define parameters used in Mill tool-path modules
- Chain geometric entities
- Apply machining commands to part geometry
- Generate numerical control code to machine the part

MASTERCAM MILL PROCESS OVERVIEW

The Mastercam CAD/CAM process involves four basic components: geometry definition, application of tool-path commands, setting the numerical control (NC) parameters, and postprocessing.

Geometry Definition

Computer-aided part programming always begins with geometry definition or part design. In previous chapters in this text, it was mentioned that you could create geometry in any one of the application areas. Mastercam Mill, Mastercam Lathe, and Mastercam Design all have part geometry creation capabilities built into them. Also, if the part were originally drawn using a CAD system, Mastercam could import in this drawing. This would allow us to bypass Mastercam geometry creation.

Tool-Path Commands

Mastercam includes five tool-path generation modules within Mastercam Mill Entry. The Contour module generates a tool path along a series of entities that are joined (chained) as a closed entity (see Figure 6–1).

FIGURE 6–1

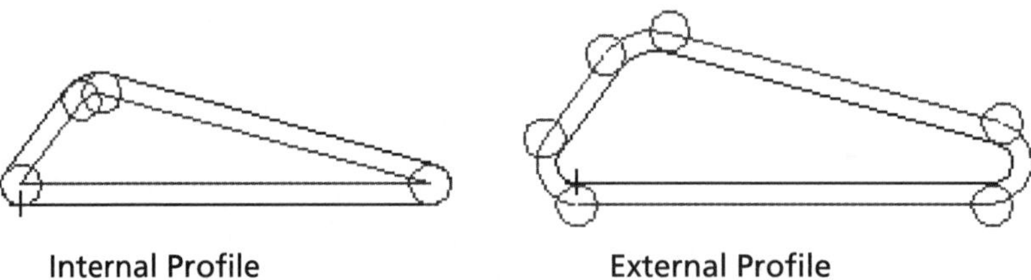

The Pocket module generates a tool path to remove materials within the confines of a series of entities that are joined (chained) as a closed entity (see Figure 6–2).

FIGURE 6–2

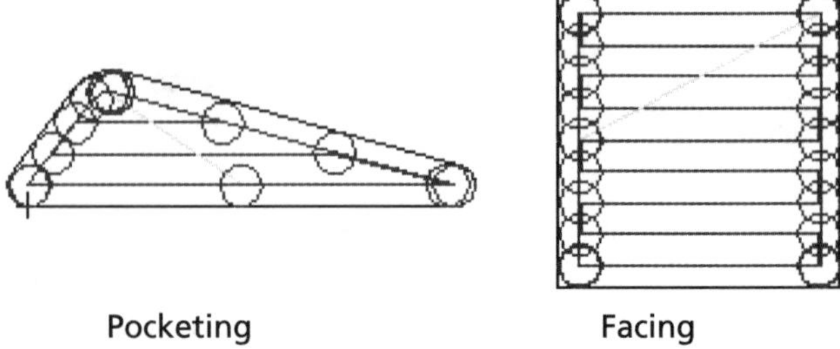

The Drill module generates a tool path to perform drilling, boring, or tapping at specified points (see Figure 6–3).

The Circle Mill module is used to create a tool path for cutting a circular feature (see Figure 6–4).

The NC Point tool path function allows you to generate a tool path by selecting points or entities using the standard Mastercam Point Entry menu (see Figure 6–5).

The following exercises will take you through a group of sample parts. Each part will show you an example of each of the mill modules that are included in Mastercam Mill Entry. We will keep the exercises that follow as simple as possible.

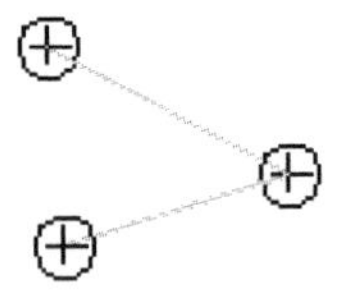

FIGURE 6–3

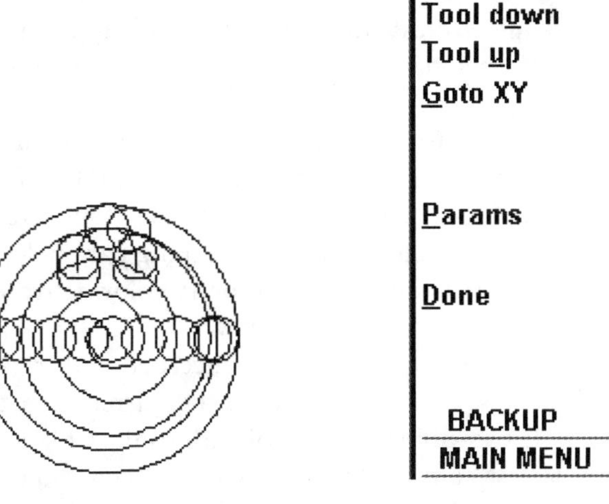

FIGURE 6–4

FIGURE 6–5

CONTOUR EXAMPLE EXERCISE

You are going to use the Contour module to generate a tool path to mill a profile around the part shown in Figure 6–6. You will use Mastercam Mill to create the part geometry. Remember that you can create geometry in any one of the application areas.

Once you have turned on your computer and allowed the system to boot up click the **Start** button using the left mouse button, and then point to the folder called **Mastercam.** Click on the **Mastercam Mill** option. Once you are in the Mastercam Main Menu area, select **File/New** to start a new file. Choose **Yes** to initialize geometry and operations. As you can see, the Mastercam Mill module looks iden-

FIGURE 6–6

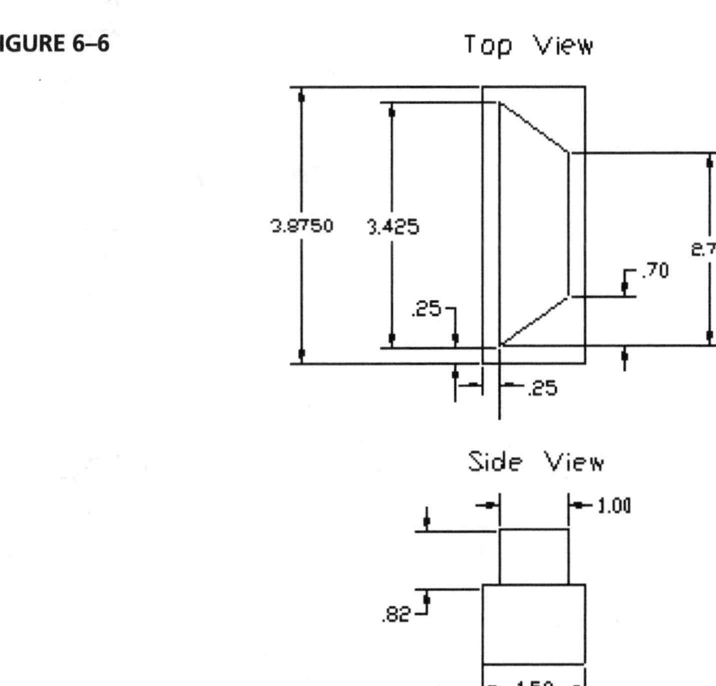

tical to the Geometry creation module. Geometry creation in Mastercam Mill is virtually identical to the Design module in Mastercam. Using your skills from the previous chapters, create the geometry for the top view of Figure 6–6.

Now that you have created the necessary geometry, let's learn about tool-path generation.

In Chapter 2 we discussed the main parts of Mastercam's working environment. One of the five main parts was the secondary menu (Figure 6–7). The secondary menu is located on the lower left side of the screen command area. The secondary menu is used to change the working parameters. The working parameters control the construction depth, geometry color, active level, mask level, tool plane, construction plane, and graphics view.

Z: 0.0000
Color:
Level: 1
Style/Width
Tplane:OFF
Cplane: T
Gview: T

FIGURE 6–7

The two parameters you are concerned with right now are the Cplane and Gview. Cplane sets the tool plane to the current construction plane. You will be doing simple two-dimensional tool path so the Cplane will be set to T for most of the time. Gview allow us to switch views. When you create a tool path it is sometimes necessary to see different views to assure that the tool path is correct. Click on **Gview** now. The Graphics menu appears (Figure 6–8).

Graphics View
Top
Front
Side
Isometric
Number
Last
Entity
Rotate
Dynamic
Next menu

FIGURE 6–8

You can also change views by selecting the appropriate icon from the tool bars. Find the tool-bar icons for the Cplane selections as well as the Gview selections. Notice that the icons for Cplane and Gview are different colors. This will help you discriminate between the two, since the icons are similar in appearance. If you try to change views right now nothing will happen because you haven't established any depth to the part yet. Before you continue, make sure that both planes are set to **Top** or **T.**

FIGURE 6–9

Main Menu:	Toolpaths:
Analyze	New
Create	Contour
File	Drill
Modify	Pocket
Xform	Surface
Delete	Multiaxis
Screen	Tools
Toolpaths	Operations
NC utils	Job setup
Exit	Next menu
BACKUP	BACKUP
MAIN MENU	MAIN MENU

Initiating the Contour Module

There are two ways to initiate the contour module. From the Main Menu select **Toolpaths** and from the Toolpaths menu select **Contour** (Figure 6–9).

You can also access the Contour module through the tool bar. Find the Contour module icon in the tool bar (Figure 6–10).

FIGURE 6–10

After initializing the Contour module, Mastercam wants you to name the NCI file that will be output (Figure 6–11).

FIGURE 6–11

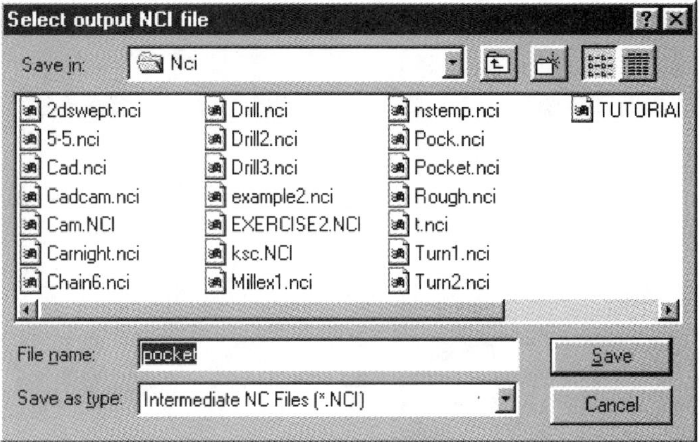

In the File name area, type **contour.** This will be an easy name to remember. Once you have typed in contour, select **Save.** Mastercam, in the dialogue box, is now prompting you to select Chain (Figure 6–12).

FIGURE 6–12

Chaining is a very important part of tool-path creation. The entities that you select become the basis for the tool path. From the Contour menu select **Chain.** Now you need to select the entities that make up the contour you want to machine. Use the mouse to select the entity shown in Figure 6–13.

Once you have selected the vertical line, the entire inner figure should become a different color and an arrow should appear (Figure 6–14).

Under the Contour chain menu you can choose a number of different chaining options, options that would have allowed us to select single entities as well as change the machining direction. Notice that the arrow is pointing in the up direction. This means that the machining will take place in a clockwise direction. To change the direction of the tool path select **Reverse** from the contour menu now. Notice the arrow direction changes. Change it back to the up direction by selecting the **Reverse** option again.

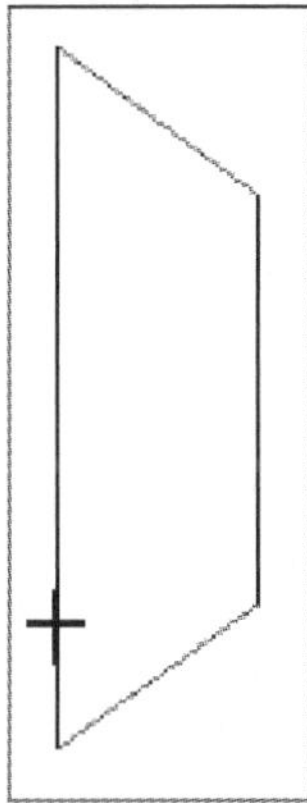

FIGURE 6–13

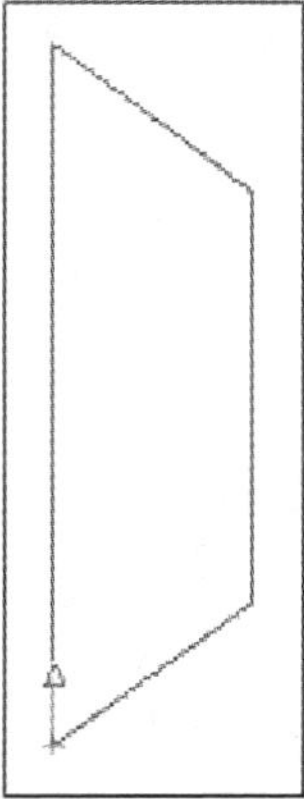

FIGURE 6–14

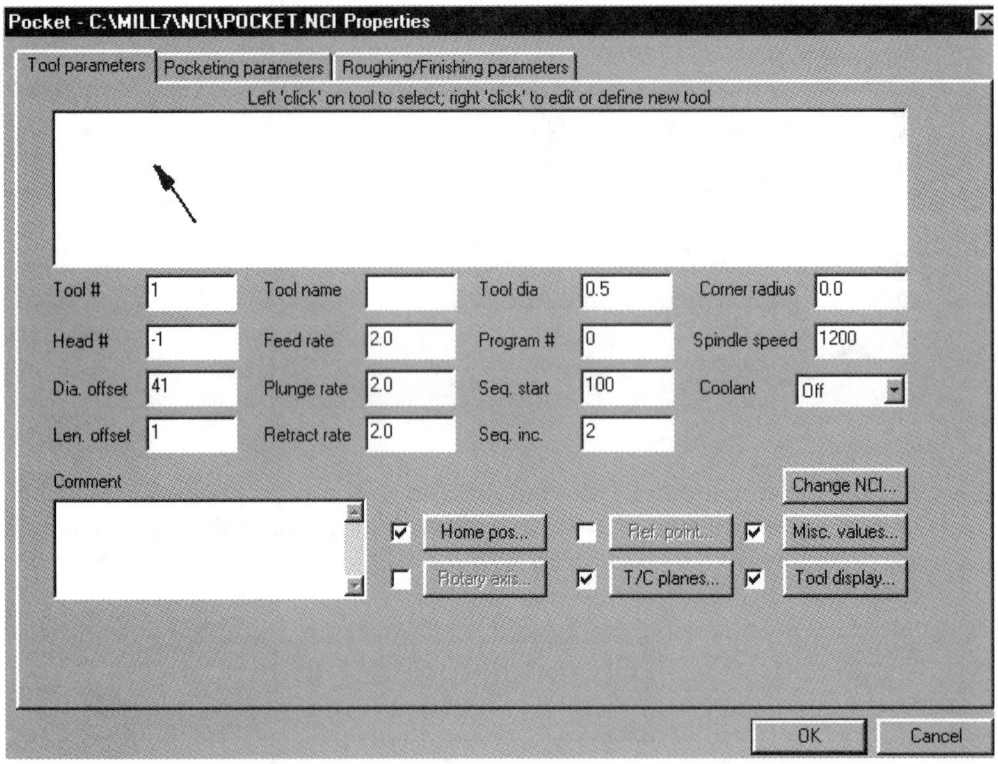

FIGURE 6–15

Now select **Done** from the contour menu. After selecting Done, the Mastercam software automatically pulls up the Tool Parameters and Contour Parameters menu (see Figure 6–15).

The Tool Parameters box is the initial box that appears. The first thing you will need to do is select a tool from the tool library. Place the mouse in the large white space indicated by the arrow in Figure 6–15. Open the tool selection menu by clicking the right mouse button. From the tool selection menu, select **Get Tool from Library.** The Tools Manager should now appear (see Figure 6–16).

FIGURE 6–16

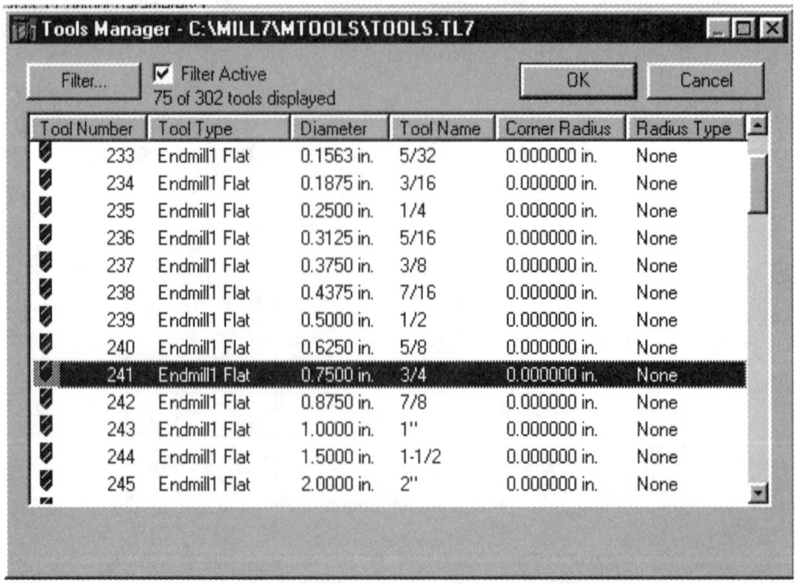

Tool Number	Tool Type	Diameter	Tool Name	Corner Radius	Radius Type
233	Endmill1 Flat	0.1563 in.	5/32	0.000000 in.	None
234	Endmill1 Flat	0.1875 in.	3/16	0.000000 in.	None
235	Endmill1 Flat	0.2500 in.	1/4	0.000000 in.	None
236	Endmill1 Flat	0.3125 in.	5/16	0.000000 in.	None
237	Endmill1 Flat	0.3750 in.	3/8	0.000000 in.	None
238	Endmill1 Flat	0.4375 in.	7/16	0.000000 in.	None
239	Endmill1 Flat	0.5000 in.	1/2	0.000000 in.	None
240	Endmill1 Flat	0.6250 in.	5/8	0.000000 in.	None
241	Endmill1 Flat	0.7500 in.	3/4	0.000000 in.	None
242	Endmill1 Flat	0.8750 in.	7/8	0.000000 in.	None
243	Endmill1 Flat	1.0000 in.	1"	0.000000 in.	None
244	Endmill1 Flat	1.5000 in.	1-1/2	0.000000 in.	None
245	Endmill1 Flat	2.0000 in.	2"	0.000000 in.	None

Tool parameters | Contour parameters

Left 'click' on tool to select; right 'click' to edit or define new tool

#1- 0.7500
endmill1 flat

Tool # 1
Tool name 3/4
Tool dia 0.75
Corner radius 0.0
Head # -1
Feed rate 24.444
Program # 0
Spindle speed 2037
Dia. offset 41
Plunge rate 12.222
Seq. start 100
Coolant Off
Len. offset 1
Retract rate 12.222
Seq. inc. 2
Comment
Change NCI...
Home pos...
Ref. point...
Misc. values...
Rotary axis...
T/C planes...
Tool display...
OK
Cancel

FIGURE 6–17

Select the **.75** end mill from the tools manager list. Now select **OK.** You can see now that the.75 end mill has been added to the Contour module (see Figure 6–17).

Next you will need to more closely define the tool and the tool holder. Put the mouse over the Tool icon indicated by the arrow in Figure 6–17. Now click the right mouse button. The Define Tool dialogue box should now appear on the screen (see Figure 6–18).

Change the settings to what is shown in Figure 6–18. Notice that Mastercam does a very nice job, through the use of arrows, of defining what each setting is going to be used for. To get these measurement settings you can either measure the

FIGURE 6–18

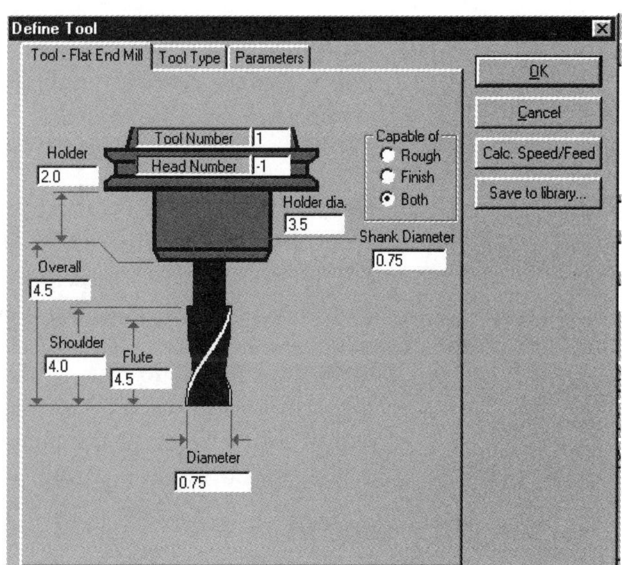

FIGURE 6–19

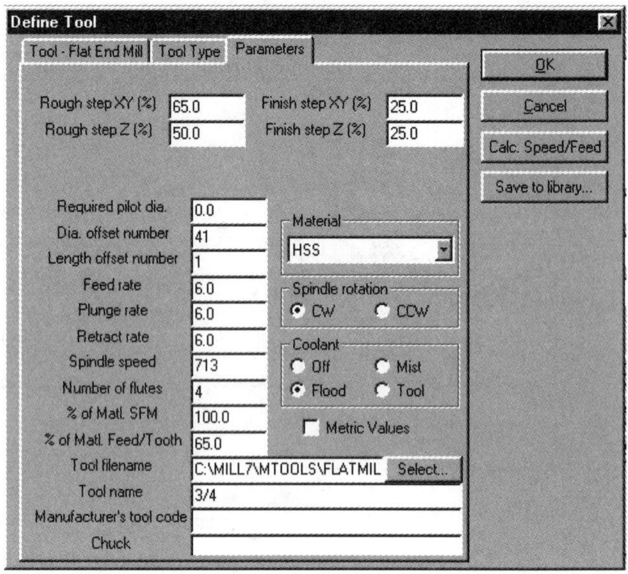

tool holder and tools yourself or get the measurements from the manufacturer's catalog. Once you have finished making the setting changes, select the **Parameters** folder heading at the top of the Define Tool dialogue box. Set the tool parameters to the values shown in Figure 6–19.

The Define Tool parameters are a set of user parameters that controls the individual tool-cutting operations. Let's take a closer look at these parameters.

Rough Step XY (%)

This parameter sets the percentage of stepover amount for consecutive roughing passes. The percentage is based on the tool size. You selected 65% of a .75-inch end mill. Our stepover amount will be about 0.480 inches.

Finish Step XY (%)

This parameter sets the percentage of stepover amount for finish passes. Again, the percentage is based on the tool size. You selected 25% of a .75-inch end mill. Our stepover amount will be about 0.180 inches.

Rough Step Z (%)

This parameter sets the depth of cut in the Z-axis direction for consecutive roughing passes. This is also based on a percentage of the tool size. You selected 50% of a 4-inch end mill. Our Z-axis depth of cut will be about .370 inches.

Finish Step Z (%)

This parameter sets the depth of cut in the Z-axis direction for finishing passes. This is also based on a percentage of the tool size. You selected 25% of a 4-inch end mill. Our Z-axis depth of finish cut will be about .180 inches.

Required Pilot Dia

This parameter is used when a pilot machining operation is needed. Pilot holes are required for plunge machining with a non-end-cutting end mill or when tapping, drilling, or boring.

Material

This pull-down menu allows you to select the cutting tool material type.

% of Mat. SFM (surface feet per minute)

Mastercam calculates the cutting speed based on suggested materials and cutting tool surface footage loaded into the database. This parameter allows you to use a percentage of the calculations.

% of Mat. Feed/Tooth

Mastercam calculates the feed rate based on material, cutting-tool material, depth of cut, and the tool diameter data loaded into the database. This parameter allows you to use a percentage of the calculations.

Tool Filename

This selection box allows you to pick a certain customized tool file to make your tool selections from. The tool files may be set up for different machine tools.

Tool Name

This dialogue box allows you to describe or name a tool.

Spindle Rotation

This option allows you to select the direction for proper spindle rotation.

Coolant

This option allows you to select a coolant mode. Accept the Define tool parameter settings by selecting **OK.**

Contour Parameters

Now you have to define the contour machining parameters. Open the contour module by clicking on the folder heading called **Contour** parameters at the top of the framed area. Looking at the Contour parameters (see Figure 6–20), you can see

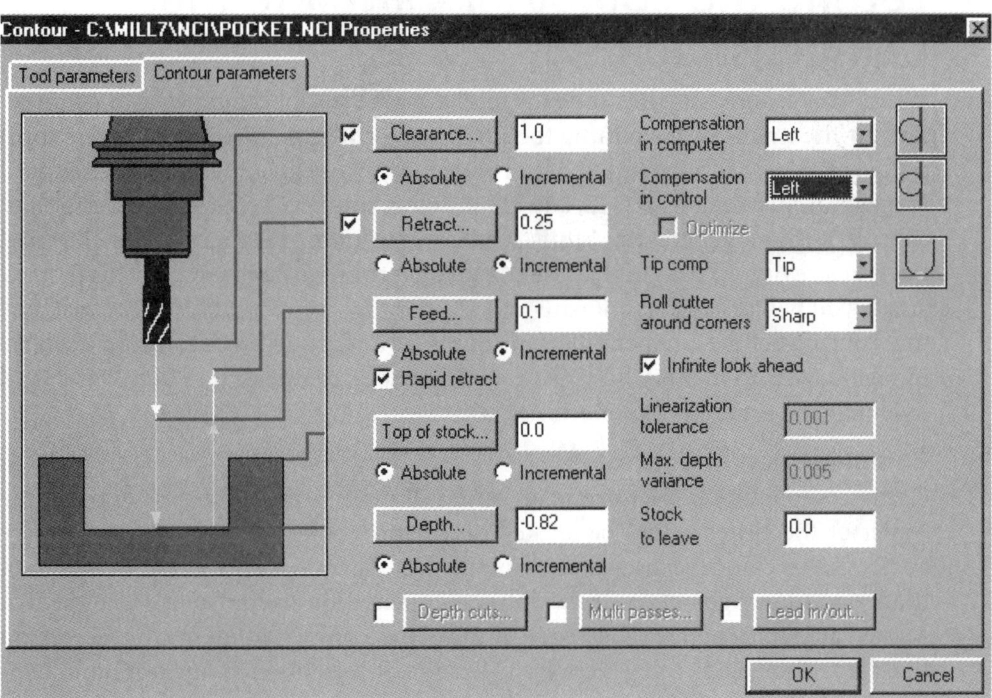

FIGURE 6–20

that these parameters control how the tool path will be generated. Let's take a closer look at them now.

Clearance

This parameter defines the safe Z-axis level above the part where the tool needs to be to travel between operations. Set the clearance to **1.0** inches.

Retract

This parameter defines the safe Z-axis level above the part where the tool will retract to between operations. Set the retract plane to **.25** inches. Use the mouse to turn on the **Absolute** setting.

Feed

This parameter defines the Z-axis position where the tool stops its rapid positioning and goes into a feed mode. Set the feed plane to **.10** inches. Use the mouse to turn on the **Absolute** setting.

Top of Stock

This parameter specifies the programming coordinate of the top of the stock. The top of our stock will be set at **0.0.** The absolute or incremental setting tells the control whether the top of stock selection is either an absolute coordinate or an incremental distance. Use the mouse to turn on the **Absolute** setting.

Depth

This parameter specifies the programming coordinate of the final depth of the contour geometry. The total depth of our profile will be −.82 inches. The absolute or incremental setting tells the control whether our depth selection is either an absolute coordinate or an incremental distance. Use the mouse to turn on the **Absolute** setting.

Letting the Computer Calculate the Compensation

When Mastercam generates code to run the machine tool it can be set to compensate for the radius of the cutting tool. Assigning cutter compensation in the computer will generate code with the tool path compensated, but it will not generate a compensation code (G41, G42, and G40) unless you have set the compensation in control. Without generating an offset code you wouldn't have any way of changing the part size or tool path in the case of tool deflection or tool wear. For this first example you will offset the tool path and use the tool compensation at the machine tool control. Set the compensation in computer to **Left.** In the future, use the table in Figure 6–21 to identify how you want the cutter compensation and Mastercam to handle the generation of machine code.

Compensation in Control

Cutter compensation is a form of an offset. Without using some type of offset the center of the cutter would be located on the programmed geometry (see Figure 6–22). Cutter compensation allows you to offset the tool to the right or to the left of the programmed geometry. If the cutter compensation in control is set to the left, Mastercam will generate a G41 code. If the cutter compensation in control is set to the right, Mastercam will generate a G42 code. If the cutter compensation in control is set to "tool on," Mastercam will generate a G40 code for no compensation.

Compensation		Machine Code Generated	Effect on Tool Path
Control	Computer		
Off	Off	None	No offset and no ability to offset the tool path.
Off	Right/Left	None	Programmed path is offset correctly by the software, but there is no ability to offset for tool wear or tool deflection at the machine control.
Right/Left	Off	G41/G42	No offset in the programmed path by the software, but the path can be adjusted through the use of the G41 and G42 that is generated. Offset will be equal to the tool radius.
Right/Left	On	G41/G42	The programmed path is offset by the software and the path can also be adjusted through the use of the the G41 or G42 code at the machine conrol. Offset will be equal to the difference between the programmed tool diameter and the actual tool diameter.

FIGURE 6–21

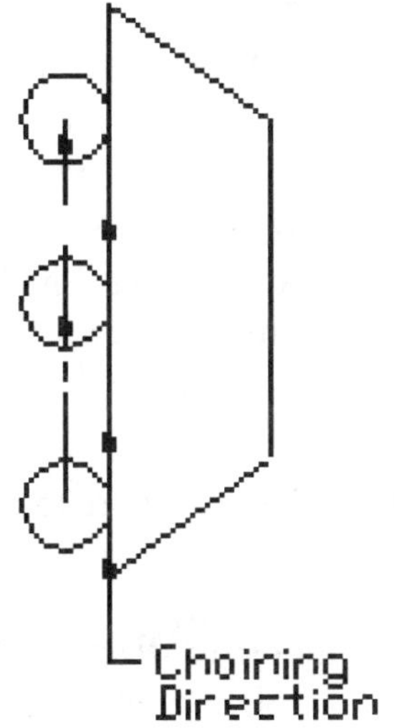

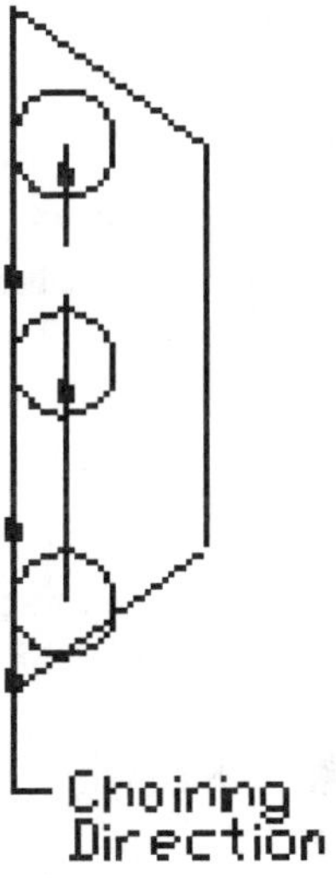

FIGURE 6–22

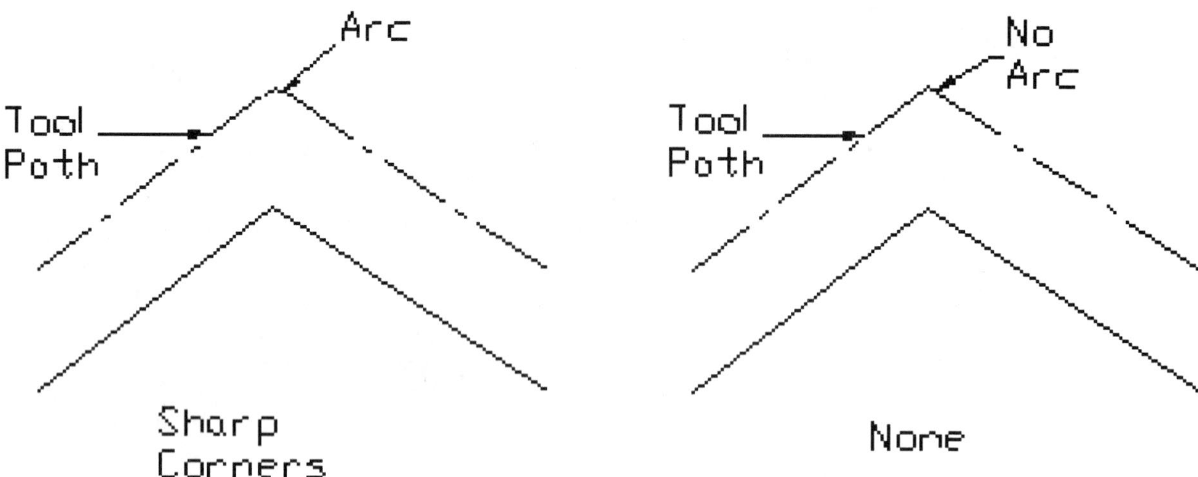

FIGURE 6-23

Cutter compensation codes not only are used to offset the cutter to the edge of the geometry profile, but also allow us to compensate at the machine control for changes in cutter size or tool deflection.

Because our chaining direction was up and you want the tool to be on the outside of the profile you needed to select **Left** for Compensation in control.

There are three different parameter settings for corners. The Sharp setting will roll the cutter around corners less than 135 degrees (see Figure 6–23). The All Corners setting will roll the cutter around all corners. This is the default setting. The None setting rolls the cutter around any corner. Set this parameter to **Sharp.**

Infinite Look Ahead

The Infinite Look Ahead parameter lets the control look ahead for tool-path intersection problems that may cause tool gouging. If this problem is encountered Mastercam will adjust the tool path to avoid the problem. This parameter is either on or off. The check mark in the empty box indicates that it is on. Turn this parameter **on.**

Stock to Leave

The Stock to Leave parameter allows you to leave stock for future or secondary finish operations. This parameter is not used as a finish stock allowance. The Finish Stock Allowance parameter setting is in the Depth Cuts control area. Set stock to leave at **0.0** inches.

Depth Cuts

You now need to activate the **Depth Cuts** dialogue box. Use the mouse to place a check mark in the empty box adjacent to the Depth Cuts dialogue box (see Figure 6–24).

Once you have activated the dialogue box, use the mouse to select the **Depth Cuts** dialogue box. The Depth Cuts parameter setting box should now appear on the screen (see Figure 6–25).

FIGURE 6–24

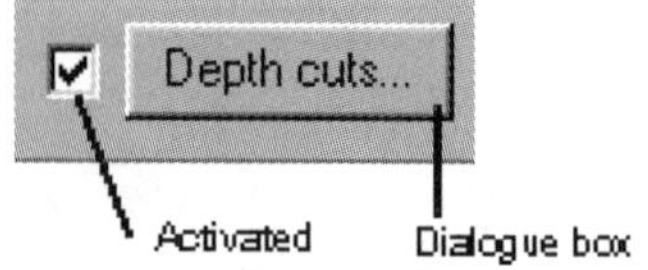

FIGURE 6–25

The parameter settings in the Depth Cuts dialogue box controls the Z-axis depth of the tool path.

Max Rough Step

This parameter sets the maximum depth of cut per pass in the Z axis. Set this parameter to **0.500** inches.

Finish Passes

This parameter sets the number of finish passes in the Z axis. Set this parameter to **1.**

Finish Step

This parameter sets the amount of material to take off per finish pass in the Z axis. Set this parameter to **0.02** inches.

Stock to Leave

This parameter setting is the amount of stock you want to leave after all of the machining passes have occurred. This is not the amount of stock to leave for finishing. The amount of stock to leave for finishing is controlled by the number of finish passes and the finish step. Set this parameter to **0.0** inches.

Keep Tool Down

The Keep Tool Down parameter tells the system whether you want to retract the tool between cuts. Keep this parameter **off** to keep the tool from gouging on depth cuts. Once you have completed these parameter selections select **OK.**

Multi Passes

You now need to activate the Multi Passes dialogue box. Use the mouse to place a check mark in the empty box adjacent to the Multi Passes dialogue box. Once you have activated the dialogue box, use the mouse to select the **Multi Passes** dialogue box. The Multi Passes parameter setting box should now appear on the screen (see Figure 6–26).

The Multi Passes parameter settings control is split into three sections: Roughing Passes, Finishing Passes, and Machine Finish Passes at final depth or all depths.

Roughing Passes

These parameter settings control the number and amount of the tool's X- and Y-axis roughing passes.

FIGURE 6–26

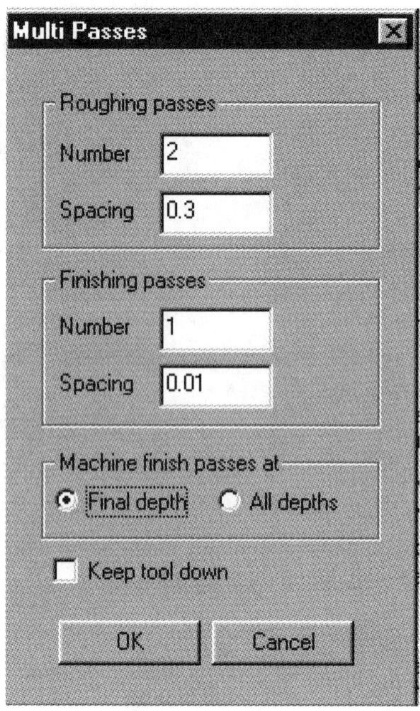

Number

This parameter sets the number of X- and Y-axis roughing passes you wish to make. A setting of zero indicates no roughing passes. You want to make two roughing passes to insure that the excess stock around the contour is removed. Set Number to **2.**

Spacing

This value represents the amount of stock to be removed per roughing pass on the X and Y axes.

Set this parameter to **0.30.** If there is not 0.30 inches of stock remaining, Mastercam will calculate the amount of stock left before the finish amount and make a cut at that depth.

Finishing Passes

These parameter settings control the number and amount of the tool's X- and Y-axis finishing passes.

Number

This parameter sets the number of X- and Y-axis finishing passes you wish to make. A setting of zero indicates no finish passes are to be made and therefore no material will be left after the roughing passes. You want to make one finish pass. Set Number to **1.**

Spacing

This value represents the amount of stock to be removed per finish pass on the X and Y axes. Set this parameter to **0.01.**

Machine Finish Passes

Finish passes can be made at either the final depth or at all depths.

Final Depth

This parameter tells the control to make finish passes only at the final depth. **Activate** this option now.

All Depths

This parameter tells the control to make finish passes after every rough pass at all depths.

Keep Tool Down

The Keep Tool Down parameter tells the system whether you want to retract the tool between cuts. Turn this parameter **on** to keep the tool down. Once you have completed the Multi Pass parameter settings select **OK.**

Lead In/Out

You now need to activate the Lead In/Out dialogue box. Use the mouse to place a check mark in the empty box adjacent to the Lead In/Out dialogue box. Once you have activated the dialogue box, use the mouse to select the **Lead In/Out** dialogue box. The Lead In/Out parameter setting box should now appear on the screen (see Figure 6–27).

The Lead In/Out parameter setting allows for a smooth transition of the cutter path to the profile of the contour. Mastercam allows you to place a combination of lines or arcs at the beginning or at the end of the roughing and finishing passes.

Overlap

Overlap allows you to add a line to go past the end of the tool path. Set this parameter to **0.0.** *Note:* This option can be used only on closed contours.

Entry

The Entry option allows you to add an arc and/or a line move to the entry of all of the roughing or finishing passes. If both line and arc options have entries other than zero, the line move will be executed first. Select the **Entry** check box to activate the Entry option dialogue box.

FIGURE 6–27

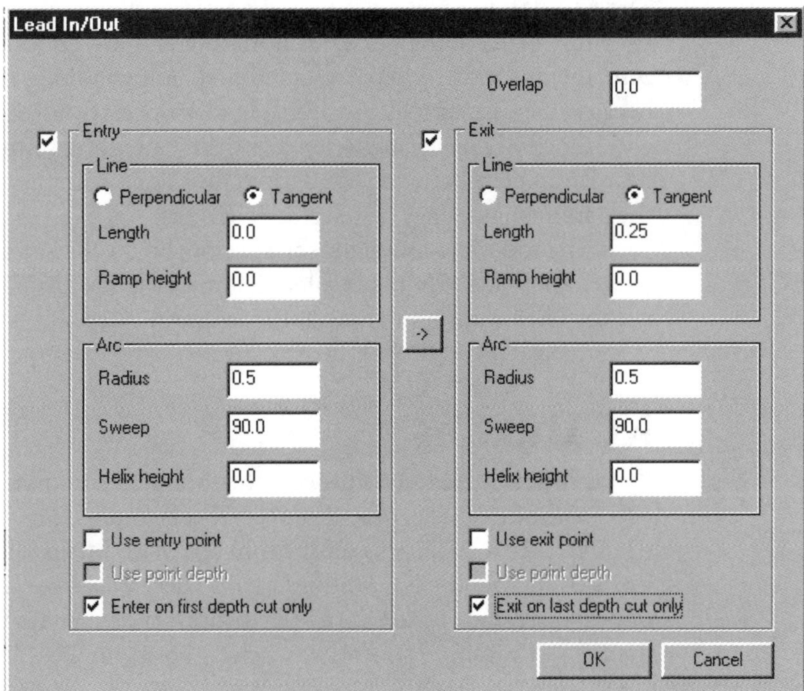

Perpendicular/Tangent This parameter setting will place an entry line perpendicular or tangent to the chaining direction. Set the Tangent option to **on** by placing a dot in the Tangent option circle.

Line Length This parameter setting sets the length of entry line. Set the Line Length to **0.0** for no entry line.

Ramp Height This parameter setting adds a depth to the entry line. Set the Ramp Height to **0.0** for no ramp height on the entry line.

Arc Radius This parameter setting will place an entry arc tangent to the toolpath. Set the Arc Radius to **0.500.**

Arc Sweep This parameter setting will set the sweep angle of entry arc. Set the sweep angle to **90.0** degrees.

Helix Height The Helix Height parameter will add a depth cut to the entry arc creating a helix entry cut. On deep cuts this allows the cutter to create clearance for itself. Set the Helix Height to **0.0.**

Use Entry Point This parameter sets the start point for the entry arc or entry line. The system automatically defaults to the last point chained in the path or the profile so you can leave this option **off.**

Use Point Depth This option starts the entry move at the entry point depth. Leave this option **off.**

Enter on the First Depth Cut Only This parameter tells the control to use the entry line or arc on the first depth cut only. Set this option to **on** by placing a check mark in this option box.

->

FIGURE 6–28

Arrow Button The arrow button (Figure 6–28) automatically copies the entries from the Entry options over to the Exit options.

Click on this button now. Notice that everything that was in the Entry option fields is now also in the Exit option fields.

Exit

The Exit option allows you to add an arc or a line move to the entry of all of the roughing or finishing passes. If both line and arc options have entries other than zero, the line move will be executed first. You will not go through the Exit options because they are virtually identical in all respects to the Entry options.

Once you have completed all of the parameter settings, select **OK.** The Contour Parameters dialogue box should now appear on the screen again. Accept all of the parameter settings by selecting **OK.**

The top-view tool path should now be on the screen. Use Figures 6–29 and 6–30 to help identify the results of some of the setting decisions you made. Now use the **Gview** option to look at the Isometric view.

NC Utilities

You will now need to postprocess the tool path into machine language. There are two methods of selecting the postprocess mode. The first method is accessed through the NC Utilities menu. From the Main Menu select **NC Utilities** (see Figure 6–31). From the NC Utilities menu select **Post Proc.** Mastercam has a number of postprocessor data files. The postprocessor file creates machine codes specific to the type of machine control you select. From the Post Proc menu select **Change** (see Figure 6–32).

FIGURE 6–29

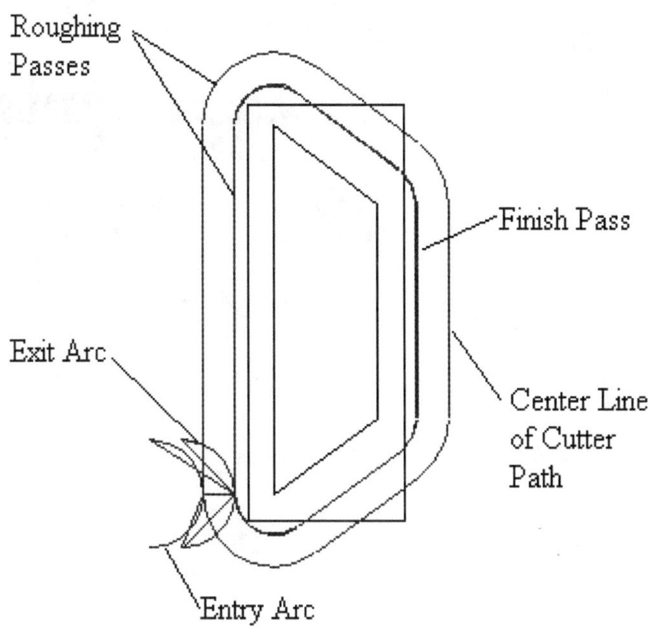

FIGURE 6–30

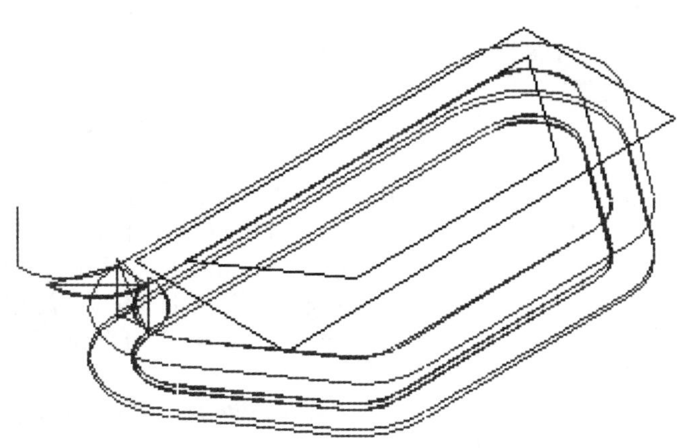

Main Menu:	NC Utilities:
Analyze	N-See 2000
Create	Backplot
File	Edit NCI
Modify	Filter
Xform	Post proc
Delete	Setup sheet
Screen	Def. ops
Toolpaths	Def. tools
NC utils	Def. matls
Exit	
BACKUP	BACKUP
MAIN MENU	MAIN MENU

FIGURE 6–31

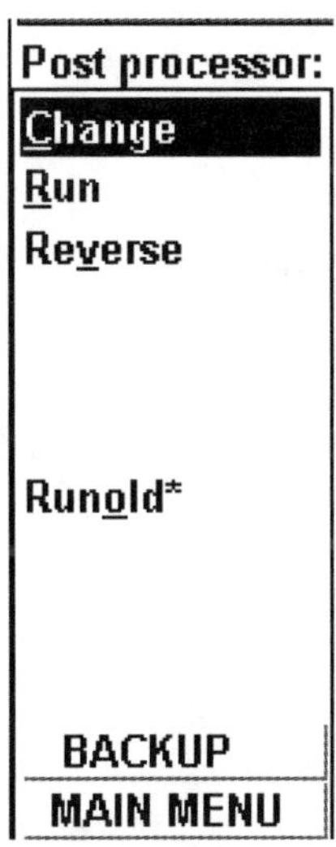

FIGURE 6–32

FIGURE 6–33

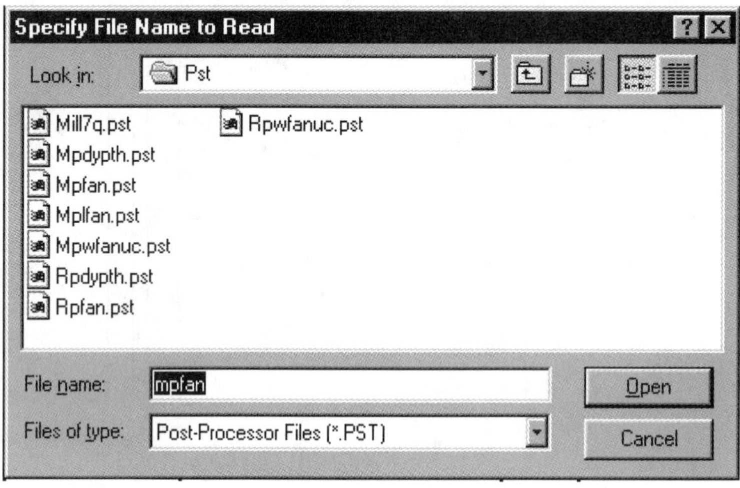

Mastercam makes it possible to take the same tool-path file and postprocess it for many different types of controls (see Figure 6–33). The postprocessor files end with a .pst extension. The number of files you see in Figure 6–33 is only a small portion of the number of postprocessor files available through Mastercam. Select the **Mpfan.pst** file and press the **Open** button.

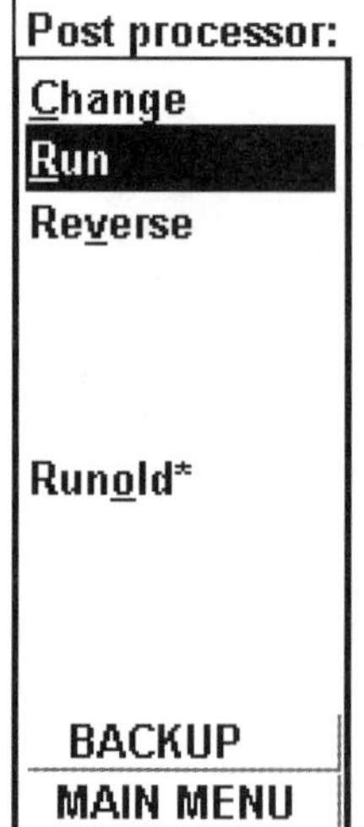

FIGURE 6–34

Once you have opened the Post Processer file select **Run** from the Post Processor menu (see Figure 6–34).

Mastercam now asks you to name the NC file that it is going to create. Name this NC file the same name as the geometry file. Mastercam now will create an NC file. This is the file that will be downloaded to the machine tool to make the part. Since the two files have different extensions you will not be writing over the top of the original file. Select **Save.** Your coded file should now appear on the screen. Take note in Figure 6–35 of how Mastercam handled our cutter compensation selections.

Maximize the Program Editor screen by using the **Maximize** button in the upper right corner of the screen. The Programmer's File Editor allows you to edit, print, and manipulate the NC file. **Exit** the Programmer's File Editor now.

You have now completed the first exercise on contour machining. You will now move onto the next exercise. The next exercise will deal with pocket machining. Pay close attention because you will receive some new information as you go along.

FIGURE 6–35

```
%
O0000
(PROGRAM NAME - 5-5)
(DATE=DD-MM-YY - 01-06-99 TIME=HH:MM - 14:08)
(3/4 TOOL - 1 DIA. OFF. - 41 LEN. - 1 DIA. - .75)
N100G20
N102G0G40G49G80G90
N104T1M6
N106G0G90G54X-.56Y-.25S2037M3
N108G43H1Z1.
N110Z.1
N112G1Z-.405F12.22
N114G2G41D41X-.06Y.25R.5F24.44
N116G1Y3.675
N118G2X.25Y3.985R.31
```

G41 (cutter compensation left)
D41 (compensation register 41)

POCKET EXAMPLE EXERCISE

The Pocket module is used to create tool paths to remove material in a closed contour or to face mill the top of a part. You are going to use the Pocket module to generate a tool path to mill a pocket in the part shown in Figure 6–36. You will use Mastercam Mill to create the part geometry. Remember that you can create geometry in any one of the application areas. Once you have turned on your computer and allowed the system to boot up, click the **Start** button using the left mouse button, and then point to the folder called **Mastercam.** Click on the **Mastercam Mill** option. Once you are in the Mastercam Main Menu area, select **File/New** to start a new file. Choose **Yes** to initialize geometry and operations. As you can see, the Mastercam Mill module looks identical to the Geometry creation module. Geometry creation in Mastercam Mill is virtually identical to the Design module in Mastercam. Using your skills from the geometry creation chapters, create the geometry for the front view of Figure 6–36.

Now that you have created the necessary geometry, let's get acquainted with the Job Setup function. From the Main Menu select **Toolpaths.** From the Toolpaths menu select **Job Setup** (see Figure 6–37).

Job Setup

The Job Setup function should now appear on the screen (see Figure 6–38). The Job Setup function sets the machining parameters for the current job. These machining parameters include the stock origin and size, material type, tool-offset registers, feed calculations, and tool-path configurations.

Stock Origin

The Stock Origin can be identified by picking the stock origin from the graphics area or by selecting the stock corners from the graphics area.

FIGURE 6–36

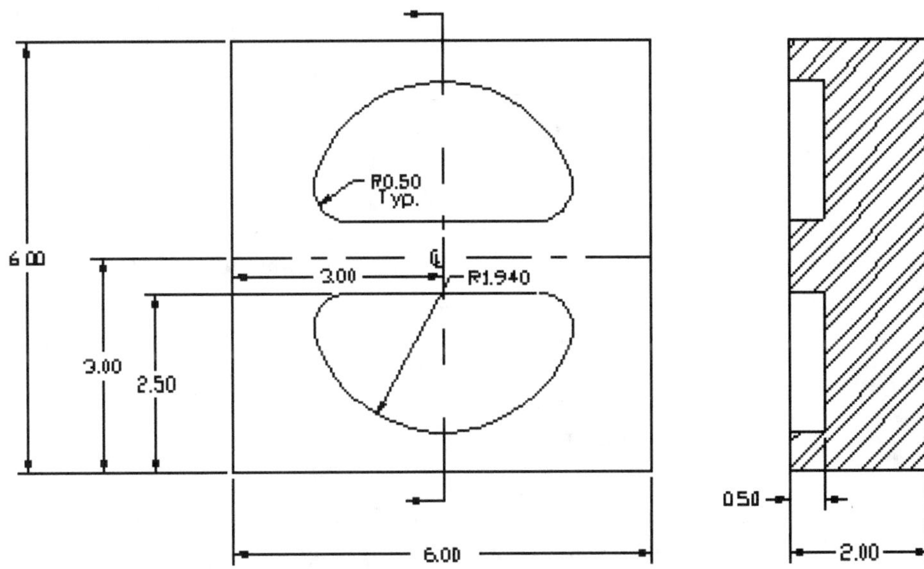

FIGURE 6–37

Main Menu:	Toolpaths:
Analyze	New
Create	Contour
File	Drill
Modify	Pocket
Xform	Surface
Delete	Multiaxis
Screen	Tools
Toolpaths	Operations
NC utils	Job setup
Exit	Next menu
BACKUP	BACKUP
MAIN MENU	MAIN MENU

FIGURE 6–38

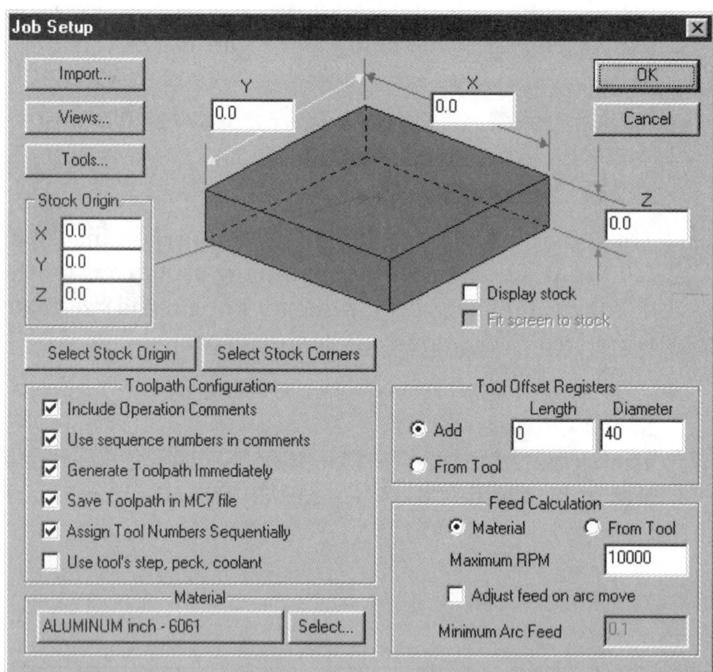

From the Job Setup parameters pick the **Select Stock Corners** button. The graphics screen will now appear on the screen. Use the mouse to pick **Corner 1,** the lower left corner of the stock as shown in Figure 6–39.

Next select **Corner 2,** the upper right corner as shown in Figure 6–39. Even though you are not going to define the stock origin, Mastercam allows you to define the stock origin this same way.

You have indicated to Mastercam that you wanted to define the stock by the corners of the part. Notice how the values for the stock corners have automatically been input (see Figure 6–40). Now input the Z-axis stock thickness of **2.0** inches as shown in Figure 6–40.

Material Type

Mastercam allows you to select the material type within the Job Setup function (see Figure 6–41). The material type you select sets the base surface footage and

FIGURE 6–39

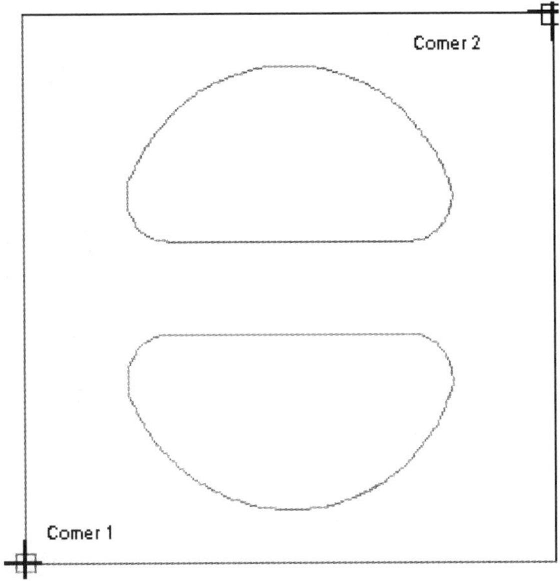

FIGURE 6–40

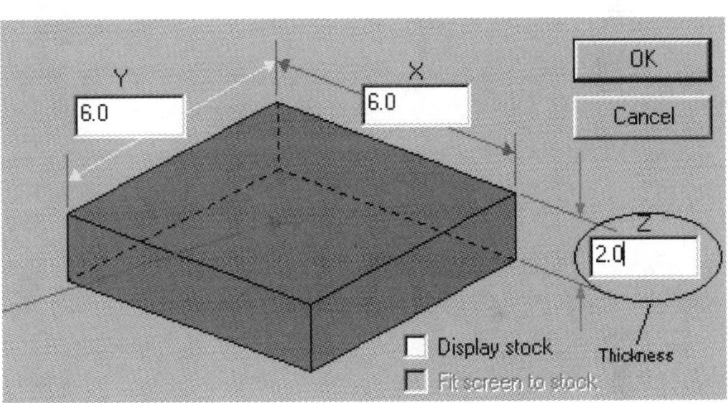

FIGURE 6–41

feed rates based on the suggested surface footage and the Brinnel hardness (BHN) number of the material.

Click on the **Select** button in the Material area. A list of material types should now appear on the screen. Use the **down arrow** scroll button along the right side of the menu to move down (see Figure 6–42).

Scroll down until STEEL inch 1010-200 BHN appears. Use the mouse to highlight this selection. Press **OK.** You should now be back in the Job Setup area. Click on the **STEEL inch 1010-200 BHN** material button. The Material Definition screen should now appear on the screen (see Figure 6–43). At this point you could change any of the material settings to fit this job.

You will not change any of these settings. Select **OK.**

Tool Offset Registers

The Tool Offset Register determines the input for the tool's diameter offset and length offset (see Figure 6–44).

FIGURE 6–42

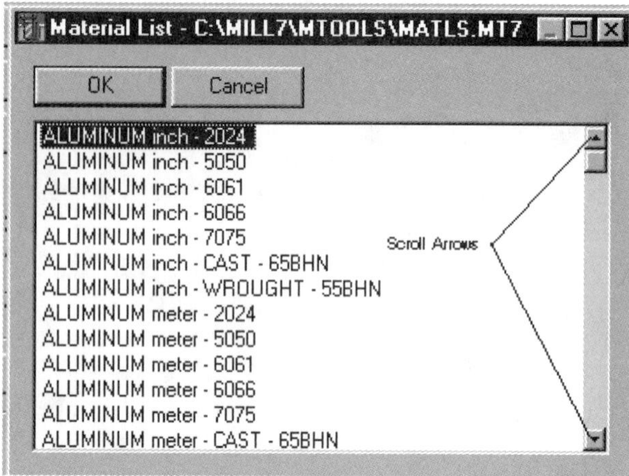

FIGURE 6–43

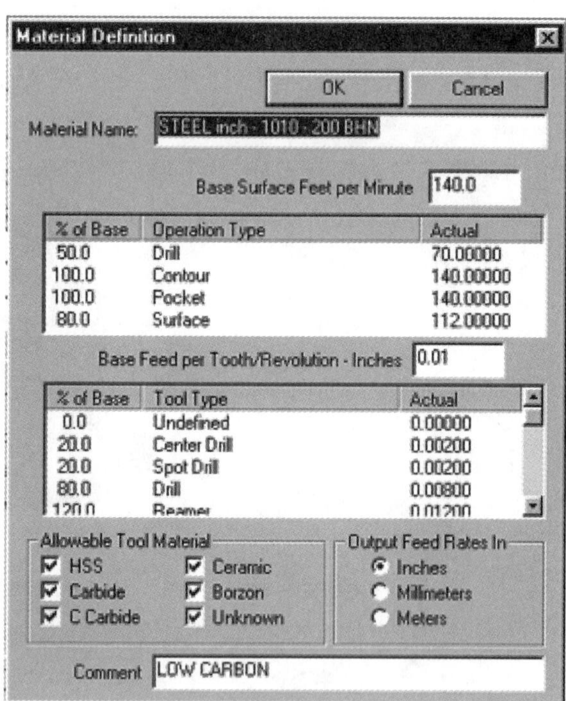

FIGURE 6–44

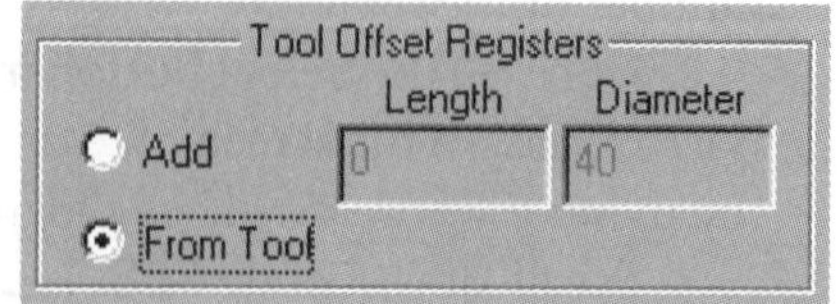

Add The Add option will add a specific number to the tool number in the Operations Manager. You will also be discussing the Operations Manager within this chapter.

From Tool The From Tool option will take the tool length and tool diameter offset number information right from the tool definition. Activate the **From Tool** option now.

FIGURE 6–45

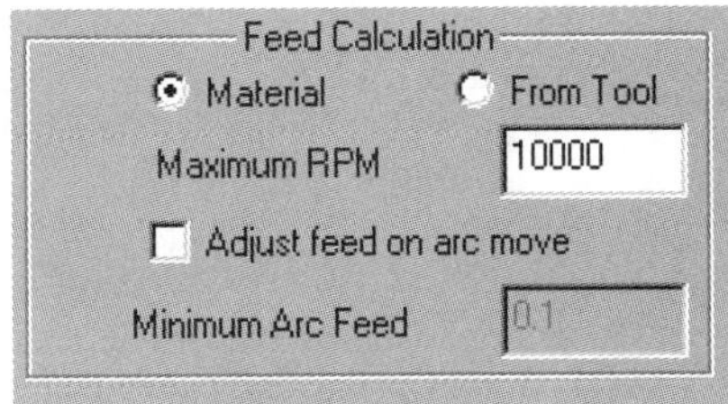

FIGURE 6–46

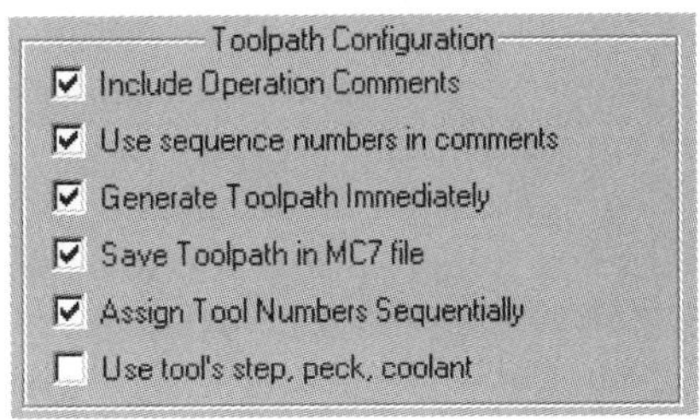

Feed Calculation

The Feed Calculation option determines where the feedrate, retract rate, and spindle speed information will be taken from (Figure 6–45). The calculation information can come from either the material file or the selected tool file. Within the feed calculations you can also set a maximum RPM limit and tell the control to calculate a slower feed rate when cutting an arc. Select the **Material** option now if it is not already selected.

Tool-Path Configurations

The Toolpath Configuration parameters section allows you to control how Mastercam will output the NCI file (see Figure 6–46).

Set the tool-path configurations as they appear in Figure 6–46. Once you have finished with these options, select **OK** from the Job Setup function menu.

Initiating, the Pocket Module

There are two ways to initiate the contour module. From the Main Menu select **Toolpath.** From the Toolpaths menu select **Pocket** (Figure 6–47). You can also ac-

FIGURE 6–47

Main Menu:	Toolpaths:
Analyze	New
Create	Contour
File	Drill
Modify	Pocket
Xform	Surface
Delete	Multiaxis
Screen	Tools
Toolpaths	Operations
NC utils	Job setup
Exit	Next menu
BACKUP	BACKUP
MAIN MENU	MAIN MENU

FIGURE 6–48

cess the Pocket module through the tool bar. Find the Pocket module icon in the tool bar (Figure 6–48). After initializing the Pocket module Mastercam wants you to name the NCI file that will be output (Figure 6–49).

In the File name area, type **Pocket.** This will be an easy name to remember. Once you have finished typing in Pocket, select **Save.** Mastercam, in the dialogue box, is now prompting you to select Chain. Use the mouse to select the entity shown in Figure 6–50.

Once you have selected the horizontal line, the entire upper figure should become a different color and an arrow should appear. Under the Contour Chain menu you can choose a number of different chaining options—options that would have allowed us to select single entities as well as change the machining direction. Notice the arrow direction. This means that normally the machining will take place in this direction, but you will find out that within the pocketing parameter settings you can tell the control whether you want to climb mill the pocket or conventional mill the pocket. Now select **Done** from the pocket menu. After selecting Done, the Mastercam software automatically pulls up the Tool parameters, Pocket parameters, and Roughing/Finishing parameters menu (see Figure 6–51).

The Tool parameters box is the initial box that appears. The first thing you will need to do is select a tool from the tool library. Place the mouse in the large

FIGURE 6–49

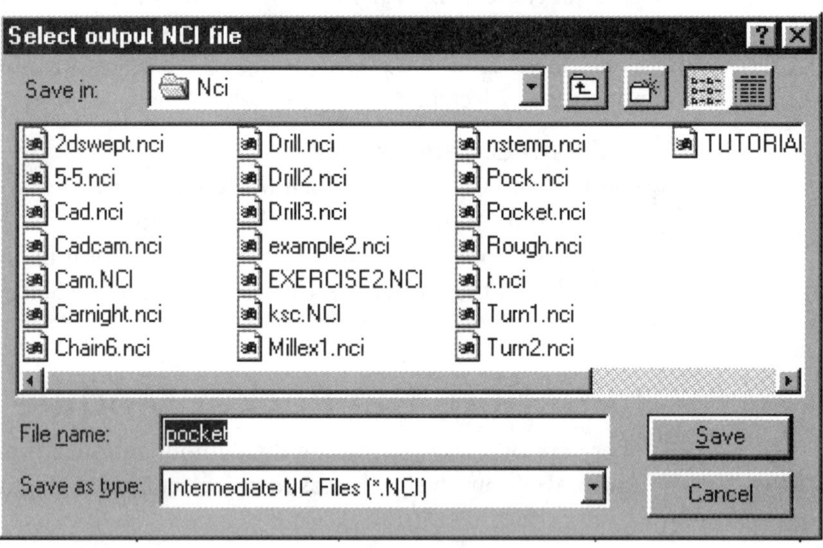

FIGURE 6–50

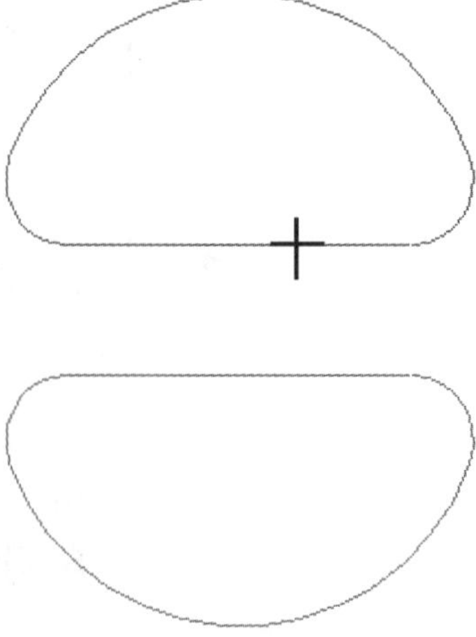

FIGURE 6–51

white space indicated by the arrow in Figure 6–51. Open the tool selection menu by clicking the right mouse button. From the tool selection menu, select **Get Tool from Library.** The Tools Manager should now appear (see Figure 6–52).

Select the 5/8 end mill from the Tools Manager list. Now select **OK.** You can see now that the 5/8 end mill has been added to the pocket module (see Figure 6–53).

FIGURE 6–52

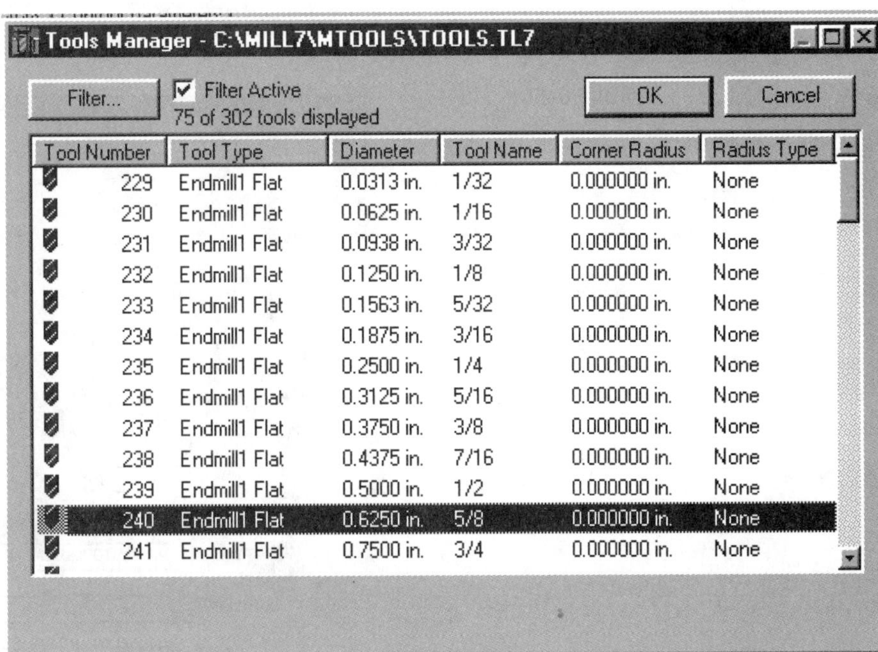

Tools Manager - C:\MILL7\MTOOLS\TOOLS.TL7

Filter... | Filter Active | 75 of 302 tools displayed | OK | Cancel

Tool Number	Tool Type	Diameter	Tool Name	Corner Radius	Radius Type
229	Endmill1 Flat	0.0313 in.	1/32	0.000000 in.	None
230	Endmill1 Flat	0.0625 in.	1/16	0.000000 in.	None
231	Endmill1 Flat	0.0938 in.	3/32	0.000000 in.	None
232	Endmill1 Flat	0.1250 in.	1/8	0.000000 in.	None
233	Endmill1 Flat	0.1563 in.	5/32	0.000000 in.	None
234	Endmill1 Flat	0.1875 in.	3/16	0.000000 in.	None
235	Endmill1 Flat	0.2500 in.	1/4	0.000000 in.	None
236	Endmill1 Flat	0.3125 in.	5/16	0.000000 in.	None
237	Endmill1 Flat	0.3750 in.	3/8	0.000000 in.	None
238	Endmill1 Flat	0.4375 in.	7/16	0.000000 in.	None
239	Endmill1 Flat	0.5000 in.	1/2	0.000000 in.	None
240	Endmill1 Flat	0.6250 in.	5/8	0.000000 in.	None
241	Endmill1 Flat	0.7500 in.	3/4	0.000000 in.	None

FIGURE 6–53

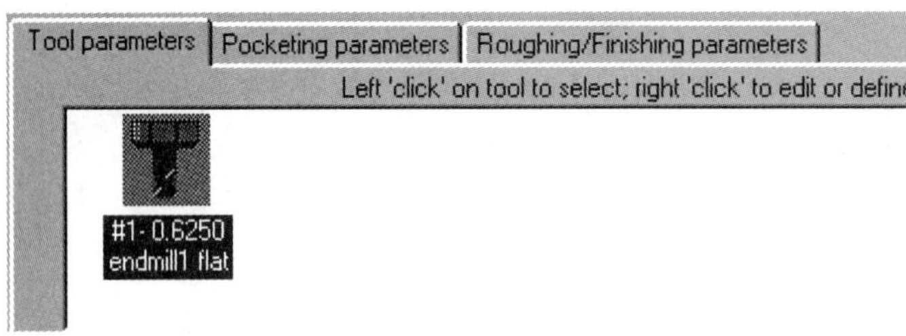

Next you will need to more closely define the tool and the tool holder. Put the mouse over the **Tool** icon and click the right mouse button. The Define Tool dialogue box should now appear on the screen (see Figure 6–54).

Change the settings to what is shown in Figure 6–54. Once you have finished making the setting changes, select the **Parameters** folder heading at the top of the Define Tool dialogue box. Set the tool parameters to the values shown in Figure 6–55. You changed the offset numbers so you would have some consistency. The

FIGURE 6–54

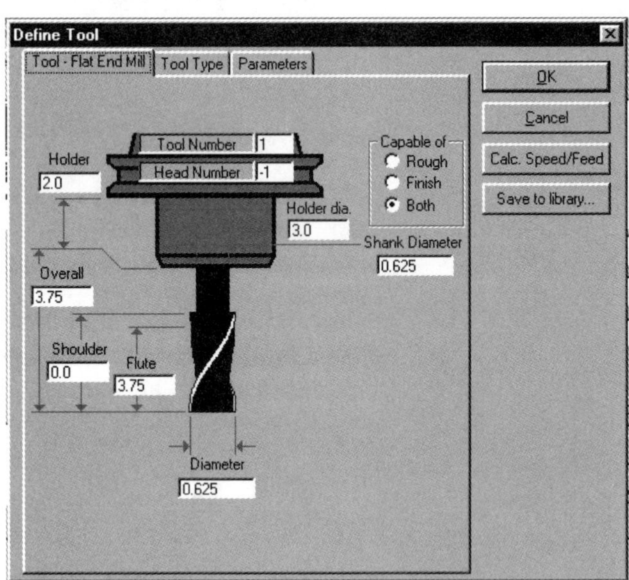

FIGURE 6–55

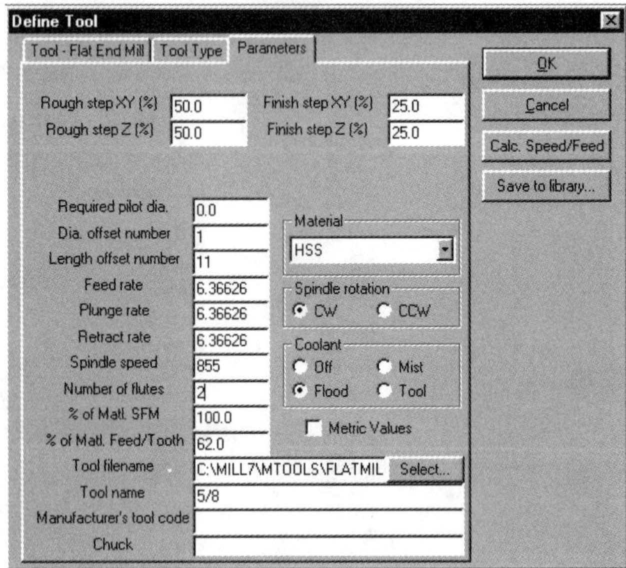

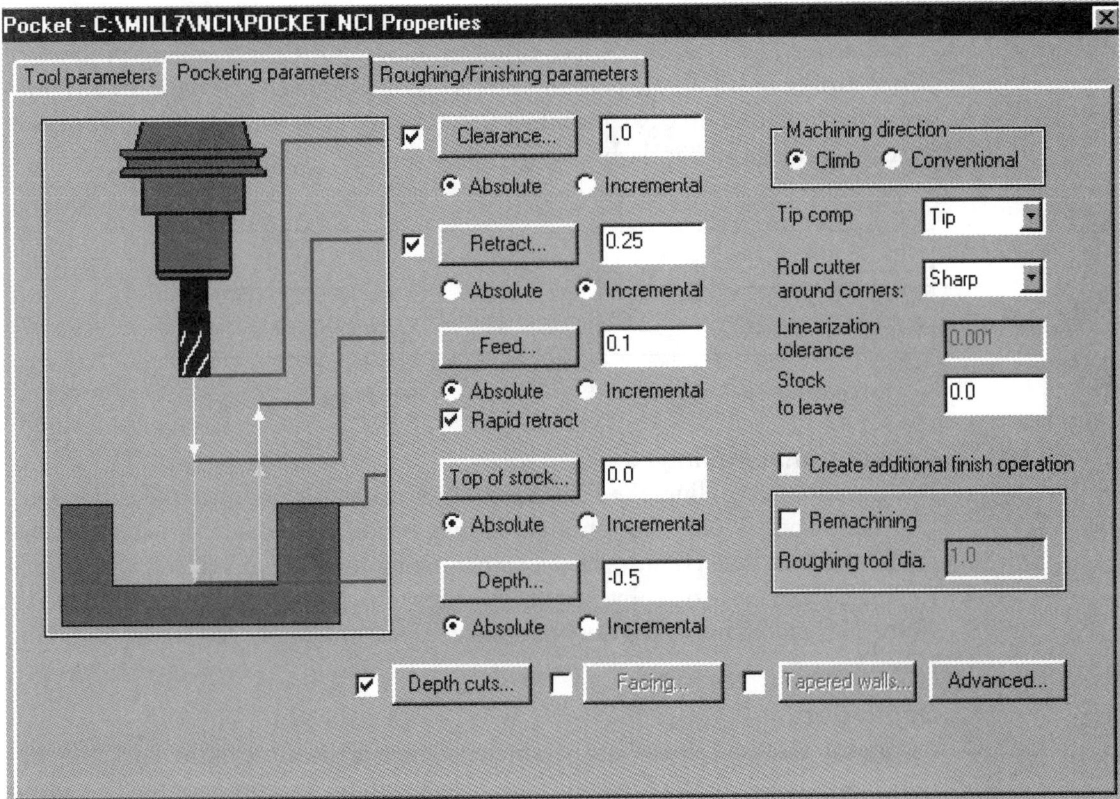

FIGURE 6–56

diameter-offset number corresponds to the tool number and the length-offset number is the tool number with a 1 in front of it.

Your facility will probably have some system set up for offset numbers. You also changed the number of flutes to 2. Select **OK** once you have made the tool parameter changes.

Pocketing Parameters

The Pocketing parameters control how the pocket is to be cut. As you can see the Pocketing parameters setting screen looks much like the Contour parameters screen (see Figure 6–56), with some exceptions. Set the parameters to the ones shown in Figure 6–56.

Machining Direction

The Machining Direction parameter (see Figure 6–57) sets the cutting direction for the pocketing operation. Numerical control programming always programs the cutter movement direction, not the direction of the machine table.

FIGURE 6–57

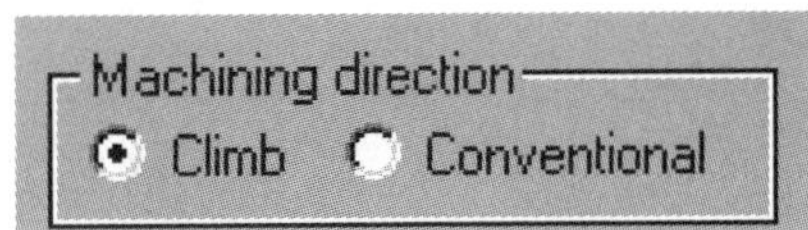

In climb cutting (climb milling) the feed direction is the same as the cutter rotation (see Figure 6–58). Select **Climb** milling now. Climb milling produces a better surface finish on the part and draws less horsepower. It is typically advantageous to climb mill on CNC machines because they have ball screws and you don't have to worry about backlash.

FIGURE 6–58

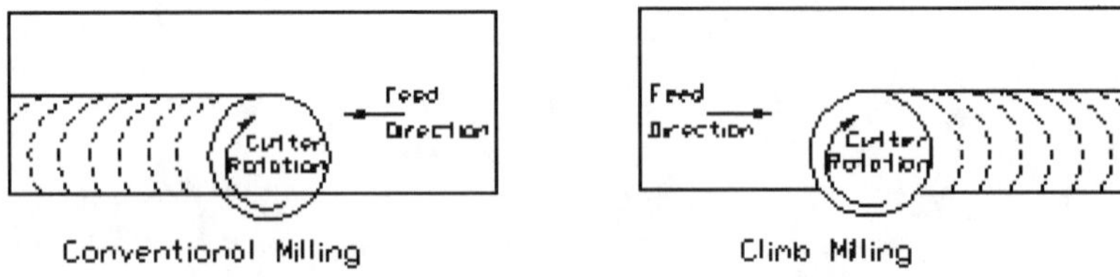

Conventional Milling

In Conventional milling, the feed direction is against or opposite the cutter rotation (see Figure 6–58). Conventional milling produces less side thrust and therefore less cutter deflection, especially when using longer end mills. Conventional milling is done more on conventional machine tools because of the backlash factor. *Note:* The machining direction parameter does not apply to Zigzag roughing passes.

Depth Cuts

As you can see, the Depth Cuts parameters screen is the same in the Pocketing parameters as it is in the Contouring parameters with the exception of the Use Island Depths parameter (see Figure 6–59). Set the Depth Cuts parameters as they are shown in Figure 6–59.

Use Island Depths

A figure inside of a pocket is known as an island (see Figure 6–60). If you set the Use Island Depths parameter, the tool will pass over the island until the system reaches the depth of the island. Since you have no islands the Use Island Depths feature doesn't have to be activated. Once you have finished making these selections, select **OK.**

FIGURE 6–59

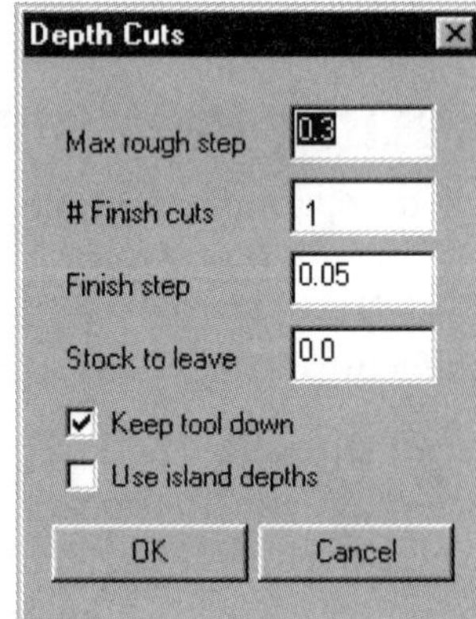

FIGURE 6–60

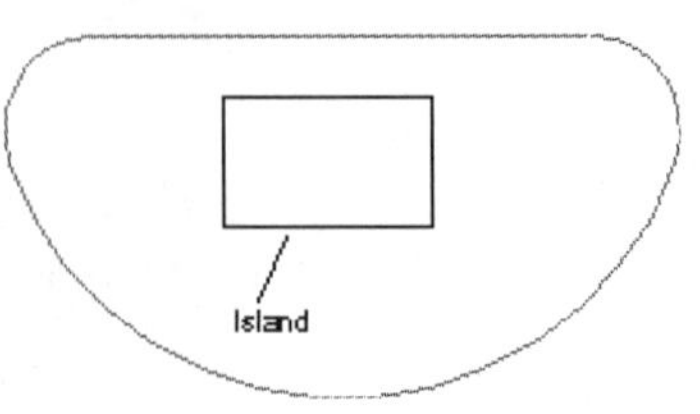

Facing

The Facing function contains options that allow for facing operations. You will not be facing the top of this part, but you will be using this option in the future. Leave this option **off.**

Tapered Walls

The Tapered Walls option allows you to clear a pocket leaving tapered pocket walls or tapered walls on the internal islands. You will not need tapered walls on this particular job. Leave this option **off.**

Advanced

The Advanced parameters are used when you want additional machining operations to be performed, such as secondary, roughing, or additional finishing operations. You have already specified a finishing pass. Leave this option **off.**

Roughing Parameters

Select **Rouging Parameters** from the Pocket properties main screen. Activate the **Rough Toggle** check box in the upper left corner of the screen (see Figure 6–61).

Cutting Method

Mastercam gives you seven different pocket-cutting methods to choose from. Select the **Constant Overlap Spiral** now. The Constant Overlap Spiral creates one roughing cut and then determines the remaining stock to cut. The Constant Overlap Spiral will keep repeating until the pocket is clear.

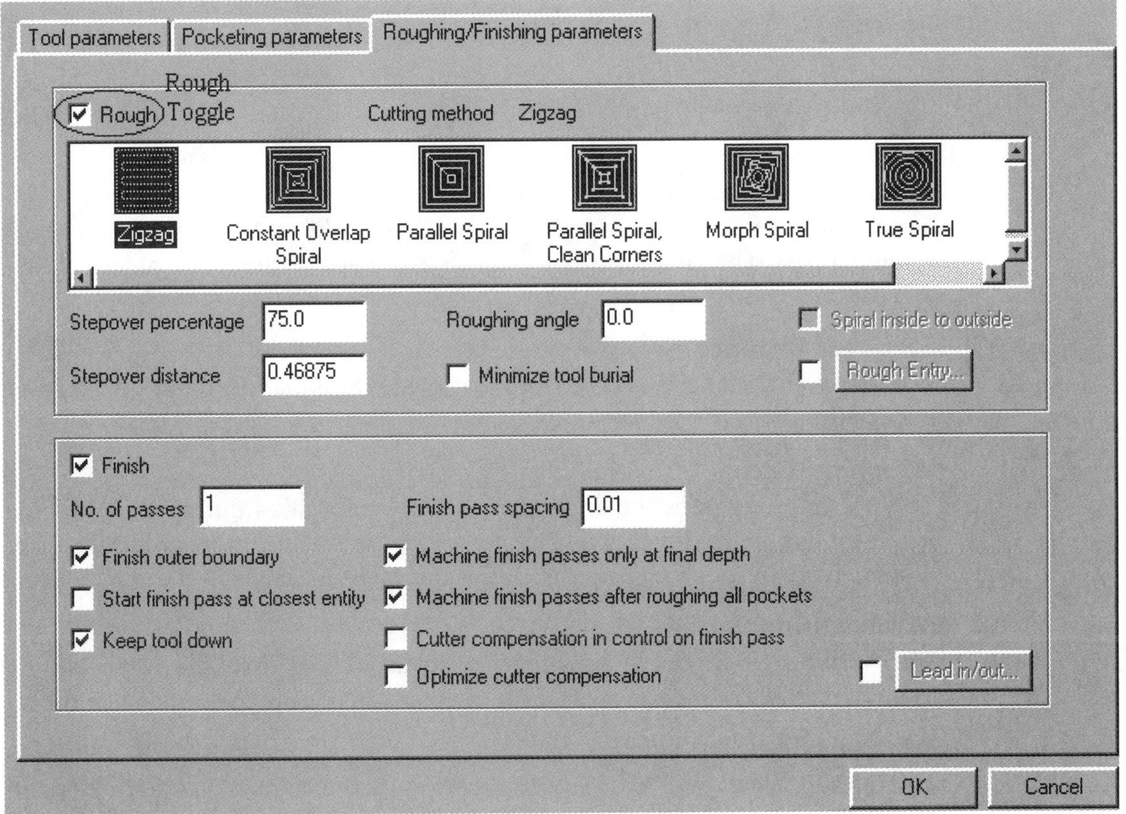

FIGURE 6–61

Zigzag

Zigzag roughs the pocket using line moves.

Parallel Spiral

Parallel Spiral roughs the pocket in a constantly overlapping spiral. This option does not guarantee clean out of the pocket.

Parallel Spiral, Clean Corners

Parallel Spiral, Clean Corners roughs the pocket in same type of constantly overlapping spiral as the Parallel Spiral. This option adds clean-out moves to the corners of the pocket, but still does not guarantee total clean out of the pocket.

Morph Spiral

The Morph Spiral roughs the pocket in a nonuniform spiral pattern. The pattern configuration is based on the island figure residing within the pocket. This option works only with a single island.

True Spiral

The True Spiral generates roughing passes with tangent arc moves. This type of pocket roughing pattern creates a clean pocket using minimal NC code generation.

One Way

The One Way roughing pattern creates tool path in one direction only. Now that you have established the cutting pattern, you must now check the other roughing parameters (see Figure 6–62).

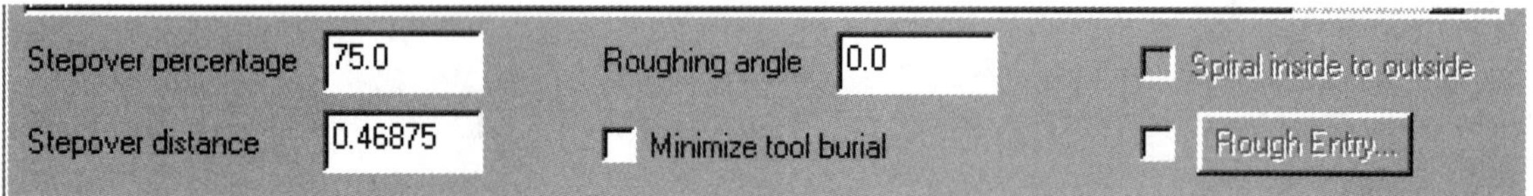

FIGURE 6–62

Stepover Percentage

The Stepover Percentage parameter sets the distance the tool moves over after each roughing pass. The amount is based on a percentage of the tool diameter. Leave this parameter at **75 percent.**

Stepover Distance

The Stepover Distance is a direct product of the tool diameter and the stepover percentage.

Roughing Angle

The Roughing Angle is the angle that the tool path takes during the roughing passes for one-way and zigzag tool paths (see Figure 6–63). You are not using either of these types of roughing patterns, so this option is not available.

Minimize Tool Burial

The Minimize Tool Burial option helps to avoid tool breakage when cutting around islands. This option is especially helpful when using small-diameter tools.

Spiral Inside to Outside

This option allows you to pick where you want the spiral-roughing pattern to begin. The default spiral pattern starts on the wall and moves toward the center. Leave this option blank.

FIGURE 6–63

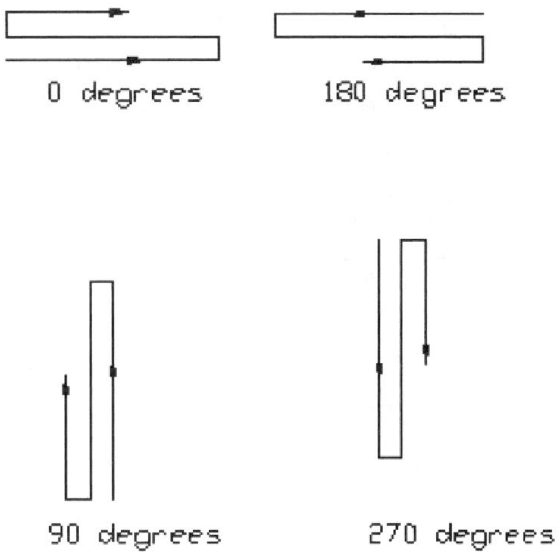

0 degrees 180 degrees

90 degrees 270 degrees

Rough Entry

The Rough Entry dialogue box allows you to add a helix or ramp entry move to the roughing tool path (see Figure 6–64). One or the other can be used, not both.

Even though you are not going to use the Rough Entry option, let's still explore the parameter settings. Select the **Rough Entry** check box. The Rough Entry button now becomes active. Select the **Rough Entry** button. The Rough Entry dialogue box should now appear on the screen (see Figure 6–65).

FIGURE 6–64

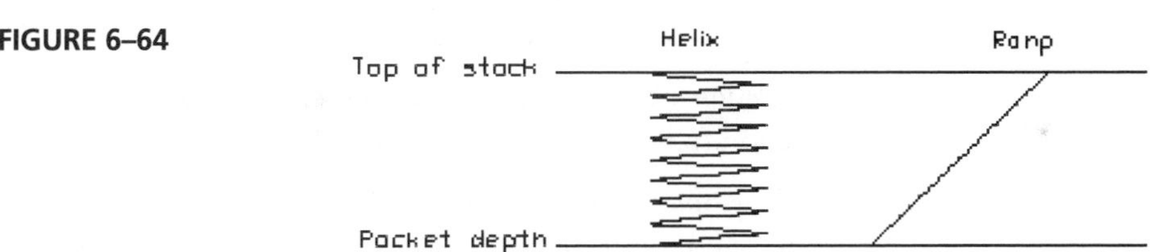

FIGURE 6–65

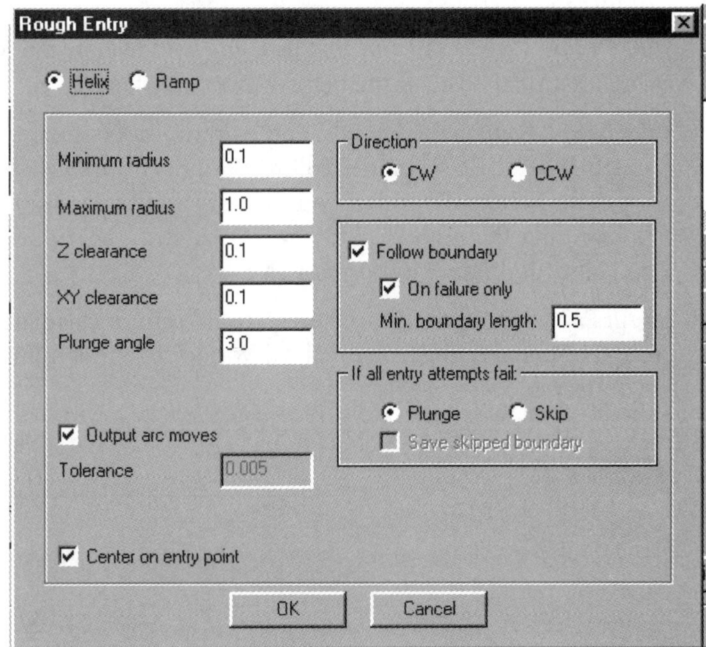

The series of parameter settings that are appearing on the screen are specific to either helix or ramp. If the Helix option is already activated, activate the Ramp option. Look at how the questions change for each of the options. Let's start with the explanation of the helix rough entry.

Helix Rough Entry

Minimum Radius This parameter sets the minimum radius of the entry helix.

Maximum Radius This parameter sets the maximum radius of the entry helix.

Z Clearance The Z Clearance is the Z-axis distance above the top of the stock where you want the helix rough plunge cut to begin.

XY Clearance The X- and Y-axis clearance sets a minimum distance between the helix rough plunge tool path and the wall of the pocket.

Plunge Angle The Plunge Angle sets the speed of the plunge helix. The greater the angle the greater the plunge distance per helix rotation (see Figure 6–66). In the figure you have a 20-degree plunge angle for clarity. This is a very aggressive angle. A typical plunge angle is 3 to 5 degrees.

Output Arc Moves The Output Arc moves option tells Mastercam to code the helix plunge tool path as arc moves instead of short linear moves. If you leave this option off, the NCI file can become quite long.

Tolerance The Tolerance parameter tells the control how exact the helix has to be. The smaller the tolerance, the longer the NCI file.

Center on Entry Point This option tells Mastercam to find the first chained point in the pocket geometry and center the plunge helix on this point.

Direction The Direction setting tells the control whether you want the helix direction to be clockwise or counterclockwise.

Follow Boundary The Follow Boundary option tells the control to abort the helix entry and follow the rough boundary if the helix rough entry fails. Helix failure occurs when Mastercam cannot calculate the helix based on the minimum and maximum radius settings.

On Failure Only The On Failure Only option tells the Mastercam to follow the rough boundary only if the helix rough entry fails.

Minimum Boundary Length The Minimum Boundary Length setting tells the control what to do when the Follow Boundary option fails.

The Follow Boundary option will fail if the Rough Boundary setting is shorter than the minimum boundary length. This option becomes active only if the Follow Boundary option is active.

If All Entry Attempts Fail If the software cannot calculate either an entry helix or rough boundary, Mastercam allows you to set either, plunge, skip, or save skipped boundary as a last resort.

FIGURE 6–66

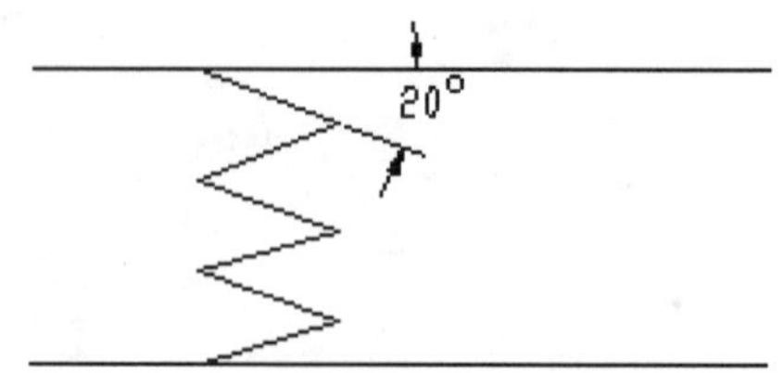

FIGURE 6–67

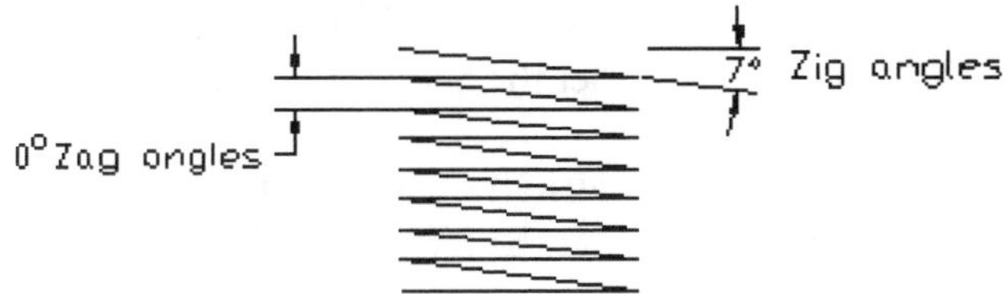

Ramp Rough Entry

Minimum Length This parameter sets the minimum line length of the entry ramp.

Maximum Length This parameter sets the maximum line length of the entry ramp.

Z Clearance The Z Clearance is the Z-axis distance above the top of the stock where you want the ramp plunge cut to begin.

XY Clearance The X- and Y-axis clearance sets a minimum distance between the ramp rough plunge tool path and the wall of the pocket.

Plunge Zig Angle The Plunge Zig Angle sets the entry plunge angle (see Figure 6–67).

Plunge Zag Angle The Plunge Zag Angle sets the last plunge angle (see Figure 6–67).

Auto Angle The Auto Angle lets the system automatically set ramp angle.

XY Angle The XY Angle setting allows you to set the plunge angle. If the Auto Angle is set, you cannot manually set the XY Angle.

Additional Slot Width The Additional Slot Width setting adds a fillet at the end of each ramp move for smooth transitional tool movement.

Direction The Direction setting tells the control which direction you want the fillet to travel when the Additional slot width setting is greater than zero.

If All Entry Attempts Fail If the software cannot calculate an entry ramp, Mastercam allows you to set plunge, skip, or save skipped boundary as a last resort.

Align Ramp with Entry Point This option tells the software to align the entry ramp with the entry point.

Ramp from Entry Point This option allows you to use a point selected in the chaining process as the ramp entry point. Even though you are not going to use the helix or ramp rough entry option, keep these options in mind for future use.

Finishing Parameters The Finishing parameters tell the control how you want to handle the finishing operations for the pocket machining process (see Figure 6–68). Select the **Finish** check box as shown in the upper left corner of Figure 6–68.

☑ Finish
No. of passes 1   Finish pass spacing 0.01
☑ Finish outer boundary   ☐ Machine finish passes only at final depth
☐ Start finish pass at closest entity   ☑ Machine finish passes after roughing all pockets
☐ Keep tool down   ☐ Cutter compensation in control on finish pass
☐ Optimize cutter compensation   ☑ Lead in/out...

FIGURE 6–68

Number of Passes

Set the Number of finish passes to **1.**

Finish Pass Spacing

Set the Finish Pass Spacing to **0.01** of an inch.

Finish Outer Boundary

Turn on the **Finish Outer Boundary** so that the pocket wall receives a finishing pass.

Start Finish Pass at Closest Entity

If you turn this option on, the finish pass will start from the point of the last roughing move. Leave this option **Off.** The finish pass will now start in the order that the boundary entities were selected in the chaining operation.

Keep Tool Down

Turn this option **On** to keep the tool down between finish passes.

Machine Finish Passes Only at Final Depth

This option is used when you have pockets with different depths. If you turn this option on, the system will perform the finish passes at the final cutting depth only. You can leave this option **Off.**

Machine Finish Passes After Roughing All Pockets

This option is used when you have multiple pocket regions. If you turn this option on, the system will rough all of the regions in the pocket before it starts the finishing operations. You can leave this option Off.

Cutter Compensation in Control on Finish Pass

If you use Cutter Compensation in Control on Finish Pass, the system will generate a cutter compensation code in the NCI file. Turning this on will allow you to compensate at the machine tool for cutter wear or tool deflection. In most cases you would want to use this option, but for clarity, later on in this unit, leave this option **Off.**

Optimize Cutter Compensation

If you had turned on the Cutter Compensation in Control on Finish Pass, Optimize Cutter Compensation would have eliminated the arcs in the tool path that are less than or equal to the radius of the tool. Doing this will help prevent tool gouging.

Lead In/Out

Select the **Lead In/Out** check box to add lead in or lead out ramp moves to the pocket tool path. The Lead In/Out parameter dialogue box should now appear on the screen (see Figure 6–69).

The Lead In/Out setting for pocketing is the same as it was for contouring. Set the parameters as they are shown in Figure 6–69. If you have any questions about the settings, go back to the Lead In/Out explanation in the Contour section of this chapter.

Once you have made the settings, select **OK.** The tool path should now be on the graphics screen. Use the **Gview** option in the secondary menu to change the view to Isometric. Use the **Fit** icon from the tool bar to size the screen to the part.

FIGURE 6–69

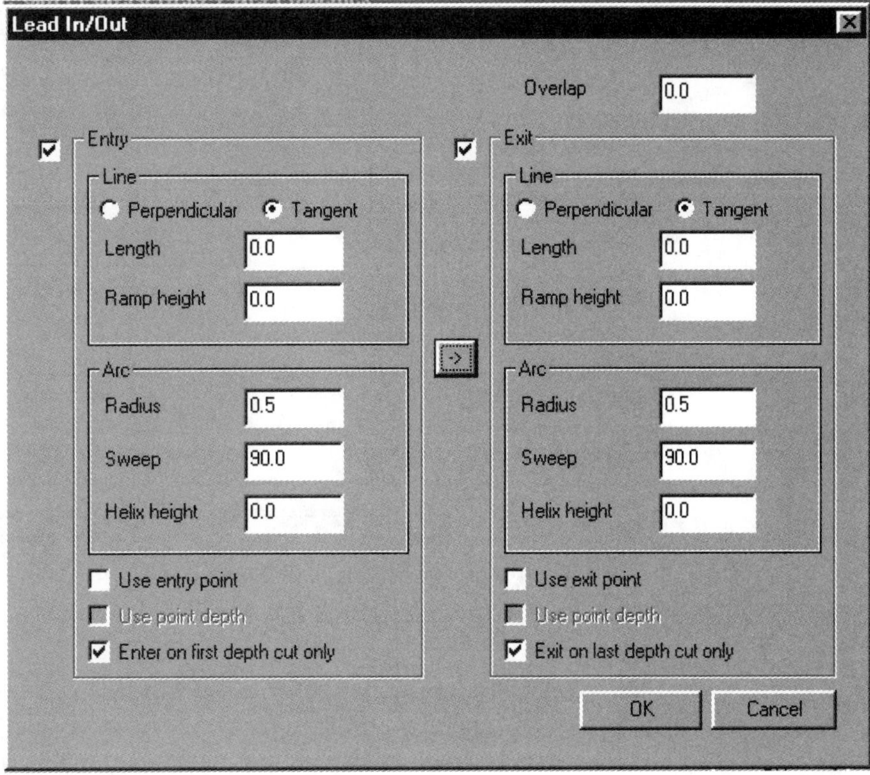

FIGURE 6–70

Main Menu:	Toolpaths:
Analyze	New
Create	Contour
File	Drill
Modify	Pocket
Xform	Surface
Delete	Multiaxis
Screen	Tools
Toolpaths	Operations
NC utils	Job setup
Exit	Next menu
BACKUP	BACKUP
MAIN MENU	MAIN MENU

Operations Manager

Now that the tool path has been generated, you can see a true graphic representation of the machining operations before you postprocess and generate NC code. The operations manager is a very powerful user interface within Mastercam. The operations manager allows you to verify tool path, backplot tool path, and postprocess, regenerate tool paths, and change or move machining parameters. To open the Operations Manager select **Toolpath** from the Main Menu (see Figure 6–70). From the Tool-paths menu select **Operations.**

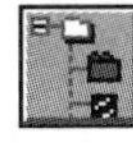

FIGURE 6–71

You can also access the Operations Manager through the Operations Manager icon in the tool bar (see Figure 6–71).

FIGURE 6–72

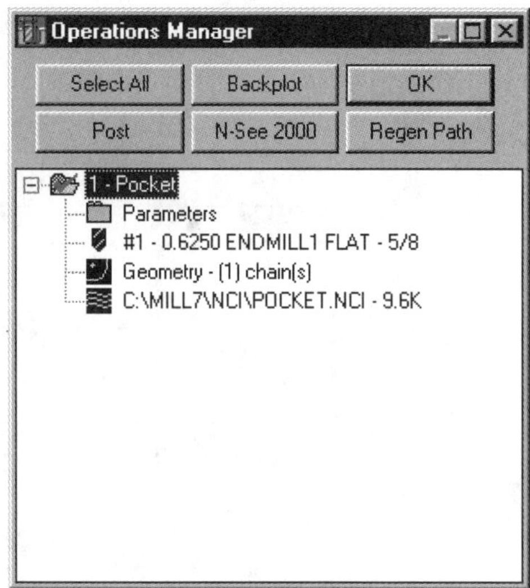

The Operations Manager dialogue box should now appear on the screen (see Figure 6–72).

Select All

The Select All button selects all of the operations listed. An operation is a particular machining operation that resides as part of the overall program. Selected operations are represented by a check mark. If you do not wish to select all of the operations, you can select individual operations by clicking on the file folder in front of the operation name (see Figure 6–73). You have only one operation, so either use the **Select All** button or select the Pocket file folder as shown in Figure 6–73.

FIGURE 6–73

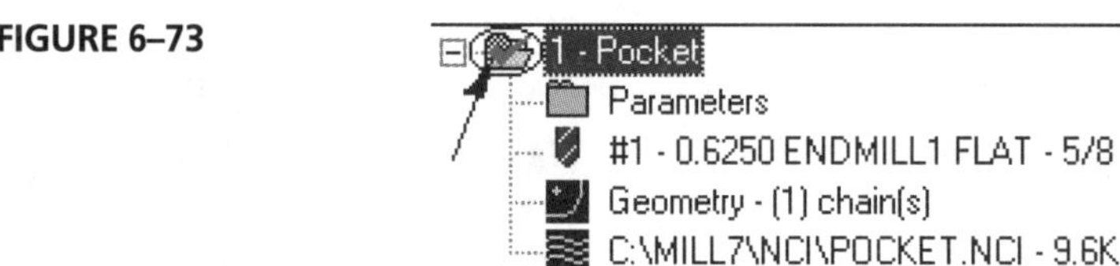

Post

The Post button creates the NCI file from the selected operations. The NCI file is the file that runs the machine tool. You can also access the Post Process menu through the Main Menu/NC Utilities/Post Proc commands. You used these commands when you postprocessed the Contour program earlier in this chapter. You are not through with this program, so you will postprocess this program later.

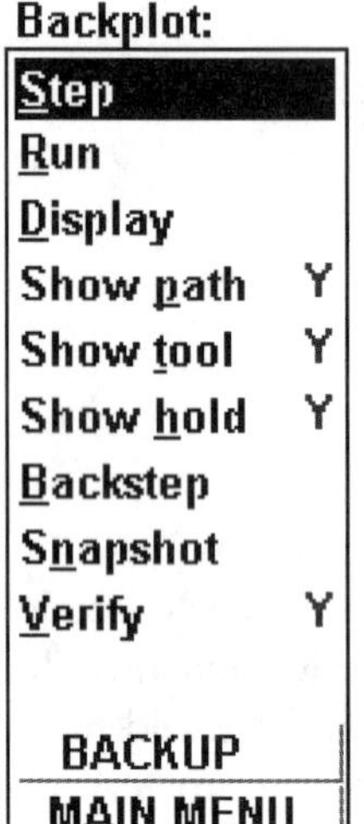

FIGURE 6–74

Backplot

The Backplot function redisplays the tool path, but under your control. Make sure that the Gview is set to **Top.** Select **Backplot** from the Operations dialogue box. The Backplot menu should now appear on the screen (see Figure 6–74).

Step

The Step function allows you to see one step of the tool path at a time. Select the **Step** backplot function now. You will need to continually select the Step function after each step is completed. Keep stepping through the Pocket routine until it is completed.

Run

Once selected, the Run function will continue the tool path until it is completed.

Display

The Display function will allow you to manipulate the tool-path display. Click on the **Display** function now. The Display dialogue box should now appear on the screen (see Figure 6–75).

Mastercam allows you a great deal of control when displaying the tool path. Let's go through the Backplot Display parameters shown in Figure 6–75.

Step Mode

There are two settings within the Step mode: Interpolate and Endpoints.

Interpolate Interpolate shows the tool path in specified step incremental lengths.

Endpoints Endpoints show the tool path at each endpoint.

Tool Motion

There are two setting within the Tool Motion mode: Animated and Static.

Animated In the Animated mode, the tool will give the appearance that it is moving. The tool will disappear when it is moving and reappear when it stops.

Static In the Static mode, the tool will appear at every point in the tool path and the tool will not disappear.

Delay

The Delay function sets how long the tool will be displayed. The Delay function is active only in the Run mode. If the file is a large one, it is best to set the delay time to 0.0.

Simulate Rotary Axis

The Simulate Rotary Axis wraps the geometry around a cylinder to simulate rotary axis machining.

Erase Toolpath in Repaint

This option erases the current plot every time the screen is refreshed.

FIGURE 6–75

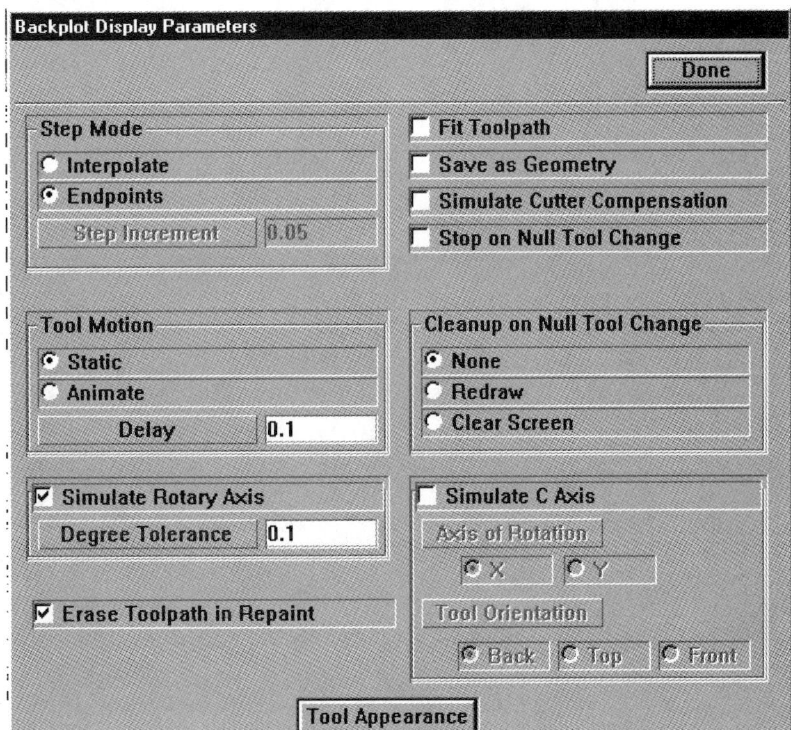

Fit Toolpath

This option fits the entire tool path to the screen. If you use the Fit Toolpath option make sure you disable it before trying to use the Zoom feature.

Save as Geometry

This option converts tool path into geometry.

Simulate Cutter Compensation

This option will simulate cutter compensation when compensation in the control is activated. When the system sees a G41 or a G42 in the NCI file the backplot is shown as if the cutter compensation was on.

Stop on Null Tool Changes

By turning this option on the backplot will stop for all tool changes.

Cleanup on Null Tool Changes

This option tells the control how to refresh the screen during tool changes. The refresh options include None, Redraw, and Clear screen.

Simulate C Axis

This option allows you to simulate a rotary axis tool path.

Tool Appearance

At the bottom of the Backplot Display parameters dialogue box there is a **Tool Appearance** button. Select this button now. The Tool Appearance dialogue box should now appear on the screen (see Figure 6–76).

Show Tool The Show Tool check box will determine whether you want the tool shown in the backplot.

Show Holder The Show Holder check box will determine whether you want the tool holder shown in the backplot.

Tool Appearance The Tool Appearance buttons determine how you want the tool to appear during backplotting. The Tool Appearance options include Plain, Fluted, and Shaded.

Tool Type

The Tool Type option sets the shape of the displayed tool.

Auto The Auto Tool Type setting uses the parameter settings from the Define Tool dialogue box to describe the tool.

FIGURE 6–76

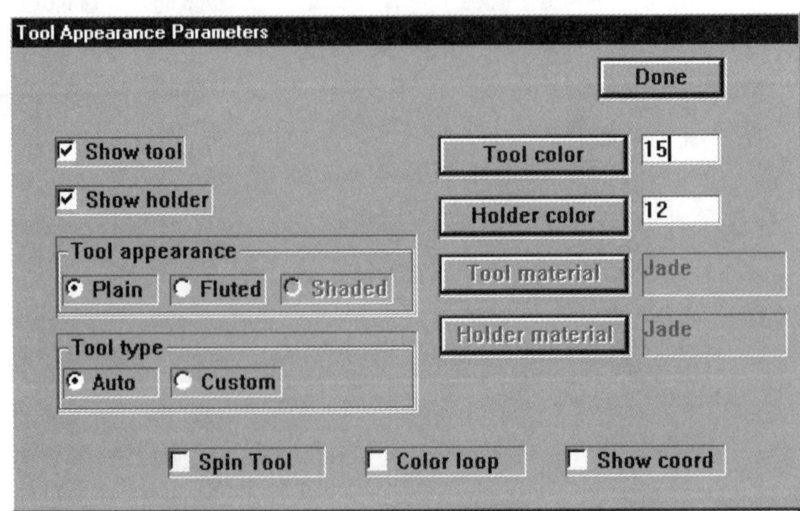

Custom The Custom Tool Type setting uses the parameter settings from a selected MC7 file. You can set the MC7 file in the Define Tool dialogue box to describe the tool.

Tool Color

You can change or specify the tool color by selecting the Tool Color button and picking the tool color from a list of tool colors. If you know the number of a specific color, you can type the number in the text box.

Holder Color

You can change or specify the holder color by selecting the Holder Color button and picking the holder color from a list of holder colors. If you know the number of a specific color, you can type the number in the text box.

Tool Material

To select the tool material color for a shaded tool, select the Tool Material button and select a color from the list of possible options.

Holder Material

To select the holder material color for a shaded holder select the Holder Material button and select a color from the list of possible options.

Spin Tool

This option spins the tool during backplotting. This option cannot be used with a shaded tool.

Color Loop

This option will cycle through a series of 6 colors, one color for each operation.

Show Coord

This option will show the X-, Y-, and Z-axis coordinates of the tool position in the prompt area. *Note:* The coordinates will be visible only during the Run mode.

Show Path

The Show Path option under the Backplot menu sets whether you want to display the tool path in the graphics. To show the tool path, the Show Path toggle should be set to (Y) for yes.

Show Tool

The Show Tool option, under the Backplot menu, sets whether you want to display the tool in the graphics. To show the tool, the Show Tool toggle should be set to (Y) for yes.

Show Holder

The Show-Holder option under the Backplot menu sets whether you want to display the tool holder in the graphics. To show the tool holder, the Show Holder toggle should be set to (Y) for yes.

Backstep

When you have the step mode on for backplotting, the Backstep option takes single steps back through the tool path.

Snapshot

When you have the Step mode on for backplotting, the Snapshot option takes a picture of the tool at each step through the tool path.

FIGURE 6–77

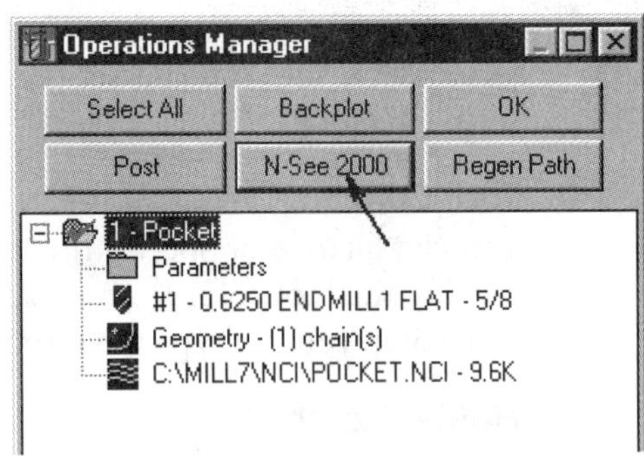

Verify

The Verify option shows you where the tool has been throughout the course of the backplot. Verify will show the programmer if any material has been missed. To show the tool positions, the Verify toggle should be set to (Y) for yes.

N-See 2000

The N-See 2000 function is a solid modeling tool-path verification utility (see Figure 6–77). The N-See 2000 verification tool allows the programmer to thoroughly inspect the NCI file for errors before sending the program to the shop floor. Select **N-See 2000** from the Operations Manager mode now.

N-See 2000 allows you to select three verification modes (see Figure 6–78): Preview, Turbo, and Verify.

Preview The preview mode provides tool animation for the selected NCI file. The tool and tool-path are both evident, but the preview has limited part inspection and machining time capabilities.

Turbo Turbo is the fastest type of verification. Turbo does not show tool any tool animation. The Turbo mode shows only the finished part and lists any errors that may have occurred during the verification process.

Verify The Verify mode creates very accurate results, but does not show tool animation. *Note:* Verify does not come with all systems.

Scan NCI File to Determine Stock Size

This option looks at the current NCI file to determine the stock size. This option looks at the X-, Y-, and Z-axis extents of the tool path and automatically changes the stock lengths in the Job Setup file.

FIGURE 6–78

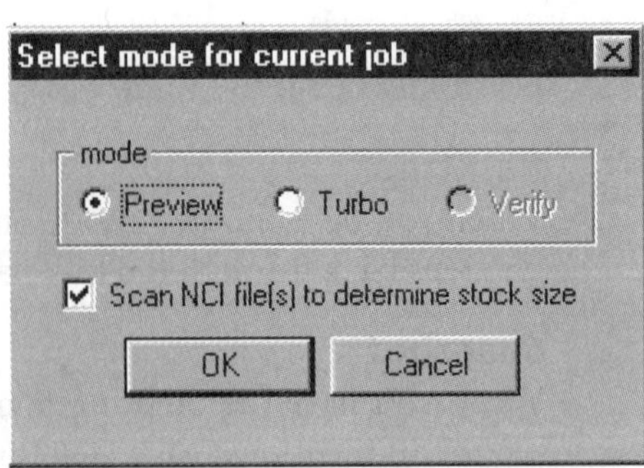

Before you demonstrate the N-See 2000 verification mode, let's make sure that you have set the view and done the job setup properly. **Cancel** the N-See 2000 mode and go back to the Main Menu/Toolpaths menu. Set the View, in the secondary menu, to **Isometric.** From the Toolpaths menu, select Job Setup. The Job Setup function should now appear on the screen. From the Job Setup parameters, pick the **Select Stock Corners** button. The graphics screen will now appear on the screen. Use the mouse to pick the lower left corner of the stock. Next pick the upper right corner of the stock. Input the Z-axis stock thickness of **2.0** inches. Select **OK** to accept these changes. Open the Operations Manager by selecting the **Operations Manager** tool bar icon (see Figure 6–79).

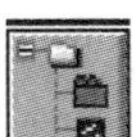

FIGURE 6–79

Select **N-See 2000** from the Operations Manager mode. Set the mode for the current job as shown in Figure 6–80.

You don't want to scan the NCI file to determine stock size because our job setup settings would change.

Select **OK.** The N-See 2000 solid modeling screen should now appear on the screen. Notice the two control boxes in the graphics area (see Figure 6–81).

FIGURE 6–80

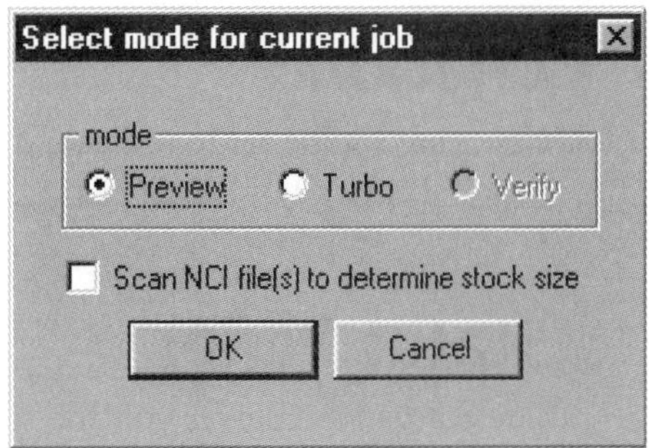

FIGURE 6–81

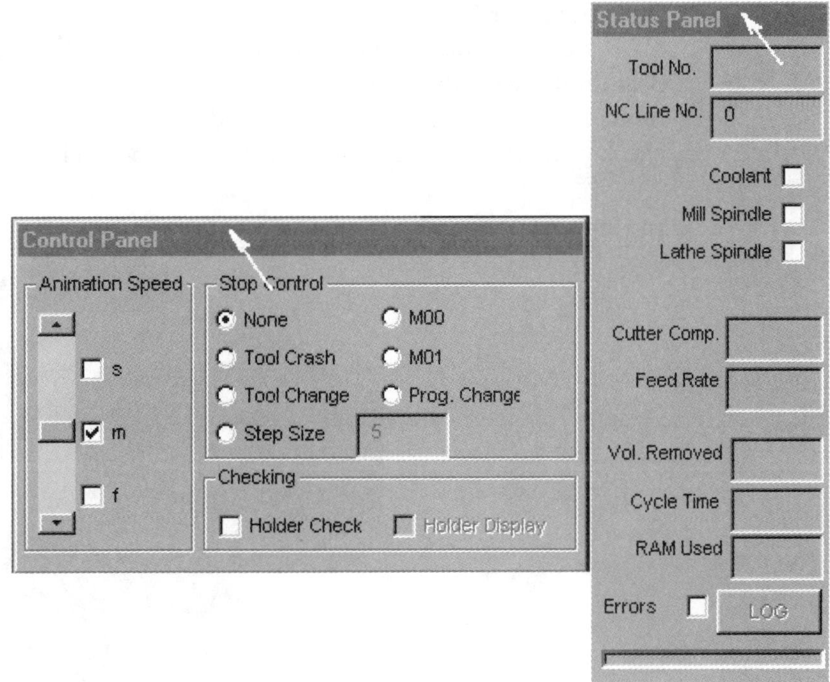

CONTROL PANEL

The Control Panel allows the viewer total control over the solid modeling verification. To move the Control Panels out of the viewing area, use the mouse to pick in the Title area (see Figure 6–81), hold the left mouse button down, and drag the panel out of the way.

Animation Speed

Set the Animation Speed to medium by selecting the **M** box as shown in Figure 6–81. You can also use the sliding button to more closely control the animation speed.

Stop Control

The Stop control can be set to indicate to the viewer if a crash, optional stop, or tool change has occurred. Set the Stop control to **None.**

Checking

Checking can be set to indicate if the tool holder becomes a problem during verification. Leave all of the Checking options **Off.**

Status Panel

The Status Panel gives you the status of the operations as they occur and a log of errors that have occurred during verification. There are no settings to be made on the Status Panel.

FIGURE 6–82

To run the N-See 2000 solid model verification, select **Do It** form the N-See 2000 menu (see Figure 6–82).

You should have been able to verify the tool path and the part should now appear on the screen (see Figure 6–83). As you can see, the N-See 2000 verification mode is very dynamic. If the solid model verification did not occur, go back and check your setting. To leave the N-See 2000 mode, select **Exit** from the menu area.

FIGURE 6–83

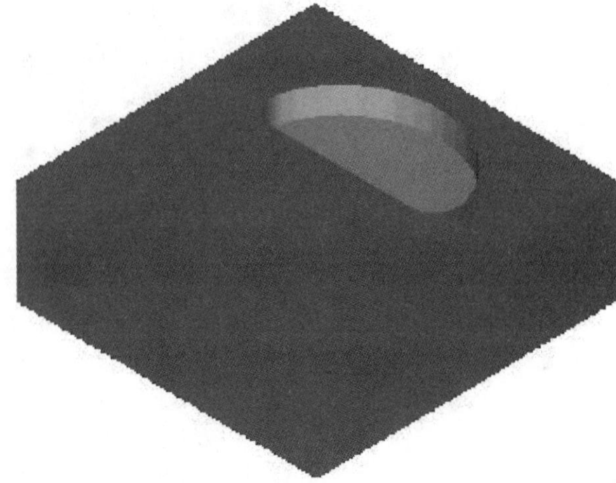

FIGURE 6–84

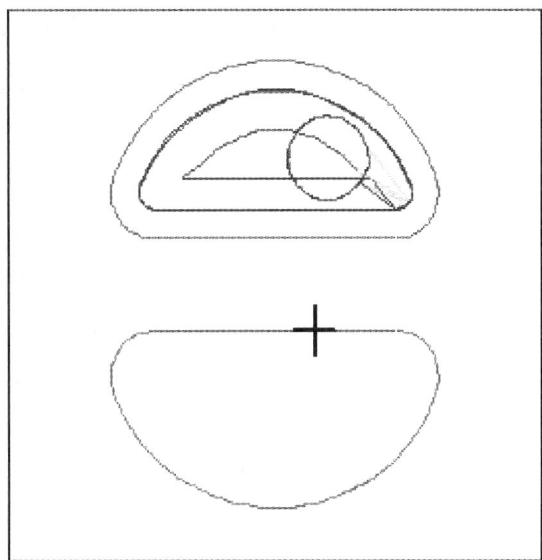

Regen Path

The Regen Path in the Operations Manager mode regenerates the tool path of the selected operations. It is typically used after changes have been made to the operations. To exit the Operations Manager select **OK.** You now need to finish programming the part. Change the Gview back to **Top.** Select **Pocket** from the Toolpaths menu.

Mastercam, in the dialogue box, is now prompting you to select Chain. Use the mouse to select the entity shown in Figure 6–84. Once you have selected the horizontal line, the entire figure should become a different color and an arrow should appear. Now select **Done** from the pocket menu. After selecting Done, the Mastercam software automatically pulls up the Tool parameters. The tool and all of the parameters will be the same for the second pocket as it was for the first. Select **OK** to accept all of the parameters associated with the first pocket. The new tool path should appear on the screen.

EDITING OPERATIONS IN THE OPERATIONS MANAGER

The Operations Manager gives you the ability to sort, move, or change any of the operations associated with the part. Open the Operations Manager using the **Operations Manager** icon in the tool bar. The Operations Manager dialogue box should now appear on the screen (see Figure 6–85).

The new pocket operation should now be visible in the Operations Manager operations list. The Operations Manager dialogue box is where you will make any necessary changes to the operations.

Use the mouse to select the **parameters folder associated with pocket number 2** (see Figure 6–85). Notice how the Contour properties dialogue box appears, allowing you to make any changes. Open the **Roughing/Finishing** parameters folder. Change the Rough cutting method to **Parallel Spiral.** Select **OK** to accept the change you just made. Now select **Regen Path** to show the new tool path. Notice that only the 2-Pocket folder has a check mark, so that was the only operation that had the tool path regenerated. To regenerate both pockets, choose the **Select All** button.

FIGURE 6–85

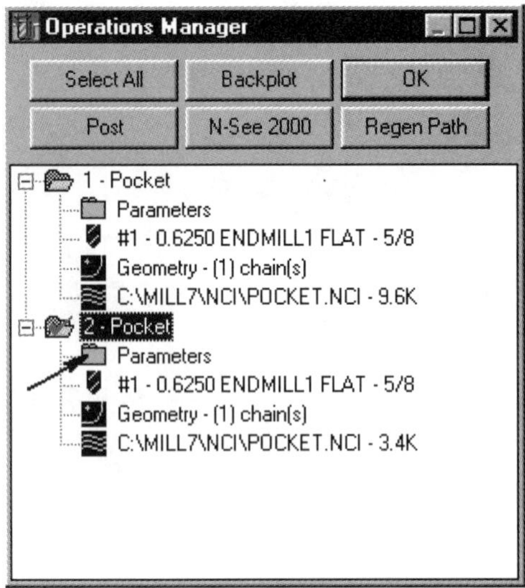

Now you will move all of the operations associated with the first pocket down to the bottom of the operations list. Use the mouse to pick the file folder associated with the first pocket (see Figure 6–86). While holding the left mouse button down, drag the file folder down and place it on top of the **2-Pocket** file folder (see Figure 6–87).

You have now changed the machining operation so that the bottom pocket gets machined first. Make sure both operations are selected before verifying the changes. Select **N-See 2000** to verify the changes. From the N-See 2000 menu select **Do It.** You will notice that the operations have been reversed, but something appears to be wrong with the machining of the lower pocket. Select Main Menu to **Exit N-See 2000.** One of the parameters that does not carry over into tool operations is the Depth in the Pocket parameters (see Figure 6–88).

Make the change in the depth to **−.500.** Select **OK** to accept the changes. Run the program through N-See 2000 to verify the changes. If everything looks correct it is time to postprocess.

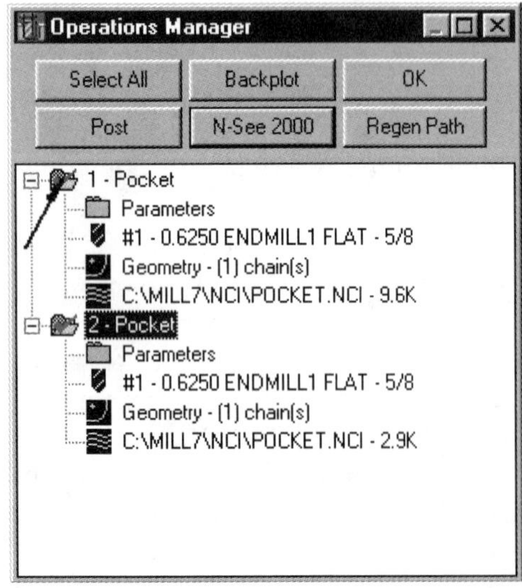

FIGURE 6–86

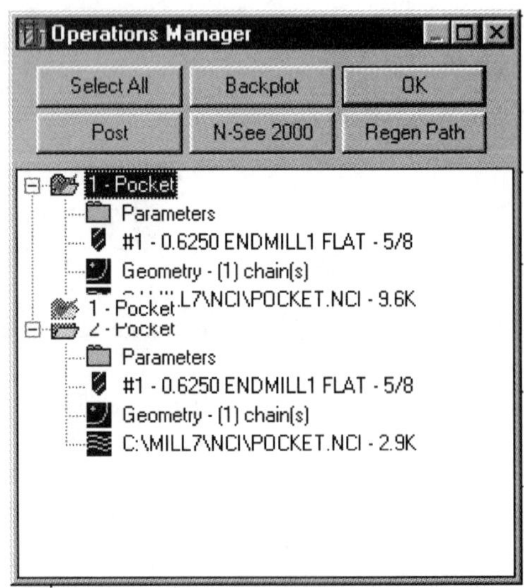

FIGURE 6–87

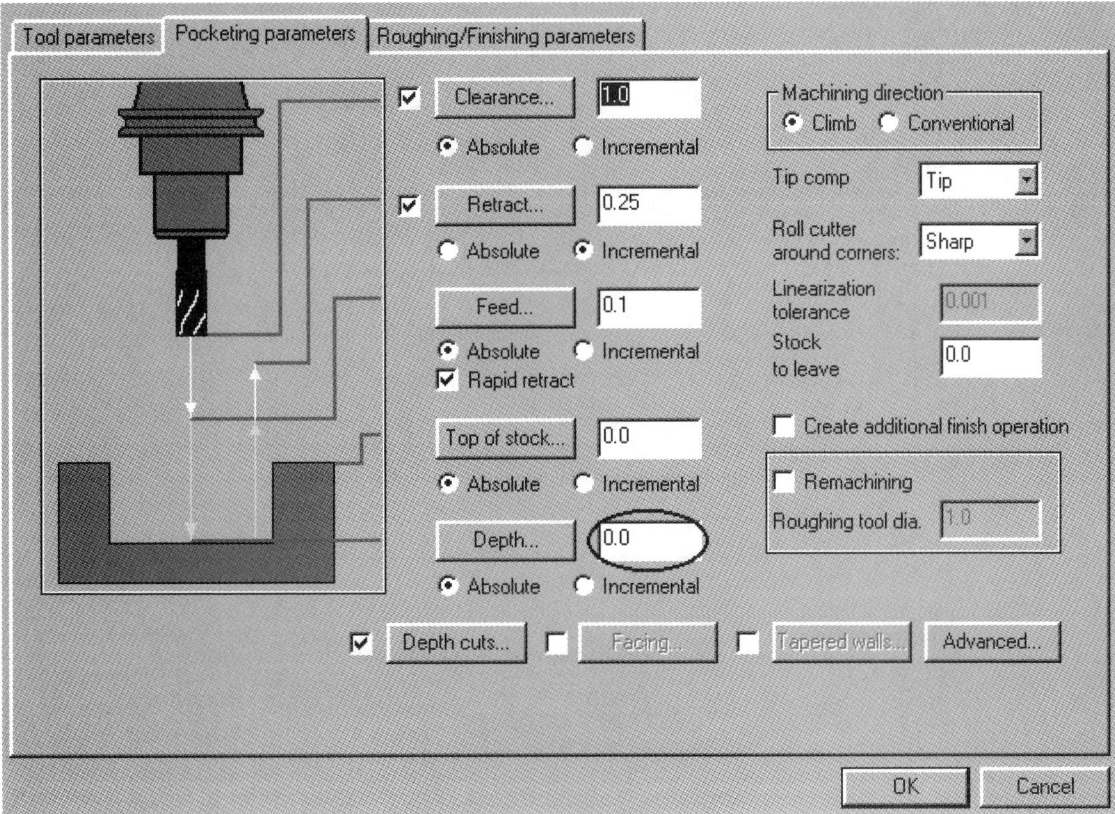

FIGURE 6–88

Post

From the Operations Manager click on the **Select All** button. From the Operations Manager, click on the **Post** button. Select **Yes** when asked if you want to run the postprocessor. Save the NC file as Pocket.

You have now completed the second exercise on pocket machining and will move on to the next exercise, dealing with the Drill module. Pay close attention because you will be receiving some new information as you go along.

DRILLING EXAMPLE EXERCISE

The Drill module is used to create tool paths for drilling, boring, and tapping. You are going to use the Drill module to generate a tool path to drill the holes in the part shown in Figure 6–89. You will use Mastercam Mill to create the part geometry. Remember that you can create the drill hole geometry as circles or just center points. Once you have turned on your computer and allowed the system to boot up click the **Start** button using the left mouse button, and then point to the folder called Mastercam. Click on the **Mastercam Mill** option. Once you are in the Mastercam Main Menu area, select File/ New to start a new file. Choose **Yes** to initialize geometry and operations. As you can see the Mastercam Mill module looks identical to the Geometry creation module. Geometry creation in Mastercam Mill is virtually identical to the Design module in Mastercam. Using your skills from the

FIGURE 6–89

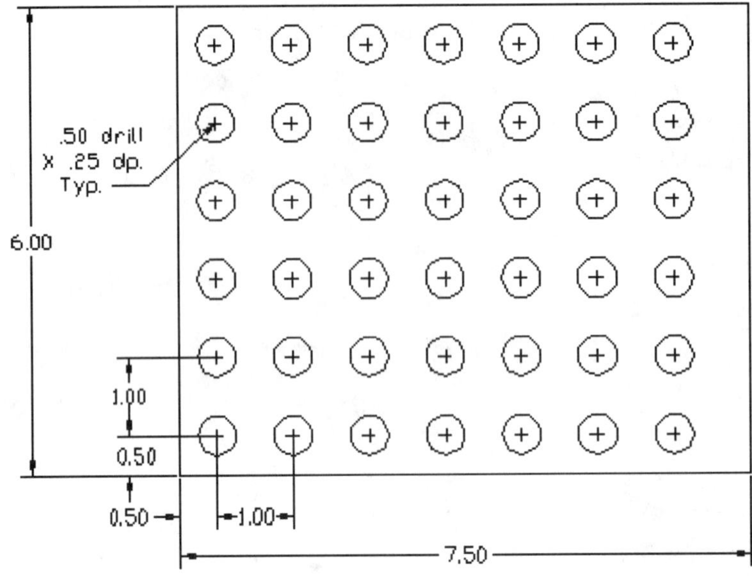

FIGURE 6–90

Main Menu:	Create:	Point:
Analyze	Point	Position
Create	Line	Along ent
File	Arc	Node pts
Modify	Fillet	Cpts NURBS
Xform	Spline	Dynamic
Delete	Curve	Length
Screen	Surface	Slice
Toolpaths	Rectangle	Srf project
NC utils	Drafting	Grid
Exit	Next menu	Bolt circle
BACKUP	BACKUP	BACKUP
MAIN MENU	MAIN MENU	MAIN MENU

geometry creation chapters create the geometry for the top view of Figure 6–89. *Hint:* Use the Points/Grid operation from the Create menu (see Figure 6–90).

Now that you have created the necessary geometry, let's go through the Job Setup function. From the Main Menu select **Toolpaths** and from the Tool-paths menu select **Job Setup.** Select the stock origin by inputting the stock corners of **0,0** and **7.50, 6.0.** Now enter the Z-axis stock thickness of **1.0** inches. Select **Steel inch 4140** as the material type.

Initiating the Drill Module

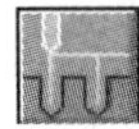

FIGURE 6–91

There are two ways to initiate the Drill module. From the Main Menu you could select **Toolpath/Drill.** You can also access the Drill module through the tool bar. Find the Drill module icon in the tool bar (see Figure 6–91).

From the Toolpaths menu select **Drill** to initiate the Drill module. After initializing the Drill module, Mastercam wants you to name the NCI file that will be output. Enter **Drill** and press **Save.** Once you have named the NCI file, Mastercam

Drill: add points

- Manual
- Automatic
- Entities
- Window pts
- Last
- Mask on arc
- Patterns
- Options
- Done
- BACKUP
- MAIN MENU

FIGURE 6–92

Point Entry:

- Values
- Center
- Endpoint
- Intersec
- Midpoint
- Point
- Last
- Relative
- Quadrant
- Sketch
- BACKUP
- MAIN MENU

FIGURE 6–93

asks you which method you want to use to add drilling points or for selecting points (see Figure 6–92).

Methods of Drill Position Selection

Manual

The Manual method allows you to select points to generate drilling tool path using the Point Entry menu (see Figure 6–93). The manual Point Entry method is used in the same manner as the Point Entry method found in the design module.

Automatic

The Automatic method allows you to select a series of points to generate drilling tool path. The Automatic method of drilling point selection uses three selection points to define an array of drilling locations. The first point defines the first point in the drilling pattern (see Figure 6–94). The second point establishes the direction of tool travel. The last point establishes the final drill hole position.

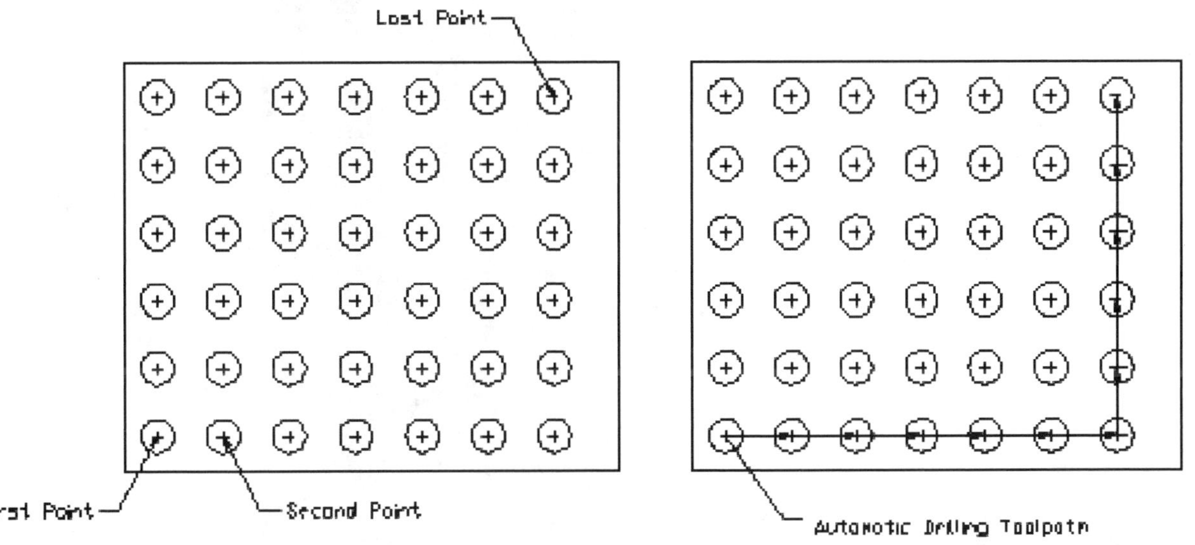

FIGURE 6–94

Entities

The Entities method allows you to select any entity to generate a drilling position. When using the entities method, you can place drilling positions at the end of lines, arcs, and splines or at the center of circles.

Window Pts

This method allows you to create a box around a series of points to create a drilling tool path.

Last

This method uses the last point or points set from the previous drilling operation.

Mask on Arc

This method uses the center points of the arcs in the mask group as the drilling locations. It is possible to specify a certain arc radius to help sort out unwanted hole locations.

Patterns

This method allows you to define drill point locations based on predetermined patterns. The pattern choices include

Grid—creates a rectangular grid of drill points

Bolt circle—creates a circular pattern of drilled holes

Options

The Option function displays the Point Sorting dialogue box (see Figure 6–95). Point sorting gives you the ability to select the drilling sequence. The Entities and Window Pts methods require a drilling sequence selection.

Editing Drill Tool Paths

The Edit option allows you to make changes to the drill tool path. The Edit option becomes active after the drill points have been selected. When you select the Edit option, the Drill Point Manager menu is displayed (see Figure 6–96). The Drill Point Manager is a very easy way to change or customize your drill tool path.

FIGURE 6–95

Drill Point Mana

Delete pts
Edit depth
Rstr depth
Edit jump
Rstr jump
Import ops

Reverse
Done
BACKUP
MAIN MENU

FIGURE 6–96

Drill: add points

Manual
Automatic
Entities
Window pts
Last
Mask on arc
Patterns
Options
Edit
Done
BACKUP
MAIN MENU

FIGURE 6–97

Delete Pts

This option removes selected points.

Edit Depths

This option changes the depth of selected points.

Rstr Depth

This option will delete any changes made using the Edit Depths option.

Edit Jump

This option adds a jump height. A jump height is a height greater than the clearance plane height. Edit Jump is used between selected holes to avoid clamps.

Rstr Jump

This option will delete any changes made using the Edit Jump option.

Import Ops

This option allows you to import drilling parameters from other MC7 files.

Reverse

This option reverses the order of the current drilling tool path.

Drilling the Holes

You will now drill the holes in our plate. Select **Window Pts** from the Drill: Add points menu (see Figure 6–97).

Once you have selected Window Pts, Mastercam prompts you to select the first corner of the window. Use the mouse to select a point outside of the upper left corner of the point grid (see Figure 6–98).

Now drag the window down to the lower right corner of the plate as shown in Figure 6–98. Click the left mouse button to accept this window. The drilling pattern should now appear on the screen. Now select **Options** from the Drill: Add Points menu (see Figure 6–99).

From the Point Sorting dialogue box, select the **Xzig+Y+** (see Figure 6–100) sorting option. Notice that the name of the pattern appears when you hold the mouse cursor over the top of each option.

FIGURE 6–98

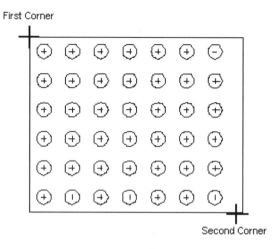

First Corner

Second Corner

FIGURE 6–99

FIGURE 6–100

Select **OK** to accept this sorting method. Now select **Done** from the Drill: Add Points menu. After selecting Done, the Mastercam software automatically pulls up the Tool Parameters/Drill/Counterbore Parameters menu (see Figure 6–101).

The Tool Parameters box is the initial box that appears. The first thing you will need to do is select a tool from the tool library. Place the mouse in the large white space indicated by the arrow in Figure 6–101. Open the tool selection menu by clicking the right mouse button. From the tool selection menu, select **Get Tool from Library.** The Tools Manager should now appear (see Figure 6–102).

Select the **1/2″** drill from the Tools Manager list. Now select **OK.** You can see that the 1/2″ drill has been added to the drill module. Now you need to select the **Drill/Counterbore** folder from the Drill NCI properties screen. Select and input the parameters as they appear in Figure 6–103.

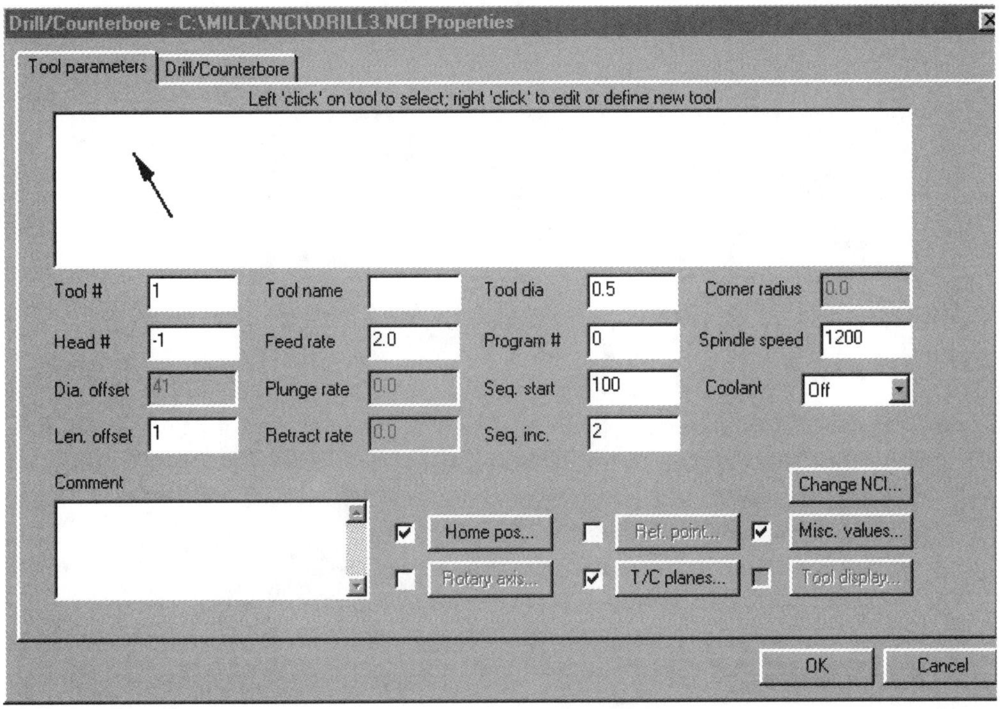

FIGURE 6–101

When you have made these parameter changes, select **OK.** The tool path should now appear in the graphics screen (see Figure 6–104).

Operations Manager

Now that the tool path has been generated, you can see a true graphic representation of the machining operations before you postprocess and generate NC code. The Operations Manager is a very powerful user interface within Mastercam. The Operations Manager allows you to verify tool path, backplot tool path, and post-

FIGURE 6–102

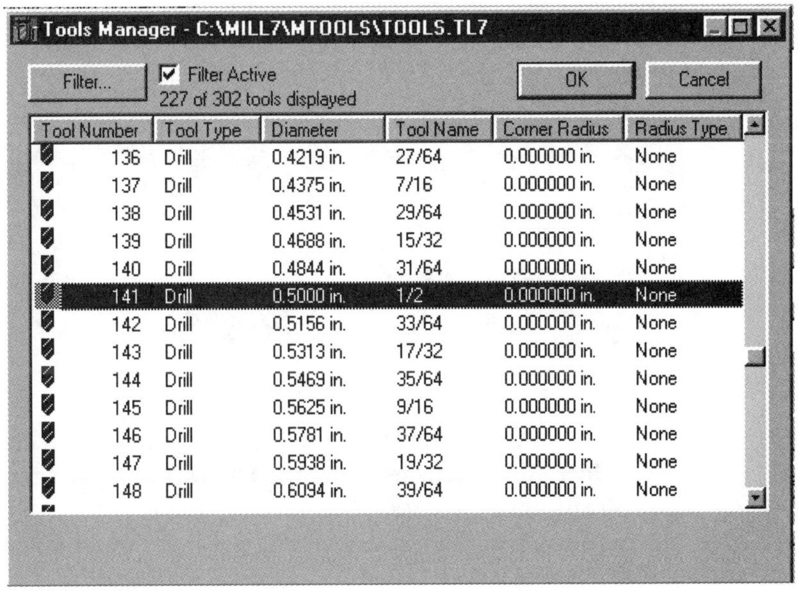

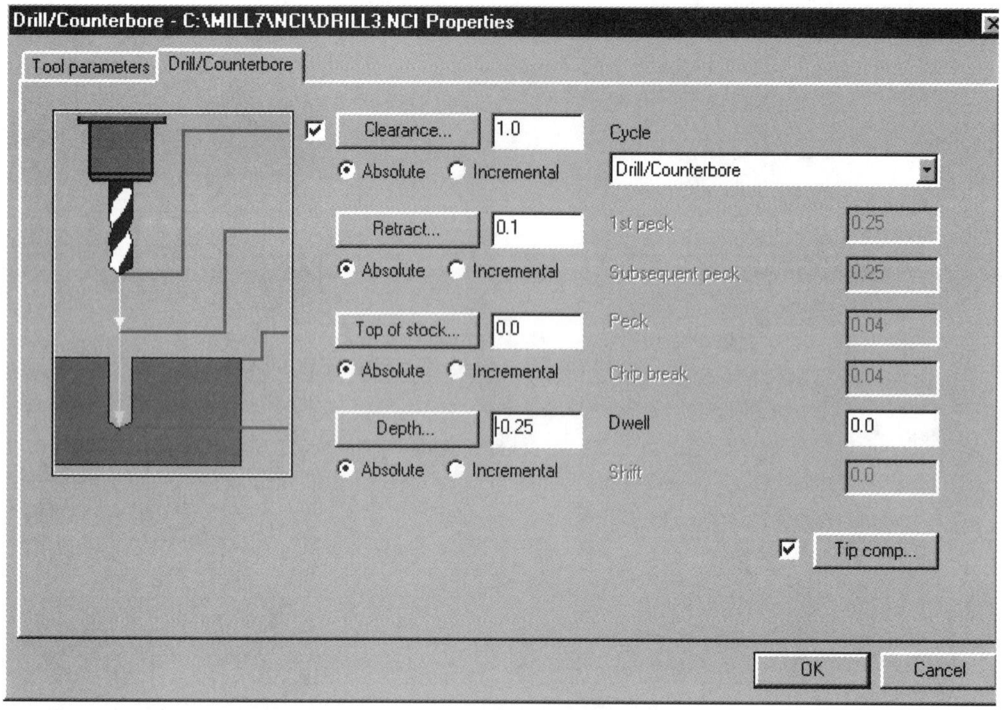

Drill/Counterbore - C:\MILL7\NCI\DRILL3.NCI Properties

Tool parameters | Drill/Counterbore

Clearance... 1.0 — Absolute / Incremental
Retract... 0.1 — Absolute / Incremental
Top of stock... 0.0 — Absolute / Incremental
Depth... -0.25 — Absolute / Incremental

Cycle: Drill/Counterbore
1st peck 0.25
Subsequent peck 0.25
Peck 0.04
Chip break 0.04
Dwell 0.0
Shift 0.0
Tip comp...

OK Cancel

FIGURE 6–103

FIGURE 6–104.

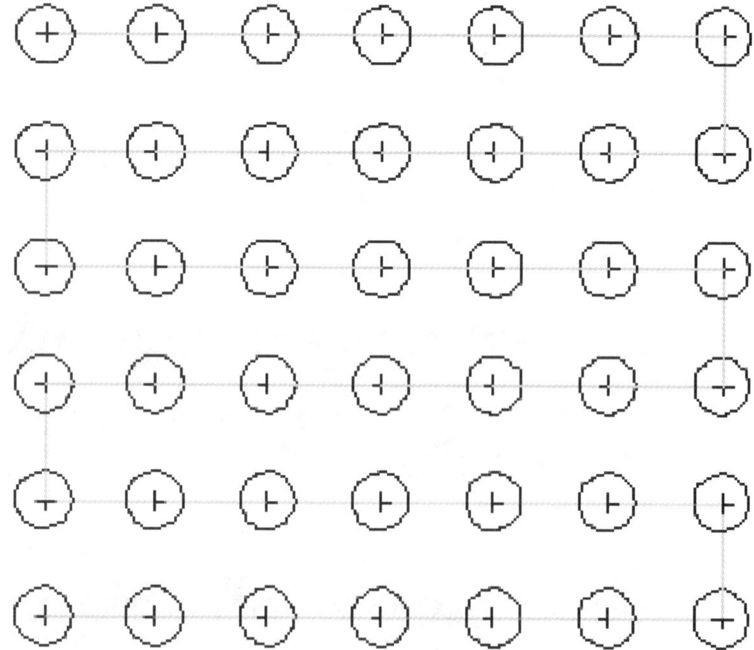

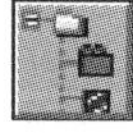

FIGURE 6–105

process, regenerate tool paths and change or move machining parameters. To open the Operations Manager select the **Operations Manager** icon in the tool bar (see Figure 6–105).

The Operations Manager dialogue box should now appear on the screen (see Figure 6–106).

FIGURE 6–106

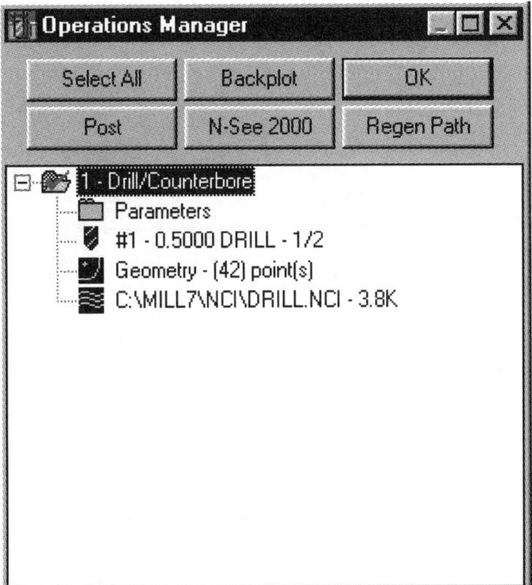

Select All

The Select All button selects all of the operations listed. An operation is a particular machining operation that resides as part of the overall program. Selected operations are represented by a check mark. You have only one operation, so use the **Select All** button or select the **Drill/Counterbore** file folder.

Post

The Post button creates the NCI file from the selected operations. The NCI file is the file that runs the machine tool. Select **Post** now. Answer **Yes** to the question, "Run the post processor?" Name the NC file Drill by typing **Drill.** Select **Save.** Your coded file should now appear on the screen. This is the file that will be downloaded to the machine to make the part.

CIRCLE MILLING EXERCISE

The Circle Mill module is used to automatically create a tool path for cutting a circular feature.

You are going to use the Circmill module to generate a tool path to mill a circular pocket in the part shown in Figure 6–108. You will use Mastercam Mill to create the part geometry. Remember that you can create geometry in any one of the application areas. Once you have turned on your computer and allowed the system to boot up click the **Start** button using the left mouse button, and then point to the folder called **Mastercam**. Click on the **Mastercam Mill** option. Once you are in the Mastercam Main Menu area, select **File/ New** to start a new file. Choose Yes to initialize geometry and operations. As you can see the Mastercam Mill module looks identical to the Geometry creation module. Geometry creation in Mastercam Mill is virtually identical to the Design module in Mastercam. Using your skills from the geometry creation chapters to create the geometry for the front view of Figure 6–107.

Now that you have created the necessary geometry, let's get acquainted with the Circmill module. To access the Circmill tool-path function, from the Main Menu choose **Toolpaths/Next Menu/Circmill.** After initializing this module,

FIGURE 6–107

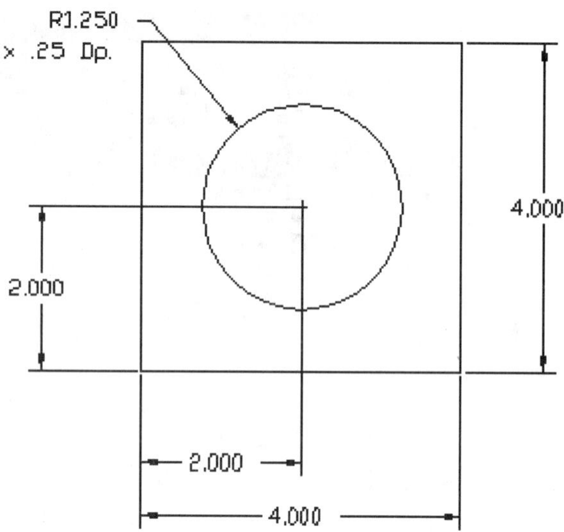

Mastercam wants you to name the NCI file that will be output. In the File name area, type **Circmill.** This will be an easy name to remember. Once you have finished typing, select **Save.** Mastercam, in the dialogue box, is now prompting you to select Chain.

From the Circmill menu, select **Chain.** Now you need to select the entities that make up the circular pocket you want to machine. Use the mouse to select the **1.250** radius. Now select **Done.** The Circmill parameters should now appear on the screen (Figure 6–108).

Entry/Exit Arc Sweep

You can define the tool-path entry and exit sweep for circle milling (see Figure 6–109). Leave the arc sweep at **180** degrees.

Absolute/Incremental

The Absolute/Incremental setting tells the system to assign the depth as either an absolute depth or incremental depth. Click the **Absolute** button.

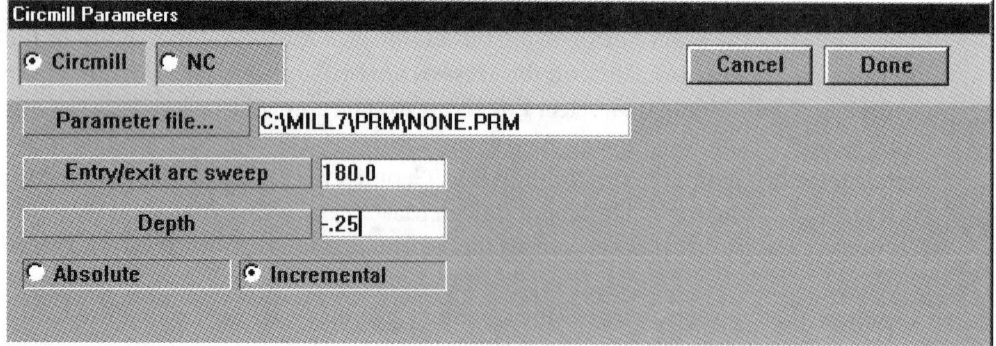

FIGURE 6–108

FIGURE 6–109

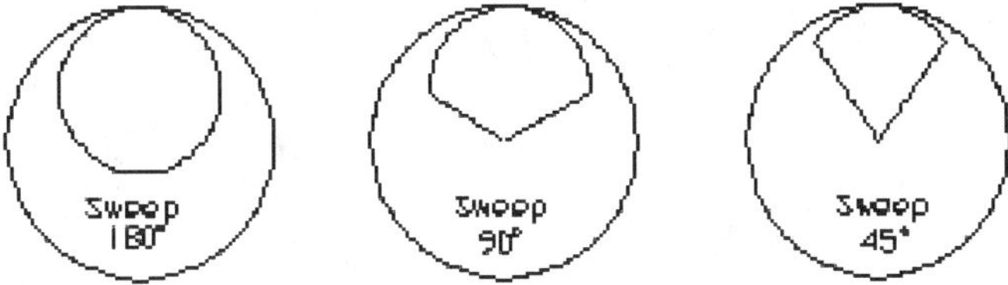

Depth

The Depth parameter sets the depth for the Circmill tool path. In the Depth dialogue box, type **−.250.** Now click the **NC** button to set the NC parameters. The Circmill parameters should now appear on the screen (see Figure 6–110).

Click on the **Tool Ref** button. Place the mouse in the large white space of the Tools Manager screen. Open the Tool Selection menu by clicking the right mouse button. From the Tool Selection menu select **Get Tool from Library.** The Tools Manager should now appear. Select the **1.0-inch** flat endmill. Accept the tool selection by pressing **OK.** At the Tools Manager screen select **OK** again. When the Circmill parameters screen reappears, select **Done.**

Operations Manager

Now that the tool path has been generated, you need to generate NC code. To open the Operations Manager select the **Operations Manager** icon in the tool bar.

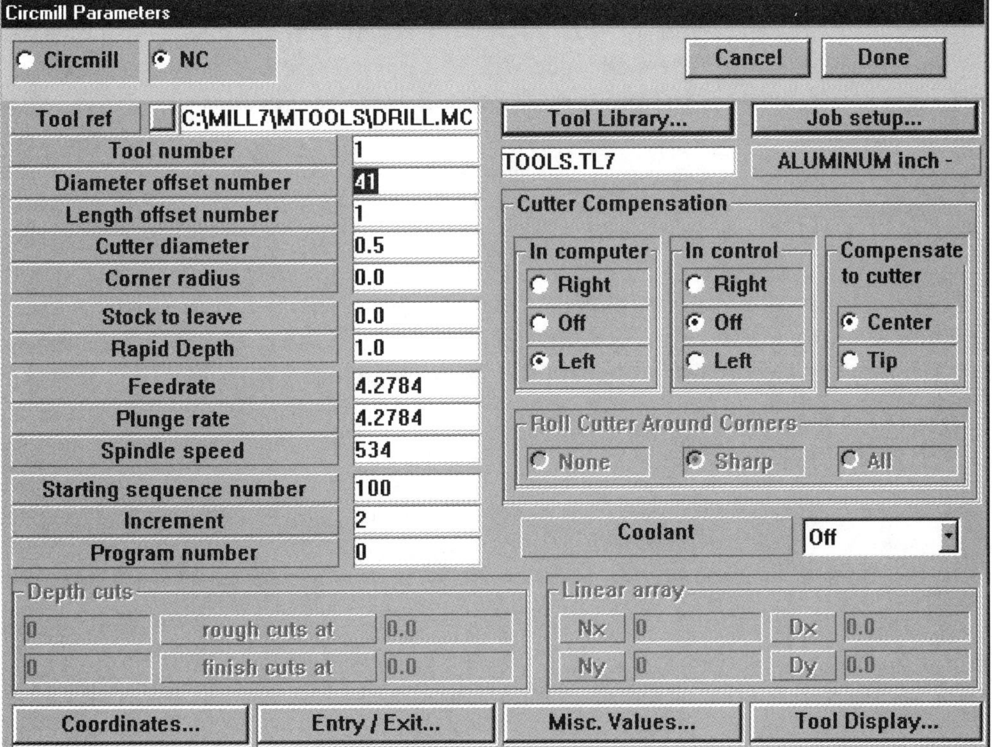

FIGURE 6–110

FIGURE 6–111

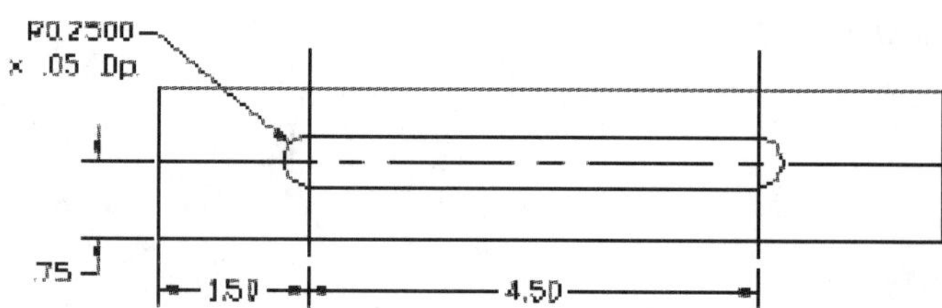

Post

The Post button creates the NCI file from the selected operations. The NCI file is the file that runs the machine tool. You can also access the postprocess menu through the Main Menu/NC Utilities/Post Proc commands. You used these commands when you postprocessed the other programming modules earlier in this chapter. Postprocess the Circmill program you just created.

NC Point Module

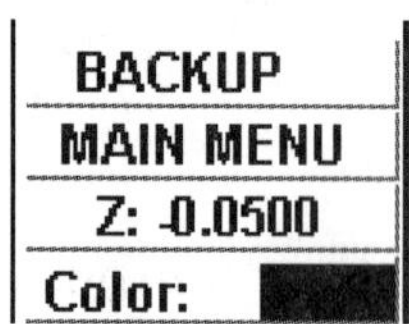

FIGURE 6–112

The NC Point module is used to generate linear tool paths for tool positioning or single-pass machining operations, such as slots or face milling operations. Let's use the NC Point module to cut a single-pass slot in the part shown in Figure 6–111. Using your skills from the geometry creation chapters to create the geometry for the front view of Figure 6–111.

To accomplish cutting the slot to the defined 0.05-inch depth, change the **Z-level** construction depth in the secondary menu to **−.05** (see Figure 6–112).

Now access the NC Point function. From the Main Menu, select **Toolpaths/Next Menu/Point.** After selecting Point, the system prompts you to name the NCI file. Type **Point** and press **Save.** The system may automatically dump you into the Point parameters dialogue area. If it doesn't dump you into the Point parameters dialogue area, from the NC Point menu select **Params.**

Params

You can choose parameters at any stage of tool-path generation and the system will display the Point parameters dialogue box. The Point parameters screen should now appear on the screen. Click on the **Tool Ref** button. Place the mouse in the large white space of the Tools Manager screen. Open the Tool Selection menu by clicking the right mouse button. From the Tool Selection menu select **Get Tool from Library.** The Tools Manager should now appear. Select the **.50 inch** flat endmill. Accept the tool selection by pressing **OK.** At the Tools Manager screen select **OK** again. When the Point parameters screen reappears, select **Done.**

Now select **Go to XY** from the NC Point menu. The Go to XY option instructs the tool to move to the XY coordinates of the point that you select. If the tool is already down, the tool moves at the feed rate; if the tool is up, the tool positions at the rapid feed rate. The system displays the tool location at the bottom of the screen. Choose **Center** from the Point Entry menu. Use the mouse to select the left arc to position the tool to the center of the arc. Now press the **Esc** (escape) key to move back to the NC Point menu. Next select **Tool Down.** The Tool Down command instructs the tool to move down to the rapid depth plane as set in the Point Parameters and then feed down to the construction plane depth. Now select **Go to XY** from the NC Point menu. Now choose **Center** from the Point Entry menu. Use the mouse to select the right arc to feed the tool to the end of the slot. Now press the **Esc** (escape) key to move back to the NC Point menu.

Next select **Tool Up.** This option instructs the system to move the tool up to the rapid depth at the plunge rate as set in the Point parameters. You have finished the slot, so select **Done** from the NC Point menu.

Now that the tool path has been generated, you need to generate NC code. To open the Operations Manager select the **Operations Manager** icon in the tool bar. Postprocess the NC Point program that you have just created.

For doing face milling operations you don't need to have existing geometry. Just input the positions you want directly from the Point Entry position menu.

Use the examples that follow to practice what you have learned in this section. If you get stuck, go back to the corresponding section in the chapter. Good luck!

REVIEW QUESTIONS

Complete questions 1–4 by correctly identifying the tool-bar icons shown below.

1.  ____________________
2. 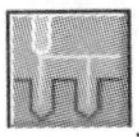 ____________________
3.  ____________________
4. 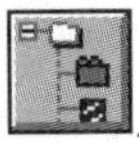 ____________________
5. Name the module used to create a tool path for cutting a circular feature.
6. The Gview command allows us to switch views. Name the two methods for selecting the Gview command.
7. The ________ are a set of user parameters that control the individual tool-cutting operations.
8. Without generating an offset code you wouldn't have any way of changing the part size or tool path in the case of tool deflection or tool wear. What code offsets the tool to the left?
9. This setting would allow you to compensate for the end radius of a cutter as in the case of ball nose or bull nose end mill.
10. The ________ creates machine codes specific to the type of machine control you select.
11. The Job Setup function sets the ____ ____ for the current job.
12. In ________ milling, the feed direction is the same as the cutter rotation.

13. A figure inside of a pocket is known as a/an ______________.
14. The ______________ function redisplays the tool path.
15. The ______________ verification mode is a very dynamic solid modeling tool for verifying tool path.

PRACTICE EXERCISES

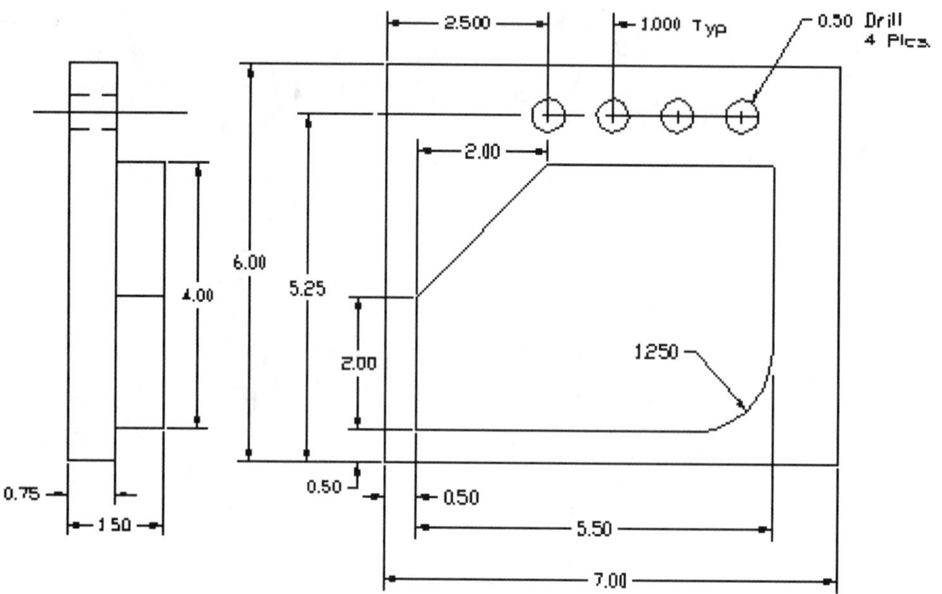

EXERCISE 6-1

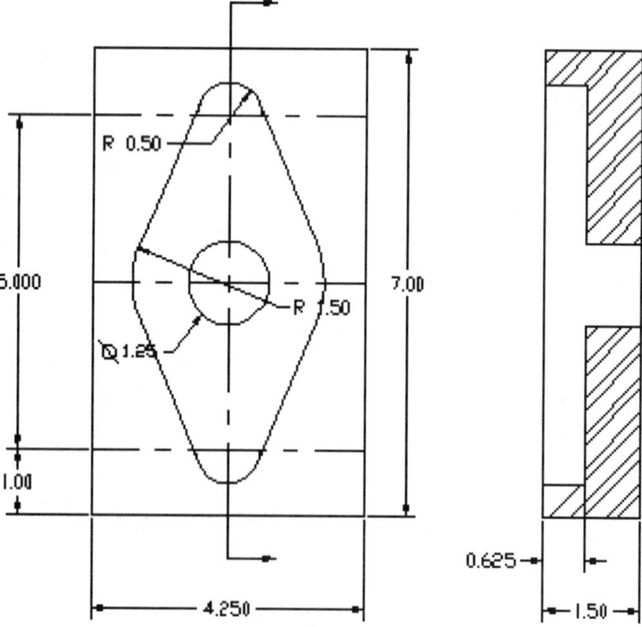

EXERCISE 6-2

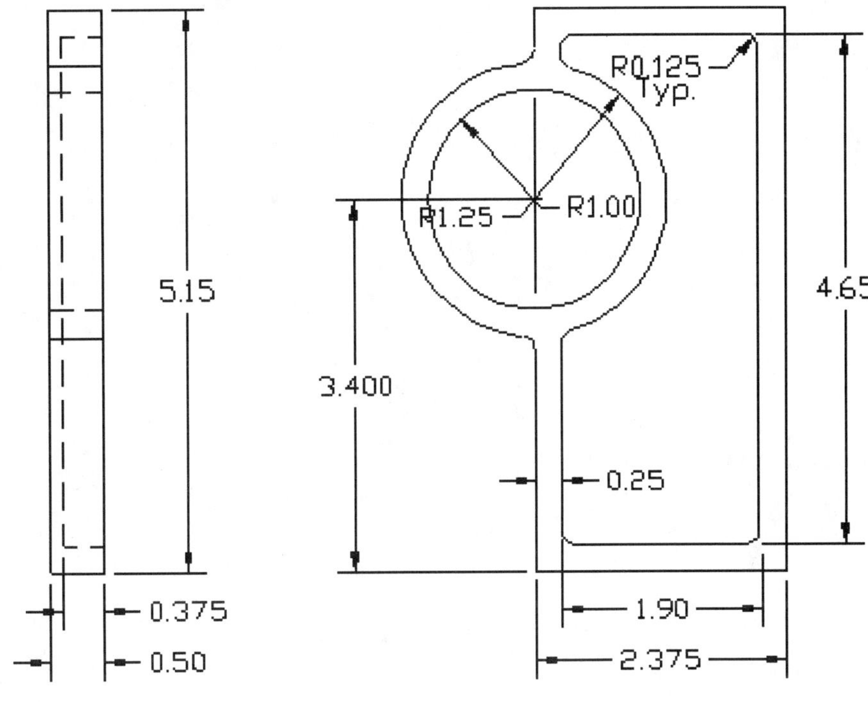

EXERCISE 6-3

CHAPTER

7

Creating Lathe Geometry

In this chapter you will be introduced to Mastercam Lathe. Mastercam lathe functions include facing, turning, profiling, grooving, drilling, boring, threading, and cutoff (parting). All of these lathe functions start with geometry creation. This chapter will concentrate on the basics of lathe part programming and geometry construction. Remember that geometry can be created in the Design area of Mastercam and also in the particular application areas. In this chapter you will examine how you can create geometry specific to turning machines. No matter which Mastercam tool you use to create geometry, it is essential that the geometry you construct be correct in all phases, including scale. Since the geometry you will be creating will be the basis for our lathe tool path, the drafting model that you create is an essential part of the CAD/CAM process.

You will also be reviewing the axes associated with turning machines and selecting the workpiece origin.

Objectives

Upon completion of this chapter you will be able to:

- Describe the coordinate system used on the lathe
- Select the system origin
- Set the proper lathe construction plane
- Explain the difference between radius and diameter programming
- Create part profiles using lines, points, arcs, fillets, and chamfers

LATHE COORDINATE SYSTEMS

Turning centers or CNC lathes manufactured today will vary in the manner in which the cross slide is mounted. On slant bed turning centers the tool turret will be mounted on the slant bed and the tool will be on the left side of the spindle centerline when viewing the machine from the headstock (see Figure 7–1). This is known as the left-handed coordinate system.

On a CNC lathe the tool turret will be mounted on the front side of the machine and the tool will be on the right side of the spindle centerline when viewing the machine from the headstock (see Figure 7–2). This is known as the right-handed coordinate system.

No matter which type of turning machine you are programming, the two basic axes you will be controlling are the X and Z axes. The Z axis is always parallel with the spindle of the machine. The X axis or cross slide is perpendicular to the Z axis and controls the diameter of the part. Keep these coordinate systems in mind when you are asked to set the coordinate system later on in this section.

Selecting the System Origin

Before beginning geometry creation you must first select the system origin. The system origin or absolute program zero is the main reference point for all geometry and tool-path creation. The absolute zero or the origin of the part is typically located at the right face and centerline of the part (see Figure 7–3).

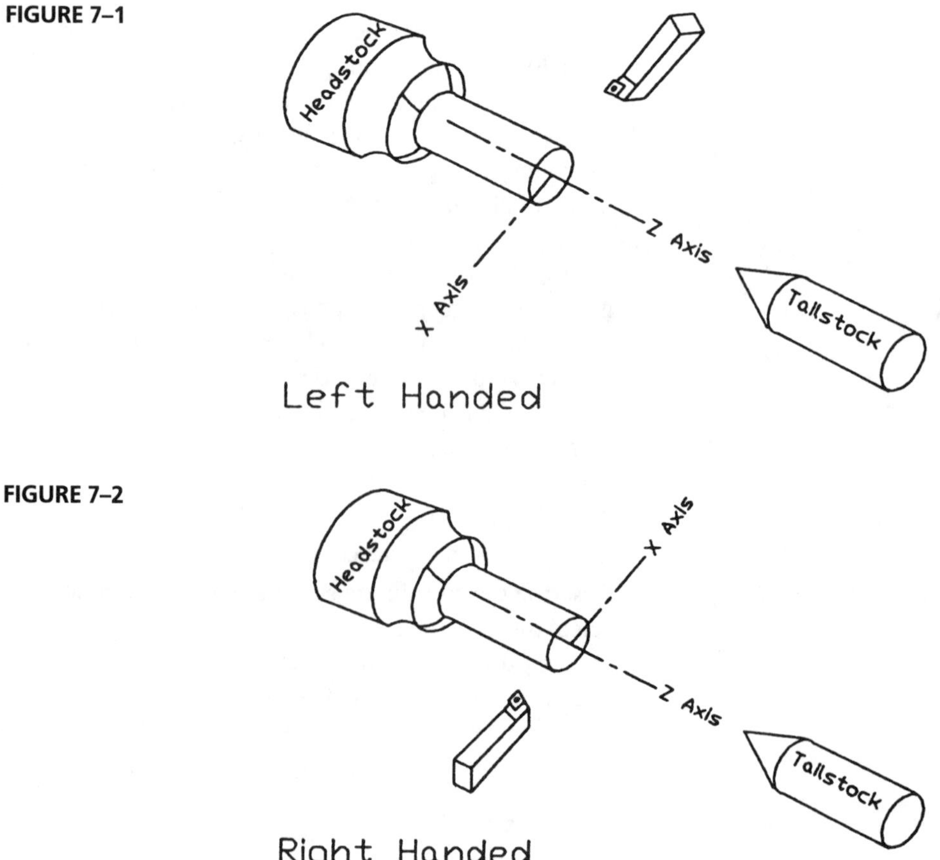

FIGURE 7–1

FIGURE 7–2

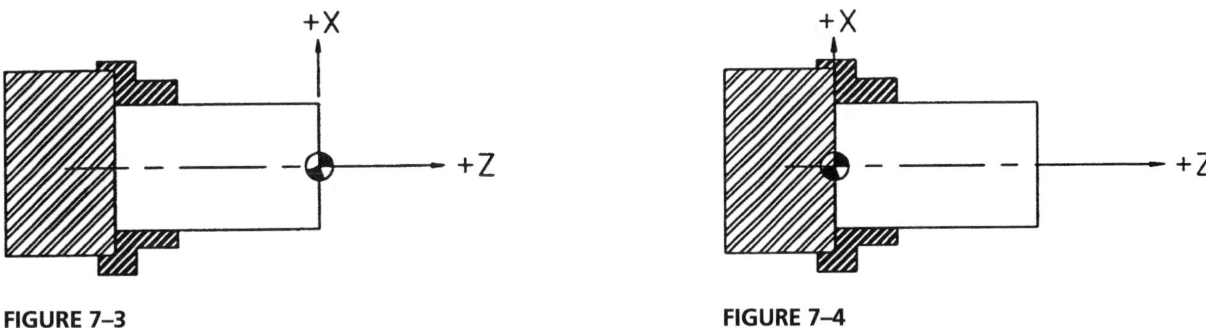

FIGURE 7–3

FIGURE 7–4

The other absolute zero or origin of the part can be located at the left face and centerline of the part (see Figure 7–4).

Construction Planes

The construction plane (Cplane) setting defines the axes construction method you wish to use. When you begin describing geometry you have to tell Mastercam how coordinate values are to be specified. When you described coordinate values in Mastercam Mill you used the X, Y, and Z axes. The values were typically absolute coordinates located from the X, Y, and Z origin point. When you describe lathe geometry you use the X and Z axes. The dimensions in the X axis can be described in two ways: radius and diameter programming (Figure 7–5).

Mastercam uses the prefix of X for radius programming and the prefix D for diameter programming.

If you wanted to describe a turned diameter of 1.00 inch and you had the Mastercam construction plane (see Figure 7–6) set to XZ or radius programming, you would need to describe the X geometry as .50 inch. If you wanted to describe a turned diameter of 1.00 inch and you had the Mastercam construction plane set to DZ or diameter programming, you would need to describe the X (D) geometry as the actual 1.0-inch diameter.

The different Cplane settings of −DZ or −XZ allow the programmer to describe points on the right side of the center line without having to use the negative signs (Figure 7–7). With the Cplane set to −X or −D, all of the coordinates on the right side of the centerline of the part are described as positive values. With the Cplane set to +X or +D all of the coordinates on the left side of the centerline of the part are described as positive values.

FIGURE 7–5

FIGURE 7–6

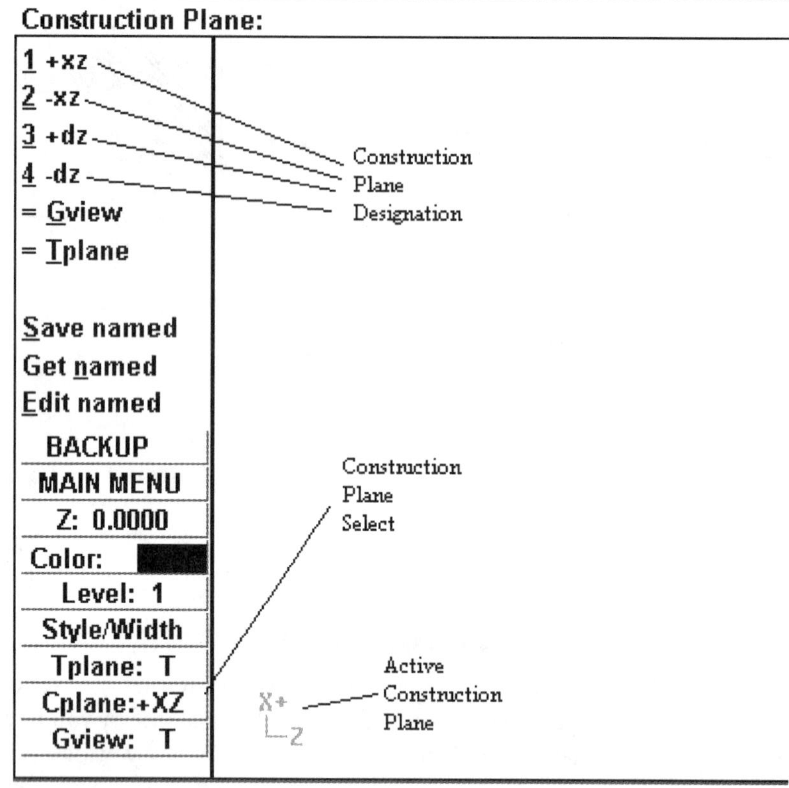

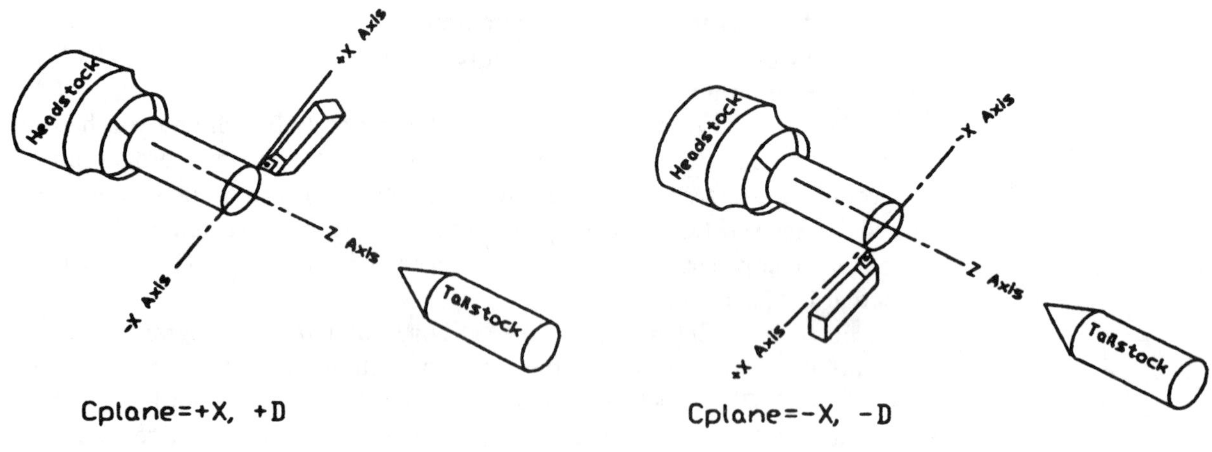

FIGURE 7–7

GEOMETRY CREATION FOR LATHE

Once you have turned on your computer and allowed the system to boot up, click the **Start** button using the left mouse button, and then point to the folder called Mastercam. Click on the **Mastercam Lathe** option. You are going to use the Lathe module to generate lathe part geometry for the part shown in Figure 7–8.

You will create the geometry for the lathe part using both radius and diameter programming methods. The first example will utilize radius programming, but since diameter programming is a much more common method of programming,

FIGURE 7–8

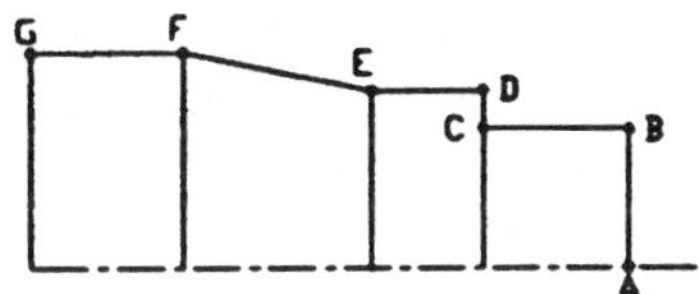

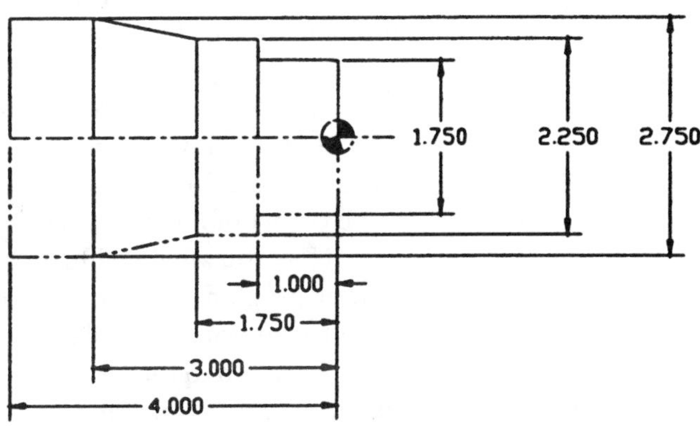

all future examples will use the diameter method. Once Mastercam Lathe appears on the screen you will notice that the Mastercam Lathe screen looks very much like Mastercam Mill. The location and the use of the graphics display, the tool bar, and the menus are identical to the other applications you have covered in this text. When you create geometry for lathe parts you need to create only one-half of the part because lathe parts are typically symmetrical. All of the geometry creation techniques you used in previous chapters apply here. Keep in mind that you are working with only two axes. The Z axis will be longitudinal, while the X axis will be vertical. When defining points using coordinates, the X axis will be input first while the Z axis will be input second, i.e., (X)1.0, (Z)1.0. Let's get started.

Creating Part Geometry for Tutorial 1

You are going to create the geometry for Figure 7–5 using the radius-programming mode first. To switch to the radius-programming mode click on **Cplane** from the secondary menu now. From the Construction Plane menu select **NextMenu.** From the next Construction Plane menu select **+XZ** (see Figure 7–9).

FIGURE 7–9

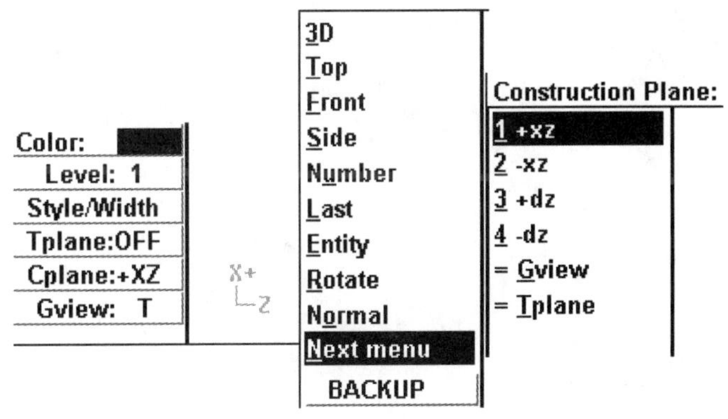

FIGURE 7–10

Notice that the coordinate indicator in the lower left corner of the display screen shows that you are using the X+,Z or radius programming system. Switch the view under Gview in the secondary menu to **Top.**

Start the Line creation either by selecting **Main Menu/Create/Line/Multi** or select the Multi-Line icon from the tool bar (Figure 7–10).

Input the point coordinates found in chart below. These coordinates correspond to the lettered points in the radius view of Figure 7–8.

When you have finished entering the coordinates, press the **Esc** key to exit the multiline mode. The image on the screen should now look like the one in Figure 7–11.

Now let's add a .100 chamfer at point B (Figure 7–11). From the Main Menu select **Create/Next Menu/Chamfer.** Select **Distances** from the Chamfer menu. At the distance prompts enter .100 for both lengths. Select the two lines that make up the B corner of the part. The chamfer should now appear on the part.

Now you are going to create the same geometry for Figure 7–5 using the diameter-programming mode. Delete all of the entities on the screen using the **Delete** icon from the tool bar.

To switch to the Diameter programming mode click on **Cplane** from the secondary menu. From the Construction Plane menu select **Next Menu.** From the Construction Plane menu select **+DZ.**

Notice that the coordinate indicator in the lower left corner of the display screen shows that you are using the D, Z or diameter programming system. Start the Line creation by selecting the **Multi-Line** icon from the tool bar.

Input the following point coordinates. These coordinates correspond to the diameter dimensions shown in Figure 7–12.

When you have finished entering the coordinates, press the **Esc** key on the keyboard to exit the multiline mode.

POINTS	RADIUS VALUE	Z VALUE
A	0	0
B	.875	0
C	.875	-1.00
D	1.125	-1.00
E	1.125	-1.75
F	1.375	-3.00
G	1.375	-4.00

FIGURE 7–11

FIGURE 7–12

POINTS	RADIUS VALUE	Z VALUE
A	0	0
B	.875	0
C	.875	-1.00
D	1.125	-1.00
E	1.125	-1.75
F	1.375	-3.00
G	1.375	-4.00

POINTS	DIAMETER VALUE	Z VALUE
A	0	0
B	1.75	0
C	1.75	-1.00
D	2.25	-1.00
E	2.25	-1.75
F	2.75	-3.00
G	2.75	-4.00

Next add a .100 fillet at point B. From the Main Menu select **Create/Fillet/Radius.** At the radius prompt enter **.100.** Select the two lines that make up the B corner of the part. The chamfer should now appear on the part.

Now let's add a rectangle to depict the rough stock boundary. To keep the stock boundary and the part geometry completely separate you will put the stock boundary on level 2. Select **Level** from the secondary menu. From the Level dialogue box select the number **2.** Select **OK.** To keep the levels visually separated, change the color of level 2. From the secondary menu select **Color.** From the Color dialogue box select any color other than the one used on level 1. Select **OK.** To add the stock boundary select **Create/Rectangle** from the Main Menu. From the Rectangle menu select **2 points.** At the prompt enter **0,−4** for the lower left corner of the rectangle. At the prompt enter **2.75,0** for the second point of the rectangle. The stock boundary should now be visible on the screen (Figure 7–13).

FIGURE 7–13

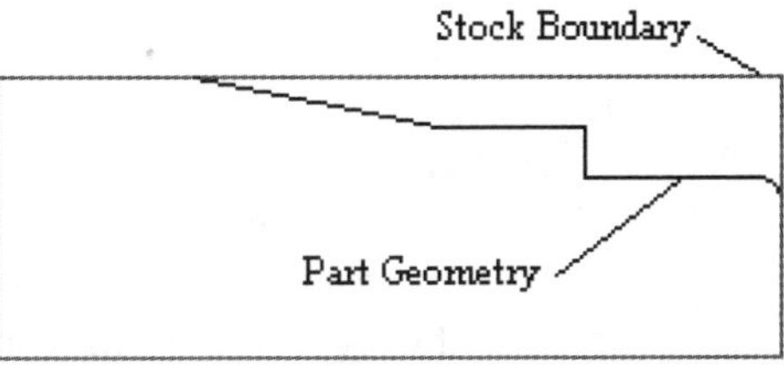

FIGURE 7–14

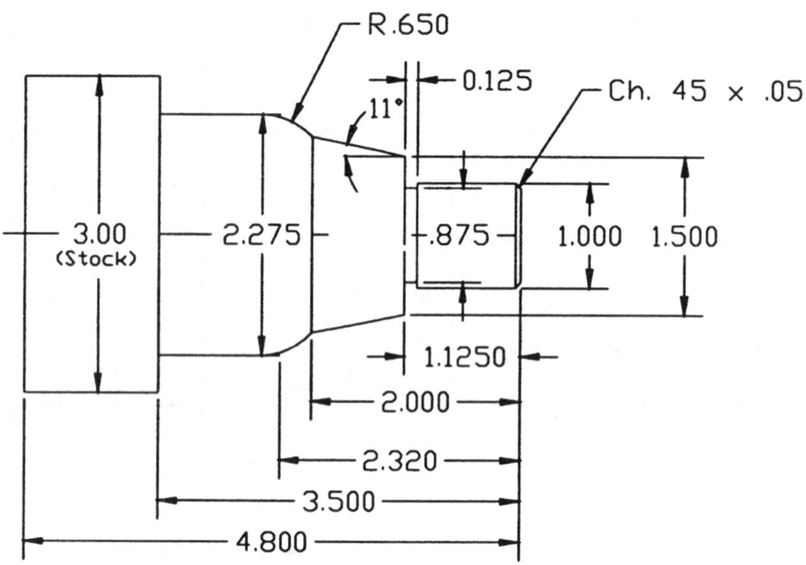

Save this file. From the main menu select **File/Save.** At the prompt, type **tutorial1.** Select **Save.**

Creating Part Geometry for Tutorial 2

Select **New** from the File menu. Initiate a new program.

You will create the geometry for Figure 7–14 using diameter programming. Check the construction plane setting in the lower left corner of the display area. It should be set to D+Z. If it isn't, switch to the Diameter programming construction plane by selecting **Cplane** from the secondary menu. From the Construction Plane menu select **NextMenu.** From the next Construction Plane menu select **+DZ.** In review, the commands were Cplane/Next Menu/+DZ. The methods you use for creating lines and arc may not be what you would normally use, but it is worthwhile to try some different methods of creating lathe geometry.

Let's begin creating the lathe part geometry shown in Figure 7–14. From the Main Menu select **Create/Line/Vertical.** Enter the first coordinate **0,0.** Enter the second coordinate **1.0,0.** At the Z-coordinate prompt hit **Enter.** Select **Backup.** To enter the second line select **Horizontal.** Use the smart mouse to select the upper endpoint of the first line to specify the first endpoint. Enter the coordinate, **1,** and **−1** for the horizontal endpoint coordinate. At the D coordinate prompt hit **Enter.** To enter the third line select **Main Menu/Create/Line/Multi.** Use the smart mouse to select the left endpoint of the horizontal line to specify the first endpoint of the multiline segment. Enter the coordinate **.875,−1** for the endpoint of the multiline. Now enter **.875,−1.125** for the next endpoint of the multiline. Now enter **1.5,−1.125** for the endpoint of multiline 4. Hit the **Esc** key to exit the Multiline mode. Use the **Zoom** window function icon from the tool bar to resize the part to the screen. Your part should now be identical to the part shown in Figure 7–15.

To create the angled line, select **Main Menu/Create/Line/Polar.** Use the smart mouse to select the top endpoint of the last line. This will be the start point of the angled lined. At the angle prompt you will use the math capabilities of Mastercam. At the angle prompt, type **180−11.** At the length prompt enter **.875.**

To create the arc select **Main Menu/Create/Arc/Endpoints.** For the start point of the arc, use the smart mouse to select the left end point of the angle line.

FIGURE 7–15

FIGURE 7–16

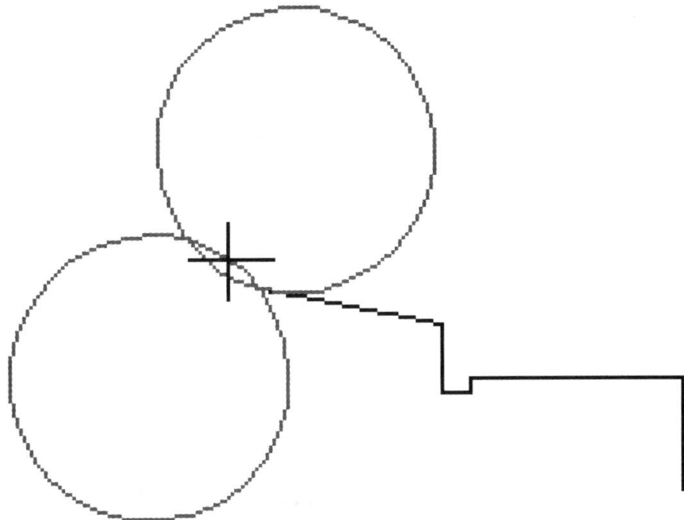

At the second endpoint prompt type in the coordinates **2.275,−2.32.** Enter **.65** for the radius. Select the **Unzoom** icon from the tool bar. On the screen you will see all of the possible scenarios for our coordinate inputs. Use the mouse to select the portion of the arc shown in Figure 7–16.

To create the next line select **Main Menu/Create/Line/Endpoints.** Use the smart mouse to select the left endpoint of the arc. Enter the endpoint coordinates of **2.275,−3.5.** To create the next line select **Backup/Vertical.** Use the smart mouse to select the left end point of the last horizontal line. At the endpoint prompt enter **3.0.** At the Z-coordinate prompt hit **Enter.** Use the **Repaint** function icon from the tool bar to update the screen. Your part should now be identical to the part shown in Figure 7–17.

You now need to add the 0.05 chamfer to the right end of the part. Select **Main Menu/Create/Next Menu/Chamfer/Distance.** At the Distance prompt enter **.05.** At the Distance Length prompt hit **Enter** to accept the .05 default. At the prompt select the first leg of the chamfered figure. At the prompt, select the second line of the chamfered figure. The chamfer should now appear on the part.

Now you are going to add the rough bar stock geometry. To keep the stock boundary and the part geometry completely separate you will put the stock boundary on level 2. Select **Level** from the secondary menu. From the Level dialogue box select the number **2.** To keep the levels visually separated we will change the color of level 2. From the secondary menu select **Color.** From the Color dialogue box select any color other than the one used on level 1. To add the stock

FIGURE 7–17

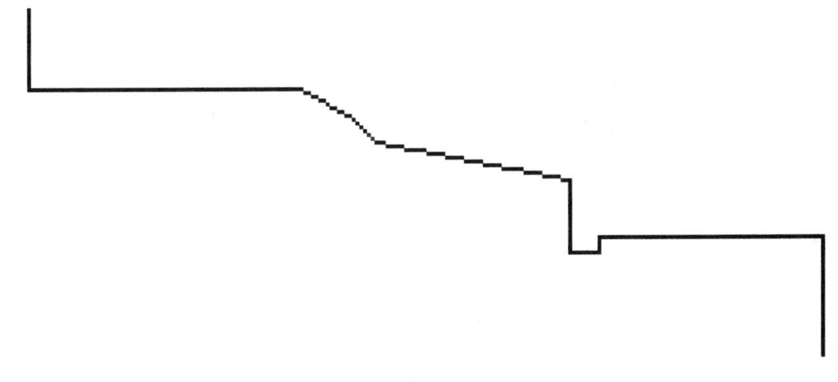

FIGURE 7–18

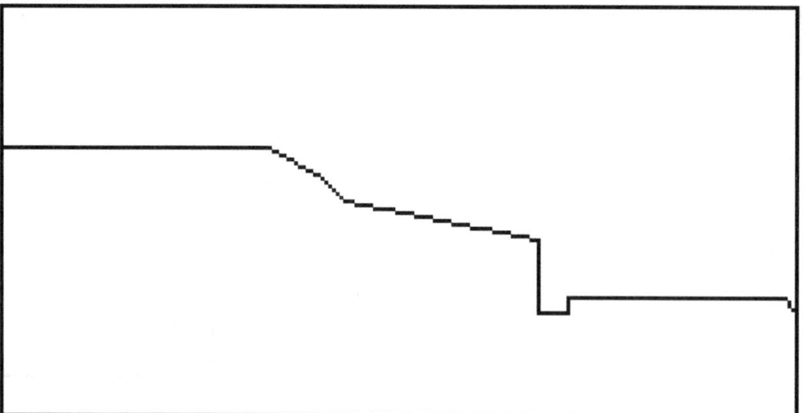

boundary select **Create/Rectangle** from the Main Menu. From the Rectangle menu select **2 points.** At the prompt enter **0,−3.5** for the lower left corner of the rectangle. At the prompt enter **3.5,0** for the second point of the rectangle. The stock boundary should now be visible on the screen (Figure 7–18). Save this file as Tutorial2.

Creating Part Geometry for Tutorial 3

Select **New** from the File menu. Initiate a new program.You are going to create the geometry for Figure 7–19 using diameter programming. Check the construction plane setting in the lower left corner of the display area. It should be set to D+Z. If it isn't, switch to the Diameter programming construction plane by selecting **Cplane** from the secondary menu. From the Construction Plane menu select **Next Menu.** From the next Construction Plane menu select **+DZ.** In review, the commands were Cplane/Next Menu/+DZ. The methods you use for creating lines and arc may not be what you would normally use, but you want to practice some different methods of creating and editing lathe geometry.

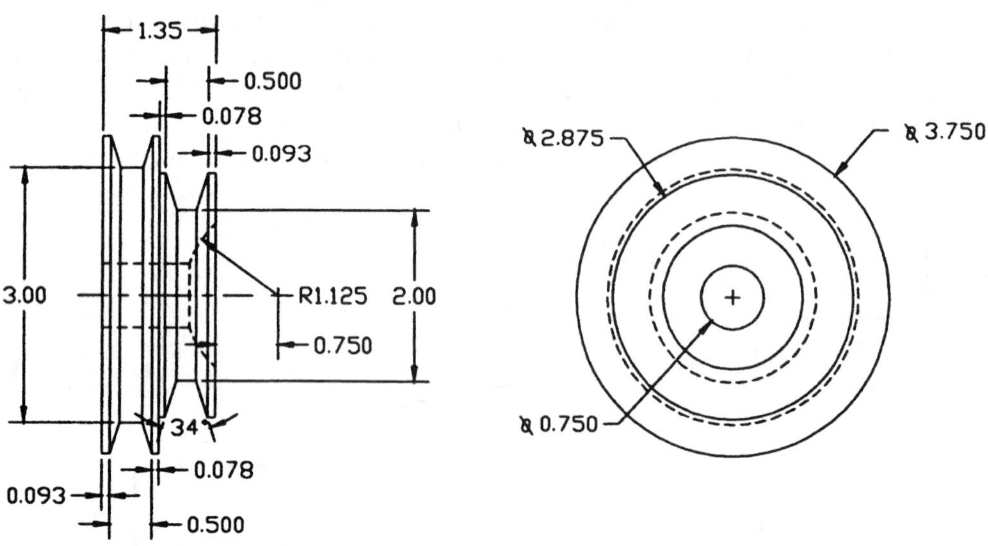

FIGURE 7–19

FIGURE 7–20

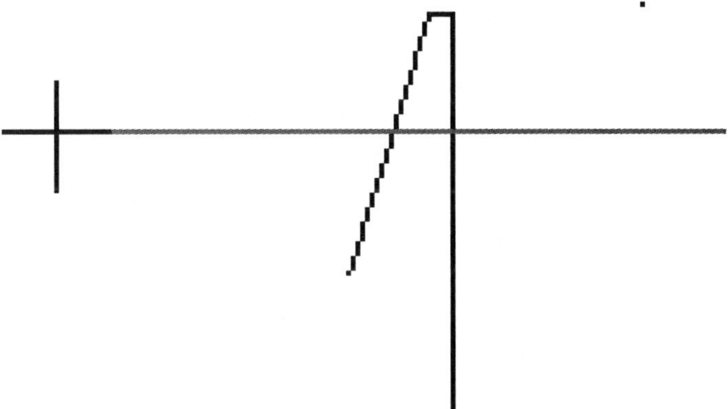

FIGURE 7–21

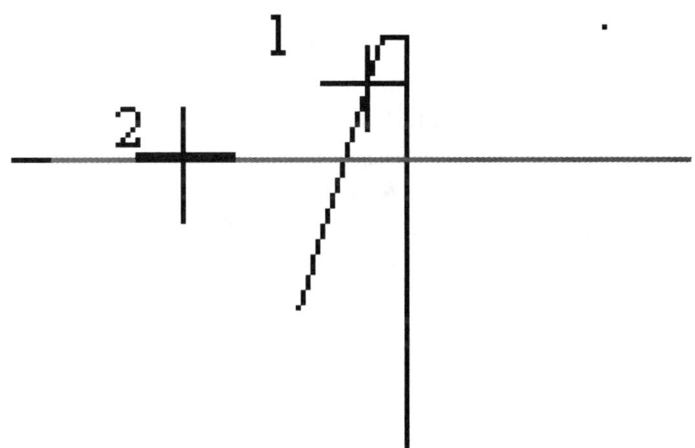

Let's begin creating the lathe part geometry shown in Figure 7–19. From the Main Menu select **Create/Line/Vertical.** Enter the first coordinate **0,0.** Enter the second coordinate **2.875.** At the Z-coordinate prompt hit **Enter** to accept the default. Select **Backup.** To enter the second line select **Horizontal.** Use the smart mouse to select the upper endpoint of the first line to specify the first endpoint. Enter the coordinates **2.875,−.093** for the horizontal endpoint coordinate. At the D coordinate 2.875, hit Enter. Select Backup. To enter the third line select **Polar.** Use the smart mouse to select the left endpoint of the horizontal line to specify the first endpoint of the Polar line segment. At the prompt for the angle, enter **270−17**. At the prompt to enter the line length, accept the default of .875. Use the **Zoom** window function icon from the tool bar to resize the part to the screen. Select **Backup.** To enter the next line select **Horizontal.** Specify the first endpoint by typing in the coordinates of **2.0,1.0.** Stretch the line to the left beyond the existing lines (Figure 7–20).

Accept the default D coordinate of 2.0 by pressing **Enter.** Now you will need to do some editing. Select the **Modify-Trim-2-Entities** icon. At the prompt to *select entity to trim,* select the entities shown in Figure 7–21.

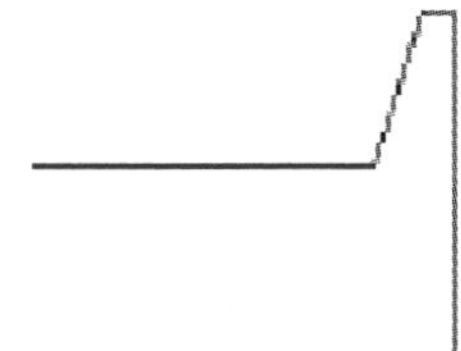

FIGURE 7–22

You should now have the geometry shown in Figure 7–22.

Select **Backup.** To enter the next line, from the Main Menu, select **Create/Line/Polar.** To specify the first endpoint, enter the coordinates **2.875,−.593.** At the angle prompt type **270+17**. At the length prompt accept the default or enter **1.**

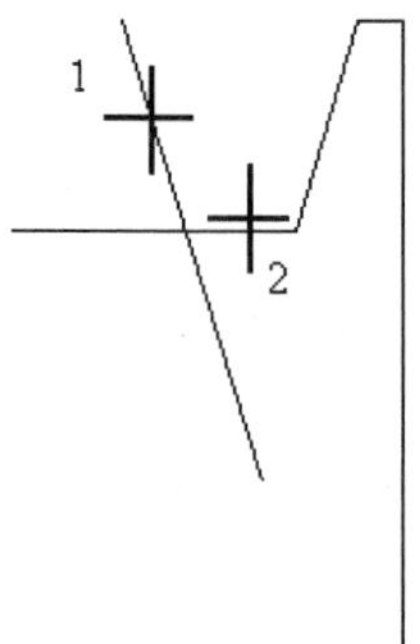

FIGURE 7–23

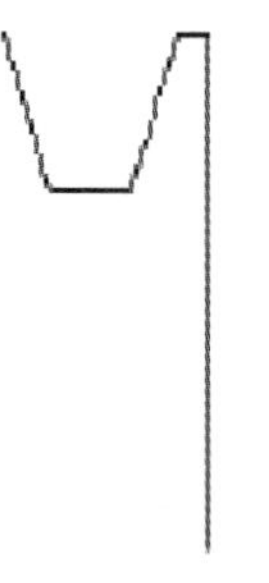

FIGURE 7–24

It is time again to do some editing. Select the **Modify-Trim-2-Entities** icon. At the prompt to *select entity to trim,* select the entities shown in Figure 7–23.

The geometry on the screen should now appear the same as Figure 7–24.

To show you how you can create free-form geometry, you will finish the profile of the part by starting from the left end of the part and work your way back. Select **Backup** from the menu until you get back to the multiline option. Select **Multi.** Type in the following coordinates:

0,−1.35 Press **Enter.**

3.75,−1.35 Press **Enter.**

3.75,−1.35+.093 Press **Enter.**

Press **Esc** to get out of the Multi mode. Now select **Polar.** Use the smart mouse to select the right end of the last line. Type **270+17** at the prompt to enter the angle in degrees. Accept the default of **1** when asked to enter the line length. Select the **Repaint** icon from the tool bar to refresh the screen. Select **Backup.** Now select **Horizontal** from the Line menu. Specify the first endpoint as **3.0,−1.5.** Stretch the horizontal line to the right, past the last angle line you put in. Press the left mouse button to secure this position. Accept the D default of **3.0.** Now select **Polar.** You are going to create the other angled line. To locate the start point of the angled line you will use the relative option. Relative means incremental distance from. The start point of the new line is .5 inches to the right of the start point of the existing angled line. Select **Relative.** At the prompt to specify an endpoint, use the smart mouse to select the start point of the existing angle line (see Figure 7–25).

At the Define Vector prompt select **Rectang.** Enter the relative coordinates of **0,.5.** When asked to enter the angle in degrees, type **270−17**. Press **Enter.** Accept the default of **1** for the line length. The geometry on the screen should now appear the same as shown in Figure 7–26.

Select the **Modify-Trim-3-entities** icon. At the prompt to *select entity to trim,* select the entities in order as shown in Figure 7–27.

The geometry on the screen should now appear the same as the geometry in Figure 7–28.

Select the **Repaint** icon from the tool bar to refresh the screen. Select **Backup** from the menu until you get back to the Multi-Line option. Select **Multi.** Use the

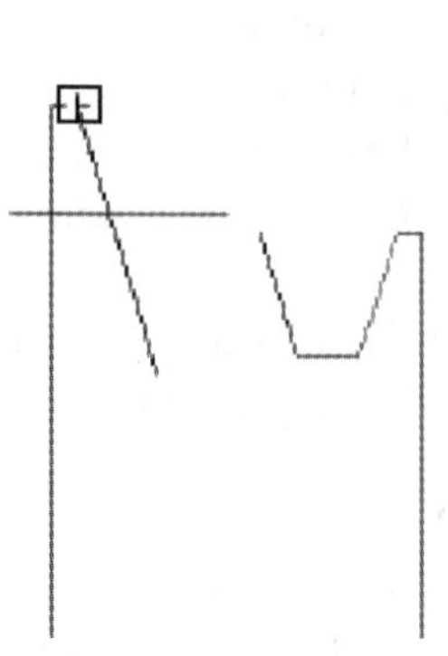

FIGURE 7–25

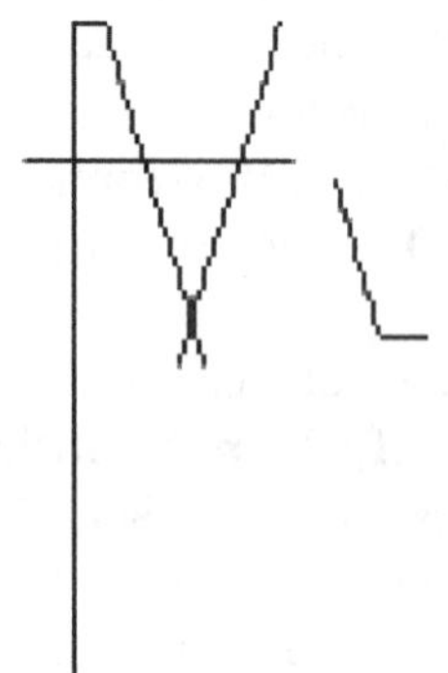

FIGURE 7–26

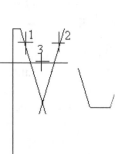

FIGURE 7–27

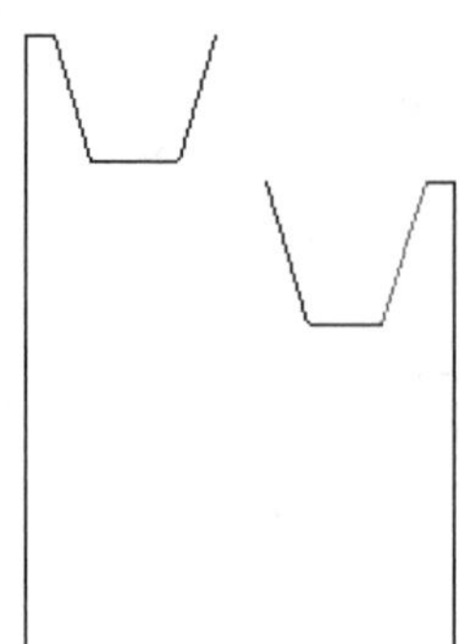

FIGURE 7–28

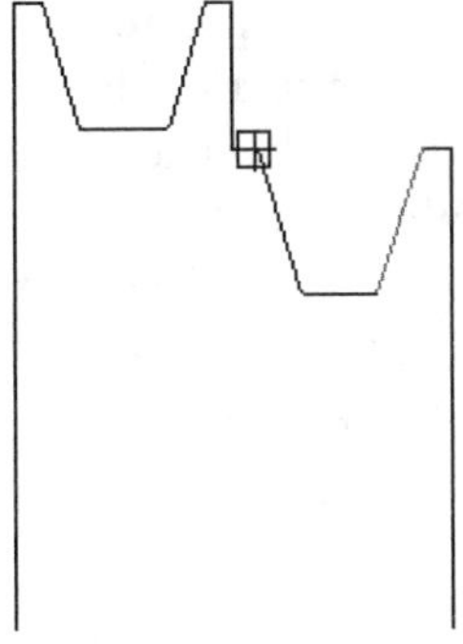

FIGURE 7–29

smart mouse to select the upper right endpoint of the last angled line you just created. Type in the following coordinates:

3.75,−.671 Press **Enter.**

2.875,−.671 Press **Enter.**

Now use the smart mouse to connect the multiline back to the endpoint of the original geometry (Figure 7–29). Press **Esc** on the keyboard to back out of the multiline mode. The Esc key works the same as the Backup button in the Main Menu.

Now you need to create the internal profile of the part. To keep the internal profile and the external profile geometry completely separate you will put the internal profile on level 3. Select **Level** from the secondary menu. From the Level dialogue box select the number **3.** To keep the levels visually separated we will change the color of level 3. From the secondary menu select **Color.** From the Color dialogue box select any color other than the ones used on levels 1 and 2.

Internal Profile Geometry

To start adding the internal profile, select **Create/Arc/Circ pt+rad.** At the prompt to enter the center point enter **0,.75.** At the prompt to enter the radius enter **1.125.** Press the **Esc** key until you get back to the Create menu. Select **Line/Horizontal.** At the prompt to specify the first endpoint enter **.75,0.** At the prompt to specify the second endpoint enter **.75,−1.35.** At the prompt to enter the D coordinate accept the default of .75 by pressing **Enter.** It is time again to do some editing. Select the **Modify-Trim-3-entities** icon. At the prompt to *select entity to trim,* select the entities in the order shown in Figure 7–30.

Select the **Repaint** icon from the tool bar to refresh the screen. The geometry on the screen should now appear the same as the geometry in Figure 7–31.

Now let's add a rectangle to depict the rough stock boundary. To keep the stock boundary and the part geometry completely separate you will put the stock boundary on level 2. Select **Level** from the secondary menu. From the

FIGURE 7–30

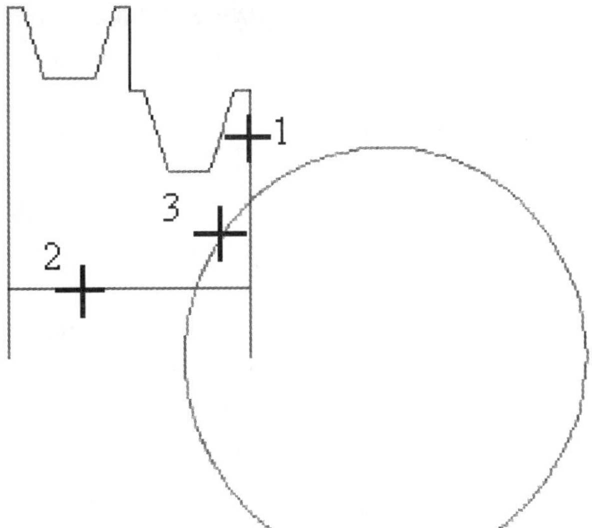

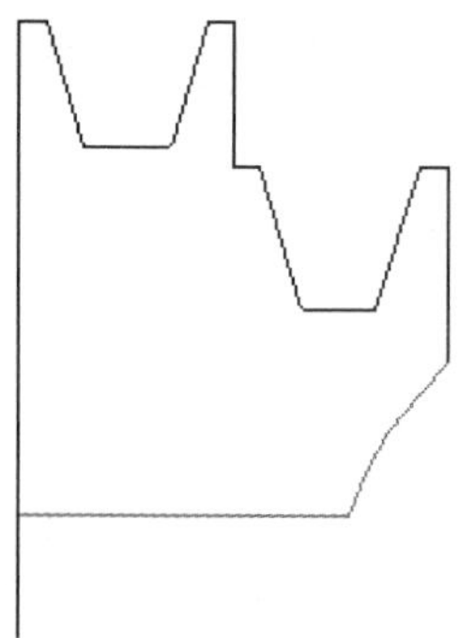

FIGURE 7–31

Level dialogue box select the number **2.** To keep the levels visually separated we will change the color of level 2. From the secondary menu select **Color.** From the Color dialogue box select any color other than the ones used on levels 1 and 3. To add the stock boundary select **Create/Rectangle** from the Main Menu. From the Rectangle menu select **2 points.** At the prompt enter **0,−3** for the lower left corner of the rectangle. At the prompt enter **4,.1** for the second point of the rectangle. The stock boundary should now be visible on the screen (Figure 7–32).

FIGURE 7–32

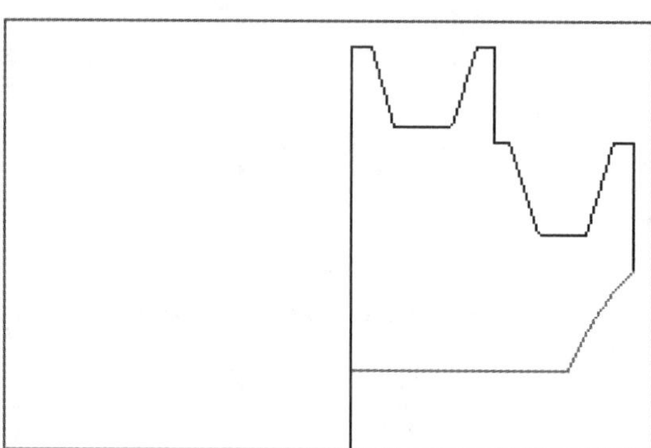

Save this file. From the Main Menu select **File/Save.** At the prompt, type **tutorial3.** Select **Save.**

Congratulations, you have finished the lathe geometry tutorial. Now it's time for you to practice. Do the exercises at the end of this chapter. Save these exercises to a diskette for use later on in the textbook.

REVIEW QUESTIONS

1. When the tool is mounted on the left side of the spindle centerline, when viewing the machine from the headstock, this is known as the __________ __________ coordinate system.
2. The two basic axes associated with the lathe are the __________ and __________ axes.
3. The __________ axis controls the diameter of the part.
4. The absolute zero or the origin of the part is typically located at the __________ and centerline of the part.
5. The construction plane setting defines __________.
6. Dimensions in the X axis can be described in two ways. Name them.
7. Mastercam uses the prefix X to describe radius programming. What prefix does it use to describe diameter programming?
8. When defining points using coordinates, which axis will be input first?

PRACTICE EXERCISES

EXERCISE 7–1

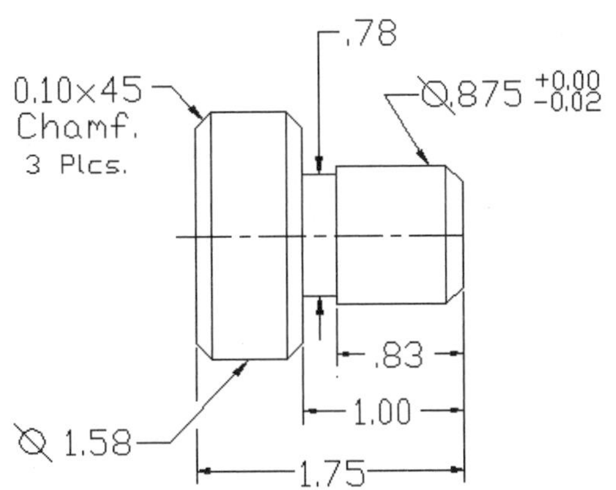

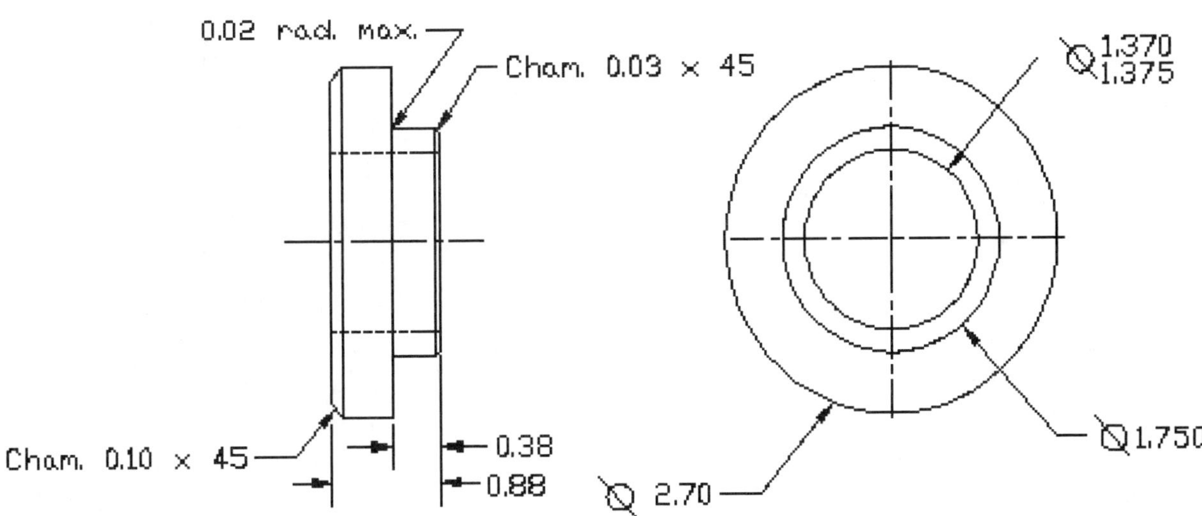

EXERCISE 7–2

EXERCISE 7–3

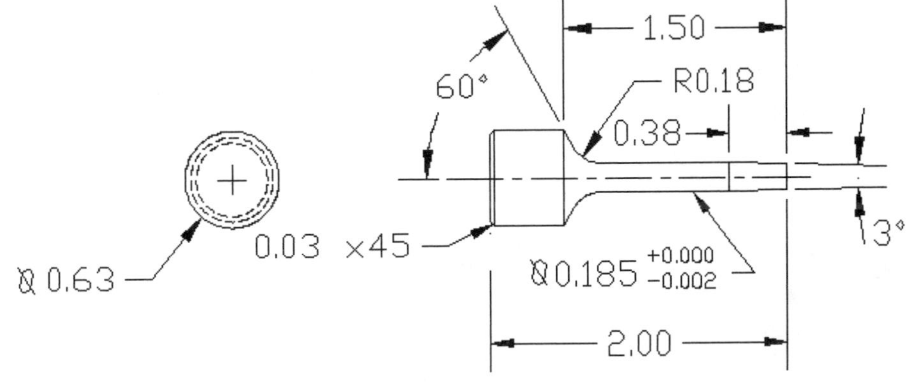

CHAPTER

8

Creating Tool Paths in Mastercam Lathe

In this section you will be led through step-by-step procedures of how Mastercam can take you from a basic part conception to generating NC code. Mastercam offers two levels of lathe tool-path programming. Turning is a basic system of programming, which concentrates on the seven basic turning operations performed on a CNC lathe or turning center. Mill-Turn includes the seven basic turning operations plus tool-path generation for milling operations performed on a combination mill-turn machine. In this chapter you will concentrate solely on the machining capabilities of turning.

Objectives

Upon completion of this chapter you will be able to:

- Define the basic components of the Mastercam Lathe module
- Use Mastercam Lathe to create part geometry
- Define parameters used in Lathe tool-path modules
- Chain geometric entities
- Apply machining commands to part geometry
- Generate numerical control code to machine the part

MASTERCAM LATHE PROCESS OVERVIEW

The Mastercam CAD/CAM Lathe process involves four basic components: geometry definition, application of tool-path commands, setting the numerical control (NC) parameters, and postprocessing.

Geometry Definition

Computer-aided part programming always begins with geometry definition or part design. In previous chapters it was mentioned that you could create geometry in any one of Mastercam's application areas. Mastercam Mill, Mastercam Lathe, and Mastercam Design all have part geometry creation capabilities built into them. Also, if the part were originally drawn using a CAD system, Mastercam could import this drawing. This would allow us to bypass Mastercam geometry creation.

Tool-Path Commands

Mastercam Lathe includes seven toolpath generation modules. The Rough module generates a series of tool paths along a series of entities that are joined (chained) together as the finish profile geometry (see Figure 8–1). The series of tool paths remove the excess stock from the finish profile geometry.

The Finishing module generates a tool path to finish cut a profile to size along a series of entities that are joined (chained) as the finish profile geometry (see Figure 8–2).

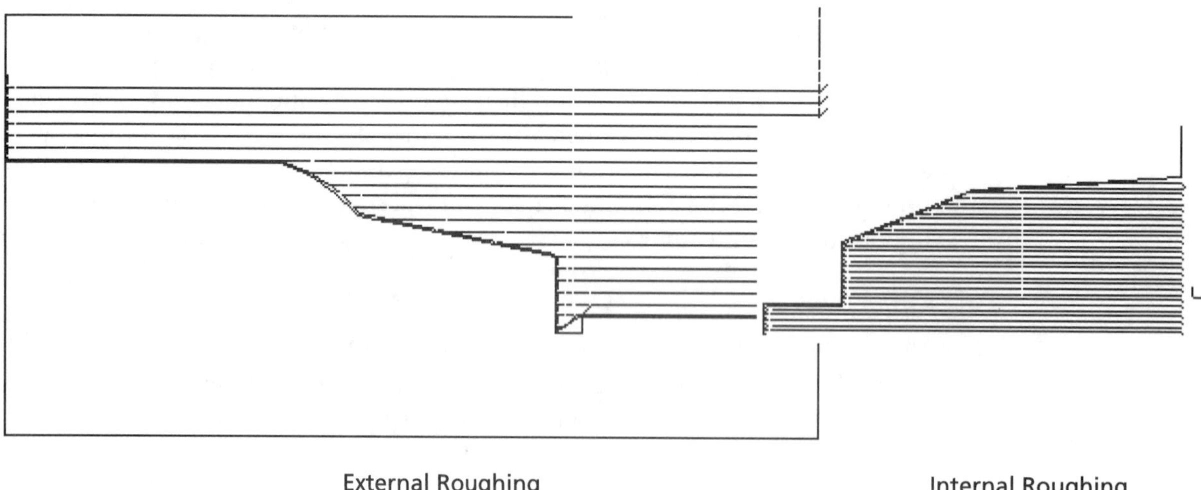

External Roughing

Internal Roughing

FIGURE 8–1

FIGURE 8–2

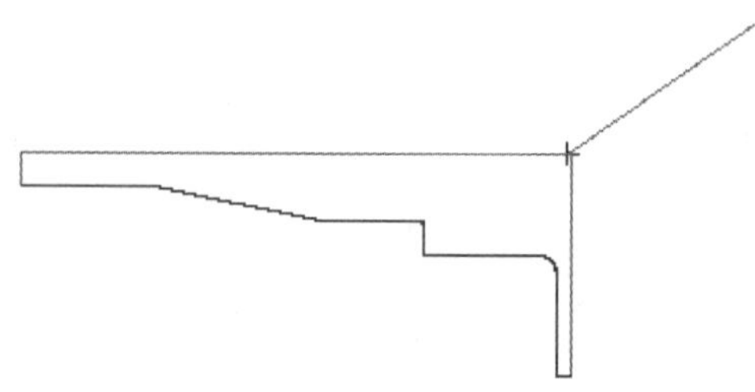

FIGURE 8–3

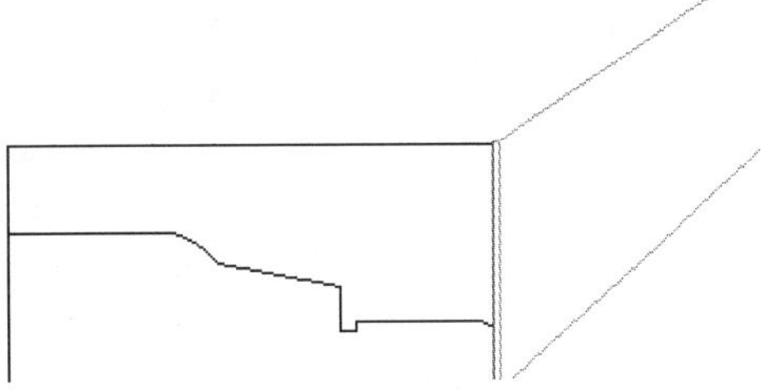

The Face module generates a tool path to clean up the face of the part (see Figure 8–3)

The Grooving module is used to create a tool path for cutting a groove in a part (see Figure 8–4).

FIGURE 8–4

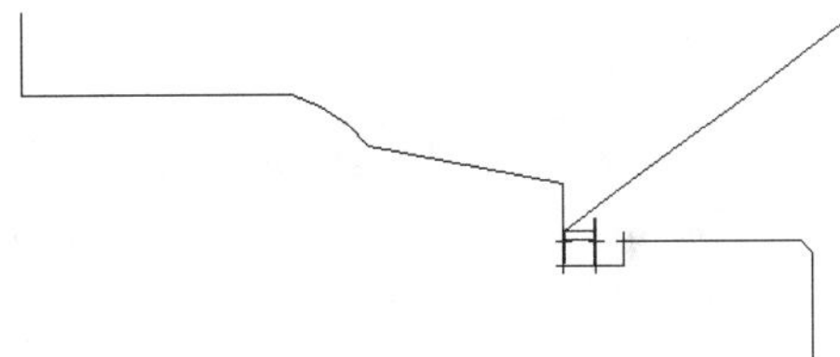

The Cut Off or Parting module is used to create a tool path for parting or cutting off the part from rough stock (see Figure 8–5).

The Threading module is used to create a tool path for various types of threads (see Figure 8–6).

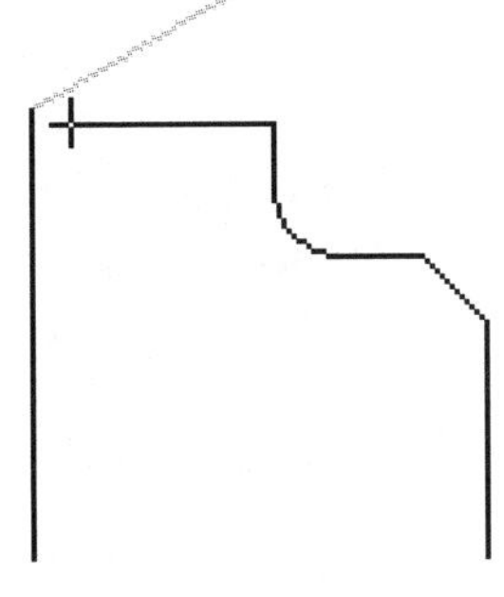

FIGURE 8–5

FIGURE 8–6

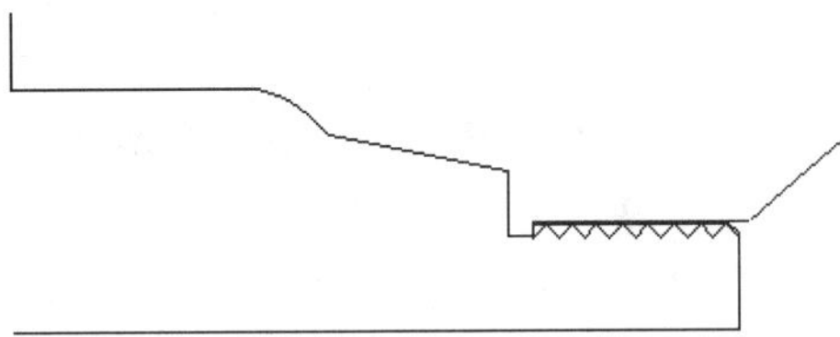

The Drill module is used to create a tool path for drilling, boring, and tapping (see Figure 8–7).

FIGURE 8–7

The following exercises will take you through a group of sample parts. Each part will show you an example of each of the lathe modules that reside within Mastercam Lathe. You are going to keep the exercises that follow as simple as possible.

ROUGH EXAMPLE EXERCISE 1

You will use the Rough module to generate tool paths to rough out the part shown in Figure 8–8. You will use Mastercam Lathe to create the part geometry. Remember that you can create geometry in any one of the application areas.

Click the **Start** button using the left mouse button, and then point to the folder called Mastercam. Click on the **Mastercam Lathe** option. Once you are in the Mastercam Main Menu area, select **File/New** to start a new file. Choose **Yes** to initialize geometry and operations. As you can see, the Mastercam Lathe module looks identical to the Geometry creation module. Geometry creation in Mastercam Lathe is virtually identical to the Design module in Mastercam. Using your skills from the previous chapters create the geometry for Figure 8–8.

Save this geometry file as Rough.

Now that you have created the necessary geometry, let's get started learning about tool path generation.

Job Setup

Lathe job setup is the area where you can choose parameters to describe the current job. To access the Job Setup parameters select **Toolpaths** from the Lathe Main Menu screen. From the Lathe Toolpaths menu select **Next Menu.** Now select **Job Setup.** The Lathe Job Setup dialogue box should now appear on the screen.

Until you get more comfortable with Mastercam Lathe, the only parameter settings you will be concerned with are the Material parameter and the Tool Clearance settings.

Material

This parameter setting allows you to choose the type of material you will be using for stock. You can either choose from the material list or you can define a material. Choose the **Select** button from the Material area of Job Setup. From the Lathe material list select **Steel Inch 4140.** Select **OK** to accept your selection. You should now be back to the Job Setup dialogue box. Find the Feed Calculation area. Activate the **Material** button to have Mastercam calculate the cutting conditions according to the material you selected. Now select **OK.**

Tool Clearance

The Tool Clearance parameter option allows you to determine the minimum amount of clearance you want to keep between the tool and the stock, chuck, and tailstock when making rapid moves and when entering or exiting the part. The sys-

FIGURE 8–8

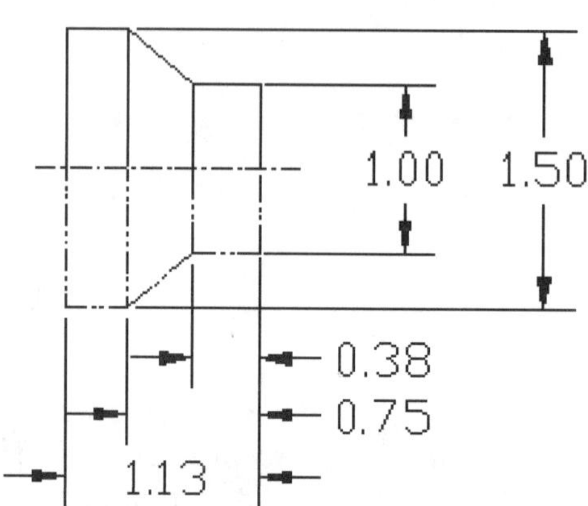

tem default is set to 0.05 inches on rapid moves and 0.01 on entry/exit moves (see Figure 8–9). If the tool clearances are not set to these values, set them now.

FIGURE 8–9

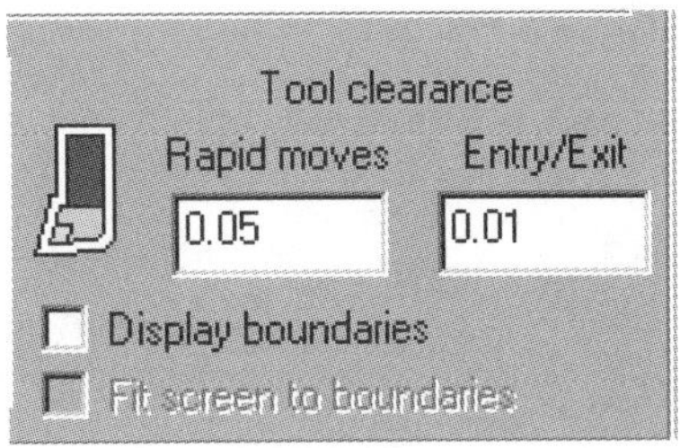

Initiating the Rough Module

From the Main Menu select **Toolpaths.** From the Toolpaths menu select **Rough.**

After initializing the Rough module Mastercam wants you to name the NCI file that will be output. The first time you begin creating a tool path for a job, Mastercam will ask you to name the NCI file. In the File name area, type in **Rough.** This will be an easy name to remember. Once you have finished typing in Rough, select **Save.** Mastercam, in the dialogue box, is now prompting you to select the entry point (Figure 8–10). The entry point is the point where the tool is going to contact material on the first pass. The entry point is the stock boundary point.

FIGURE 8–10

Rough: select the entry point or chain the inner boundary

You will be using 1.50-diameter stock and the right end of the workpiece is Z zero. From the Main Menu select **Point.** At the Point prompt, type in **1.50,0.** The entry point should now appear on the screen (Figure 8–11).

Chaining is a very important part of tool-path creation. Chaining is the selection of a set of connected lines, points, or arcs. The entities that you select become the basis for the tool path. Mastercam will now prompt you to Chain the inner boundary. This means you need to select the entities that make up the chained profile you want to machine. Use the mouse to select the vertical line entity shown in Figure 8–12.

Once you have selected the vertical line, the entire inner figure should become a different color and an arrow should appear (Figure 8–13).

Under the Contour Chain menu you can choose a number of different chaining options. These options allow you to select single entities as well as change the machining direction. Notice that the arrow is pointing in the up direction. This

FIGURE 8–11

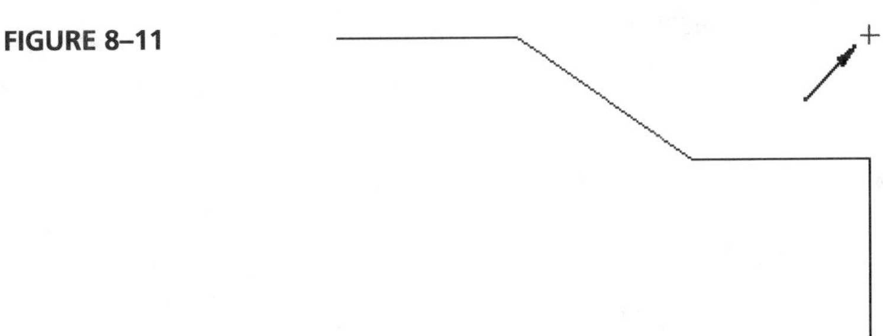

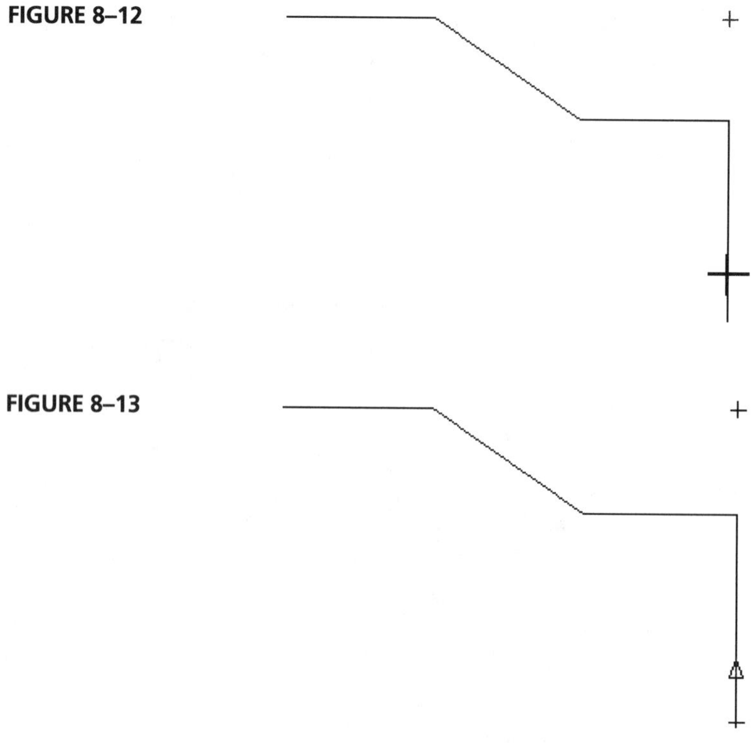

FIGURE 8–12

FIGURE 8–13

Rough: chain th
Chain
Window
Polygon
Area
Single
Section
Point
Last
Unselect
Done
BACKUP
MAIN MENU

FIGURE 8–14

means that the machining will take place between the part profile and the stock boundary. To change the direction of the tool path, select **Reverse** from the Contour menu now. Notice that the arrow direction changes. Change it back to the up direction by selecting the **Reverse** option again. Now select **Done** from the Chain menu. After selecting Done, the Mastercam software asks you to select the next chain boundary or the retraction point. You have selected the boundary you want to machine, so now you need to select the retract point. Select **Point** from the menu (see Figure 8–14).

After selecting Point from the menu, select the actual retraction point using the mouse. The retraction point will be the same as the Entry Point (Figure 8–15). Select this point now. After selecting the retraction point, Mastercam will be prompting you that the Rough chaining is complete. Select **Done** from the menu.

After Done is selected, the Rough Parameters screen will appear (Figure 8–16).

The Rough Parameters screen is the area where common numerical control parameters are set. The first thing you will need to do is select a tool. Use the mouse to select the large **Tool Select** button. The Tool Manager box should now

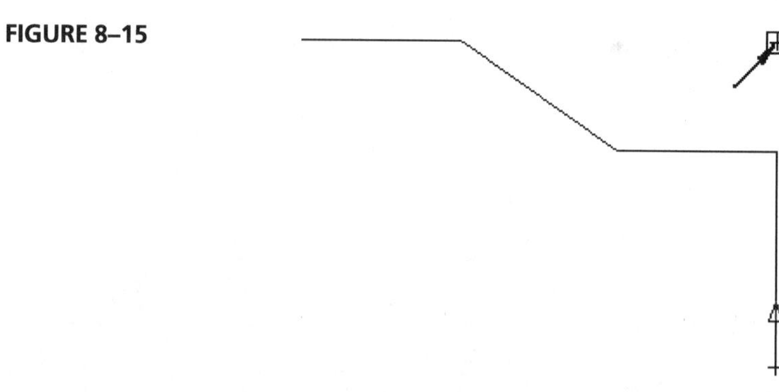

FIGURE 8–15

Roughing Parameters

Parameter file... ROUGH.PRM Cancel Done

Roughing Method: One way | Zigzag

Rough Direction: OD

Roughing angle 0.0

Overlap amount 0.01

Tool Parameters

Tool Select | Current Tool: Not Defined

Number	1	Offset	1
Radius	0.03125	Width	1.25

Equal steps

Coolant: Flood

Cutter Compensation

In computer: Right | Off | Left

In control: Right | Off | Left

Roll Cutter Around Corners: None | Sharp | All

Linearization tolerance	0.001
Amount of each cut	0.05
Stock to leave in X	0.02
Stock to leave in Z	0.01
Start seq. n. 10 Increment	10
Program number	1330

Feedrate	0.015	Inches / Rev	Inches / Min
Slow Feedrate	0.0075	Inches / Rev	Inches / Min
Spindle speed	300	CSS	RPM
Maximum spindle speed	5000	RPM	

Coordinates | Entry / Exit Vectors | Misc. Values | Tool Display

FIGURE 8–16

appear on the screen. Place the mouse in the large white space indicated by the arrow in Figure 8–17. Open the Tool Selection menu by clicking the right mouse button.

From the Tool Selection menu select **Get from Library.** The Tool Manager should now appear (see Figure 8–18).

FIGURE 8–17

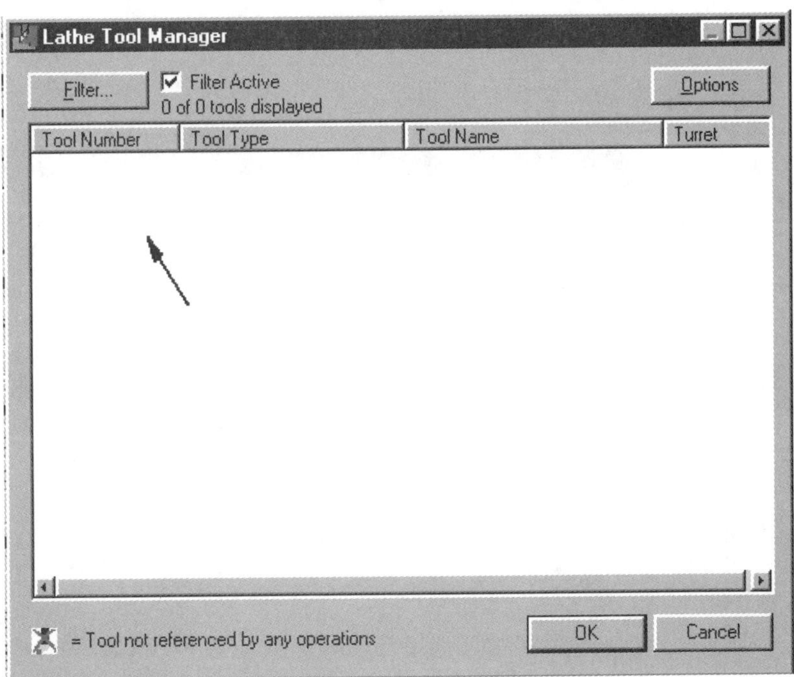

FIGURE 8–18

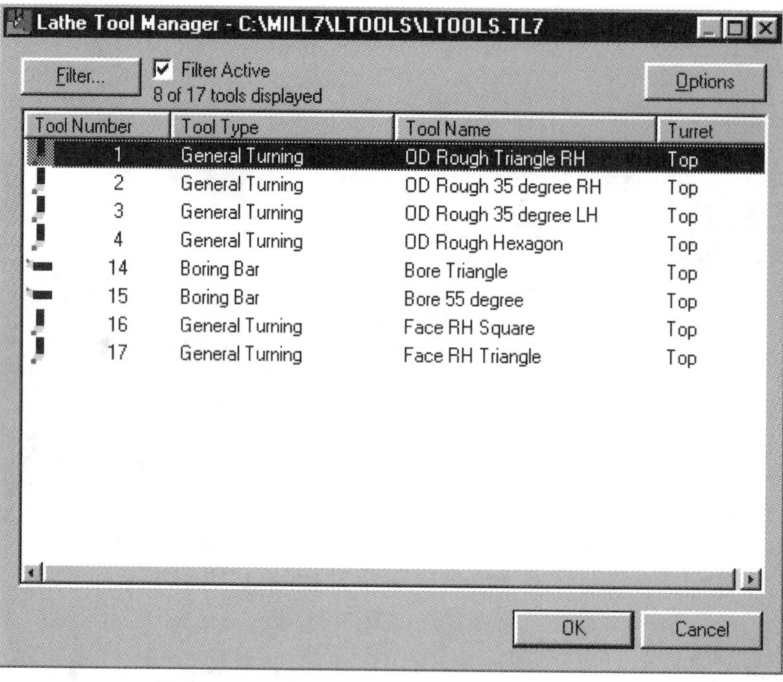

Select tool number **1.** This should be the right, triangular shaped roughing tool. Now select **OK.** You can see that this tool has been added to the lathe tool manager. A number of tool files reside within Mastercam. This is the simplest and easiest tool file, so it is a good one to begin with.

Next you will look more closely at the tool you have chosen. Put the mouse over the Tool icon indicated by the arrow in Figure 8–19. Now click the right mouse button.

The Define Tool dialogue box should now appear on the screen (see Figure 8–20).

FIGURE 8–19

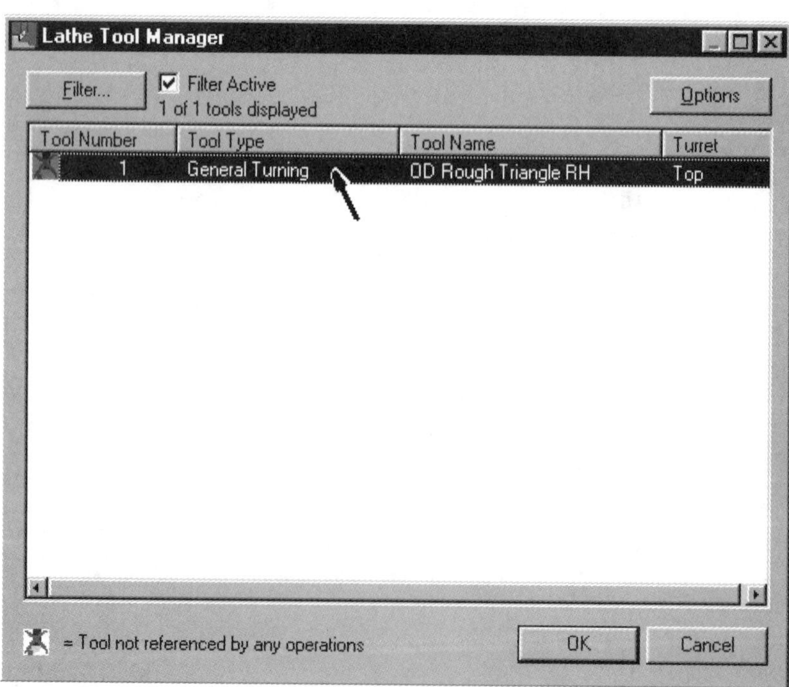

FIGURE 8–20

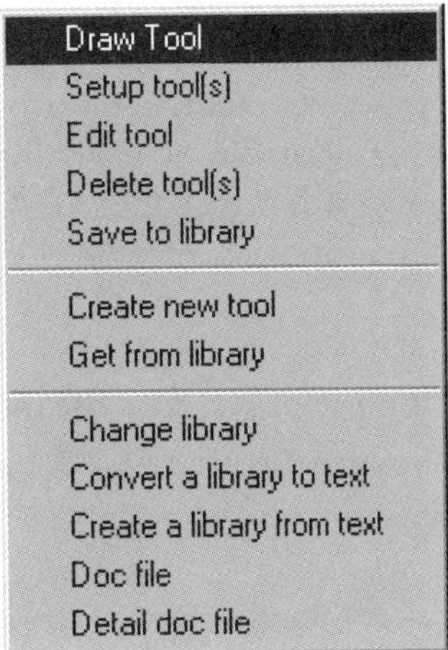

Select Draw Tool from This Menu

Notice that Mastercam switches back to the geometry creation screen and your tool appears on the screen. You could change the geometry of this tool the same way you create geometry in the main area of Mastercam. You don't need to change this tool, so either press the **Esc** key or select Continue. You should now be back at the Lathe Tool Manager menu. Select **OK.** You can look at any tool in the tool library using the same technique. This feature comes in very handy when you are looking for the correct tool.

Now you need to go back and look at the Roughing Parameters menu.

Roughing Method

Find the Roughing Method area. This parameter lets you set the method in which you want to cut the part. If you select One Way, the tool will cut in one direction only. The tool will start at one end of the cut, lift up, rapid back, and start the cut back at the beginning. If you choose Zigzag, the tool will cut in both directions. This could save time, but it can be done only with the proper tooling. See Figure 8–21 for an illustration of both roughing methods. Select **One Way,** if it is not already selected.

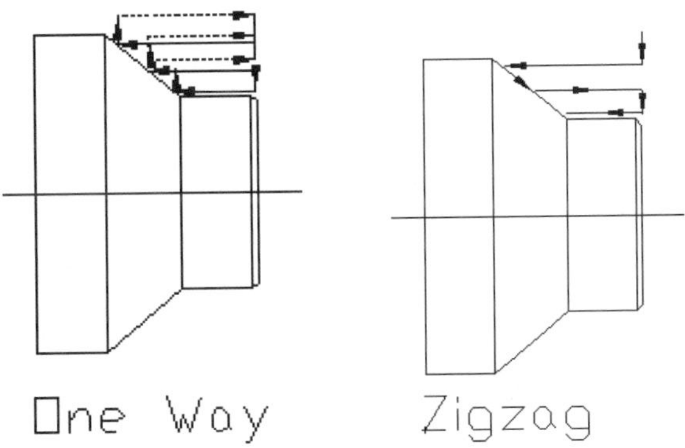

FIGURE 8–21

Rough Direction

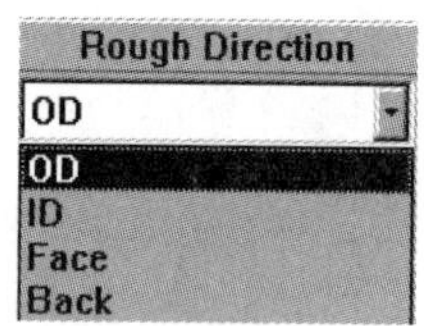

FIGURE 8–22

This pull-down menu allows you to select the cutting direction for rough cutting the part. The choices of roughing directions are OD, ID, Face, and Back (see Figure 8–22). You will notice that Mastercam looks at the tool and defaults to the rough direction it thinks is most likely to be correct.

Choosing OD creates the tool path on the outside of the part profile.

Choosing ID creates the tool path on the inside of the part profile.

Choosing Face creates the tool path in the facing direction (see Figure 8–23).

Choosing Back creates the tool path from the back face of the part.

Accept the default of **OD** rough cutting direction.

Roughing Angle

This parameter sets the cut direction angle. The Angle text box allows you to type in the cut direction angle relative to the roughing direction (see Figure 8–24). The typical rough cutting angle is parallel to the Z axis of the part. The parallel angle is zero. Type **0** or accept 0 as the default.

Overlap Amount

Activating the Overlap Amount check box allows you to choose the overlap amount. The overlap amount determines how far above the previous cut the tool will retract before the tool repositions for the next cut (Figure 8–25).

If you are using the Zigzag roughing method and turn off the retract amount, the tool will plunge to the next cut depth without retracting. If you are using the One Way roughing method and turn off the retract amount, the tool will retract to the previous cut depth. Check the **Overlap Amount** check box and set the retract amount to **.01.**

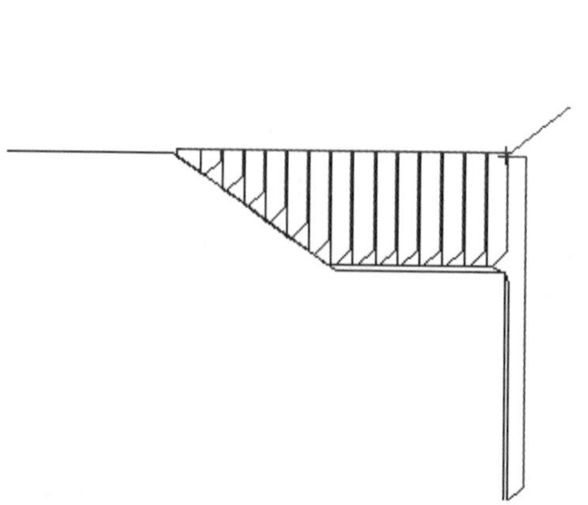

FIGURE 8–23

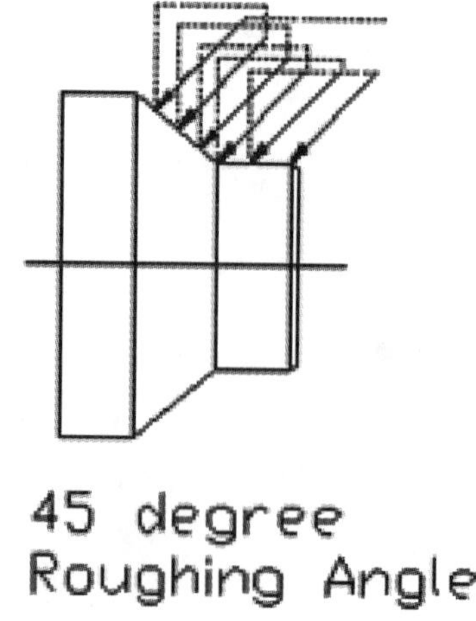

FIGURE 8–24

FIGURE 8–25

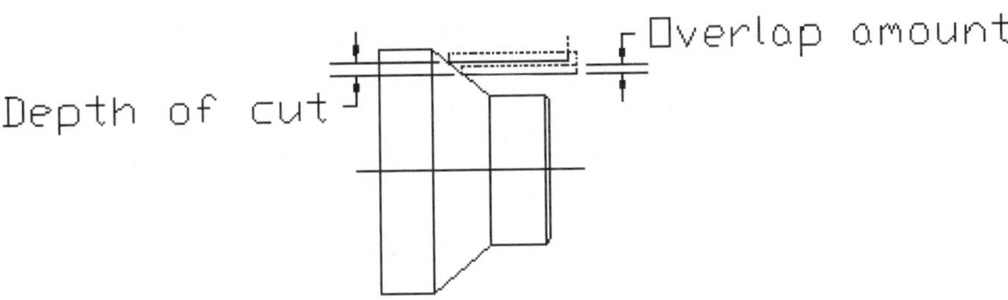

Cutter Compensation

Cutter compensation is a type of offset. All lathe tools have some type of tool tip radius. The tool tip radius helps to strengthen the tool and give the part a better finish. Without using some type of offset, the imaginary tip of the tool would be located on the programmed geometry (see Figure 8–26). This would cause tapers or radii on the part to be cut improperly.

FIGURE 8–26

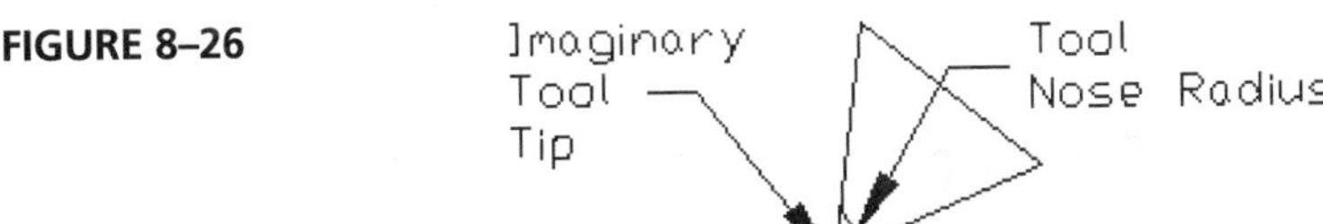

Cutter compensation allows you to offset the tool to the right or to the left of the profile of the part. The direction of the compensation depends on position of the tool in conjunction with the profile of the part (see Figure 8–27). An easy way to figure cutter compensation direction is to think of yourself as walking on the edge of the part in the direction of the cut: Do you want the cutter on your right side or your left side?

FIGURE 8–27

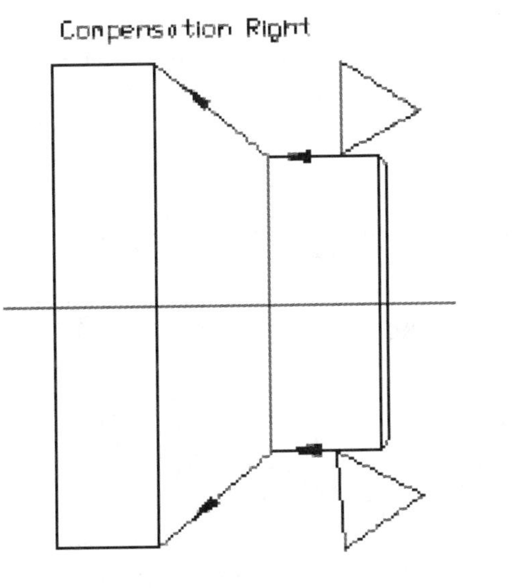

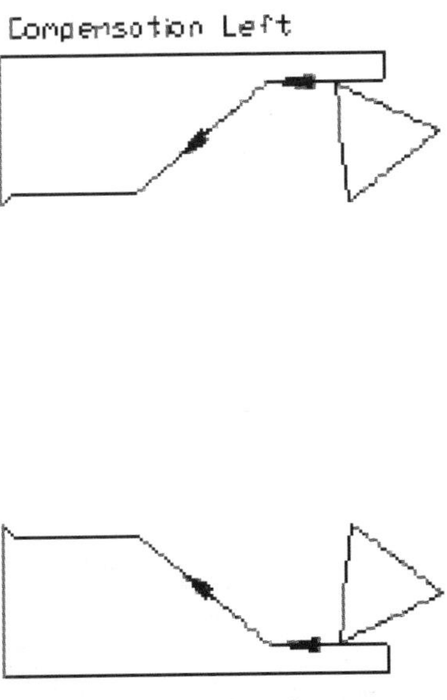

Letting Mastercam Generate Tool Compensation

When Mastercam generates code to run the machine tool it can be set to compensate for the tool tip radius of the cutting tool. Assigning cutter compensation in the computer will generate code with the tool path compensated, but it will not generate a compensation code (G41, G42). For this first example you will offset the tool path at the machine tool control using the G41 or G42 code that will be generated. Set the compensation in computer to **Off.**

Letting the Machine Generate the Tool Compensation

The compensation in the control will be set to Right. With these settings set the way they are, Mastercam will generate a G42 tool nose radius compensation code. The amount of tool nose radius compensation will need to be input at the machine. If the cutter compensation in control is set to the left, Mastercam will generate a G41 code; if the cutter compensation in control is set to the right, Mastercam will generate a G42 code.

Knowing which compensation is correct may seem confusing, but after you have postprocessed your first program it will become much clearer. After you have converted this program to machine language take a look at how Mastercam handled your cutter compensation parameter settings.

Offset

Offset generates the number of the offset associated with the tool. Normally, when the tool is called in the program, it corresponds to the tool number. An example of a tool call is T01. This tells the machine to index to or call tool number 1. In lathe programming there is always an offset number associated with the tool number. A normal tool call for a lathe would look like T0101. T means tool call. The first 01 stands for tool number 1. The second 01 stands for offset 01. The offset 01 corresponds to an offset table in the control. The amount of tool offset for such things as tool wear or tool deflection is set in the control under this offset number. Set the Offset to **1.**

Amount of Each Cut

The amount of each cut is the depth of cut per pass. This depth is per side. If you set the depth at 0.05 inches, the diameter of the part will be reduced by 0.100 inches per cut pass. Set the amount of each cut to **0.05** inches.

Stock to Leave in X

The Stock to Leave parameter allows you to leave stock on the X axis for future or secondary finish operations. This parameter is used as a finish stock allowance. Set Stock to Leave in X at **0.02** inches.

Stock to Leave in Z

The Stock to Leave parameter allows you to leave stock on the Z axis for future or secondary finish operations. This parameter is used as a finish stock allowance. Set Stock to Leave in Z at **0.01** inches.

Start Seq. n.

Starting sequence number for line numbers. Enter **10.**

Increment

Increment values for each line number. Enter **10**.

Program Number

This parameter sets the program number. The program number will appear in the beginning of the NCI program. Input any 4-digit number for the program number.

Feedrate

This is the feedrate setting for the roughing passes. You have set the feedrate in Job Setup. Make sure that the type of feedrate is set to **Inches/rev.**

Slow Feedrate

The Slow Feedrate option allows you to slow the plunge tool move to a feedrate lower than the rough-cut feedrate. This parameter setting is used when the plunge tool path will be cutting stock. Our tool does not contact rough stock when moving down to cut depth. Leave the Slow Feedrate parameter at the default setting. Turn on **Inches/Rev** to set the type of feedrate.

Spindle Speed

The Spindle Speed can be set to surface footage for the tool and material, or you can input an RPM. For roughing cuts, constant surface footage is the most economical. Constant surface footage will automatically speed up the spindle as the tool gets closer to the center of the part, maintaining constant surface footage. When drilling or thread cutting you will want to set the spindle speed in RPM. You have stated the material type in Job Setup, so the surface footage should already be set.

Maximum Spindle Speed

When using constant surface footage the spindle will speed up as the tool gets closer to the center of the part. You can set a maximum to which the spindle will speed up. This is done for safety reasons. Set the maximum spindle speed to **5000 RPM.**

Entry/Exit Vectors

Entry and Exit Vectors are the paths the tool enters and exits the part for each cut. The Entry/Exit Vector parameter settings allow for a smooth transition of the tool into and out of the cut (Figure 8–28). The Entry Vector is the path that the tool makes when entering the stock for each roughing pass. The Exit Vector is the path the tool takes after each roughing pass.

Choose the **Entry/Exit Vectors** button at the bottom of the Roughing Parameters page. The Entry/Exit Vectors dialogue box should now appear on the screen (Figure 8–29).

The Entry/Exit Vectors dialogue box has three pages: the Entry Vector page, the Exit Vector page, and the Auto Entry/Exit page.

Entry

The Entry Vector page is the initial page that you enter upon choosing the Entry/Exit Vectors dialogue box. There are a number of ways to set the entry/exit vectors: the angle dial, the line button, Intelli-Set, and points.

Angle Dial You can use your mouse to click on the dial hand and move it so that it points in the direction you wish the tool to enter or exit the cut. Put the mouse on the dial hand. Click and hold down the left mouse button and move the dial to the **6:00** position (the straight down direction).

Line This parameter brings you back to the graphics screen and allows you to draw or select a line that you wish to use as your entry and exit vector. When you complete the line vector settings you will return to the dialogue box and the angle dial will reflect your direction vector, line length, and the X and Z components.

Intelli-Set Intelli-Set automatically sets the entry and exit vectors based on the orientation of the tool. Choose this option only if you know the entry/exit vector angle relative to the part. When you complete the Intelli-Set vector settings the angle dial will reflect your direction vector.

Points If you choose the Points option, you will return to the graphics screen. Once in the graphics screen you can choose two points that will define the angle direction vector, line length, and X and Z components.

Clear

If you choose clear, Mastercam will set all of the variables back to zero.

Length

The Length parameter setting sets the length of the entry/exit vector.

FIGURE 8–28

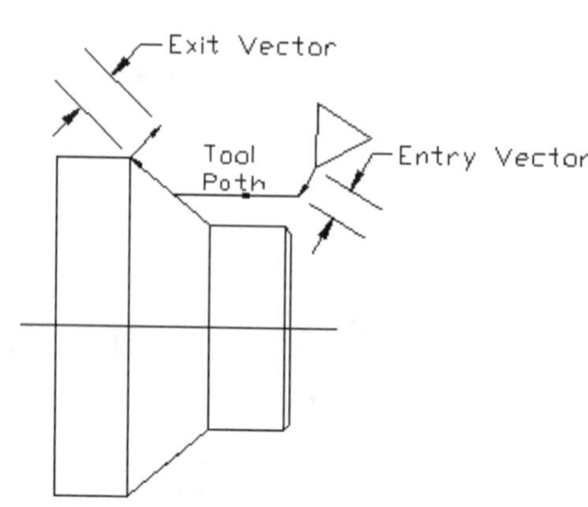

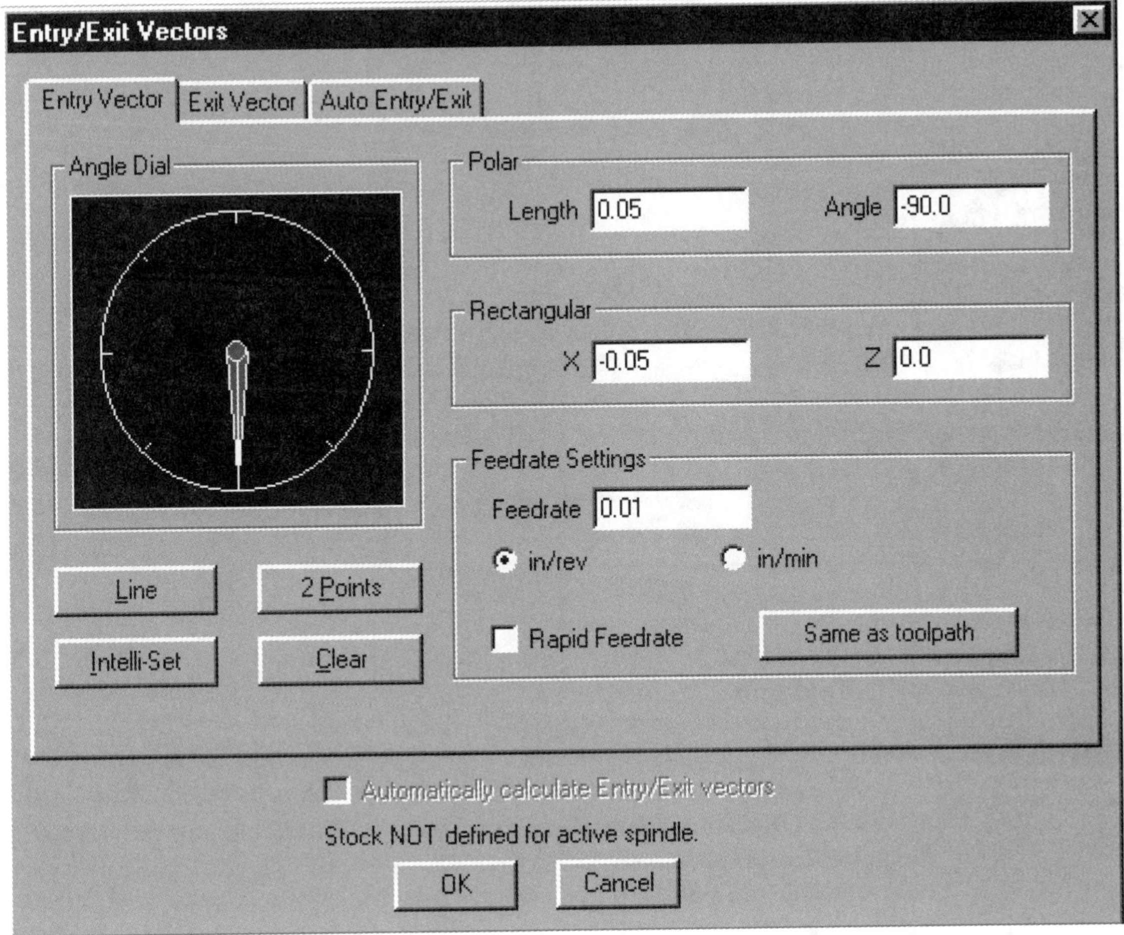

FIGURE 8–29

Angle
The Angle parameter setting sets the angle of the entry/exit vector.

X
The value you enter under X is the X-axis incremental distance of the entry or exit vector.

Z
The value you enter under Z is the Z-axis incremental distance of the entry or exit vector.

Feedrate
The Feedrate parameter setting sets the feedrate of the entry/exit vector.

Rapid Feedrate
The Rapid Feedrate parameter sets the feedrate of the entry/exit vector to the rapid rate of the machine.

Exit Vector
Select the Exit Vector tab above the angle dial. Set the Exit Vector Angle Dial to the **12:00** position (the straight up direction). Set the X rectangular distance to **0.05** and press **Enter** (Figure 8–30). You will notice that the Polar Length updates itself.

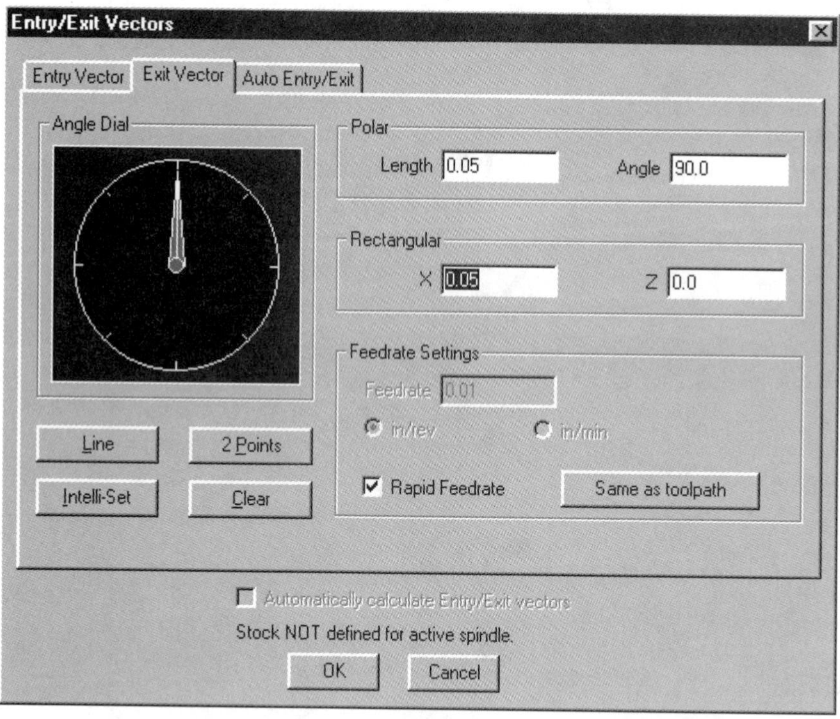

FIGURE 8–30

Select **OK** from the Entry/Exit Vectors screen. You should now be back to the Roughing Parameters screen.

Coordinates

Before you generate a tool path you must look at the Coordinates dialogue box. Choose the **Coordinates** button now. From the Coordinates dialogue box you can set the active spindle, the machine home position, and the tool origin position.

Active Spindle

The Active Spindle setting allows you to choose the type of spindle direction orientation you are using. Set the Active Spindle to **Left** if it is not already set to left.

Home Position

The Home Position is the position the tool travels to for tool changes. On smaller turning machines the home position and the machine home position are the same. On larger machines, with longer beds, the programmer will set up an intermediate home position. This speeds up noncutting time. As you become familiar with your machine and the procedure you use for setting the home position, the home position will become very clear. For our purposes type **10.00** and **10.00** in the Home Position D and Z boxes.

Tool Origin

The Tool Origin setting corresponds to the D0.0 Z0.0 coordinates of the part. The tool origin value is automatically set according to the tool selected. You can change these values by inputting the corresponding values in the text boxes. If you don't know the tool origin, choose the **Tool Origin** button to return to the graphics window. From the graphics window you can choose the Tool Origin. For our purposes, type **0.0** and **0.0** in the Tool Origin D and Z boxes.

Select **OK** to accept the coordinate settings. Now select **Done** from the Roughing Parameters dialogue box. You should now be back at the Mastercam Main Screen. Select **Yes** to accept this tool-path segment.

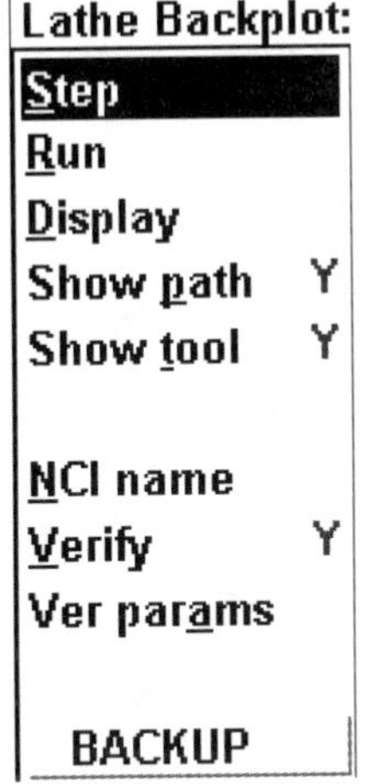

FIGURE 8–31

Backplotting the Tool Path

Select **Operations** from the Lathe Toolpaths menu. The Operations Manager dialogue box should appear on the screen. Select **Backplot.** The Lathe Backplot menu should now appear (Figure 8–31).

Set the Show Path, Show Tool, and Verify parameter to **Y** for yes. From the Lathe Backplot menu select **Step.** Step generates the tool path in step intervals. Every time you select step using the left mouse button you get the next tool move. If you want to see the tool path in the Run mode, press the **Esc** key, select **OK,** and select **Run.** You have now completed the Roughing module. Press the **Esc** key to get out of the Run mode. You will now finish turn the part. Select **OK** to exit the Operations Manager area.

Finish

The Finish module creates a finish tool path on the part. The finish tool path follows the part geometry making the final pass on the part. To enter the Finish mode select **Toolpaths** from the Main Menu. Now select **Finish** from the Toolpaths menu. Mastercam now asks you to select the Entry Point. The entry point is the point where the tool is going to contact material on the finish pass.

You have roughed the right end diameter to 1.02 and right end of the work piece is Z zero. From the Main Menu select **Point.** At the point prompt type **1.02,0.** The entry point should now appear on the screen (Figure 8–32). Remember you have built in clearance values for the tool in Job Setup.

Chaining is an important part of tool-path creation. Chaining is the selection of a set of connected lines, points, or arcs. The entities that you select become the basis for the tool path. Mastercam will now prompt you to Chain the contour. You don't want to finish the face of the part so you are going to leave the right end face of the part off of the finishing pass. Select **Chain** from the menu. Mastercam now prompts you to select Chain in the Chain 2 menu. Select **Partial** from the Chain 2 menu. You need to select Partial because you don't want the finish pass to follow the whole part geometry. Use the mouse to select the first horizontal line (see Figure 8–33).

FIGURE 8–32

FIGURE 8–33

FIGURE 8–34

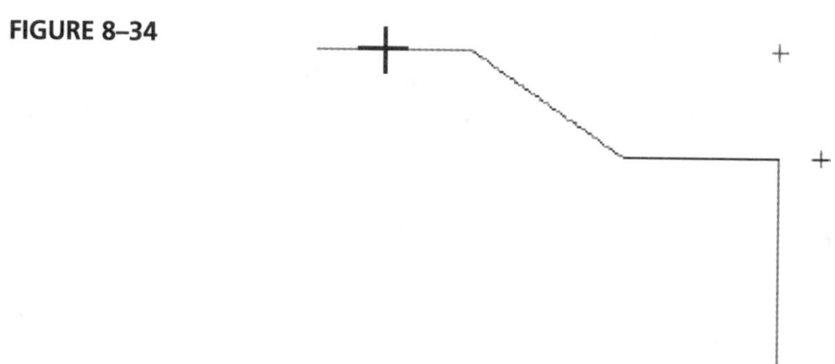

Mastercam now prompts you to select the last entity. Select the last entity. This is the other horizontal line (see Figure 8–34).

Only three entities should be selected at this point. Now select **Done** from the menu. Mastercam now prompts you to select the retract point. Select **Point** from the menu. Use the mouse to select the retract point from the roughing module. This will give you a clear intermediate point. Mastercam now tells you that the chaining is complete. Select **Done.**

Finishing

Upon selecting done the Finish parameters screen will appear (Figure 8–35).

The Finish Parameters screen is the area where common numerical control parameters are set. The first thing you will need to do is select a tool. Use the mouse to select the large **Tool Select** button. The Tool Manager box should now appear

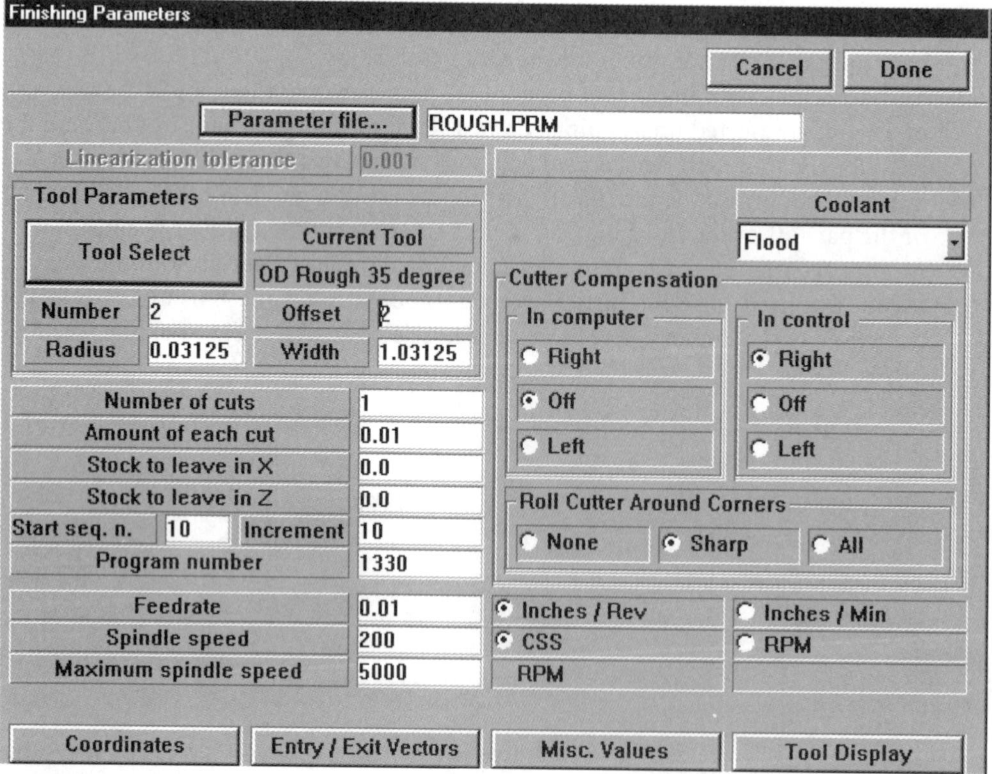

FIGURE 8–35

on the screen. Place the mouse in the large white space and open the tool selection menu by clicking the right mouse button. From the Tool Selection menu select **Get from Library.** The Tool Manager should now appear. Select tool number **2.** This should be the right-hand, 35-degree finishing tool. Select **OK.** You can see now that this tool has been added to the lathe tool manager. Select **OK.** Now you need to go back and look at the Finishing Parameters menu.

Offset
Set the Offset to **2.**

Number of Cuts
The number that you put in this box is the number of finish cuts you want to make. Set the number of cuts to **1** if it has not defaulted to 1.

Entry/Exit Vectors
Set the Entry dial to the **9:00** position if it has not already defaulted to this position. Set the Exit dial to the **3:00** position if it has not already defaulted to this position. Set the Exit Vector X rectangular amount to **0.02** and press **Enter.** Select **OK** from Entry/Exit Parameters screen.

That concludes our work in the Finishing Parameters area. Select **Done** from the Finishing Parameters dialogue box. After you select Done, Mastercam returns to the graphics area and the Change menu appears (Figure 8–36).

Change:
Write
Feedrate
Rapid
Manual ent
Can'd text
Spindle sp
Dwell

FIGURE 8–36

You need to look at the options available in the Change menu.

Dwell
The Dwell option allows you to pick a point where you want the tool to pause. You also have the ability to set the amount of time you want the tool to dwell for.

Spindle Speed
The Spindle Speed option allows you to pick a point where you want the spindle speed to change. You also have the ability to set the new speed for the spindle.

Canned Text
Canned Text is an area in the postprocessor where you can assign special commands such as an optional stop. This command will then be output in the NCI file. Mastercam allows you to set up ten of these variables.

Manual Entry
Manual Entry allows you to insert comments to the operator. Choosing this option allows you to pick a point where you want the comment to occur in the NCI file.

Rapid
The Rapid option allows you to pick a point where you want the tool to go from a feedrate to a rapid rate.

Feedrate
The Feedrate option allows you to pick a point and change the feedrate for that point. All of the other points retain their original feedrate.

Write
Choosing Write tells the system to enter the finish tool-path data, which you just compiled in Finish Parameters, in the NCI file. If you don't choose Write, the tool path will not be converted to NC data.

Choose **Write.** Mastercam now asks you if you want to select this tool-path segment. Select **Yes.**

Backplotting the Rough and Finish Tool Paths

Select **Operations** from the Lathe Toolpaths menu. The Operations Manager dialogue box has now appeared on the screen. Click on the **Select All** button to plot both the rough and finish paths. Select **Backplot.** The Lathe Backplot menu should now appear. Set the Show Path, Show Tool, and Verify Parameter to **Y** for yes. Type the **S** button on your keyboard to achieve the step tool path. Step generates the tool path in step intervals. Every time you type S you get the next tool move. If you want to see the tool path in the Run mode, press the **Esc** key, select **OK,** and select **Run.** You have now completed the Roughing module. Press the **Esc** key to get out of the Run mode.

Facing

Normally, the first operation you would perform when turning a part is facing. We postponed covering the facing operation unit: you could see how to move operations using the Operations Manager. You will now face the part. Select **OK** to exit the Operations Manager area. Select **Face** from the Toolpaths menu. Choosing Face tells Mastercam that you want to generate tool path on the face of the part.

Upon selecting Face, Mastercam prompts you to select the first boundary point. The facing module uses the creation of a rectangle. The two points of the rectangle make up the rough stock boundary and the face of the part (Figure 8–37). The first point is where the facing cycle starts and the second point is where the facing cycle ends.

For the first point type **1.50,.03** and press **Enter.** These values represent the diameter of the rough stock and the amount rough stock on the face of the part. Mastercam is now prompting you to select the second point. Type **0,0** and press **Enter.** These values represent the end and center of the workpiece. Upon selecting the second point the Facing Parameters dialogue box will appear (Figure 8–38).

The appearance of the Facing Dialogue box is similar to the other parameter dialogue boxes you have covered. Let's take a closer look at the parameters that are unique to facing.

Face Rough

Choosing the Face Rough button will allow you to make face roughing passes. If you have a great deal of stock on the face of the part, use this parameter to remove material on the face of the part. It is possible to select both the Face Rough and Face Finish option check boxes. Activate the **Face Rough** button now.

FIGURE 8–37

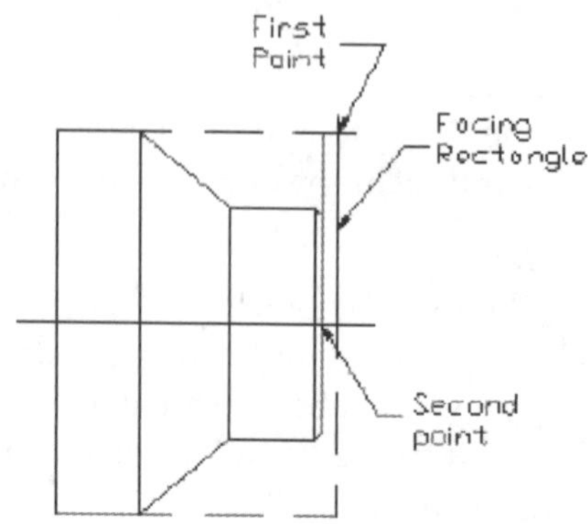

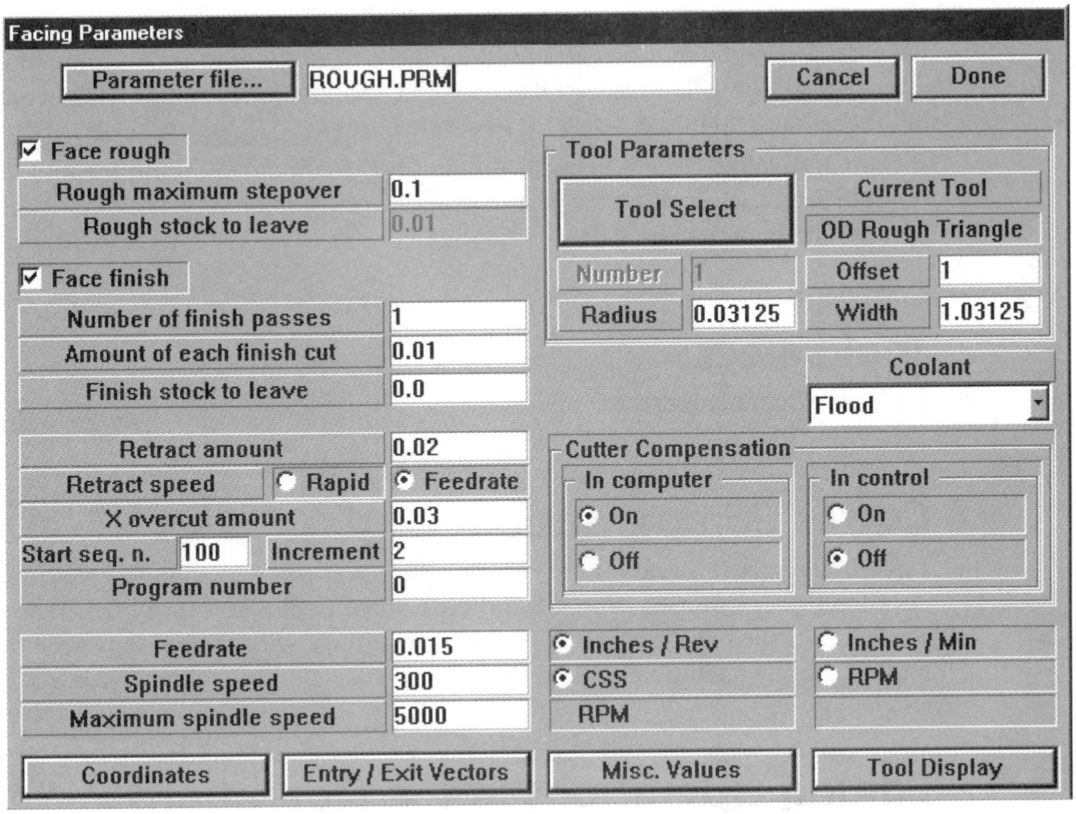

FIGURE 8–38

Rough Maximum Stepover If you activate the Face Rough check box the Rough Maximum Stepover parameter setting becomes active. The maximum stepover value is the largest cut the roughing tool pass will make. Since you only have 0.03 stock to face, accept the default.

Rough Stock to Leave In this area you can input a value for the amount of finish stock to be left on the part after roughing. The Rough Stock to Leave parameter becomes available only if you activate the Face Rough check box and de-activate the Finish check.

Face Finish

Choosing the Face Finish button allows you to make finish facing passes. It is possible to select both the Face Rough and Face Finish option check boxes. If you choose both Face Rough and Face Finish, separate parameters settings will become available for both sets of tool paths. Activate the **Face Finish** button.

Number of Finish Passes The number you input in this area will determine the number of facing finish passes the tool will make. Enter **1** for the Number of Finish Passes.

Amount of Each Finish Cut This parameter setting controls the amount of each finish cut pass. Set this parameter to **0.01** inches.

Finish Stock to Leave This parameter setting controls the amount of material that will be left on the face of the part after the last finish-facing cut. Enter **0.0.**

Retract Amount The value that is entered here will be the distance that the tool backs away from the part before the tool repositions for the next facing cut. Enter **0.02** for the Retract Amount.

Retract Speed The Retract Speed is the speed at which the tool backs away from the part. The rapid choice would position the tool at the maximum positioning rate of the machine. The feedrate choice would position the tool at the feedrate set in the Feedrate text box. Activate the **Feedrate** button.

X Overcut Amount The X Overcut Amount is the amount you want the tool to travel beyond the center of the part to avoid leaving a nubbin on the face of the part. Set this parameter to **0.03.**

Tool Select

Set the tool number and offset to **1**.

Cutter Compensation

Typically, you want Mastercam to calculate the cutter compensation when facing. Turn the Cutter Compensation **On** and the Compensation in Control **Off.** When you have finished with the Facing parameter settings select **Done.** It is time to move the facing operation to the proper position using the Operations Manager.

Editing Operations in the Operations Manager

The Operations Manager gives you the ability to sort, move, or change any of the operations associated with the part. Open the Operations Manager using the **Operations Manager** icon in the tool bar. The Operations Manager dialogue box should now appear on the screen (see Figure 8–39).

The new facing operation should now be visible at the bottom of the Operations Manager operations list. The Operations Manager dialogue box is where you will move the facing operation. Use the mouse to select the parameters folder associated with the facing operation (see Figure 8–40).

FIGURE 8–39

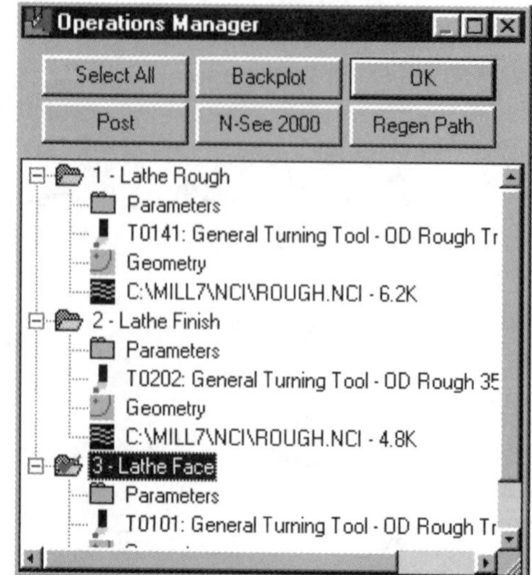

FIGURE 8–40

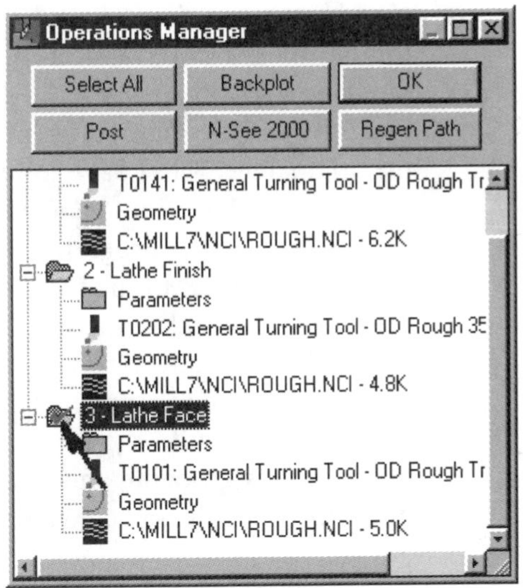

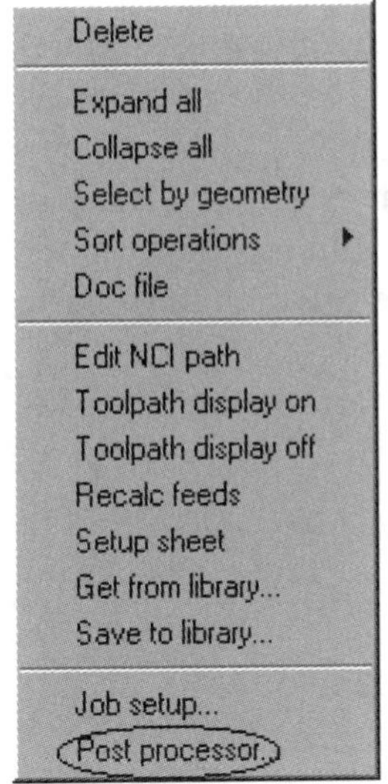

FIGURE 8–41

While holding the left mouse button down, drag the file folder up and place it on top of the **1-Lathe Rough** folder (see Figure 8–41). Notice that the Face operation has not moved to the top. You cannot place an operation at the top of the list; you must move the number 1 rough operation down. Use the mouse to select the **Parameters** folder associated with the 1-Lathe Rough operation. While holding the left mouse button down, drag this file folder down and place it on top of the **2-Lathe Face** folder. The Operations Manager should now be in the proper order.

You have now changed the machining operation so that the facing operation occurs first. Make sure all operations are selected before verifying the changes in Backplot. Press the **Select All** button now. Backplot the program. Verify the tool path in Backplot. Unzoom the graphics screen so you can see the full tool path. If it doesn't look correct, go back and look at the parameter settings. Once the tool path looks correct, it is time to postprocess the tool path into numerical control machine language.

NC Utilities

You will now need to postprocess the lathe tool path into machine language. From the tool bar select the **Toolpaths-Operations Manager** icon. The Operations Manager dialogue box should appear on the screen. Place the mouse cursor in the **Operations Manager** dialogue box and press the right mouse button. The operations edit dialogue box should now appear on the screen (Figure 8–41).

Mastercam has a number of postprocessor data files. The postprocessor file creates machine codes specific to the type of machine control you select. From the Operations Edit dialogue box select **Post Processor.**

Mastercam makes it possible to take the same tool-path file and postprocess it for many different types of controls. The postprocessor files end with a .pst extension. The number of files you see are only a small portion of the number of postprocessor files available through Mastercam. Select the **Mplfan.pst** file and press the **Open** button.

Choose **Select All** to make sure you postprocess all of the tool paths associated with our part program. Select **Post** from the Operations Manager.

Mastercam now asks you to name the NC file that it is going to create. Name this NC file the same name as the geometry file. Mastercam now will create an NC file. This is the file that will be downloaded to the machine tool to make the part. Since the two files have different extensions you will not be writing over the top of the original file. Select **Save.** Your coded file should now appear on the screen. Take note of how Mastercam handled our tool nose radius compensation selections.

Maximize the Program Editor screen by using the **Maximize** button in the upper right corner of the screen. The Programmer's File Editor allows you to edit, print, and manipulate the NC file. Exit the Programmer's File Editor by selecting the exit **X** in the upper right corner of the screen.

You have now completed the first exercise in Mastercam lathe machining. You will now move onto the next exercise. The next exercise will deal with the same modules plus grooving and threading. Pay close attention because new information will be added as you go along.

EXAMPLE EXERCISE 2

Figure 8–42 will be used to demonstrate the Threading and Grooving modules. You have to complete the Face, Rough, and Finish modules before you can groove and thread the part.

Using your skills from the previous chapters, create the geometry for Figure 8–42. Make sure that the Cplane is set to Diameter programming. Your geometry creation should look like the part in Figure 8–43. Save this geometry file as **Exercise2.**

Now that you have created the necessary geometry let's start creating tool path.

FIGURE 8–42

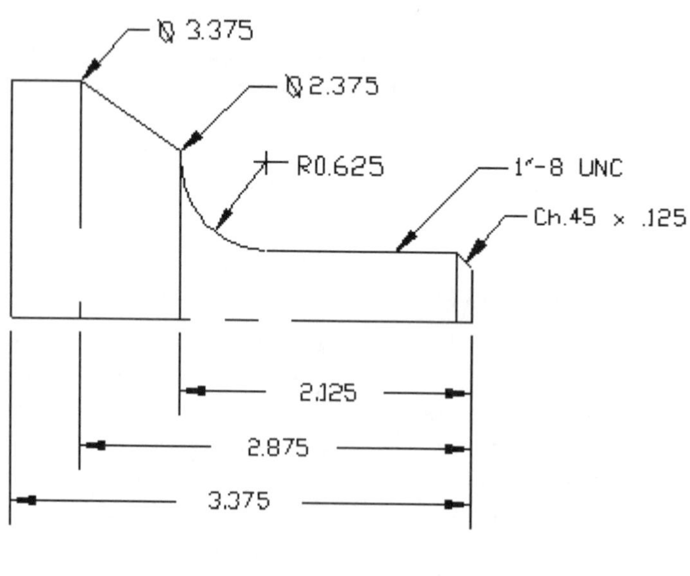

FIGURE 8–43

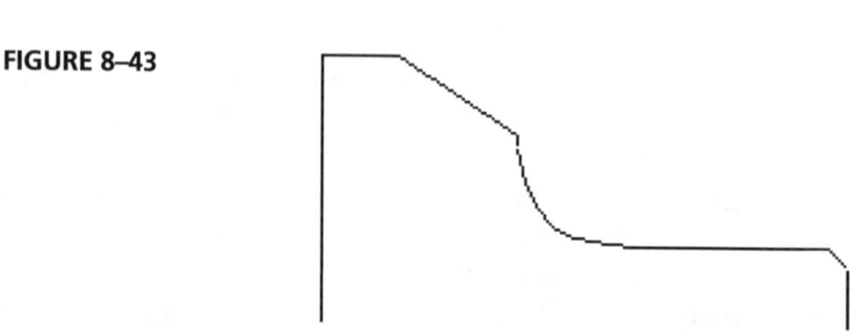

Job Setup

Access the Job Setup parameters by first selecting **Toolpaths** from the Lathe Main Menu screen. From the Lathe Toolpaths menu select **Next Menu**. Now select **Job Setup**. The Lathe Job Setup dialogue box should appear on the screen. In review, the commands were Toolpaths/Next Menu/Job Setup.

Material

Choose the **Select** button from the Material area of Job Setup. From the Lathe material list select **Aluminum Inch-6061.** Select **OK** to accept your selection. You should now be back to the Job Setup dialogue box. Activate the **Material** button to have Mastercam calculate the cutting conditions according to the material you selected. Next select **OK.**

Tool Clearance

The system default is set to 0.05 inches on rapid moves and 0.01 on entry/exit moves. If the tool clearances are not set to these values, set them now.

Facing

You will now face the part. Select **Face** from the Toolpaths menu. Upon selecting face, Mastercam prompts you to name the NCI file. Name the NCI file **Exercise 2.** The facing module uses the creation of a rectangle. The first boundary point of the rectangle is 3.50 and .05. Type **3.50** and **.05** and press **Enter.** This means you are using 3.50-inch-diameter stock with 0.05-inch excess stock on the face of the part. The second boundary point is the end and center of the part. Type **0,0** and press **Enter.** The Facing Parameter box should now appear on the screen.

Face Rough

You will not be activating the Face Rough button. You will make only one finishing cut.

Face Finish

Activate the **Face Finish** button now.

Number of Finish Passes The number you input in this area will determine the number of facing finish passes the tool will make. Enter **1** for the number of finish passes.

Amount of Each Finish Cut Set this parameter to **0.05** inches.

Finish Stock to Leave Input **0.0.**

Retract Amount Input **0.02** for the Retract Amount.

Retract Speed Activate the **Feedrate** button.

X Overcut Amount Set this parameter to **0.03.**

Tool Select

Use the mouse to select the large **Tool Select** button. The Tool Manager box should now appear on the screen. Place the mouse in the large white space. Click the right mouse button. You are going to change tool libraries, so select **Change Libraries.** From the tool libraries list select **Kennamet.tl7.** Save this file. The Tool Selection menu should still be on the screen. Place the mouse in the large white space and click the right mouse button. From the Tool Selection menu, select **Get from Library.** Put the mouse over the tool named **DCGNR-164D** and press the right mouse button. Select **Draw Tool.** The tool should appear on the graphics screen. The tool should be a right-hand roughing tool. Select **Continue** to return to the

Tool Manager dialogue box. Now select **OK.** You can see that this tool has been added to the lathe tool manager.

Tool Offset

Change tool offset to **1.**

Entry Vector

Entry Vector dial should be set to the **6:00** position.

Exit Vector

Exit Vector should be set to the **3:00** position.

Cutter Compensation

Typically, you want Mastercam to handle the cutter compensation when facing. Turn the cutter compensation in computer **On** and the compensation in control **Off.** When you have finished with the Facing Parameter settings select **Done.**

Initiating the Rough Module

From the Main menu select **Toolpaths.** From the Toolpaths menu select **Rough.** Mastercam should now be prompting you to select the Entry Point. Use the same position as the first point you used for the facing module. Type **3.50,.05.**

Chaining

You don't want to rough machine the face of the part, so you are going to leave the right end face of the part off of the roughing module. Select **Chain** from the menu. Mastercam now prompts you to select Chain in the Chain 2 menu. Select **Partial** from the Chain 2 menu. You need to select Partial because you don't want the finish pass to follow the whole part geometry. Use the mouse to select the chamfer on the right end of the part. Mastercam is now prompting you to select the last entity. Select the last horizontal line (see Figure 8–44).

Select **Done** from the menu. Mastercam now prompts you to select the retract point. Select **Point** from the menu. Use the mouse to select the same point you used as the entry point. Mastercam now tells you that the Rough chaining is complete. Select **Done** from the menu. The Rough Parameters screen will appear.

The first thing you will need to do is select a tool. Use the mouse to select the large **Tool Select** button. The Tool Manager box should now appear on the screen. Select the same tool you used for facing, tool number **1.** Select **OK.**

Roughing Method

Select **One Way,** if it is not already selected.

Rough Direction

Accept the default of **O.D.** rough cutting direction.

FIGURE 8–44

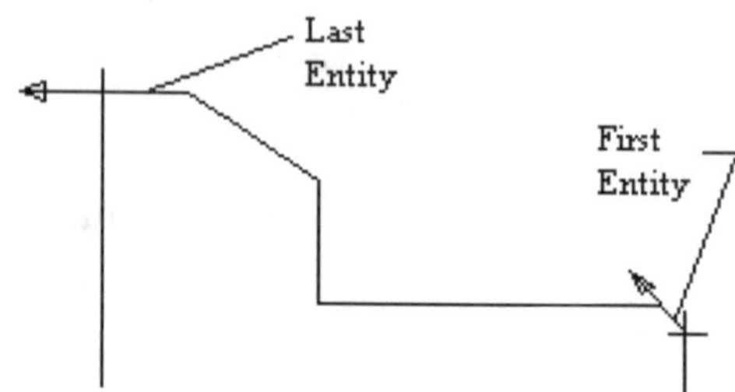

Roughing Angle
Type **0** or accept 0 as the default.

Overlap Amount
Check the **Retract Amount** check box and set the retract amount to **.01.**

Cutter Compensation
To see how the compensation selections affect the outcome of the NCI file, set the compensation in computer to **Right** and the compensation in the control to **Off.** This is opposite of our first example program. Compare the two when you are done with this program.

Offset
Set the offset to **1.**

Amount of Each Cut
Set the amount of each cut to **0.100** inches.

Stock to Leave in X
Set Stock to Leave in the X axis at **0.02** inches.

Stock to Leave in Z
Set Stock to Leave in the Z axis at **0.01** inches.

Start Seq. n.
Starting sequence number for the line numbers. Enter **10.**

Increment
Enter **10.**

Program Number
Enter **1000** for the program number.

Feedrate
Make sure that the type of feedrate is set to **Inches/Rev.**

Spindle Speed
Surface footage should already be set from our Job Setup selections.

Maximum Spindle Speed
When using constant surface footage the spindle will speed up as the tool gets closer to the center of the part. You can set a maximum to which the spindle will speed up. This is done for safety reasons. Set the maximum spindle speed to 5000 RPM.

Entry/Exit Vectors
Choose the **Entry/Exit Vectors** button at the bottom of the Roughing Parameters page.

Angle Dial Put the mouse cursor on the **9:00** position and press the right mouse button. This will move the dial to the 9:00 position.

Exit Vector Select the **Exit Vector** tab above the angle dial. Set the Exit Vector Angle Dial to the **3:00** position. Set the X Rectangular distance to **0.05** and press **Enter.**

Coordinates
Open the Coordinates dialogue box by choosing the **Coordinates** button now.

Active Spindle Set the Active Spindle to **Left** if it is not already set to left.

Home Position The Home Position is the position the tool travels to for tool changes. For our purposes type **10.00** and **10.00** in the home position D and Z boxes.

Tool Origin For our purposes type **0.0** and **0.0** in the Tool Origin D and Z boxes. Select **OK** to accept the coordinate settings. Select **Done** from the Roughing Parameters dialogue box. You should now be back at the Mastercam main screen. Select **Yes** to accept this tool-path segment.

Finishing

From the Toolpaths menu select **Finish.**

Mastercam is now prompting you to select the Entry Point. Select **Point.** Type in **1.03,.05.**

Chaining

You don't want to finish machine the face of the part, so you are going to leave the right end face of the part off of the Facing module. Select **Chain** from the menu. Mastercam now prompts you to select chain in the Chain 2 menu. Select **Partial** from the Chain 2 menu. You need to select Partial because you don't want the finish pass to follow the whole part geometry. Use the mouse to select the chamfer on the right end of the part. Mastercam is now prompting you to select the last entity. Select the last horizontal line.

This is exactly the same procedure you learned in the Rough module.

Select **Done** from the menu. Mastercam now prompts you to select the retract point. Select **Point** from the menu. Use the mouse to select the same point you used as the Rough entry point. Mastercam now tells you that the Finish chaining is complete. Select **Done.** The Finish Parameters screen will appear.

Use the mouse to select the large **Tool Select** button. The Tool Manager box should now appear on the screen. Place the mouse in the large white space and open the Tool Selection menu by clicking the right mouse button. From the Tool Selection menu select **Get from Library.** The Tool Manager should now appear. Select the tool named **NVLCR-163D.** This should be the right-hand, 35-degree finishing tool. Select **OK.** You can see that this tool has been added to the Lathe Tool Manager. Select **OK.** Now you need to go back and complete the Finishing parameters.

Offset

Set the Offset to **2.**

Number of Cuts

Set the number of cuts to **1** if it has not defaulted to 1.

Entry/Exit Vectors

Set the Entry dial to the **9:00** position if it has not already defaulted to this position. Set the Exit dial to the **3:00** position if it has not already defaulted to this position. Set the Exit Vector X rectangular amount to **0.02** and press **Enter.** Select **OK** from Entry/Exit Parameters screen.

That concludes our work in the Finishing parameters area. Select **Done** from the Finishing Parameters dialogue box.

After selecting Done, Mastercam returns to the graphics area and the Change menu appears.

Write

Choose **Write** now. Mastercam now asks you if you want to select this tool-path segment. Select **Yes.** Let's check to see how you are doing so far before you begin the grooving module.

Backplotting the Rough and Finish Tool Path

Select **Operations** from the Lathe Toolpaths menu. The Operations Manager dialogue box has now popped up on the screen. Click on the **Select All** button to plot both the rough and finish paths. Select **Backplot.** The Lathe Backplot menu should now appear. Type **S** on your keyboard to achieve the step tool path or type **R** on your keyboard to achieve the run tool path. When the tool path looks correct, move on to the Grooving module.

Grooving

Choose **Groove** from the Lathe Toolpaths menu. Mastercam offers many methods for groove creation. The Groove creation module allows you to groove a simple rectangular groove or a groove that follows a complex profile of a part.

1 Point

The Groove menu should now be displayed on the screen. The first groove option in the menu is 1 point. Choosing 1 Point or 2 Point tells Mastercam that you want to create a simple rectangular groove. In the 1 Point or 2 Point groove module you don't need to have created the groove ahead of time; you can create the point where you want the groove to be located. Select **1 point** now.

Choose **Manual** from the 1 Point menu. Upon selecting manual, the Point Entry menu appears. From this menu you can select a point, endpoint, midpoint, or intersection. Any type of point can be selected as groove location. You can also just type in the location of the groove. Type **1.00,−1.25.** Press **Enter.** Choosing Window instead of Manual would have allowed you to use your mouse to select more than one point at a time by drawing a rectangle around them. Each point that is selected in the window becomes the position for a new groove.

Our manual point should now appear on the screen. I know that this groove doesn't appear on the screen, but I needed to show you how to create points for grooving. You have completed the locating point for the groove. Press the **Esc** key.

The Grooving Parameters dialogue box should now appear on the screen (Figure 8–45).

Activate the **Groove Rough** check box and click on the **Groove Rough** button. By checking the box you have added a roughing cycle to the grooving module. The Groove Rough dialogue box should now appear on the screen (Figure 8–46).

Most of the parameter settings throughout Mastercam are very similar. You will concentrate on the parameters that are specific to the Grooving module.

Step Direction

Step Direction is the cut direction. The cut direction is the direction in which the tool will cut to achieve the width of the groove (Figure 8–47). Positive step cuts from left to right. Negative step cuts from right to left. Center cutting starts at the center of the groove and moves left and right until the rough groove path is finished. Select **Positive Step** now.

Stock Clearance

Stock clearance is the incremental distance that the tool retracts above the top of the groove between plunges (Figure 8–47). Type **.05** inches and press **Enter.**

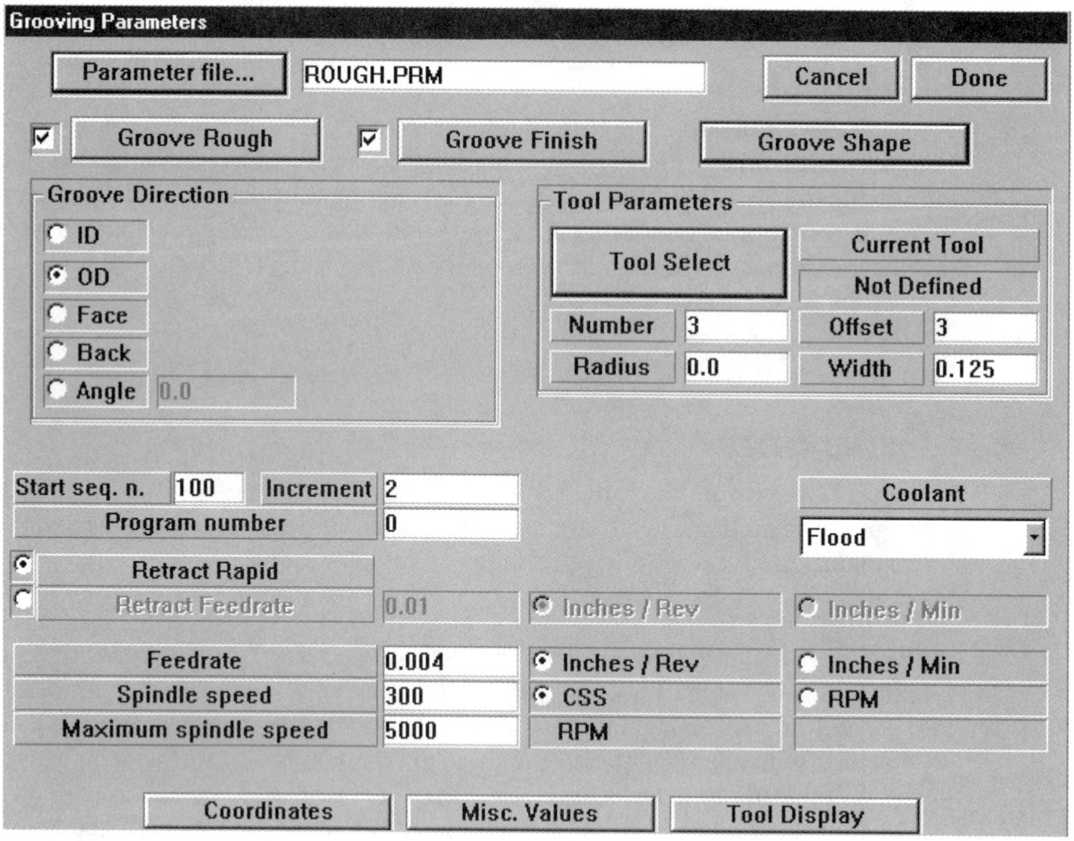

Grooving Parameters

Parameter file... | ROUGH.PRM | Cancel | Done

☑ Groove Rough | ☑ Groove Finish | Groove Shape

Groove Direction
- ○ ID
- ◉ OD
- ○ Face
- ○ Back
- ○ Angle 0.0

Tool Parameters

Tool Select	Current Tool
	Not Defined
Number 3	Offset 3
Radius 0.0	Width 0.125

Start seq. n. 100	Increment 2		Coolant
Program number	0		Flood
◉ Retract Rapid			
○ Retract Feedrate	0.01	◉ Inches / Rev	○ Inches / Min
Feedrate	0.004	◉ Inches / Rev	○ Inches / Min
Spindle speed	300	◉ CSS	○ RPM
Maximum spindle speed	5000	RPM	

Coordinates | Misc. Values | Tool Display

FIGURE 8–45

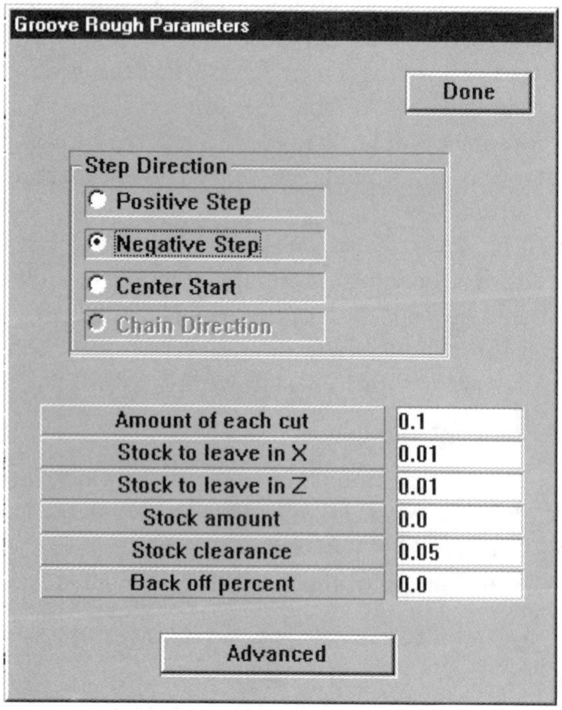

Groove Rough Parameters

Done

Step Direction
- ○ Positive Step
- ◉ Negative Step
- ○ Center Start
- ○ Chain Direction

Amount of each cut	0.1
Stock to leave in X	0.01
Stock to leave in Z	0.01
Stock amount	0.0
Stock clearance	0.05
Back off percent	0.0

Advanced

FIGURE 8–46

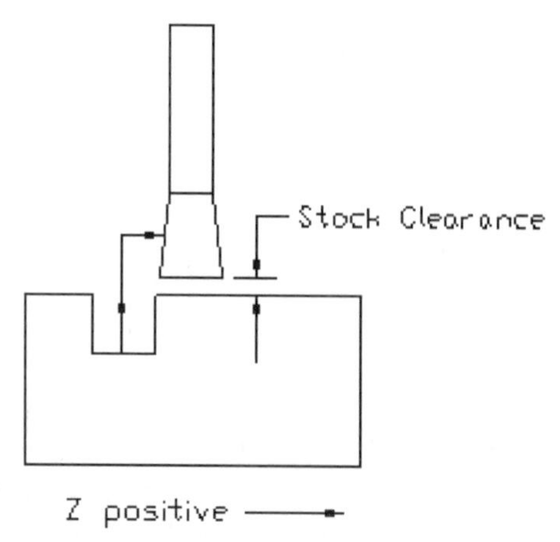

FIGURE 8–47

Back Off Percentage

This is the amount that the tool backs away, at a 45-degree angle, from the wall of the groove before it retracts (Figure 8–48). The amount that is input is the percentage of the amount of each cut. Type **0.0** for the Back Off Percentage.

Advanced

The Advanced button opens up the Advanced Roughing Parameters dialogue box. Select **Advance.** You are not going to use advance, but you need to understand it.

Groove Peck

Activating Groove Peck tells Mastercam you want the tool to peck away the stock. Pecking allows the chips to get cleared from the groove. Peck is typically used on deep grooves. Mastercam allows you to control how you want the tool to peck groove through a series of Peck parameters.

First Plunge Only If this parameter is activated the tool pecks only on the first plunge. If it is not activated, the tool will peck each time it plunges.

Peck Number The Peck Number is the number of times you want the tool to peck.

Peck Increment The Peck Increment is the amount you want the tool to peck each time.

Last Increment The number you input in the Last Increment dialogue box works along with the Peck Increment. The amount that is input here assures that the last peck will be equal to the last increment value.

Retract Amount This is the incremental distance that the tool retracts between each peck.

Dwell Time Dwell Time is the amount of seconds you want the tool to dwell at the end of each peck plunge. Dwelling helps to clear chips out from the groove.

Multiple Depth Cuts

When you select this option the Depth Cut Parameters dialogue box appears. The depth cut parameters allow you to set the depth of cut and how many passes you want the tool to make.

Number of Depth Cuts

The value that you enter here is the number of passes the tool will make to rough out the material. Our groove does not need to be peck machined. Make sure that neither Groove Peck nor Multiple Depth Cuts is activated and select **Done** to return to the Rough Parameters dialogue box. Set the final Rough parameters to those found in Figure 8–46. Going through these parameters would be repetitive. The groove roughing parameters are very much like other roughing parameters you have already covered.

FIGURE 8–48

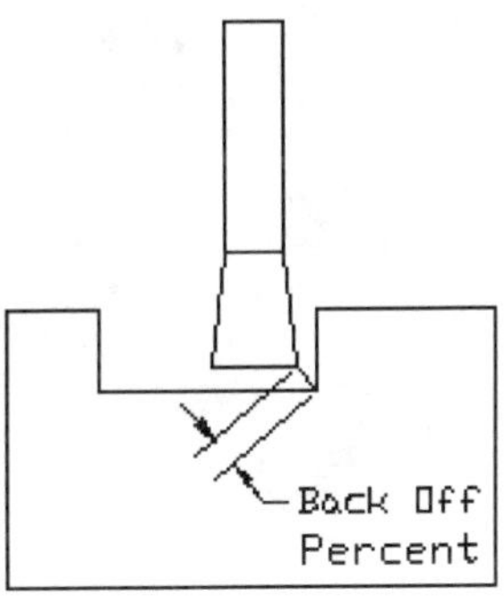

The Rough Groove parameters are set; now you have to set the Finish Groove parameters.

Groove Finish

Activate the **Groove Finish** check box and click on the **Groove Finish** button. By clicking on the Groove check box you have added a finish groove pass to the program. The Groove Finish dialogue box should now appear on the screen (Figure 8–49).

For all of the groove types, except the 2 Boundary-type groove creation, the grooving finish pass will cut down the wall of the groove, retract, come down the other wall to the bottom of the groove, and then cut across to the far wall of the groove. Most of the parameter settings are identical to past parameter settings. You will concentrate on the parameters that are specific to Groove Finish.

Lengthen First Pass This parameter sets the distance that the grooving tool moves along the bottom of the groove on the first pass. Set to **0.0.**

Shorten Second Pass This parameter sets the distance the tool stays away from the far wall of the groove on the second pass. Set to **0.0.** The tool cuts down to depth and moves across the bottom of the groove to within the setting distance of the opposite groove wall and then the tool retracts.

First Pass CW If you activate the First Pass Clockwise option, the tool will cut from the negative end of the groove to the positive end of the groove. The tool then backs out of the groove and cuts from the other side. You won't activate this option.

First Pass CCW If you activate the First Pass CounterClockwise option, the tool will cut from the positive end of the groove to the negative end of the groove. The tool then backs out of the groove and cuts from the other side. You won't activate this option.

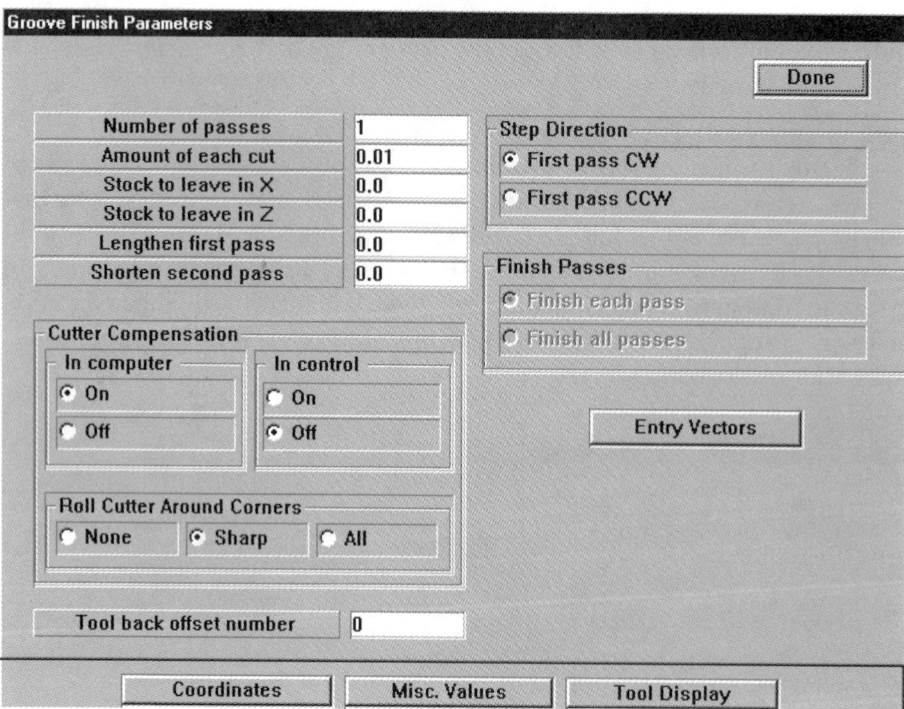

FIGURE 8–49

Finish Each Pass This option is used when you have more than one groove. If you activate this option, the tool will complete all of the finish passes of one groove before it makes the grooving passes for the next groove.

Finish All Passes This option is also used when you have more than one groove. If you activate this option, the tool will complete all of the first passes on each groove and then make the second grooving passes on each groove. Leave this option off.

Tool Back Offset Number This is the offset number you want to assign to the backside cutting edge of the tool. This option is needed only when you have programmed a finishing pass that cuts with the backside of the tool. Set this option to **0.**

Set the remaining Groove Finish parameters to those found in Figure 8–49.

Entry Vectors Choose the **Entry Vectors** button now. Notice that the names for the grooving vectors are Positive Side and Negative Side entry vectors. These entry vectors work the same as other vectors you have worked with.

The Positive Side Entry vector is the path that the tool will make when entering the stock on the positive side of the groove. The Negative Side Entry vector is the path that the tool makes when entering the stock on the negative side of the groove. Set both vectors to the **6:00** position (straight down). Now select **Done** to accept the vector selections.

That concludes the Groove Finish parameters. Select **Done** to accept these parameter settings. You will now return to the Grooving Parameters menu.

Groove Direction

Groove Direction is the direction in which you want the tool to cut (Figure 8–50).

ID The ID selection cuts the groove on the inside diameter of the part.

Face The Face selection cuts the groove on the front face of the part.

Back The Back selection cuts the groove on the back face of the part.

Angle The Angle selection cuts the groove at the selected angle. The Angle selection is measured relative to the centerline origin of the machine. You need an external groove. Select **OD** for outside diameter grooving.

FIGURE 8–50

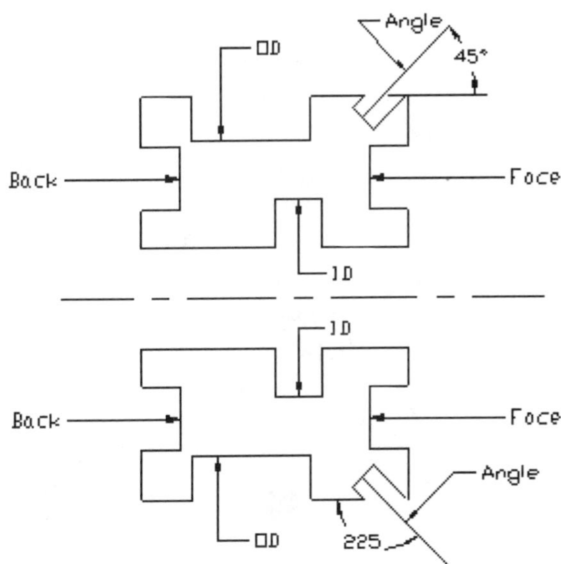

Groove Shape

The Groove Shape button allows you to add chamfers and radii to the groove shape when you are using all of the groove creation types except the 2 Boundary type. Selecting Groove Shape will also draw a picture of the groove for you. Select the **Groove Shape** button now.

Asymmetrical Versus Symmetrical The Groove shape and Groove Shape parameters will change considerably, depending on whether you select asymmetrical or symmetrical. With the symmetrical-shaped groove, you need only describe the inside and outside corners as shown on the right side of the Parameters dialogue box. The symmetrical dialogue box should be on the screen now (Figure 8–51).

You are creating a single-point groove so the Single Point Groove option appears and allows you to input the groove Depth and Width.

Depth The depth of the groove is measured on radius. This means if you have a .100-inch-deep groove, the difference on the diameter is .200 inch. Type **.100** for the depth of the groove.

Width The width of our groove is 0.25. Type **.25** for the width of the groove.

Wall Angle The value you enter is the angle of the walls of the groove. Type **0.0.**

Outer Corners Does the groove have a radius or chamfer on the outer edge? If you activated either the radius or chamfer, a dialogue box would appear and you would be prompted to input the values for the radius or chamfer. Our groove has no radii or chamfers on the outer corners. Leave the Outer Corners parameter setting at None.

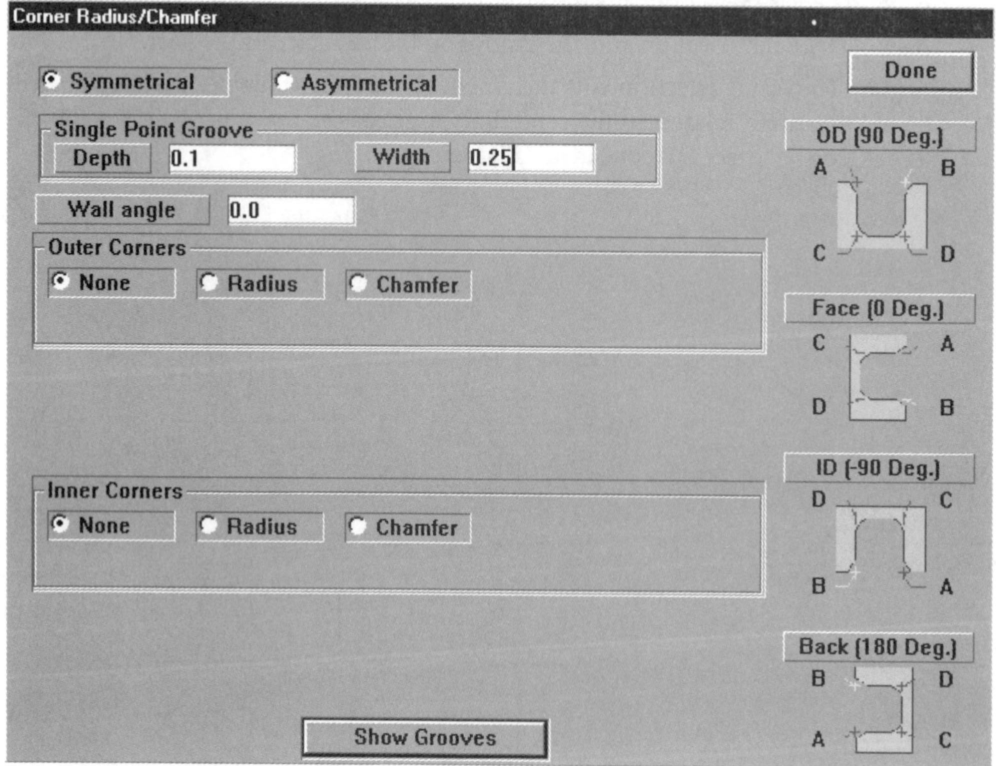

FIGURE 8–51

Inner Corners Does the groove have a radius or chamfer on the inner corners? If you activated either the radius or chamfer, a dialogue box would appear and you would be prompted to input the values for the radius or chamfer. Our groove has no radii or chamfers on the inner corners. Leave the Inner Corners parameter setting at None.

Show Grooves

Select the **Show Groove** button to see what the groove looks like. If the groove looks correct, select **Save the Groove.** Now select **Done** to return to the Groove Shape Parameters screen.

Select the **Asymmetrical Groove** setting now just to see what this menu looks like. From this menu you can see that you have the option of describing each one of the groove walls and corners. Change back to **Symmetrical.**

That concludes Show Grooves. Select **Done.**

Tool Select

You should now be back at the Grooving Parameters screen. Click on the **Tool Select** button. The Tool Manager box should appear on the screen. Place the mouse in the large white space and open the Tool Selection menu by clicking the right mouse button. From the Tool Selection menu select **Get from Library.** Put the mouse over the number 58 tool named **NGDHR-16** and press the right mouse button. Select **Draw Tool.** If you don't see tool number 58, make sure the tool library is the Kennametal library. The tool should appear on the graphics screen. This should be the right-hand grooving tool. Select **Continue** to return to the Tool Manager dialogue box. Select **OK.** You can see that this tool has been added to the lathe tool manager. Select **OK** to accept the tool settings. Return to the Groove Parameter dialogue box.

Current Tool This area tells us which tool you selected.

Number This will be the tool identification number for your machine tool turret. Let's keep the tool number at **3.**

Offset Set the Offset to **3.**

Radius The radius value is set when you select the tool from the tool file. It should be set at **0.01** for the corner radius of the grooving tool.

Width The width value of the tool is set when you select the tool from the tool file. It should be set at **0.156** for the width of the grooving tool.

All of the other groove parameters should already be set as defaults. Check the spindle speed and feed parameters against the settings in Figure 8–45. Select **Done** after checking the grooving parameters.

The Change menu now appears on the screen. Select **Write.** To accept the grooving path that was created select **Yes.**

Backplotting the Tool Path

Select **Operations** from the Lathe Toolpaths menu. The Operations Manager dialogue box will pop up on the screen. Click on the **Select All** button to plot both the rough and finish paths. Select **Backplot.**

Before you move on, lets cover the groove types you did not use in this exercise.

2 Point Groove

Two-point groove creation is nearly identical to one-point groove creation. The two-point groove creation is done by using two points. For every two points you create or select, Mastercam creates a groove.

FIGURE 8–52

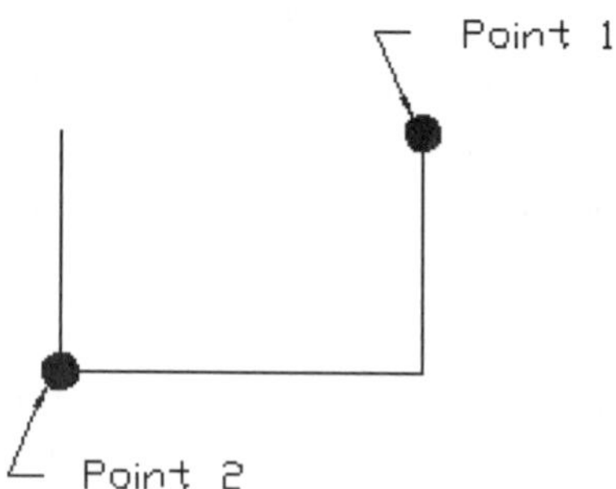

You can create as many grooves as you want using the 2 Point creation method, but you must define each groove by selecting or creating the top corner and the opposite bottom corner (Figure 8–52).

3 Line Groove

This type of groove creation must start with existing geometry. You can't create the points while you are creating the groove tool path. Upon selecting the 3-Line Groove option, Mastercam displays the Chaining methods menu. The groove elements that you chain must have three, and only three, sides. The first and third must be parallel and equal in length (Figure 8–53) This is the type of groove creation you will most likely use on parts with precreated grooves in the design or geometry creation phase when Mastercam asks you for chaining methods. If your part has more than the three elements that make up the groove, select Partial. Pick the first entity and then the last entity that make up the groove.

FIGURE 8–53

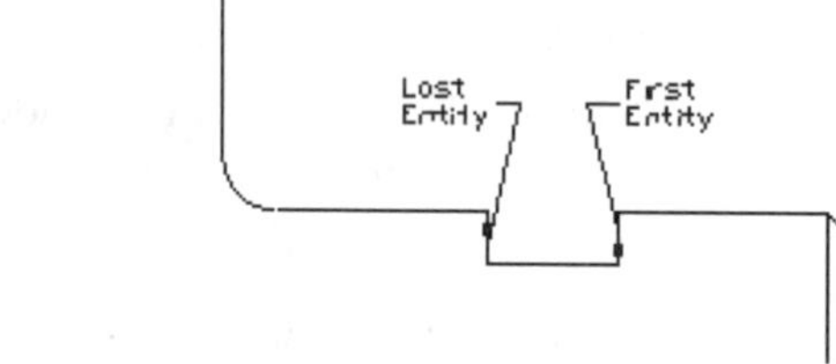

2 Bdry

The 2 Bdry groove method allows you to create a groove tool path of any shape. This type of groove tool path needs part geometry and a stock boundary. The 2 Boundary method of groove tool-path creation is much like creating the Rough tool path. You will need an inner boundary and an outer or stock boundary. A typical 2 Boundary type groove tool-path creation would consist of selecting an entry point, chaining an inner boundary, selecting an outer boundary, and selecting a retraction point (Figure 8–54). Follow the prompts at the top of the screen. As you do the exercises at the end of this chapter, try using these other methods of groove creation.

If everything looks correct, it is time to move on to the Threading module. If everything does not look correct, go back and check your parameter settings.

Threading

Mastercam's Threading module can create a threading tool path for internal, external, face, or tapered threads. The Threading module is completely parameter

FIGURE 8–54

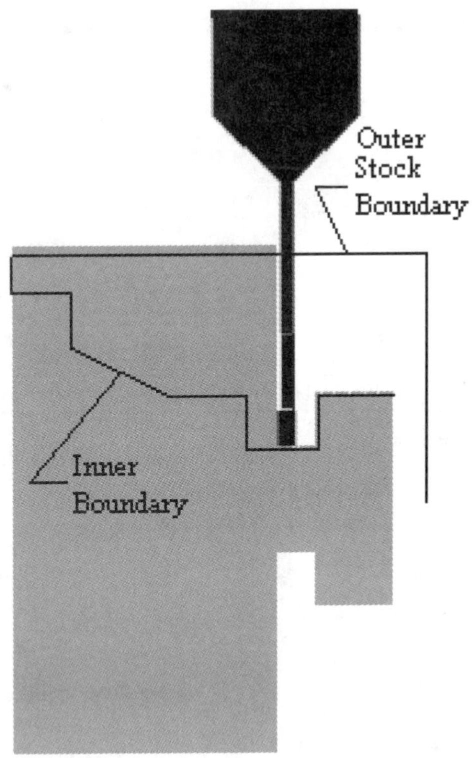

driven, so you don't need to have geometry created for the thread. If you do have geometry already created for the thread, this is also acceptable.

Choose **Thread** from the Lathe Toolpath menu.

Upon choosing Thread, the Threading Parameters dialog box will appear on the screen (Figure 8–55).

Thread

As was stated earlier, Mastercam is able to create a tool path for a number of thread types. The choice of the type of thread brings about a set of parameters specific to that type of thread. The thread type choices are ID, OD, and Face/Back.

ID The choice of ID would be used when you want to create a tool path for an internal thread.

OD The choice of OD would be used when you want to create a tool path for an external thread.

Face/Back The choice of Face/Back would be used when you want to create a tool path on the end or face of the part. The face of the part can either be on the left end or right end face.

Figure 8–42 specifies cutting a 1″-8 UNC external thread. Activate **OD** for Thread.

Thread Size

The thread size parameters control the size of the thread. There are a number of different methods of defining the thread size. You can enter values in the text box. You can also choose the Select button, which would allow you to pick points from the graphics area. The Select from Table and the Compute from Formula buttons are the other methods of defining the thread size.

Threading Parameters

Thread | NC | Cancel | Done

Thread: ID | OD | Face/Back

Thread Size
Lead 8.0 | Inches / thread | Threads / inch
Major diameter 1.0 | Select | Adjusted Major 1.0
Minor diameter 0.8647 | Select | Adjusted Minor 0.8647
Select from table | Compute from formula

Thread Endpoints
Start Z 0.0
End Z -1.0
Taper angle 0.0
Negative X
Select

Allowance
Major Allowance 0.0
Minor Allowance 0.0
Select from table
Tolerance 0.0

Stock Clearance
Clearance 0.0
Compute acceleration clearance

Thread Parameters | Draw geometry

FIGURE 8–55

Thread Lead

The thread lead is the distance that a nut would travel in one revolution. The lead value can be represented in two ways: threads/inch or inches/thread. Figure 8–56 illustrates the parts of a thread. Activate the **Threads/Inch** so you can put in the number of threads per inch directly from the part drawing. Input an **8** for eight threads per inch. To calculate the lead or inches/thread, you would divide 1 by the number of threads per inch. In our case it would be 1/8, which calculates to .125. This would be the distance from one thread to the next thread.

Select from Table

Once you have input the lead, choose the **Select from Table** button. The Select from Table button is an option when you are cutting ID or OD threads only. The Thread Table dialogue box should now appear on the screen (Figure 8–57). This dialogue box contains information for all of the common thread forms.

FIGURE 8–56

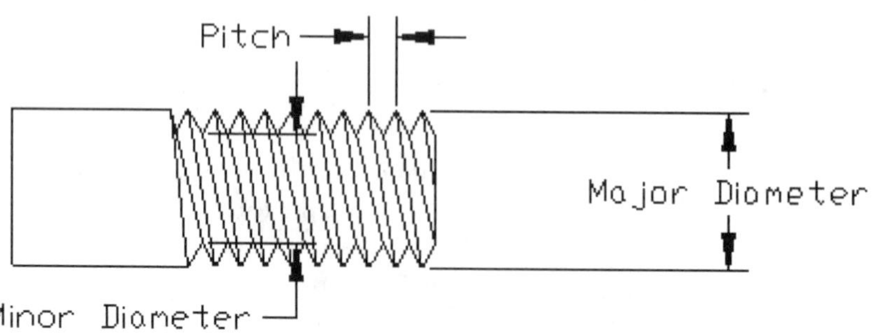

Thread Table

Cancel Done

Thread Form: Unified - UNC, UNF

Unified - UNC, UNF
Unified - UNRC, UNRF
Unified - UN, UNC, UNF, UNEF
Unified - UNR, UNRC, UNRF, UNREF
Acme General Purpose
Acme Stub

Common diameter/lead

Basic Major	Lead Threads/in			
0.7500	16.00			
0.8750	9.00	0.8750	0.7547	7/8, 9, UNC
0.8750	14.00	0.8750	0.7977	7/8, 14, UNF
1.0000	8.00	1.0000	0.8647	1, 8, UNC
1.0000	12.00	1.0000	0.9098	1, 12, UNF
1.1250	7.00	1.1250	0.9704	1-1/8, 7, UNC
1.1250	12.00	1.1250	1.0348	1-1/8, 12, UNF
1.2500	7.00	1.2500	1.0954	1-1/4, 7, UNC
1.2500	12.00	1.2500	1.1598	1-1/4, 12, UNF
1.3750	6.00	1.3750	1.1946	1-3/8, 6, UNC
1.3750	12.00	1.3750	1.2848	1-3/8, 12, UNF
1.5000	6.00	1.5000	1.3196	1-1/2, 6, UNC
1.5000	12.00	1.5000	1.4098	1-1/2, 12, UNF
1.7500	5.00	1.7500	1.5335	1-3/4, 5, UNC
2.0000	4.50	2.0000	1.7594	2, 4.5, UNC
2.2500	4.50	2.2500	2.0094	2-1/4, 4.5, UNC
2.5000	4.00	2.5000	2.2294	2-1/2, 4, UNC

FIGURE 8–57

Select the **Thread Form** pull-down arrow. These are the common thread forms that are included in Mastercam's Threading module. Select **Unified-UNC, UNF.** Our thread is a Unified National Coarse thread. All of the common Unified thread forms are now shown in the table. Scroll down the table and select the **1.00-8** thread. Select **Done** to accept the parameter settings that go with this selection.

You should now have returned to the Threading Parameters dialogue box. Notice that most of the thread size parameters have been filled in for you.

Major Diameter

The Major Diameter of the thread is the large diameter of the thread (Figure 8–56) The large diameter for our thread is 1.00. Verify that the Major Diameter parameter is set to **1.00.**

Minor Diameter

The Minor Diameter of the thread is the diameter across the bottom of the thread (Figure 8–56). The minor diameter for our thread is 0.8647. Verify that the Minor Diameter parameter is set to **0.8647.**

Adjusted Minor

The adjusted minor diameter is the minor diameter with allowance and tolerance values applied to it. These adjusted values cannot be edited.

Thread Endpoints

The Thread Endpoints parameter area allows you to input or select the points that make up the thread start points and endpoints (Figure 8–58).

FIGURE 8–58

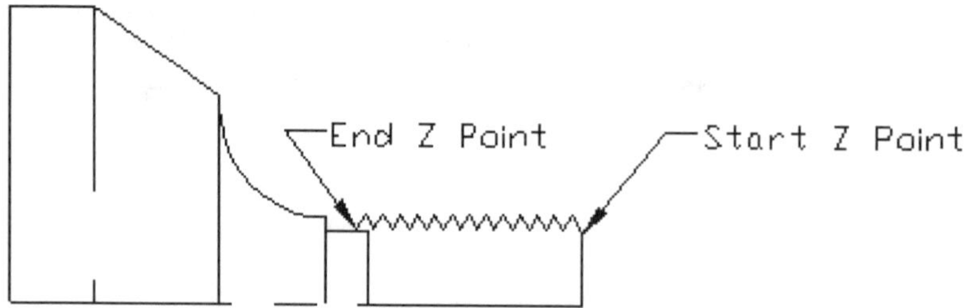

Start Z The Start Z is the point on the Z axis where the thread starts. You can either type in these coordinates or use the Select button to go back to the graphics area and use the Point Entry menu to pick the Start Z point. Type **0.0** in the Start Z parameter area.

End Z The End Z is the point on the Z axis where the thread ends. You can either type in these coordinates or use the Select button to go back to the graphics area and use the Point Entry menu to pick the End Z point. Type **−1.300** in the End Z parameter area. This will end the thread in the groove.

Taper Angle

The Taper Angle text box allows you to input the angle you want on the thread. Tapered threads are use for sealing-type threads such as pipe threads. A positive value will cause the thread diameter to increase from the start of the thread to the end of the thread. A negative value will cause the thread diameter to decrease from the start of the thread to the end of the thread. You can either type in the angle or use the Select button to go back to the graphics area and use the Point Entry menu to pick the start point and endpoint diameters of the thread. You are cutting a straight thread. You can disregard this entry.

Negative X

The Negative X text box allows us to indicate to Mastercam that the thread will be cut on the negative side of the centerline of the machine.

Thread Parameters

Click on the **Thread Parameters** button. The Thread Parameters dialogue box allows you to enter the parameters that control stock removal and thread lead issues (Figure 8–59).

FIGURE 8–59

Thread Parameters

Amount of first cut	0.01
Amount of last cut	0.001
Lead in angle	29.0
Lead out angle	29.0
Number of starts	1
Number of spring cuts	1
Finish pass allowance	0.0
Anticipated pull-off	0.0

Done

Amount of First Cut The value that is entered here is the amount of the first cut pass of the threading cycle. The depth that is entered here is expressed as a radius value. The amount of the first cut is usually the heaviest cut and each cut after the first cut will be decreasing in depth. The amount of the first cut determines the number of cut passes that will need to be taken to reach the full thread depth. Enter **.01** inches for the Amount of First Cut.

Amount of Last Cut The value that is entered here is the amount of the last cut pass of the threading cycle. The depth that is entered here is expressed as a radius value. Enter **.001** inches for the Amount of Last Cut.

Lead In Angle The value that is entered here is the angle of the front side of the thread. The lead in angle also determines the position of the tool as it enters the thread cut pass. The lead in angle is usually half of the included angle of the thread, but this can change with the type of threading tool you are using. Enter **29** degrees for the Lead In Angle.

Lead Out Angle The value that is entered here is the angle of the backside of the thread. The lead out angle is usually half of the included angle of the thread, but this can also change with the type of threading tool you are using. Enter **29** degrees for the Lead Out Angle.

Number of Starts The value that is entered here depends on the whether you are cutting a single lead or multilead thread. If you were cutting a triple-lead thread, you would need to use three start positions. You are cutting a single-lead thread. Type **1** for the Number of Starts.

Number of Spring Cuts Spring cuts are tool passes with no depth specified. Spring cuts are used to remove material that is left on the part due to tool or part deflection. Set the Number of Spring Cuts to **1.**

Finish Pass Allowance The value entered here is the amount of stock you wish to leave for the spring cuts. Enter **0.0.**

Anticipated Pull-off The value entered here is the distance beyond the end of the thread that the tool will travel retracting out of the thread pass. Enter **0.0.** Select **Done** to accept these parameter settings.

Find the Allowance area of the Thread Parameters page.

ALLOWANCE: The Allowance parameters determine the class of fit you want between the mating parts of the thread.

MAJOR ALLOWANCE: The value entered here is either added to or subtracted from the major diameter of the thread. When applied to an ID thread, the allowance would be added to the major diameter. When applied to an OD thread, the allowance would be subtracted from the major diameter.

MINOR ALLOWANCE: The value entered here is either added to or subtracted from the minor diameter of the thread. When applied to an ID thread, the allowance would be added to the major diameter. When applied to an OD thread, the allowance would be subtracted from the major diameter.

SELECT FROM TABLE: The Select from Table button opens the Allowance Table dialogue box. The dialogue box includes a standards table for allowances for certain thread class of fit combinations.

TOLERANCE: Tolerance is the amount that a nominal dimension can vary in size. When applied to an ID thread, the tolerance would be added to the major and minor diameters. When applied to an OD thread, the tolerance would be subtracted from the major and minor diameters.

Stock Clearance The Stock Clearance parameter sets the acceleration clearance. The acceleration is the speed of the tool as it enters the thread-cutting pass. When the threading tool makes a cut pass it is very important that the timing of tool be perfect because the tool must fall into the same thread groove each time. If the tool does not have enough time to drop into position before reaching the part, the thread pattern will be wrong.

CLEARANCE: Clearance is the incremental distance you wish to have from the stock to the start of the thread.

COMPUTE ACCELERATION CLEARANCE: If you choose this check box, Mastercam automatically calculates the acceleration clearance distance required. The calculation is based on the spindle speed and the lead of the thread. Activate this check box if it is not already selected.

Draw Geometry

The Draw Geometry check box draws an outline of the thread on the geometry graphics screen.

NC Parameters

The NC Parameters area allows you to choose how you want the thread to be cut. The NC Parameters area is where you select which tool you want to use and what type of code you want to have generated in the NCI file. Select the **NC** button in the upper left corner of the screen.

Tool Select Click on the **Tool Select** button now. The Tool Manager box should appear on the screen. Place the mouse in the large white space and open the Tool Selection menu by clicking the right mouse button. From the Tool Selection menu select **Get from Library.** Put the mouse over the number 145 tool named **NASR-082D** and press the right mouse button. Select **Draw Tool.** If you don't see tool number 145, make sure the tool library is the Kennametal library. The tool should appear on the graphics screen. This should be the right-hand threading tool. Select **Continue** to return to the Tool Manager dialogue box. Select **OK.** You can see that this tool has been added to the Lathe Tool Manager. Select **OK** to accept the tool settings. You now will return to the NC Threading Parameters dialogue box.

CURRENT TOOL: This area tells which tool you selected.

NUMBER: This will be the tool identification number for your machine tool turret. Let's keep the tool number at **4.**

Offset Set the Offset to **4.**

NC Toolpath Thread creation on the machine takes many tool passes. The NC Toolpath parameter allows you the opportunity to choose how the threading portion of the NCI file will be output.

LONGHAND: Choosing Longhand will generate one or two lines of code for every thread-cutting pass. The EIA/ISO preparatory code that is generated is a G32.

CANNED CYCLE: Choosing Canned Cycle will generate one or two lines of code for the entire thread-cutting operation. The EIA/ISO preparatory code that is generated is a G76. Canned cycles greatly reduce the size of the program, but they reduce the amount of flexibility you have when editing the program. Select **Canned Cycle.**

BOX THREAD: Choosing Box Thread will generate one or two lines of code for every thread-cutting pass. The EIA/ISO preparatory code that is generated is a G92. It should be noted that not all machine controls recognize the G92 code as a thread-cutting code.

CSS or RPM When thread cutting and drilling, you want to use RPM input instead of constant surface footage (CSS). Make sure that the RPM button is activated. The rest of the parameters are the same or similar to parameters you have set before. Select **Done.**

The threading tool path should now appear on the screen. Accept the threading tool path by selecting **Yes.**

Drill

The Drilling module from the Lathe Toolpaths menu will create tool path for drilling, tapping, reaming, and other types of operations associated with the Z axis. Select **Drill** from the Lathe Toolpaths menu. The Drilling Parameters dialogue box should now appear on the screen (Figure 8–60).

Drilling Parameters

The initial screen that appears is the Drilling Parameters screen. The Drill parameters button in the upper left corner of the screen should be activated. The drilling parameters begin with Cycle.

Cycle Click the down arrow next to the Cycle Parameter dialogue box. The pull-down list contains the most common drilling cycles. These cycle selections are the equivalent the G81, G82, and G83 series of the EIA/ISO drilling cycle codes.

Drill/Counter Bore This is a straight drilling cycle. The drill feeds to depth and then retracts at a rapid feedrate. Choose the **Drill/Counter Bore cycle.**

Peck Drill The Peck Drill cycle is used when you are drilling deep holes. The drill feeds in to a certain depth, stops to break the chips, and then begins feeding again.

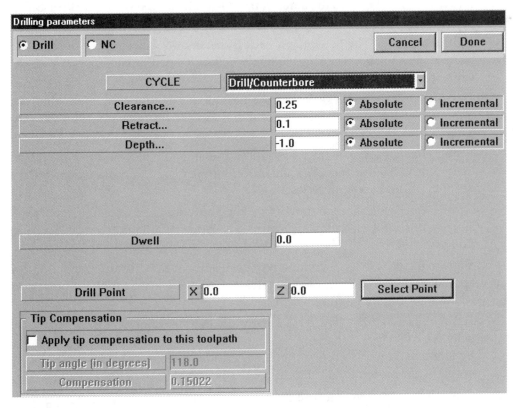

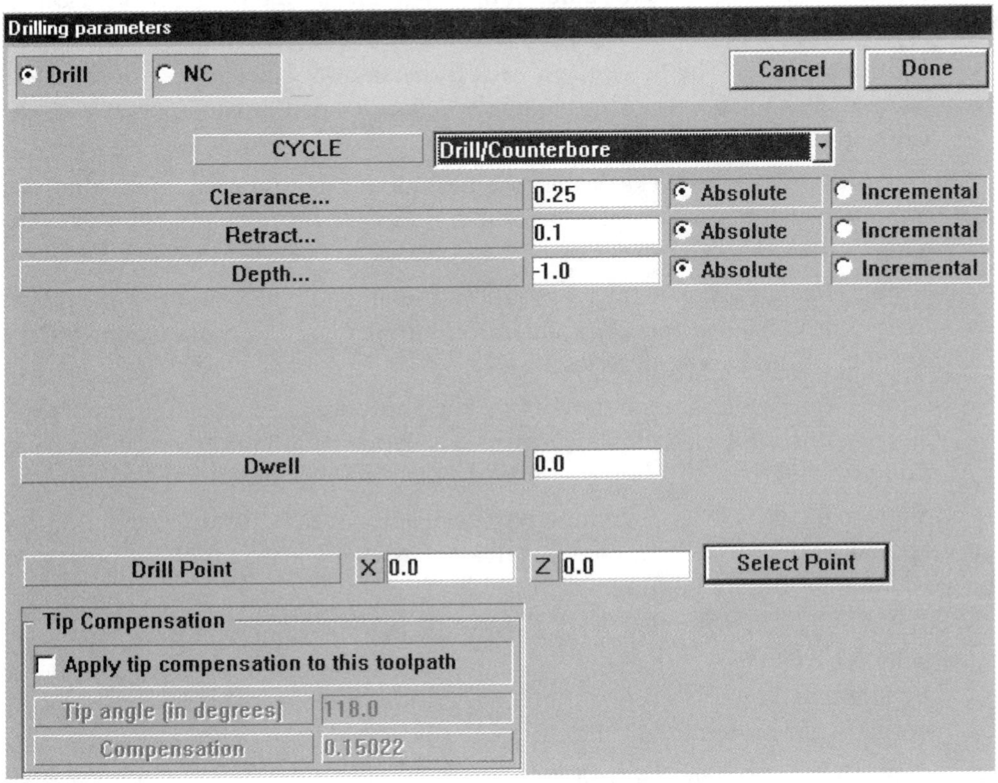

FIGURE 8–60

Chip Break The Chip Break cycle is used to drill deep holes. It is similar to the Peck Drill cycle in that it stops feeding in, but it can be set to retract to clear the chips before it begins feeding in again.

Tap The Tap cycle is used to cut internal threads. When the tap reaches the programmed depth, the spindle stops and reverses.

Bore #1 The Bore cycles are customizable drilling cycles.

Bore #2 The Bore cycles are customizable drilling cycles.

Bore #3 The Bore cycles are customizable drilling cycles.

Misc #1 The Misc cycles are customizable drilling cycles.

Misc #2 The Misc cycles are customizable drilling cycles.

Clearance Clearance is the point to which the tools will rapid traverse. Absolute sets the distance value from the Z origin point. Incremental sets the distance value from the hole. In some cases these two points may be the same. Set the Clearance at **.25 Absolute.**

Retract Retract is the point at which the tool will stop rapid traversing and begin moving at the selected feedrate. The tools travel in line with the center point of the part until it reaches the programmed depth and then the tool retracts to the retract point. Absolute sets the distance value from the Z origin point. Incremental sets the distance value from the face of the hole. Set the Retract to **.10 Absolute.**

Depth The depth value you enter determines the depth of the hole. Activating the Absolute button sets the depth distance from the origin point. Activating the Incremental button sets the distance the tool must travel from the face of the hole to the bottom of the hole. In some cases these two points may be the same. Set the Depth to **−1.00 Absolute.**

1st Peck The 1st Peck is the amount that the tool will feed on the first peck. This parameter setting is used in conjunction with the Chip Break and Peck Drill cycles.

Subsequent Peck The Subsequent Peck is the amount of each peck the tool will make after the first peck. This parameter setting is used in conjunction with the Chip Break and Peck Drill cycles.

Peck Clearance The Peck Clearance is the amount that the tools will rapid back into after each peck. This parameter setting is used on in conjunction with the Chip Break and Peck Drill cycles.

Retract Amount The Retract Amount is the amount that the tool will retract every time it makes a peck. This parameter setting is used in conjunction with the Chip Break and Peck Drill cycles.

Dwell The Dwell is the amount of time that the tool will pause after the tool stops at full depth or for each peck movement. The Dwell option is not available with all drilling cycle types.

Shift Shift allows the programmer to set an amount that the tool will back off of the wall of the part before retracting the tool. Not all machine tool postprocessors will support the Shift option.

Drill Point (X and Z) The Drill Point is the exact position you want the drilled hole. You can type in values or you can select the point from the graphics window by choosing the Select Point button. Mastercam defaults to 0,0 because this is the normal drill location for a lathe. Accept the default of **0,0.**

Apply Tip Compensation to This Tool Path This option will activate the tip compensation feature. Tip compensation calculates the amount the drill point will have to travel to achieve the full diameter depth. The compensation is automatic once you input the drill point angle. Activate the **Tip Compensation** check box.

Tip Angle The Tip Angle is the included angle of drill point. Most general-purpose drills are ground to 118 degrees. Enter **118** for the tip angle of the drill.

Compensation Compensation is the value generated by the system. The value is based on the drill diameter and the tip angle. The tip angle compensation amount will change as soon as you select your tool.

NC Parameters Activate the NC Parameters button in the upper left corner of the Drilling Parameters screen. NC parameters are the same or similar to other NC parameters you have been using. You need to select a tool from the NC Parameters area.

Tool Select Click on the **Tool Select** button now. The Tool Manager box should now appear on the screen. Place the mouse in the large white space. Click the right mouse button. You are going to change tool libraries, so select **Change Libraries.** From the tool libraries list select **LDrills.tl7.** Save this file. The Tool Selection menu should still be on the screen. Place the mouse in the large white space and click the right mouse button. From the Tool Selection menu, select **Get from Library.** Put the mouse over tool number **163** the .5 drill and press the left mouse button. Select **OK.** You can see now that this tool has been added to the Lathe Tool Manager. Select **OK** to accept this tool.

You should now have returned to the NC Parameters screen.

Tool Offset Change the tool offset to **5.**

RPM Make sure that the RPM option for the Spindle Speed setting is activated and not the CSS option.

Select **Done** to accept the drilling parameters.

Accept the drilling tool path by selecting **Yes.** The drill tool path should now appear on the screen.

Backplotting the Drilling Tool Path

Select **Operations** from the Lathe Toolpaths menu. The Operations Manager dialogue box has now popped up on the screen. Click on the **Lathe Drill** folder to plot just the drilling tool path. Select **Backplot.** Now select **Step** or **Run.** Does the drill path look correct? If it doesn't, go back and check your drilling parameters. Press the **Esc** key and select **OK** to close the Operations Manager.

Cutoff

The Cutoff module is used when you want to cut pieces off of the stock or you want to separate the finished part from the rough stock. Select **Cutoff.**

Point Entry

After selecting Cutoff, Mastercam displays the Point Entry menu. The dialogue box is asking you to select the boundary point. The boundary point determines where the tool will cut through the part. Select the point shown in Figure 8–61.

The Cutoff Parameters screen should now appear (Figure 8–62).

Tool Select

Click on the **Tool Select** button now. The Tool Manager box should appear on the screen. You are going to change tool libraries, so select **Change Libraries.** From the tool libraries list select **Iscar.tl7.** Save this file. The Tool Selection menu should still be on the screen. Place the mouse in the large white space and click the right mouse button. From the Tool Selection menu, select **Get from Library.** Put the mouse over tool number **12(DGTR-25.4-6)** and press the right mouse button. Select

FIGURE 8–61

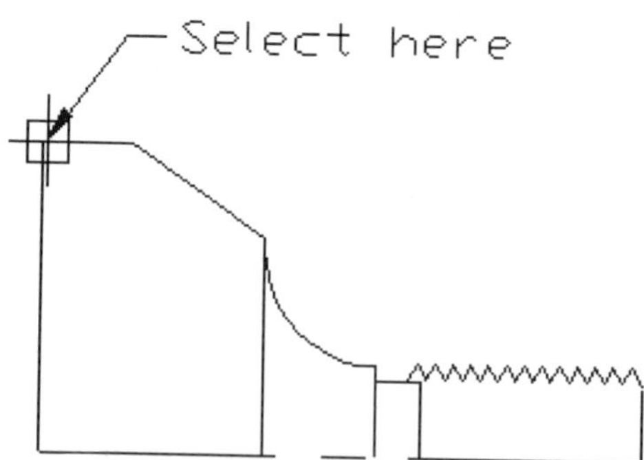

Draw Tool. This is the cutoff tool you will use. Select **Continue** to go back to the Iscar Tool Library. Now select **OK.** You can see now that this tool has been added to the Lathe Tool Manager. Select **OK** to accept this tool. You should now have returned to the NC Parameters screen.

Tool Offset

Change the tool offset to **6.** There are a number of parameter settings, as well as Entry/Exit Vectors, that you have covered already. You will concentrate on the parameter settings that are used in the Cutoff module and not used in other modules.

Cutoff Chamfer

If you choose the Cutoff Chamfer button, you activate the Cutoff Chamfer dialogue box. In this dialogue box you can enter a chamfer angle and amount. This will create a chamfer to be to be put on the cutoff part.

If you have existing geometry for a chamfer on the part, you can use the Select button to return to the graphics area and select the chamfer you wish to create.

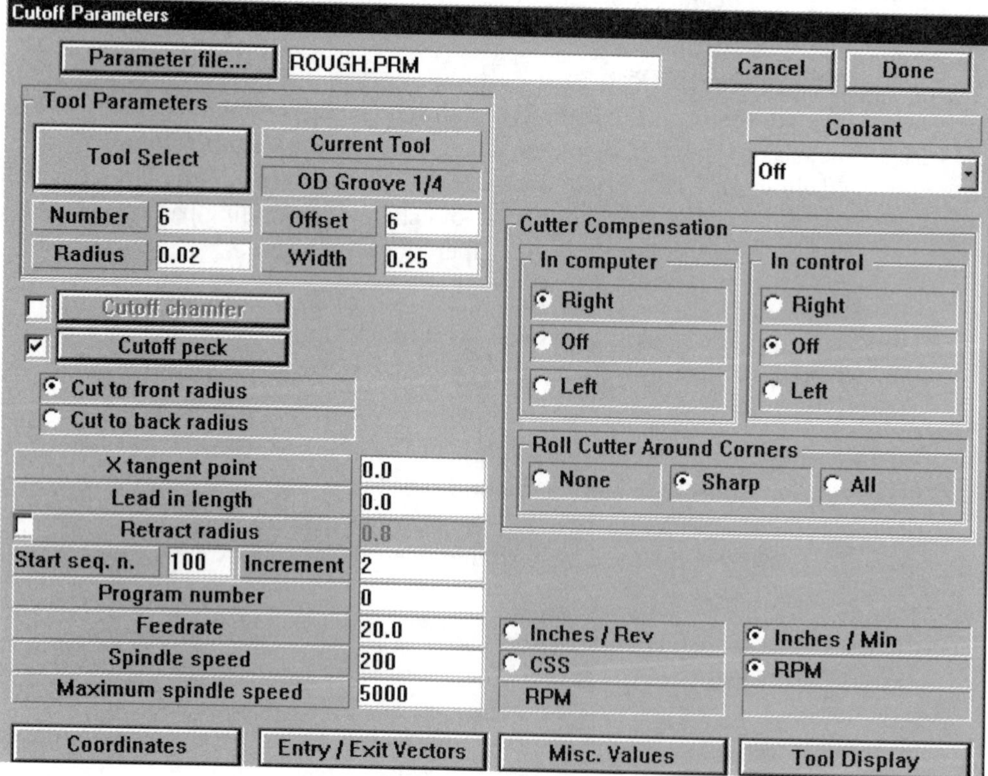

FIGURE 8–62

FIGURE 8–63

Cutoff Peck

Done

Peck Amount
Peck Number 5
Peck Increment 0.1
Last Increment 0.05

Retract/Dwell
Retract Increment 0.1
Dwell Time (sec) 0.0

Cutoff Peck

If you choose the Cutoff Peck button, you activate the Cutoff Peck dialogue box. In this dialogue box you can enter a set of parameters that create a pecking cutoff cycle. This type of cycle is especially useful when creating deep cutoff tool path. A peck is a tool move that feeds the tool into the part at a programmed feedrate and then retracts out of the stock to clear the chips. The cutoff peck parameters are very much like the peck parameters you saw in the peck drill cycle. Choose the **Cutoff Peck** button to activate the Cutoff Peck dialogue box and set the parameters to match those in Figure 8–63.

Cut to Front Radius/Cut to Back Radius

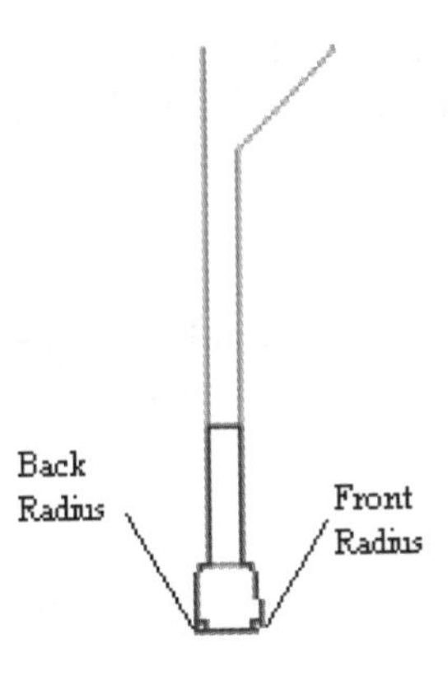

FIGURE 8–64

Choosing the Cut to Front Radius option tells Mastercam that you wish to have the tool enter the part only as deep as the center of the radius on the front side of the tool tip. The front side of the tool tip is the first side to enter the part. Choosing the Cut to Back Radius option tells Mastercam that you wish to have the tool enter the part only as deep as the center of the back radius on the backside of the tool tip. The backside of the tool tip is the trailing side of the tool tip (Figure 8–64).

X Tangent Point

The X Tangent Point is the point on the parts radius that you want the parting tool to cut to. If you are cutting a tube or a part with a hole through it, you only need the cutoff tool to go through the material.

When you are through inputting parameters, check the Entry/Exit parameters. They should be defaulting to the proper direction. Select **Done** from the Cutoff Parameters screen. At the prompt, accept the tool path by selecting **Yes.**

Make sure the tool-path creation looks correct before you postprocess the program.

Backplotting the Tool Path

Select **Operations** from the Lathe Toolpaths menu. The Operations Manager dialogue box has now popped up on the screen. Click on the **Select All** button to plot all of the tool paths. Select **Backplot.** Now Run or Step the tool path. Does it look correct? If not, check the parameter settings for the area that is in question. If it looks correct, it is time to postprocess the tool path.

NC Utilities

You will now need to postprocess the lathe tool path into machine language. From the tool bar select the **Toolpaths-Operations Manager** icon. The Operations

Manager dialogue box is now appearing on the screen. Place the mouse cursor in the **Operations Manager** dialogue box and press the right mouse button. The Operations Edit dialogue box should now appear on the screen.

Mastercam has a number of postprocessor data files. The postprocessor file creates machine codes specific to the type of machine control you select. From the operations edit dialogue box select **Post Processor.**

Mastercam makes it possible to take the same tool-path file and postprocess it for many different types of controls. The postprocessor files end with a .pst extension. The number of files you see are only a small portion of the number of postprocessor files available through Mastercam. Select the **Mplfan.pst** file and press the Open button.

Choose **Select All** to make sure you postprocess all of the tool paths associated with your part program. Select **Post** from the Operations Manager.

Mastercam now asks you to name the NC file that it is going to create. Name this NC file the same name as the geometry file. Mastercam now will create an NC file. This is the file that will be downloaded to the machine tool to make the part. Since the two files have different extensions you will not be writing over the top of the original file. Select **Save.** Your coded file should now appear on the screen. Take note of how Mastercam handled your tool nose radius compensation selections.

Maximize the Program Editor screen by using the **Maximize** button in the upper right corner of the screen. The Programmer's File Editor allows you to edit, print, and manipulate the NC file. Exit the Programmer's File Editor by selecting the Exit **X** in the upper right corner of the screen.

Use the examples that follow to practice what you have learned in this chapter. If you get stuck go back to the corresponding section in the chapter. Good luck!

REVIEW QUESTIONS

1. What are the tool-path modules found in Mastercam Lathe?
2. The ______ ______ parameter option allows you to determine the minimum amount of clearance you want to keep between the tool and the stock.
3. Lathe ______ ______ is the area where you can choose parameters to describe the current job.
4. To change the tool-path chaining direction, you would select ______ from the Contour menu.
5. There are two Roughing parameter settings that allow you to select the method in which you want to Rough turn the part. One method is called One Way roughing, the other is called ______.
6. The ______ amount determines how far above the previous cut that the tool will retract before the tool repositions for the next cut.
7. ______ ______automatically sets the Entry and Exit vectors based on the orientation of the tool.
8. To postprocess the lathe tool path into machine language you would have to be in what area?

9. In the Lathe Backplot menu, ______ generates the tool path in short tool moves.
10. In the Finish mode, Entry Point is the point where ______.

PRACTICE EXERCISES

EXERCISE 8–1

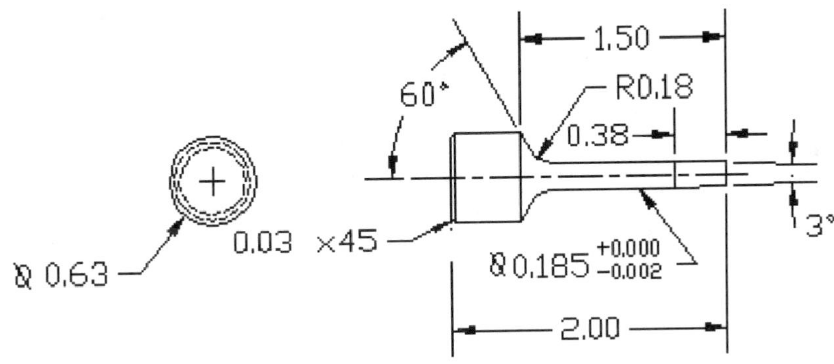

EXERCISE 8–2

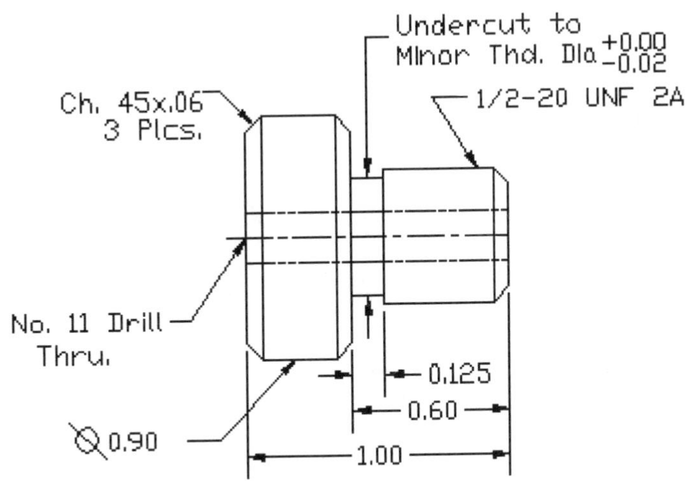

Material: 1090 Steel

EXERCISE 8–3

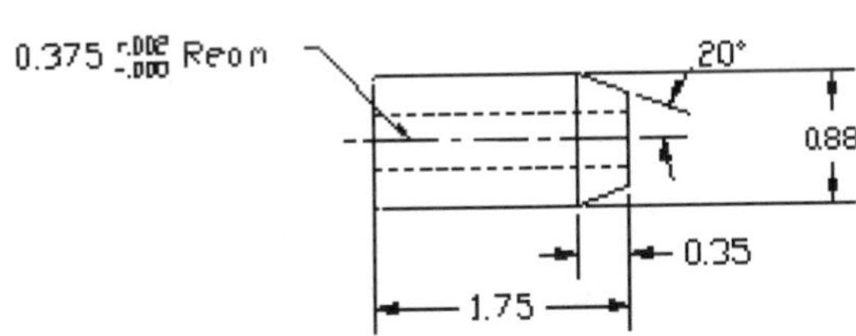

Material: 6061 Aluminum

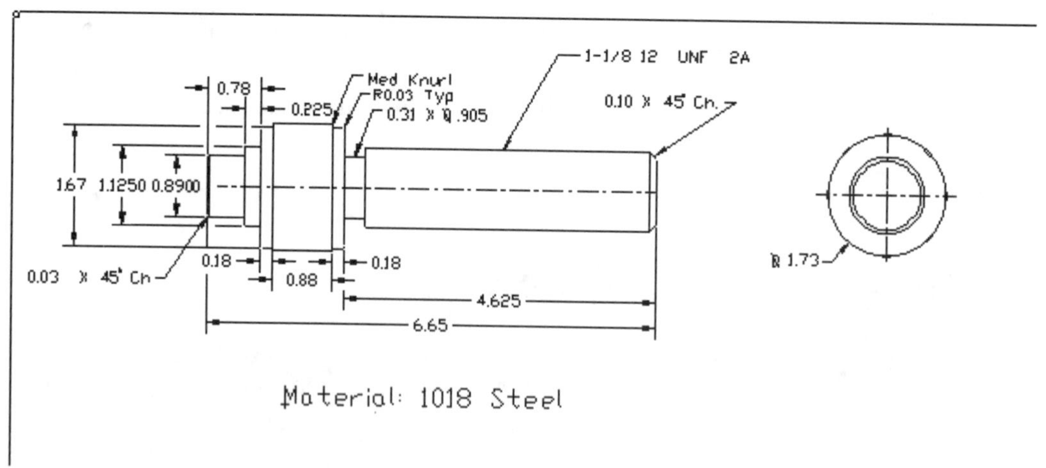
1-1/8 12 UNF 2A
0.78
Med Knurl
R0.03 Typ
0.225
0.31 X Ø.905
0.10 X 45° Ch.
1.67
1.1250
0.8900
0.03 X 45° Ch
0.18
0.88
0.18
4.625
6.65
Ø 1.73
Material: 1018 Steel

EXERCISE 8–4

CHAPTER

9

Importing CAD Files

This chapter describes how to take a CAD file and convert the drawing file into Mastercam geometry. Once the CAD file is converted, you can then assign tools and tool path to the geometry. The process of converting drawing files into machine files has become a significant part of the manufacturing environment.

Objectives

Upon completion of this chapter you will be able to:

- Convert an AutoCad geometry (DXF) file into a Mastercam file
- Separate machining entities from nonmachining entities
- Create the tool path to machine a part
- Postprocess the tool path into numerical control program language
- Verify the tool path using the Backplot module

CREATING FIGURE 9–1

The part that you will be programming is shown in Figure 9–1. You will be using a DXF file from and AutoCad drawing of this part.

Click the **Start** button using the left mouse button, and then point to the folder called Mastercam. Click on the **Mastercam Mill** option. From the Mastercam Main Menu area select **File/Converters.** Choose **Dxf** to initialize the conversion utility for Autocad drawings.

Mastercam supports a number of different file conversion utilities. See the product manual to identify the type of file that your CAD system outputs. In this chapter you will be using the DXF (drawing exchange file) format. Under the DXF menu select **Read File.** In review, the commands were Main Menu/File /Converters/ DXF/Read File.

Mastercam in the dialogue box is now asking you to select the DXF file you want to convert to Mastercam.

Place the disk that came with this textbook in drive A: . To change your target drive and directory you need to work in the Look In: file area.

Click on the down arrow button on the right side of the Look In: file area as shown in Figure 9–2. Use the up arrow button to move up the list of target areas until the 3½ Floppy (A:) appears. Click on this option using the mouse. The computer now checks to see if a disk is in the disk drive. Once the processor finds the disk, it now looks for a file with the extension of DXF. You should now see a list of all the files on your disk that have a DXF extension. Use the mouse cursor to click

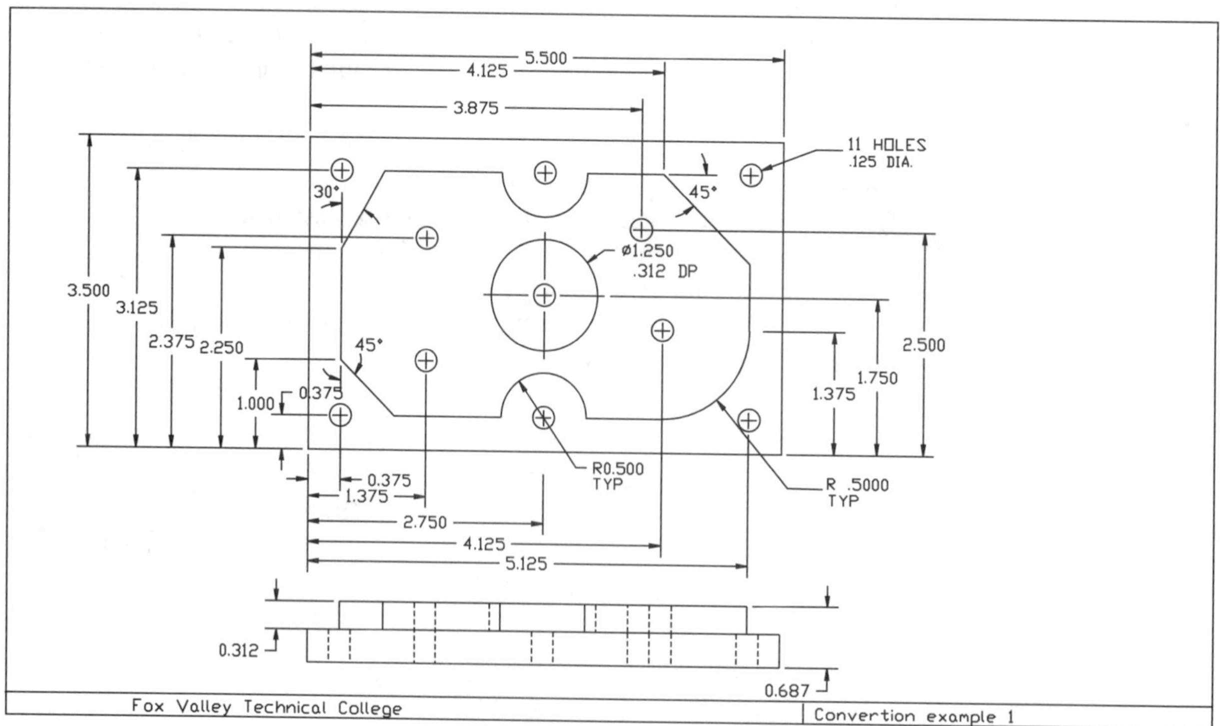

FIGURE 9–1

FIGURE 9–2

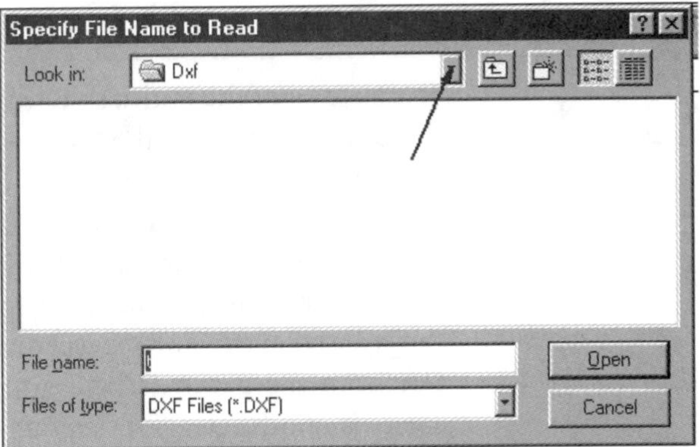

on the file named **Figure 9–1.DXF**. You can either double click on the file name or click the **Open** button also shown in Figure 9–2. Do either option now. Your file should now appear on the screen.

Push and hold down on the **Alt** key and then press the **F1** key. This screen should now have resized itself to fit your part.

ANALYZING NONESSENTIAL LEVELS

FIGURE 9–3

You now need to delete all nonessential entities. The nonessential entities are those entities that you don't want to have tool path assigned to (i.e., dimensions, title block, front view, etc.). Before you can delete the entities you don't want, you need to analyze the entities to find out what level or layer they are on. From the Main Menu select **Analyze** or select the **Analyze** icon from the tool bar (see Figure 9–3). Press the **Esc** key until you get back to the main menu.

From the Analyze menu select **Only**. Next under the Only menu select **Level**. In review, the commands were Main Menu/Analyze/Only/Level. Upon selecting Level, the Level Selection box appears on the screen (see Figure 9–4). Since you don't know the level you want, activate the **Select** box using the mouse cursor. Mastercam now prompts you to select an entity. Use the mouse cursor to select one of the dimensions from the dimensioning layer (level). The Level Selection box again appears on the screen, but this time the level number should appear on the screen in the Level dialogue box. Make note of this number. Once you have noted the level on which the dimensioning resides, select **OK** from the Enter Level dialogue box.

FIGURE 9–4

DELETING NONESSENTIAL ENTITIES

FIGURE 9–5

To delete all of the entities on this level from the Main Menu select **Delete** or select the **Delete** icon from the tool bar (see Figure 9–5).

From the Delete menu, select **All**. Next, under the All menu, select **Level**. In review, the commands were Main Menu/Delete/All/Level. Upon selecting Level, the Level Selection box appears on the screen. In the level dialogue box, type in the level (layer) that the dimensions are on or use the mouse to select the number of the layer from the Enter Level dialogue box. Once you have selected the level, select **OK** from the dialogue box. You will notice that there are still unwanted layers. There is another way of deleting unwanted layers. Select **Level** again. After selecting Level, the Level Selection box appears on the screen. Activate the **Select** box using the mouse cursor. Mastercam now prompts you to select an entity. Use the mouse cursor to select another one of the unwanted entities. The unwanted level will appear in the box. Select **OK** from the Enter Level dialogue box. Delete everything except the Top view. Now refresh the screen by choosing the **repaint** icon.

CREATING TOOL PATH

Your screen should look like Figure 9–6.

From the Main Menu select **Toolpaths** to apply tool path to the geometry of the part. Next select **Contour**. After selecting Contour, Mastercam prompts you to create a file name under which to save the Numerical Control (NCI) file. In the File Name box type **CAM**. This will be the name of our NCI file. Once you have typed in the file name, select the **Save** button. After creating the file name Mastercam prompts you to select the chain geometry you wish to apply tool path to.

The contour profile you wish to machine is the portion between the raised area of the part and the outside boundary. This is depicted by P1 in Figure 9–6.

Use the mouse to select this entity now. Since this entity is connected or is a closed profile you created in Autocad, Mastercam recognizes it as a chained profile. This is evidenced by the way Mastercam changes the whole profile into a separate selection color. Make sure that the chaining arrow is pointing in the up direction (see Figure 9–7). If it is not, use the Reverse option from the Contour menu area. You need to remove all of the material out away from this profile all the way out past the stock boundary. Once the profile has been highlighted, select **Done** from the Contour menu.

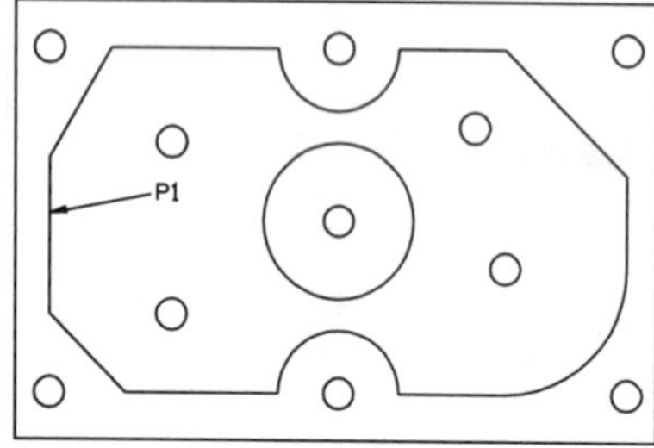

FIGURE 9–6

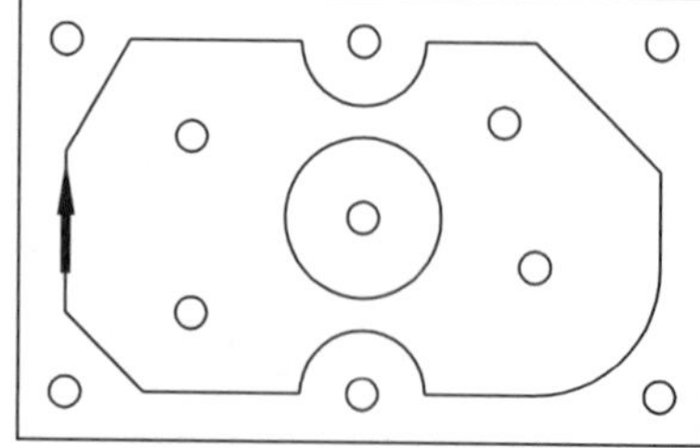

FIGURE 9–7

FIGURE 9–8

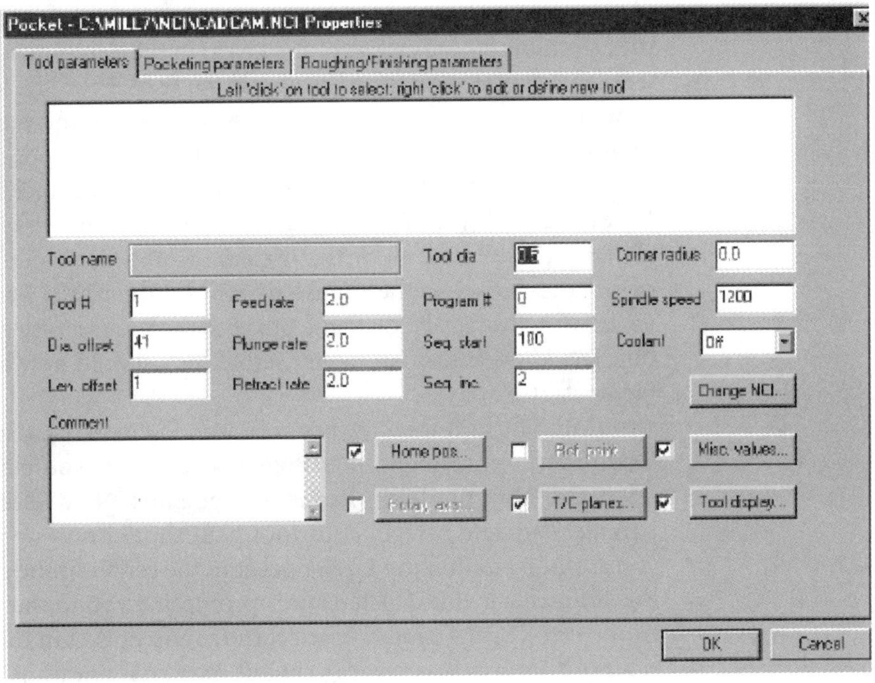

After selecting Done, the Mastercam software automatically pulls up the Tool parameters and Contour parameters menu (see Figure 9–8).

The Tool Parameters box is the initial box that appears. The first thing you will need to do is select a tool from the tool library. Place the mouse in the large white space indicated by the arrow in Figure 9–8. Open the Tool Selection menu by clicking the right mouse button. From the Tool Selection menu select **Get Tool from Library**. The Tool Manager should now appear (see Figure 9–9).

Select the **1/2 end mill** from the tool manager list. Next select **OK** from the Tool Manager menu. You should see that the 1/2 end mill has been added to the contour module. Toggle the **Coolant** arrow to Flood. Once you have made these Tool parameter changes it is time to set the Contour Parameters. Select **Contour Parameters** located in the upper left corner of the screen. Activate the clearance plane by selecting the small box next to the **Clearance** button. Activate the retract

FIGURE 9–9

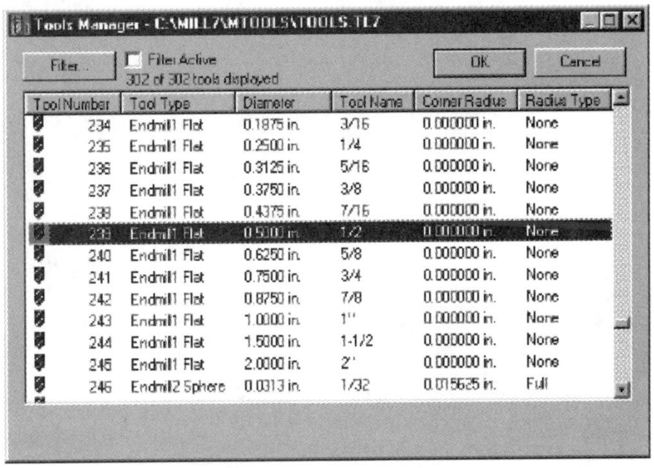

plane in the same manner. Change the Depth in the window to **−.312**. Don't select the Depth button; just type in the depth in the depth dialogue box. If you inadvertently hit the Depth button, just press the **Esc** key on the keyboard to return to the contour parameters. Activate the **Depth Cuts** box and then select the **Depth Cuts** button. The Depth Cuts dialogue box should now appear on the screen. Change the Maximum roughing steps to **.200**. Set the Number of finishing passes to **1**. Now select **OK**. You now need to activate the Multi Passes dialogue box. This will allow you to remove all of the material from this profile all the way out past the stock boundary. Use the mouse to activate the **Multi Passes** dialogue box. Once you have activated the dialogue box, use the mouse to select the **Multi Passes** button. The Multi Passes parameter setting box should now appear on the screen (see Figure 9–10).

Input the numbers as they appear in Figure 9–10. Use the **Tab** key on the keyboard to move through the dialogue boxes. Once you have entered these choices, select **OK** from the Multi Passes dialogue box. Now select **OK** from the Contour parameters menu screen. Your tool path should now appear on the screen. Now you are going to mill the 1.125 pocket in the center of the piece. Select **Pocket** from the Toolpaths menu. Mastercam is prompting you in the Chaining mode to select the pocket. Use the mouse to select the round pocket in the middle of the part. Notice the direction Mastercam's chaining arrow is pointing. It should be pointing up or in a counterclockwise direction. If the arrow isn't pointing in this direction, press **Reverse**. If it is already pointing up, select **Done** from the pocket menu. You will be using the same tool to machine the pocket that you used to machine the contour profile. You will also be using the same machining parameters.

There is no need to change the feed, speed, or plunge feed rates. Turn the coolant type to **Flood**. Once you have made this change, select pocketing parameters located in the upper left corner of the screen. Turn the clearance and retract planes on, if they are not already on. Change the depth to **−.312** in the same manner you did in the contour section. Also turn on Depth Cuts and change the parameters to the same as the contour parameters. Next select the **Roughing/Finishing Parameters** file folder at the top of the screen. Select **True Spiral** from the cutting method dialogue box. Now select **OK**.

The pocket toolpath should now appear on the screen.

Next you will drill the six 0.125-diameter holes on the outside step of the piece and the one in the center of the pocket. Select **Drill** from the Toolpaths

FIGURE 9–10

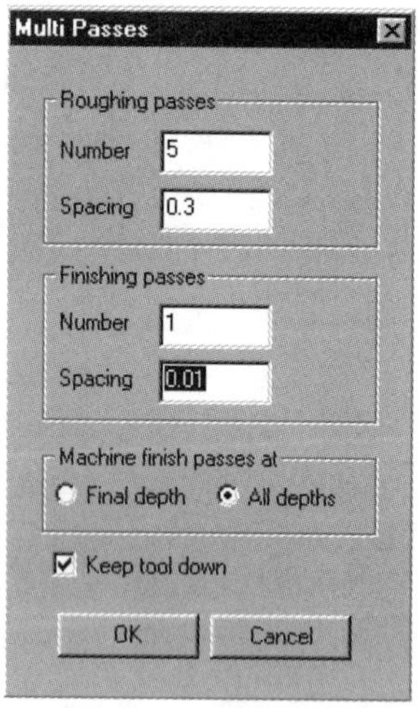

menu. From the Drill menu select **Manual**. From the Point Entry menu select **Center**. Mastercam is prompting you to select the arc. Use the mouse to select the hole in the upper left corner. Mastercam is now prompting you to select more entities. Select the rest of the holes in a clockwise direction using the center point entry method. Do the one in the center of the pocket last. Make sure that the pick box is located in the center of the hole before pressing the mouse button to accept the location. Press the **Esc** key when you are finished. Now select **Done** from the drill menu. The Tool parameter box should now appear on the screen. Use the tool selection method you used previously to get the .125-diameter drill from the tool library. Turn the coolant type to **Flood**. Once you have made these changes, select **Drill/Counterbore Parameters** located in the upper left corner of the screen. Change the Top of the Stock to **−.312**. Change the depth to **−.725**. Now select **OK**. The drilling tool path should appear on the screen.

Now you are going to drill the four 0.125-diameter holes on the top of the piece. Select **Drill** from the Toolpaths menu. From the Drill menu select **Manual**. From the Point Entry menu select Center. Mastercam is prompting you to select the arc. Use the mouse to select the **holes**. Make sure that the pick box is located in the center of the hole before pressing the mouse button to accept the location. Press the Esc key on the keyboard when you are finished. Now select **Done** from the drill menu. The Tool parameter box should now appear on the screen. You will be using the same tool to drill these holes. Everything else that deals with the tool is the same as the previous holes. Now select **Drill/Counterbore Parameters**, located in the upper left corner of the screen. Change the Top of the Stock back to **0.0**. Change the depth to **−.312**. Now select **OK**. The drill tool path should appear on the screen.

VERIFYING TOOL PATH USING BACKPLOT

You now need to verify that tool path is correct. From the Operations Manager dialogue box press the **Backplot** button. From the Backplot menu select **Run**. The plot should now appear on the screen. You can look at the Backplot path from different views. Use the **Gview** option in the secondary menu to look at the tool path from different view settings. Does it look right? If it looks correct, you are ready to postprocess the tool path. If not go back and recheck what you did.

POSTPROCESSING THE TOOL PATH

The toolpath should be complete. You now need to convert this toolpath into NC code. From the tool bar select the **Toolpaths Operations Manager** icon (see Figure 9–11).

From the Operations Manager dialogue box press the **Select All** button. Now select **Post** to postprocess the tool path. You would like to postprocess the CAM file you just created. Select **CAM** from the Look in: file dialogue box. Also save the file as CAM. Select Yes when asked, "Do you want to run the post processor?" The NC file should now appear on the Program file editor screen. Exit the Program file editor screen. Exit the file editor screen by using the **X** exit button on the upper right corner of the screen.

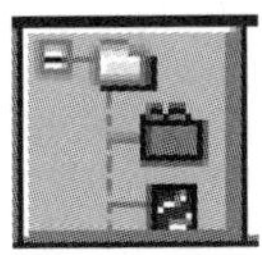

FIGURE 9–11

Index